Vulgar Eloquence

BY THE SAME AUTHOR

Living Adult Education: Freire in Scotland
(with Gerri Kirkwood)
published by Open University Press, 1989

Adult Education and the Unemployed
(edited with Sally Griffiths)
published by WEA South-east Scotland, 1984

Vulgar Eloquence:
from labour to liberation
essays on education, community and politics

Colin Kirkwood

Polygon
EDINBURGH

© Colin Kirkwood 1990
Polygon
22 George Square, Edinburgh

Set in CRTronic Sabon
by Polyprint, Edinburgh and
printed and bound in Great Britain by
Bell and Bain Limited, Glasgow

British Library Cataloguing
in Publication Data
Kirkwood, Colin
    Vulgar Eloquence: essays in education,
    community and politics.
    1. Scotland – Education
    I. Title
    370.9411

ISBN 0 7486 6043 7

Contents

in chronological order

Acknowledgements

I want to thank Peter Kravitz of Polygon for the welcome he gave to this project when it was first proposed in January 1989. He has been patient and constructive every step of the way. His support has helped me find the energy, in the midst of other tasks, to do the necessary editing and write the introductory notes.

Thanks also to Gerri for her love and understanding, to Paul and Anna, our children, and to my father, Hugh Kirkwood. Thanks to the many people who have contributed in various ways to the experiences and reflections gathered here, including Janet Hassan, Alan Harrow, Mary and Maureen Harkin, the Vaccario, Caenazzo and Marcuzzo families, Anthony Ross, Robert Tait, David and Carol Godwin, Tom and Sonya Leonard, Ken and Larraine Worpole, Neil Tempest, Robert Hunter, Joan Turner, Eric Edwards, Muriel Easton, Tom Lovett, Richard and Pauline Kurcewicz, Nicholas Nunn, Kay Carmichael, Richard and Barbara Bryant, Chris Clarke, Molly Johnston, Margaret Kyle, Cathie Thompson, Agnes Devlin, Bill Towill, Archie Hamilton, Christine Pardoe, Pat Devitt, John and Mary Miller, John and Carol Cooper, Andrew Parker, Eddie Graham, Irene and Neil Graham, Freddy and Isobel Anderson, Sheila Sim, Janette McGinn, Jean and Brian Barr, Paulo Freire, David Alexander, Tim Steward, Leo and Margaret Valdivia, Peter Wass, Ian Martin, Kenneth King, Nigel Grant, Ken Logue, Carol Craig, Pearl Henderson, Alan Swan, Joyce Connon, Kathy Turner, Kate Kinninmont, Chris Aldred, Shelagh Doonan, Harry Andrew, George Reid, Peter Gilmore, Willie Colligan, Jennifer Rodger, Craig Robertson, Sally and Nigel Griffiths, Gordon Brown, Sadie Rooney, Mike Tait, Tony Graham, Ronnie Turnbull, Craig Beveridge, Hugh and Grace Miller, Iain Glen, Bill Forbes, Colin Boyd, Raymond Ross, Duncan Toms, Stephen Maxwell, Linden West, Susan Moffat, Susan Maciver, Colin White, Charlie McConnell, Ian McGowan, Jim Sillars, Margo MacDonald, Stan Reeves, Joan Bree, Fiona McCall, Fraser Patrick, Douglas Shannon, Mike Rosendale, Gerry Cairns, Vernon and Dawn Smith, Pablo and

Colin Kirkwood

Jenny Foster, Barbara Darcy, Lalage Bown, Elisabeth Gerver, Cathy Sandler, Mona MacDonald, Judith Brearley, Jane Jones, Jennifer Gray, Sheila Main, Jane Chisholm, Liz Perry, Norman Shanks, Judith Fewell, Ronald Beasley, Jean Malcolm, Tom Carruthers, Ian Thompson, Mike Church, Ray Woolfe, Jim Griffin, Ruth Addinall, Christopher Whyte, Marion Sinclair and Tony Carty.

Finally, I want to honour the memory of my mother, Madge Kirkwood, and of Ian Towill, Geoff Shaw, Maurice Blythman and Derek Bowman.

Colin Kirkwood, September 1989

this is thi
six a clock
news thi
man said n
thi reason
a talk wia
BBC accent
iz coz yi
widny wahnt
mi ti talk
aboot thi
trooth wia
voice lik
wanna yoo
scruff. if
a toktaboot
thi trooth
lik wanna yoo
scruff yi
widny thingk
it wuz troo.
jist wanna yoo
scruff tokn.
thirza right
way ti spell
ana right way
ti tok it. this
is me tokn yir
right way a
spellin. this
is ma trooth.
yooz doant no
thi trooth
yirsellz cawz
yi canny talk
right. this is
the six a clock
nyooz. belt up.

We will endeavour . . . to be of
service to the speech of the
common people. . . We call the
Vulgar Tongue that to which
children are accustomed by
those who are about them when
they first begin to distinguish
sounds; or, to put it more
shortly, we say that the Vulgar
Tongue is that which we acquire
without any rule, by imitating
our nurses. We afterwards have
another secondary speech,
which the Romans called
Grammar. And this secondary
speech the Greeks also have, as
well as others, but not all. Few,
however, acquire the use of this
secondary speech, because we
can only be guided and
instructed in it by the
expenditure of much time, and
by assiduous study. Of these
two kinds of speech also, the
Vulgar Tongue is the nobler, as
well because it was the first
employed by the human race, as
because the whole world makes
use of it, though it has been
divided into different forms of
utterance and words. It is also
the nobler as being natural to us,
whereas the other is rather of an
artificial kind; and it is of this
nobler form of speech that we
intend to treat.

Tom Leonard,
'Unrelated Incidents' (3)
from *Intimate Voices 1965-83*

Dante Alighieri,
De Vulgari Eloquentia
(translated by
A. G. Ferrers Howell)

Introduction

Vulgar eloquence, the idea, is about the meaningfulness of what ordinary people say and the need to listen. Vulgar Eloquence, the book, is history from inside the oven, history as the process of being there, asking questions, responding, engaging. It is about history as a struggle to move forward served by investigation, retrospect and reconstruction. The pieces included here are moments in the twenty years from 1968 to 1988. Sometimes they are like stepping stones and the logic of the steps is clear. But some of the steps are leaps. To help the reader follow them, each piece is prefaced by an introductory note, setting the scene.

Can we influence the shape of the future, personally and communally, or are we determined by forces beyond our control? I believe that we *are* determined, both by our own early personal history and by those wider social processes we are caught up in: *unless*. We are determined *unless* we take on the task of knowing ourselves, that is to say both the inner potential self, and the self that we have become through our responses to environmental impingements. We are determined *unless* we take on the task of knowing our context, the interacting forces and themes of our society and the world as a whole. We are determined *unless* we make the move from an orientation of passivity to one of reflective engagement.

This can only be done in collaboration with others. But we cannot genuinely collaborate unless we seek to know ourselves. The personal and the communal are not alternatives: they are co-essential dimensions of human emergence. On this fundamental point I differ both with the collectivists of the left and the individualists of the right.

The key themes of our time have to do with the search for identity, the meaning of authority, the nature of democracy, and the exercise of power. Is power the capacity to dominate, directly or indirectly, or is it the ability to act, personally and communally, on the world we inherit? The history of all human societies is the history of the exercise of power. Far too much of it has been the history of imperial power. I believe it is possible to make a different kind of history.

Is authority something only a few people have, or does every human being potentially have authority? The etymology of the word (*auctoritas*, from *augere*, to increase, promote, originate) suggests the latter possibility. But linguistic usage and our experience of the behaviour of those in authority (parents, professionals, employers) suggests the former. I think everyone has potential authority and can use it, without negating the importance of leadership.

Is democracy a ballot paper given to adults every few years, to be aggregated or harvested by the political caste with a little help from their friends in the media? Or is it possible to exercise control of society's processes by *humanly* sophisticated means of exploring and communicating aims and values, and by direct — personal and communal — enterprise?

What is exciting about our times is the way these issues of identity and authority, of power and democracy, have become intertwined with another set of themes — or more precisely, relationships. I am thinking here of our increasing sensitivity to the dialectics of inner and outer reality, subjectivity and objectivity, self and others, and men and women.

The reader will find in these pages evidence of an option, a preoccupation, a certain identification with working-class people, with the underclass, and with groups and individuals who are excluded or lost. This is not the place to discuss the motives for this choice, except to say that it is a considered one. It is made at the level of the needs and interests of actual human beings, not as a result of political analysis, which is an insufficient basis for moral orientation. But it is not a naïve choice: it becomes in itself a major element in a political analysis. I see excluded people in the context of society, and particularly in relation to the acts and attitudes of the managerial, professional and political castes. Paulo Freire's idea that human beings can be seen and treated either as subjects who know and act, or as objects which are known and acted upon, is pivotal. Reflecting upon Latin American particularities, Freire writes:

> To immobilise peasants by promoting a welfare syndrome is not a viable approach to overcoming their difficulties. Through this approach peasants at best would be incorporated as objects into the agrarian reform process but never . . . as real subjects.
>
> (*The Politics of Education*, pp. 32/33, Macmillan, 1985)

This comment is relevant to the ways in which ordinary people in

Scotland, England, Wales and Northern Ireland have been treated throughout the post-war period by both Labour and Conservative parties, in line with two distinct but equally Victorian rationales.

In trying to understand the failure of hope in the 1970s, the key to the puzzle is that the new wine, after an initial phase of oppositional riot, poured itself voluntarily into the old bottles; by which I mean those ways of thinking, forms of organisation and modes of action characteristic of the trade union movement, the Labour Party, the Communist Party, and the British state. Even the Trotskyist sects, though livelier in style, held rigidly to the old centralist concepts and forms. The rest of the energy was burned off in hedonism or evaporated into style. This paradoxical revival of patriarchal-military-hierarchical order, having brushed off the feather-weight challenges of the early community action and feminist movements, evoked a more fundamentalist version of feminism which did succeed in shaking male self-confidence, but at a cost. The labour movement lost its vision and its drive, and the feminists became divided against themselves, consuming their energies in sectarian conflict.

The forces of change which flowered in the late '60s and '70s thus failed to facilitate a genuinely exploratory dialogue between the generations and the sexes, which might have created new forms and concepts out of the old. They failed to know themselves, read the signs, and listen to ordinary people. Following the triumph of Thatcher, many spent the 1980s in shock, recuperation, CND, and the pursuit of self-interest.

That is a harsh note on which to end the introduction to a hopeful book. But it is a true note. Only by confronting the truth in its complexity — including the truth of failure — can we share in the process of creating better ways of thinking, learning, acting and organising. These essays record a series of attempts to understand that complexity and shape of some of the new ways. The basis of hope and possibility as I see it now is outlined in the Afterword.

Colin Kirkwood
October 1989
Edinburgh

1. Italy 1969

This piece is an ideogram made by juxtaposing two extracts from a longer, previously unpublished article written in 1969.

After teaching for a year in secondary schools in London and Glasgow, my wife Gerri and I decided to go abroad. A transitional opportunity came up, in the form of a summer job teaching English to young adult students in Bournemouth. It was a lucky accident, because it brought us into contact with some of the revolting students of Western Europe, fresh from their battles on and off campus. Their confidence contrasted sharply with my tendency to self-doubt, their sociability with my solitary preoccupation with reading and writing poetry. What was also stimulating, though I didn't understand its full significance at the time, was their challenge to the state and its figures of authority.

That there were implications for adult education in these events was obvious. It became clearer still when we moved to Treviso, a small town north of Venice, to teach English in the Scuola Interpreti. Having your classroom teaching interrupted by the joyful noise of a strike by students from a local secondary school, waving banners and blowing trumpets, is not an everday occurrence in Scotland or England, but it was commonplace in Italy that year.

Until then my interest had been in personal creativity. Although a Labour voter, I had little interest in politics, which I dismissed as part of the realm of the inauthentic. Now, for the first time, I began to think in terms of a social creativity, an education that would replace the rule of the belting teacher, and a politics of direct democracy.

But there was a contradiction, a complexity in my reality, of which I was only dimly aware. My main interest in poetry was in the work of Ezra Pound, the Imagist and Objectivist traditions he had fathered, and the ways in which his influence was having an impact on the current writing scene. I knew of his hatred for the dominant culture in Britain and the USA after the first world war and his views on education, language and order. I even knew something of his fascism and anti-semitism. Could these contradictory attractions be resolved? At this stage in my development they were simply juxtaposed, and I was wrestling with them. I realise now that what was declaring itself in terms of my personal interests was a key theme, the relationship between authority and democracy. It continues to work itself out in the dynamics of our lives twenty years on, and we have not got very far with clarifying it.

*

During the last eighteen months I've been teaching English to foreign students, mostly from Europe. Some were involved in the May events of 1968 in France, and in the preceding struggles. Others were involved in similar actions in West Germany, Austria and Italy. There is, among them, a spirit of challenge and democracy, and a sense of the responsibility of everyone in every area of life. They're hostile to the dominance of the ideas or style of any one person. They believe in the development of everyone's creativity, and in the primary value of personal relationships. They seem unaware that they live off the labour of millions, imagining that soon all the dirty work will be done by machines. They criticised me as authoritarian when I chose a subject of discussion or a method of teaching myself, instead of consulting the class.

The Italian teacher who was the key link in the chain that led to my meeting with Ezra Pound spoke of the change in his own orientation. He teaches Latin and Italian literature. He's a man of about fifty who was feared for his severity. The slightest disturbance of classroom peace would provoke him to exclude the offender. That was before the *contestazione*. Since then he has become milder and more democratic. Before, his students worked alone, in class and at home. Cheating, copying, telling the answer, talking, were all forbidden. Now they sit in groups, each of which consists of more and less successful students. They do written work together, helping each other, talking it through. Homework is done in pairs, not alone. His daughter told us how they reorganised the classroom situation in her secondary school. From his position on a platform facing rows of students receding into the distance, the teacher has been brought down to floor level and placed at the centre of a semi-circle of desks just two rows deep.

In my own classes in Treviso, I was initially faced with the problem of the Italian incapacity to stop talking. I used the question and answer method, requiring the student to *use* English rather than parrot it. When a student didn't understand, she would invariably ask a friend who would do her best to help. I resisted at first, but gave up under a rain of 'it's still learning'. This was at least partly true. Freedom to talk makes students more alive, responsible, connecting the new with what they already know, *more engaged* in the learning process.

*

Alongside these experiences I want to juxtapose my encounter with Ezra Pound and Olga Rudge, which took place in the spring of 1969.

I took the train from Treviso to Venice in mid-afternoon, and walked all the way to the church of La Salute. Near it was Albergo Cici, and just along the canal, Calle Querini, where Ezra Pound lived.

This calle is an alley, about twenty yards long and three yards wide. The name on the first door was Scottish, and on the next were the words

E. Pound
O. Rudge
Telegrammi e
espressi in boca

written with a black pen running dry, on a small piece of paper, under glass. Cloud-patches of ochre plaster were flaking from the wall. The place was totally unimpressive.

Having found his lair, I went off to await the appointed hour. I found a bar round the corner called Al' Abazia and sat down outside with a roll and coffee, aware of a need for a pee (no toilets in sight) and a daft fear that Ezra would catch me eating. Would he come striding round the corner, a tall, strong man with a confident gaze and a swinging stride? Or would he be doddery? I reverted to an old fear of freezing up with embarrassment at important meetings. I must concentrate on *him*, I decided: *I* didn't matter.

When I returned, I found only a garrulous American called Lester Littlefield, who informed me that Pound and he had just exchanged: the Pounds had gone to Albergo Cici, leaving him in their house. They were about to leave Venice. I would catch them there, he thought. He proceeded, without much prompting, to fill me in on Pound's personal relationships, and the approach I ought to adopt. Pound won't say much, he said, you'll have to do the talking. He'll listen, and if he wants to, he'll reply. It might be better if you addressed your remarks to Olga. I asked him why Pound didn't reply. He said that it often seemed to be a problem of articulation: he couldn't form the words he wanted to say. I felt a rush of embarrassment, that a man of such powers should have lost a power so basic, and have to be with others for whom talking was effortless.

Then Lester Littlefield told me about Pound and Olga, how he met her in Paris when he moved there from London, and how she went to Rapallo and lived on the hillside behind the town, where Pound visited her on his afternoon walks. It had all happened forty years ago, but I experienced a profound shock, revealing the extent to which I had idealised Pound and his marriage to Dorothy Shakespear.*

I left Lester Littlefield in Pound's house with the beautiful white statue of a mother and child, and walked round to the Albergo Cici

---

* A good account of Pound's lifestyle, and his theories about the relationship between sex and creativity, is to be found in E. Fuller Torrey's *The Roots of Treason* (McGraw-Hill, 1984). According to Torrey, Pound and Olga first met in London, not Paris.

to find the Pounds had gone out for a walk. Emotionally, I decided I
had missed them — almost as if I wanted to, after the shock I'd had
— and left a note plus a selection of poems by Derek Bowman,
Robert Tait, Tom Leonard and myself. In something approaching
distress I walked to the landing stage at La Salute, hovering round a
shaky, handsome old gent whose wife turned out to be speaking
German. I waited, looking at faces, aware of powerful swings of
emotion: if that old man was Ezra Pound — how dignified, what a
fine gaze, what a humiliating tragedy old age is, loss of power. If he
wasn't, I swung to feelings of disgust. The strange middle-aged man
in the shelter at the landing stage — thoughtful, a hinterland of
understood experience behind the face — or someone leading an
unextended life of habitual sensations?

I took the vaporetto back to the station, checked the next train,
and then thought I'd phone on the off chance. In a moment I was
speaking to Olga, a posh English voice: would I like to come over for
dinner? Yes I would — I'll be over in half an hour. I rushed out of the
station, ran back to the toilet, checked the last train, and rushed over
to the landing stage. An age of slow hops and long stops later, I was
walking along the narrow streets to Albergo Cici. I stepped in
tentatively, suddenly terrified. It's full of yahyah English voices, in
the right wall an entrance, a tiny sittingroom: Ezra Pound. Sunk in a
chair, hands bowed over a stick. Grooved face. Thin beard. White
frizzy hair flying off his head. Ezra Pound in a good blue suit and a
white shirt. Withered. Across from him is Olga reading. She smiles at
me. Mr Kirkwood? Come and sit down. This is Mr Kirkwood, Ezra.
Grunt. Looks up, looks away. Polite enquiries. Shall we go and have
dinner? I walk behind them, feeling benevolent, pitying,
embarrassed, elated, frightened. He's smaller than me — but he was
six feet, I'm sure! Slightly stooped, but not that much. He must have
shrunk.

Olga takes a table near the open door to the garden. It's quite cool.
Ezra sits down on the seat nearest the door. Olga says he should
swop with her because of the draught. He doesn't want to. She
insists, gets up, goes round, come on Ezra, you go round there. Ezra
is re-placed. A few minutes later she says, oh Ezra, you *did* want to
sit here, didn't you? I should've let you. She gets up, goes round to
Ezra, shakes him up from his glazed sit, moves him back. She and I
examine the menu: what would you like? Soup, chicken, white wine.
The waitress is a bit off-hand with her because she's old. Olga has to
be almost ingratiating.

It was as Lester Littlefield forecast. Not much would be said if I sat
passive. So I talked — about teaching in Glasgow, about teaching in
Treviso, the paintings of Paolo da Venezia that had so interested me,

about cheating, about creativity, about education in general. Olga was attentive, and critical. Cheating was cheating. Did you ever cheat, Ezra? No. If you copy, you don't understand. Education democratised is degenerate — the Italian peasants were much more interesting and intelligent before they were forced to learn to read and write. People who are stupid shouldn't be taught. I remembered Yeats: aristocracy and peasantry. I responded with a description of education as a reflection of a competitive society, a system involving failure and success. It could be compared to a pyramid, I said. On the bottom step a mass: some succeed, most fail, and mostly remain failures. Next step up, more of the successful fail. No rest for the successful, they must continue to succeed, or they fail. Sooner or later, nearly everyone peels off. And so on, out through the formal education system into the world of work. Grasping the pyramid image from his own point of view, Ezra put in, quietly: when you get to the top, there's nowhere else to go.

Scotland was mentioned. Had Ezra ever been to Glasgow? Passed through it when I was sixteen. Hugh MacDiarmid. I admired his poetry, I said, but thought he was cruel to people whose work he didn't like. At least you know where you are with him, Olga replied.

Olga once or twice had to go off to answer the phone, and then I tried stumblingly to tell Pound what I — what we — had learned from him: economy, clarity, to know your own address in time, to relate ideas to particulars, juxtaposition of the apparently unconnected or perception of relations as he called it, independent study, to go beyond the aesthete's shut-off field, to have the nerve to evaluate. It felt like an embarrassment of the obvious, but I wanted to offer some other-than-banal gratitude. He heard me attentively, offering no reply.

I wanted to talk to him about *Hugh Selwyn Mauberley*, that astonishing review of his early poetic life, since there is some confusion about what it means. What I asked in the heat of the moment was an apparently banal question: is *Mauberley* a comparison and contrast of H. S. Mauberley and Ezra Pound? He replied: it's an observation. I think I understand what he meant: as when, in a conversation, someone makes a statement radically questioning and reformulating the assumptions underlying the discussion, so Pound in that poem made a telling observation on the criticism that he was an aesthete shying away from the modern world.

We came to the coffee, with little packets of granular sugar in the saucer. I tore off a strip of paper inattentively and poured it into my cup, then caught sight of Ezra, who was absorbed. He grasped the packet deliberately with difficulty, and tore slowly. When the last threads of the paper gave, his hands jerked apart. Some sugar sprayed onto the table, into the saucer. I wanted not to have seen it. But I also enjoyed it. Had I come to kill the king? No, I'd gone to meet the hero. But did I then, ever so slightly, enjoy seeing his decline?

Was it a meeting, anyway, or a mutual viewing, with one-sided harangue from me? Not much two-way communication. Didn't I go for what I could get? Of course. But somehow I felt my behaviour was lacking in respect. I had gone to meet Ezra Pound, naively expecting a man in his full powers. Instead he was at the far end of his time.

I had to go then, to catch my train. Ezra and Olga saw me to the door of the hotel, shook hands, and said goodnight. I bowed awkwardly, but they were already turning away.

2. Do-it-yourself local newspaper— is this adult education?

In November 1969 I became Area Principal for Adult Education in the Staveley district of north-east Derbyshire, responsible for a programme of adult classes, but with scope for taking other initiatives as well. The most important of these was the local paper, *Staveley Now*, one of the earliest community newspapers in Britain. A special feature was the use of transcriptions of tape-recorded interviews with residents on a range of issues. The paper group linked in with other organisations — the Disabled Group, the Festival, the Community Centre, and a cluster of playschemes. I learned a lot from people in Staveley, and am grateful for the experience I had there. This essay was written in haste, at the request of the Assistant Director of Education, for the Journal of the National Institute of Adult Education (September 1971 issue). It catches something of the spirit of the project and the energy of the people involved.

*

The context
Staveley — a small coal-steel-chemicals town in north-east Derbyshire. Population, 18,480; 95 per cent working class, as they say. The main housing estate tacked on to the old town centre. A circumference of isolated patches completes the urban district (two mining villages, a company estate, a company village, a 1950s council estate, a 1960s council estate).

An energetic urban district council has pulled down the terraced rows of the old centre, replacing them with new shops round a new square, open market, a big car park and an industrial estate. Top priorities: to put a new heart in the town centre and to attract new industry ('diversify employment opportunities'). Play, leisure and entertainment facilities come lower down the list, though the whole urban district can and does boast of its voluntary provision for old people.

Centre v. region tensions — officials want everyone to see themselves as belonging to Staveley, but there are plenty who have lived all their lives in the little settlements and will do nothing of the sort. The villagers and the estate dwellers complain of lack of amenities and inadequate services.

Six schools used as adult education centres. One (the central factory) has over thirty classes a week; the rest have one, two, three, six. Occasional demands for more classes in the 'outlying areas', as the administrator tends to describe them. Sometimes, when you put on a class they have asked for (in an old junior school, say) only two or three turn up.

But Poolsbrook, a mining village, an educational priority area, gets a new community school with coffee bar, adult and youth rooms and all mod. cons. If them, why not us?

The project
In my first months as area principal I discussed with people the idea of producing a local paper, devoted to fact-finding and debate on live local issues. Robert Hunter, the local Young Volunteer Force Foundation worker, co-operated throughout. Later, I crystallised the suggestion in a letter, sent to about thirty people: (1) inviting them to meet and talk it over in the upstairs room of the Elm Tree; (2) listing possible things they could write about as a basis for discussion; (3) philosophising — again to stir discussion. Our newspaper could be *prospective,* describing and influencing matters as yet unsettled, not *retrospective,* describing events already past. It would not use information as entertainment (like most newspapers). We might assert the individual's right to control anything that affects him/her. The thing would have to take root among local people, become *their* paper.

A tape recorder would be available for anyone wanting to do interviews.

The people
Who were the thirty? At that early stage we chose carefully (later it was open to all). Criteria: not too many power figures, representative selection of types and jobs, as many working class as possible, as many under 40 as possible, large majority of 'natives'. Main aim — not to produce a tame, middle-class, middle-aged establishment group. A lot of work went into this selection.

On the Saturday there were: a Church of England cleric, a National Coal Board clerical worker and his wife, an NCB lab-worker, four miners, a housewife/youth club leader, two housewife/playgroup workers, a managing director, a Post Office technical officer, a local councillor/lecturer in a nearby technical college, a steelworks draughtsman, a general foreman in construction (last five having worked their way up), three teachers, three sixth formers. We failed to get more women, any secondary modern kids, rockers or skinheads.

Later we discovered that one woman didn't come because it was in a pub.

We sat in a circle. Stiffness quickly relaxed. A number of points helped to establish their relationship with me. For example, I proposed that we should produce a cheap, student-type duplicated paper without adverts. But no, they were set on a real, posh newspaper, with photos — and adverts would be needed to pay for that. I was cast not as decision-maker, but as chairman and adviser.

The prospective/retrospective idea, being far too intellectual, was accepted without discussion. My assertion about the individual's right to control worried people. That's how it ought to be, the feeling was, but you won't get people in positions of power to agree. Soft pedal that idea.

Then an argument blew up. The vicar didn't want anything contentious in the paper. He was a builder of unity, fanner of the community spirit, respecter of institutions — 'a royalist and a Christian'. This tune was energetically counterpointed by a teacher, who detected strains of 'paper over the cracks'. The meeting came down heavily on the side of the individual. We would print anybody's views, left, right, up or down — but people must speak for themselves, not as representatives of the council, the church or any other body. However, we agreed it must not be 'just a knocking paper'. We must, as one of our poets later wrote, describe 'the good things of our town, and what it lacks as well'. The paper itself would not take sides. Contributions to be signed.

Getting down to it

How to get down to it was the next problem. I suggested forming groups based on interests. Each would fix a date and place to explore its subject. This was accepted and they formed the following groups: 'Playgroups and Young Children', 'Politics and Local Government', 'Secondary Education/Youth Clubs/Young People', 'Sports Facilities', 'Poolsbrook', 'Future of Staveley'.

'Playgroups' was small from the start. Someone thought it was to do with acting. One of the playgroup workers was a little deaf. Another was perhaps a little suspicious of this outsider trying to get people to start a newspaper. My wife and I invited them home to see if they felt there was anything to write about. Our relationship with the deaf supervisor was gradually warming into friendship, and she decided to write about what goes on in playgroups, and why you have them anyway. Eventually she found the time to write a mild-toned, concise exposition along those lines.

The secondary education group and the sports group both died the death, apparently because people didn't have the time (most of them were also involved in other groups). A PE master, member of both, produced, after a series of discussions, an article decribing the Bingham experiment in community use of expanded secondary school sport-and-social facilities, calling for the same in Staveley and pointing out how deficient local facilities were.

These are both examples of work by individuals (off a springboard of encouragement and co-operation). There were other such efforts: the photo of the derelict car against the pit tip, under a pylon; the poem 'Staveley Now', written during a depressing meeting about how to raise money, giving those who attended a retrospective sense of light out of darkness; and the other poems. The garnering of these as publishable items was a spin-off from the development of personal friendships between myself, or Robert Hunter, and their creators, involving regular meetings at one or other home or in some pub.

But the bulk of the material finally published as issue no. 1 was produced co-operatively.

Two co-operatives

First there was the Poolsbrook group, consisting of a villager and his wife who said little at the first meeting, but decided to write about Poolsbrook's grouses. I arranged to drop in on them as soon as possible. Meanwhile I took delivery of the new tape-recorder and, without having read the assembly instructions, drove down one evening to Poolsbrook. Within half an hour Les had the machine working and we were talking over big mugs of tea about how it could be used. He wasn't in favour of interviewing people in the street. Well, you could go to people you know, to their homes. He knew plenty of people with strong views, but this word 'interview': just not on, interviewing people you knew. Too official. You would have 'a bit of a chat, like'.

Fair enough. What'll you talk about? Well — what they think to t'village. What's needin' done to improve t'village. What about this new school you're getting — d'you think they know much about it — do they know it'll have a coffee bar? We can ask them what they think to't — if they think t'money could be put to better use, like. And — well — what they'd like to see going on int' new school.

Next time I called they had ninety minutes of tape. They were still fascinated by the actual contents, playing it over and over, saying, 'It's true', laughing at the wit, explaining silences or the fridge's hum — fascinated by their own image, their minds revolving round themselves and their fellows, their accents, their views.

'Me and Bett was reckonin' that the next thing was to edit the stuff.'

'How'll you go about it?'

'Well — get all t'answers to each o' t'questions, and write 'em down together.'

We listened to the tape again, Les laughing at his own voice, me enthusing over this and that — 'When y' used to livin' in muck, then y' doan't mind muck'; the roads 'sludged up in t'winter, an' dusted up int' flamin' summer'.

The idea of selecting, of omitting bits, came out naturally. A (to me) crucial thing came last. Next time she said 'that's *just* 'ow they talk' I butted in. 'Don't you think it'd be a good idea, when you're writing it down, to write it exactly as they speak — not change it into English — because it's Derbyshire, pure Derbyshire dialect.' Bett agrees, enthusiastically. Les is not so sure — 'they might feel, eh, you know, insulted. I mean — even if they *do* speak like that, probably don't *realise* it'. 'But it's not something to be ashamed of,' says I, 'I've got a dialect, it's just ignorant schoolteachers try to knock it out of people.' 'All right, yeh, give it a try,' Les takes the point.

The other 'co-operative' was the Politics and Local Government group. Their first meeting coincided with a local Young Volunteer Force occasion. The few who did turn up were a bit annoyed with the rest. So I asked around for an acceptable date and arranged a new meeting in the public bar of the Elm Tree. They all turned up. The juke box was blaring, dominoes and darts in progress. We sat craned forward around two tables pushed together. They fired good ideas, but no definite plans for action, and no agreement. So when the next good idea — a 'Do You Know?' page — appeared, I plonked my notebook on the table and asked for specific topics. There was a spate. What are the aims of our paper? What facilities are there at Mastin Moor? How can you contact a doctor at weekends? Where can you get the following social services? How many long-term unemployed are there in Staveley? Why must we have subsidence? Why is there a shortage of smokeless fuel? What would be an economic rent for council houses in Staveley? And so on. Who's going to answer which? We went down the list: the educational welfare officer took the social services; the local councillor took economic rents; I'd write the NCB on subsidence; Phil on smokeless fuel; two miners on Mastin Moor; young Labour Party chap on aims of the paper. . . Gradually, over months, the answers filtered back.

General meetings continued at intervals to let everyone see what progress was being made. A problem at all these meetings was a tendency to doubt decisions already made — to ask all the questions again. I see this, now, as lack of confidence due to lack of experience, as well as being an expression of individual differences. My own behaviour could be criticised: I tried to avoid playing the all-powerful leader, not wanting to create a subjected group and aiming at gradual disengagement.

We swerve to miss the ditch

One wrong direction we did take might have ditched us. We got it into our heads that we'd have to raise money to guarantee the first issue against non-sale, and met to discuss how. After a lot of argument and some near bullying from me, we chose three means of fund-raising. But I forgot to get them to decide precisely how, when and by whom it would be done. Left with the organising, I decided it just wasn't on. Neil Tempest persuaded me that fund-raising could kill the whole thing so we quietly forgot it. Instead, we collected plenty of advertising (to go on inserted duplicated sheets, thus freeing space).

Here we found that letters inviting adverts didn't work. You had to call on people. The urban district council took one side of a sheet, to advertise home improvement grants and complain about vandalism. Adult education (in the person of me) took another, to introduce the autumn programme of courses. Three competing builders bought two sides between them. The rest were shops, a family engineering business, a plastics firm, a pub with jazz club and a good old Black and Decker hedge-trimming attachment.

The first issue

Came the time when we had enough to fill four sides of the *Daily Mirror* — i.e., a single folded sheet. We decided to go ahead, publish and be damned, to give people a result of their work. A fairly fascist approach now seemed to be called for. I fixed up an evening meeting, with myself, a friendly local journalist and the group's elected 'co-ordinator'. Between us we edited the material (criteria: readability, clarity, brevity), headlined it and laid it out over four pages. A quick general meeting called to inspect and rubber-stamp our efforts, final retyping, and off it goes to the printer.

Afterwords

1. Since then: 1,900 sold at 2½p out of print run of 2,000.

2. A public meeting on 'The Future of Staveley' (arranged to coincide with distribution) attracted eighty people to the council chambers to cross swords with the town clerk. A meeting the group held to discuss the contents of the first issue attracted thirty — older,

more 'conservative', and less articulate than most of the original group members. It was a complaint session, 'them' expecting 'us' to fight their battles with the council — a classic case of alienation. We aim gradually to transform complaint into action by encouraging people to treat their grouses seriously, check their facts, get in touch with others who think alike and act together.

3. Very soon, a meeting to discuss a second issue. Keep the pot boiling. Lucky attack of 'flu, so I withdrew from role of chairman. Meeting chaired successfully by the 'native' co-ordinator.

4. Group accepts rector's suggestion that the church and other bodies be allowed to buy bulk space in paper, at advertising rates.

5. Issue no. 2 has eight pages, 2,900 sold at 2 ½p. Branching out into reminiscences, short story, thoughts on representative democracy, reports on play schemes for various ages, attack on new road route.

6. Issue no. 3 has contributions from schoolchildren, an interview with local Hell's Angels, an attack on housing department inefficiency in doing repairs and a statement on UDC policy. 2,900 sold.

7. Issue no. 4 has some good social comment photography, more history, more kids' stuff and typographically adventurous information about the Staveley Festival. The most attractive looking issue.

8. Issues 2, 3 and 4 have been edited by an 'editorial group' (i.e. anyone who wants to have a go), usually of half a dozen people.

9. I have now (July 1971) withdrawn completely from the activities of the group. The paper will be published from Staveley Community Centre, Rectory Road, Staveley, near Chesterfield. Write there for back issues or to subscribe to future ones (25p per year).

3. Hell's Angels Talk

This 1970 interview with members of a local group of Hell's Angels was the most dramatic to appear in the pages of *Staveley Now*. In it they talk frankly about their aspirations, wishes, fantasies, and relationships with their parents, their leader, the youth service, and their bikes. Joan Turner, Muriel Easton and I were the interviewers. Joan was a part-time worker at the 'greebo' youth club they frequented, and Muriel was the mother of one of their girlfriends. The pseudonyms used were chosen by the Angels themselves.

*

Voices: Colin, Neptune, Fred, Solly, Caesar, The Hun, Thor,
Muriel, Joan.

Colin: Anybody who wants to ask questions can ask questions, and anybody who wants to give answers can give answers. How old are you?
All: 19, 35, 19, 21, 27, 20, 21.
Colin: What's your job?
All: Labouring, bricklayer's labourer, welder, garage manager, labourer, supervisor.
Colin: Anybody out of work regularly?
Laughter
The Hun: Me.
Colin: Anybody else?
Fred: From time to time, me.
Colin: Anybody not much interested in their job?
Silence
Fred: If you haven't got a job to be interested in how can you be interested?
Colin (to Neptune): Are you interested in the job?
Neptune: Yes.

Colin: What's your job then?
Neptune: Welder.
Colin: How long have you been in the job?
Neptune: Two years.
Colin: It's interesting to you, you enjoy the welding?
Neptune: Yes.
Colin: You work in the evenings as well as in the day time?
Neptune: Yes.
Colin: When you're free, when you aren't working, what do you do?
Neptune: Work on motor bike, or go out, you know, odd times.
Colin: Do you stay in a lot, in the house?
Neptune: I am doing now because I'm saving money like, for holidays and that.
Colin: Do you watch TV when you're in?
Neptune: Not very often.

Colin: Is there anything you like on TV?

Neptune: Not, not really.

Colin (to The Hun): What do you do again?

The Hun: When I'm working, I'm a builder's labourer.

Colin: Are you interested in it, or do you just do it because you have to do it?

The Hun: Well, because I have to do it.

Colin: Yeh, if you had a choice of doing something else, what would you do, or do you not know?

The Hun: I'd go over to America and be one of the Angels over there, be free.

Colin: You would be one of the . . .?

The Hun: American Angels, they're free man, you know?

Colin: What do you like about bikes?

The Hun: Power.

Colin: Power, anything else?

The Hun: Yeh, yeh, well when you're on a hog, it's something out of the ordinary, you know?

Colin: What's a hog? Is that a bike?

The Hun: Chopper, yes.

Colin: As powerful as possible, the bigger the better eh?

The Hun: Yeh.

Colin: What is it about it?

The Hun: Well, when you're riding down the road or highway, you know, you're just there, and the wind is in your face and everything, and you just feel free. You know, there's people looking at you.

Colin: Do you like being looked at when you're on the bike?

The Hun: Yeh, yeh, I like everybody to look at me. That's why I've got me hog.

Colin: Would it be true to say that you don't get any of the satisfactions in your job that you get on a bike?

Caesar: Well, it's like a woman, isn't it, a bike. It's like a woman, it's bike comes first, everything else comes, a woman comes second, jobs come third. Even wives comes second to a bike.

Muriel: I think most of them have built their own bikes, haven't you?

All: Yes.

Muriel: Neptune's building his.

Colin: How long did it take you?

Neptune: Well, I've been building it for two years and I've spent £400, and it isn't finished yet.

Colin: And you haven't ridden it in all that time?

Neptune: No.

Colin: Have you got a bike to go about on?

Neptune: No.

Colin: Anybody else want to ask questions? Don't forget it's as much your right to ask questions as me. (Pause) Can I ask you something different? What do you think of schoolteachers?

Raspberry

Colin: Say that again.

The Hun: They are alright, you know. As squares go.

Colin: Squares?

Solly: Some are alright, some aren't. Some can teach, some can't. Those that can put it over are alright but them that can't, don't.

Colin: How long is it since you were at school?

Solly: I'm still at Tech.

Colin: You're still at Tech? Does the same apply to teachers at Tech?

Solly: Yes, because I nearly had a battle with one other week.

Colin: A physical fight, you mean?

Solly: Well, he's got this attitude that he was looking for a punch in the nose.

Colin: Go on, tell us about it, this is interesting. What is it exactly that you don't like about him.

Solly: Well, it's just his attitude. He comes round.

Colin: Does he try to boss you?

Solly: Well, he just makes you feel inferior, the way he goes about talking to you.

Colin: What does he teach?

Solly: Tech drawing.

Colin: Does he make you feel you know nothing about it and he knows everything?

Solly: Well, it's how he comes about it

. . . We've had him straightened out once and we had the head of department down on us.

Colin: What do you mean, down on you? For making a noise in his class, for disturbing him?

Solly: For telling him where he can go.

Muriel: Does everybody feel like this about him, or is it just you?

Solly: Well, it's his attitude. I mean, he comes up, you ask him something technical about the job, and he probably says, Oh, do you know it all, and walks off, you know? It's just his attitude.

Colin: Do you mean he doesn't like you asking him anything he isn't sort of teaching you at the moment? He just likes you to be very quiet?

Solly: Well, if you ask him about anything you're drawing, if you don't take notice of him, the way he says, if you question it, he just walks off.

Colin: He doesn't want any questions?

Solly: Well, he's been on holiday for two weeks, and this other bloke has come, they're both at Rolls Royce in Chesterfield, they're both, you know, proper blokes. Well, this bloke came other week and he turned round to me and says, Oh, you know it all do you? I says no, but you don't either. We had a discussion, week after he come back and were calling us by our christian names, come round, and it were as different again. Just because we put it straight, our way of thinking, you know? You've got to give and take a bit, I know, but that bloke, you know, he needs a poke in the mouth sometimes, you know. He nearly got it once before, with another youth.

Colin: You say teachers are squares.

The Hun: Well, everybody normal, as the high and mighty call it, are squares.

Colin: You see yourselves as separate and everybody else as normal?

Neptune: Yes, we are. Hell's Angels to everybody else are just scum, aren't we?

Joan: Not to everybody.

Thor: Well, not to you three, but to other people if they see us.

Joan: Why, why are you?

Thor: That's what we'd like to know.

Solly: Well, look what's been in papers this Sunday. I mean, they have only to see that, these old folks, and they go OOOH.

Colin: Everybody's terrified of Hell's Angels.

Joan: Yes, but isn't it your appearance?

Solly: Why should they be terrified though?

Colin: It says in the newspapers that Hell's Angels are violent and assault people.

Neptune: Do we look violent? You don't take notice of what it says in newspapers.

The Hun: We can be violent, when we're bugged.

Neptune: But now we're doing good things such as these big technical dances and that. We're invited to these dances instead of Securicor because we don't cause trouble. We went to a dance at Christmas, a big technical dance, there were about 600 people there and we kept everybody in order at the dance, you know? We didn't even have any trouble ourselves.

Colin: You mean you acted as bouncers?

Neptune: Yes. They thanked us for that, and now they've invited us to two more dances this weekend. There weren't a single fight at that dance, there could have been three or four fights, everything went smooth. We smoothed everybody out, there weren't any trouble. We had a good night and they got £100 more for Mencap or some charity than they usually get, you know.

Solly: They started off £30 down and ended up £25 up on this dance.

Colin: What do you think of your parents? Your father and mother, do you like them?

Solly: Yes, I like them, but they think if I'm wearing this, I'm daft.

Colin: They think that you're queer?
The Hun: A freak.
Solly: Well, they do, yes.
Joan: Do they think that you're letting the family down, seeing as your family had a good name in Staveley?
Solly: Well, they think I ought to marry the vicar's daughter, yes. If you know what I mean by that.
Joan: Yes.
Solly: But I told them not to try and run my life, this is it.
Joan: And have they accepted that now?
Solly: Yeh. Well put it this way, if I were going with a bird like, you know, and they don't like the family, oh I don't like her, you know, and all this lot, but they leave me alone now. I mean now I'm doing me chopper and me brother is helping me like, me and our youth have spent three months now building it up from scratch. Well, we just started with a straight bit of metal actually. They leave me alone now, me mother wants to see it on the road, and me dad keeps going 'on the idiots'. You just take no notice.
Caesar: We like these squares to think that we're . . . we like to shock them, that's the whole concept of Hell's Angels anyway. It's to shock the rest of the world.
Colin: You think the rest of the world needs a shock?
Joan: How much could you take, Caesar? We went down to Poolsbrook last week and as soon as we walked through the door they said Greebo and that was it. Now does this make you mad, as soon as you go into anywhere?
Solly: I were talking to three birds in a pub in Sheffield, I were talking to them like, and we asked them where they had come from, and one of them came from Cresswell, and as soon as I said Staveley, she said Greebo, and walked off. And I thought, you know.
Joan: Why have Greebos got this name? What have they done to get it?

Solly: Because Staveley is known as a leather-jacket town.
Thor: Everybody's in the same position, there's good and bad. We don't try to do good, we don't try to do bad, we're just trying to do what we want to do.
Joan: Yes, but the Jack O'Diamonds did good and they had leather jackets, didn't they? So why didn't that good character carry on?
Thor: I know, but such as those people, people talk about them as cissies some of them. For example, Tim Swain were doing a good deed, he were in that club where they did, and running about for people, he went hell for leather and they phoned him up to let him know, he went to Worksop and run straight back to Chesterfield and he had done about 100 miles for a pair of false teeth or something like that. Just fetched it like that, I mean they come to you.
Joan: Yeh, so you think that the rest of society is just using you then, when they want to use you?
Thor: Well, we don't want to do that sort of thing, do we? We don't want to be goodies and we don't want to be baddies.
Colin: I'd like to hear more about that.
Caesar: I don't give a damn what people think, as long as they don't break the law, you know, go and smash some shops, but I don't care, they could stand on their heads for me. That's it.
Colin: Do you want to shock people?
The Hun: Yes, yes, I want to shock 'em all, I mean that's what I wear me colours for.
Colin: Seriously, do you want to shock people, hit them over the head, I don't mean literally, what do you want to hit them for?
The Hun: It's why I wear these — it's why I wear these.
Colin: That's a swastika, do you know what that means? What does it mean?
The Hun: Well, you know, Hitler like,

you know. I'm not a Nazi, I'm not a Nazi at all, it's just that these old ones, you know, well anybody out of our seam, they think OH a Nazi, you know, they think he's a bad lot.

Thor: We don't respect Nazis, I don't think, we just respect their uniform, we don't try to be like a Nazi.

Neptune: We just wear medallions so that old folks, you know, go ooff.

Joan: So you are literally against old people then?

All: No. Not old people. Anybody else.

Solly: All I want to do when I get my bike going. I'd like to go down the centre of town on a Saturday afternoon, and mine looks queer as it is, because it's completely different, with a car engine, with horns blowing, full revs in second gear, down the centre of town, and make everybody turn round and notice, you know.

Caesar: Blow their minds?

Solly: Yes.

The Hun: I mean with things like Edward Heath and Prince Charles, those with money what these lads have to earn, and they give it them in tax. Because Charles, he's a right poof, that's what he is, literally a poof.

Solly: It isn't the background you come from, it's how you feel yourself. Look at me, I'm completely different to you in background life, but as it comes to it now I'm the same as you — definitely.

Colin: Fred now, do you want to shock people?

Fred: Well, I appear to do. (*Laughter*) Quite often, no, I think — I get a kick out of shocking them, I mean I don't do it intentionally, I mean it's . . .

Colin: What's missing in your life?

Fred: Well I mean it's dead isn't it? It's dead from start to finish. I mean the average bloke's life, he starts work at what? Say fifteen. He works till he's sixty-five and if he lives long enough he draws his old age pension.

Thor: Yes, but life is what he makes it.

Fred: I know, but I mean I want to make something out of it, I want to have a bit of fun, I have had a bit of fun and I'm going to have some more.

Thor: I mean, let's face it man, as soon as you're born you start dying, don't you, and your life in between is what you make it. I mean if you want to make a bum, I mean we aren't bums, I mean we run our life, same as Caesar, he's got a good job and Solly comes from a good background, we all know what we're on with. In fact I don't really want to shock anybody, but I want to make people know I'm there. I mean I'm no Prince Charles or King of England or Queen of England.

Solly: I mean let's put it this way. If I didn't want to be one of these, I could be going round with big nobs from firms in Sheffield, concrete plants, I know most of them, you know, by first names now. The background I come from — I run a garage. I could have no end of work from Sheffield firms if I wanted it. I've got a car out there — a Super Snipe.

Colin: Do you live in Staveley?

Neptune: No.

Colin: Where do you live then?

Neptune: Newbold.

Colin: What's wrong with this part of the world, what do you dislike about it most?

Neptune: Well, such as the Government and all that, I don't agree with anything like that, I don't agree with Government or police or any of their ways or anything like that. I don't agree with their ways — definitely not. Well, such as police, I mean you get into trouble with police, you've lost to start with, whether you're guilty or innocent, you've lost. I mean I've been to courts lots of times, I mean I have been to prison and everything but, and that for things I really shouldn't have gone to prison for.

Colin: You mean you were innocent?

Neptune: Yes, in a way but it's no use saying well, I didn't do this, because all

all you do — and they say that police don't beat you up and that. But I mean, I've had all that.

Colin: You mean you've been beaten up?

Neptune: Yes, at least four times.

Colin: For not doing anything?

Neptune: Yes. Just because they know me, they know me in Chesterfield, the know me name so I'm guilty. If they see somebody in a fight and I'm walking past I mean, I'm guilty to start with because they don't like me, none of them do in town. It's the same with lot of them. I mean, last time I got into trouble I was talking to a lad at top of a public yard like, you know, just talking. Police car stopped, dragged us both in, we were only talking. I mean I had known him for about eight years, lad. Because there's £35 in it I nearly went down for two years. It were just this one certain policeman and because it were me. It could have been a lot more serious but it cost me enough as it were, and I hadn't even done nothing. We were only arguing, but we have no say in it.

Colin: Seriously though, if you had the chance of doing it, what sort of society would you like to live in, positively like to live in?

The Hun: A Labour Government — I should a Labour Government.

Colin: Seriously, though, if you could change society,

Thor: I would like plenty of money and if I'd got the same life as I've got now, I would like to live as I have now, but with plenty of money.

Colin: So you are happy doing the things you're doing now?

Thor: I am, I'm dead happy, I enjoy what I'm doing now, and I respect what I do now, but I'd like plenty of money.

Neptune: It's true, like I'm doing now, building my own bike.

Colin: Yes, but I'm asking you to try and be more specific.

Neptune: You get people saying good

old days, don't you? But what were good about the old days? What were good about good old days?

Colin: Poverty, depression.

Neptune: Poverty, what's good about that?

Colin: It's what they remember when they were young. Like when you're old, you'll remember.

Muriel: You had more respect for things, you see, when you hadn't got much money. Your money comes easily now, I know it isn't worth much, but people seemed to have more respect for things.

Solly: But money's not everything, it just takes the worry away.

Muriel: Is there anything you respect? Any person or anything that you respect, you would like to be like them?

Thor: Well, me parents, parents more than anything else.

The Hun: Mick Jagger.

Caesar: Solly Barger.

Colin: Who's he?

Caesar: Who's he! He's the President of the Hell's Angels in America.

Colin: Now, same question to you, if you could change the world to the way you want it to be, what would you change it into?

Caesar: If I could change the world?

Colin: Yes, you know, I mean genuinely, the society you live in to something you like better.

Caesar: A National Socialist State run by Hell's Angels.

Colin: You mean the socialist bit as well as the national bit?

Caesar: Right-wing.

Colin: Right-wing? What do you mean by Socialist then? What sort of country then — tell us about it.

Caesar: Well, National Socialist.

Colin: Same as in Germany?

Caesar: Yes.

Colin: Kill Jews?

Caesar: Yes.

Joan: Why?

Caesar: Because I don't like Jews.

Joan: Why don't you like Jews?
Caesar: I don't like them.
Joan: You can't just say that.
Caesar: I can, I just said it haven't I?
Joan: There must be some reason.
Caesar: I just don't like them.
Colin: What role would you like to have played in Germany, you know, in the country?
Joan: You can compare yourself with Hitler, can't you? The position you've got with the youngsters around here, you've got Hitler's position. Do you enjoy that?
Caesar: Yes. If I were in Germany before the war, I should have liked to have been in the SS.
Thor: Pardon?
Caesar: I should have liked to be in SS.
Joan: You would?
Caesar: Yes.
Joan: Did you do National Service?
Caesar: Yes. It was a good organisation but it went wrong.
Colin: The SS?
Caesar: Yes. You wouldn't get none of these immigrants, would you? I mean, look at mess this country's in now. I mean, they did wrong, admitted, but they did a lot of good. Autobahns and all that.
Thor: I mean, let's face it. Hitler in twenty years done more than Germany has done in last 200 years. I mean they built autobahns, I mean some people say he were mental, but, he *were* mental in some ways, but he taught us to build autobahns. In fact, he wanted English to join war with him, and he said we would rule world with him, but English said they had got more sense and didn't want to do it, but if they had have joined I mean, in fact only thing that were wrong with Hitler, he wanted to rule world, but if he had ruled world and not wanted to *own* it, if he had have ruled it, it would have been a better world, a lot better country, this would.
Joan: Yes, but would you have the freedom that you've got now to do

what you want to do, so would you have been happy?
The Hun: No.
Caesar: We'd have been in the Hitler Youth. We don't do what we want to do now do we?
Joan: Ah, but you do a lot more now than you would've been able to do say in a Communist country.
Caesar: We don't know, you're brainwashed. We don't know what they do in China, it's only what we're told. It's alright saying Russia is this and Russia is that, but who's been to Russia?
Colin: Would you like to go to Russia?
Caesar: I mean take Russia, like Germany, everybody works for the Fatherland and for Mother Russia. Who cares about England? Nobody.
Thor: I hate Communists.
Neptune: Look at that film on China. When that reporter went in for two weeks, he were only shown what they wanted him to see, you never see what happens in other places, what it were really like. How could you tell?
Fred: This is it. How can you tell?
Neptune: This is it.
Colin: Fred, if you could change society round, what you wanted it to be, what would you change it to?
Fred: Well, I think in a way I'm different to most. Me, I mean, I think I told you before, money means nothing to me. It's got no value, I mean it's just nothing. I'm of non-violent nature, I've a tendency to go my own free way, and to hell with every bugger else.
Colin: I'm asking a slightly different question, if you could change society to what you wanted it to be, you know, to something that was right, you know. Caesar said they would like to change it into Hitler's Germany. What would you like to change it to?
Fred: Well, I mean it's a hell of a mix-up to do anything with but —
Colin: It's too mixed up to do anything with?
Fred: Yes.
Thor: I should abolish all Royalty to

start with.

All: Definitely, first thing to be abolished.

Thor: All they do when anything goes wrong is go on holiday. I mean all they're doing now is going on holiday, nearly six months of the year, they're going on holidays. Spending money, that's our money they're spending.

The Hun: Why can't we pay our debts what we owe to other countries like America, instead of that poof Prince Charles going to Africa for a safari for five days? He's a big bum.

Colin: Do you resent the fact that there are people who don't work?

The Hun: Yes, well, I don't work, but his mother works, and his mother works. Now. I go into their house and his mother asks if I'm working, I mean man, I'm that ashamed I said I'm on holiday, I were that ashamed because his mother works harder than most any bloke in this room.

Thor: Listen. His mother, I mean Neptune's mother, she's a hard-working woman, she does work, my mother works.

Muriel: I think what The Hun is saying is that he doesn't work and in his own way he's living like Prince Charles, and in a way because he doesn't want to work, no I'm not saying he doesn't want to work.

The Hun: I want to work.

Muriel: He wants to work but he can't get a job.

Colin: It's genuinely true?

The Hun: That's true, yes.

Thor: I mean Prince Charles, he is a bum, I mean he's taking our tax money, he's going on holidays all year round, I mean we paid for his schooling, I mean we've paid for everything for Royal family don't we? I mean whole thing about society is a load of balls, I mean this Conservative job and that, I reckon that's a load of balls an' all.

Colin: Anybody want to ask anybody any questions, I mean, I've been asking all the bloody questions.

The Hun: Well, I want to ask you a question.

Colin: Right, come on.

The Hun: Now, what do you think of this stuff? Swastikas and Iron Crosses.

Neptune: Straight, now, straight.

Colin: Well, I'll tell you. Four years ago I found swastikas and all the insignia of the Third Reich in a historical magazine, and I found it fascinating, you know, I found it really beautiful and interesting. I'll tell you why, because it's hard and it represents action.

Caesar: You know there is a mistake in the swastika? It should have been the other way round.

Thor: I mean, it's come through some years, I mean Greeks used to use the swastika, didn't they?

Caesar: Yes. That's where it come from, didn't it, originally?

Thor: It's a sign drawing everything into the middle, drawing everything into the centre.

Joan: What's it for?

Thor: Drawing everything into the centre, like he's going round drawing everybody to himself, you know, like we want.

The Hun: What do you think of Hell's Angels?

Colin: Well, I don't know much about Hell's Angels. To me the Hell's Angels are a mixture, of what I know personally of him and him, and one or two others, and when I read in the newspapers. To me Hell's Angels are people who are reacting against a rotten society. Let me finish this. I'm serious. Hell's Angels must be people who are bored by their work, bored by conventional people, and they want a different image, a live image, an image of action, and energy. I think it's a natural desire, I want a live life.

Thor: I'll tell you what I know. We're saving up for this out of club funds, I mean I'm not supposed to tell you this, what we do and what we aren't supposed to do, but what we want in our club is a place of us own where we can go, such as this place, there's people respect us down here, they don't throw us out, we don't cause trouble down here unless somebody says anything to us, and we're saving up for a club now, a club of our own, and we'll get one.

Colin: This is a youth club?

Thor: It is not a youth club, it isn't a centre for bums or anything. It's more organised than people think. We can't go into detail and tell you but our group is more organised than any other group that has ever been formed. We're wanting a place. We don't want no bum of a youth club leader. We're saving up for it.

Colin: Can I just ask you, when you say your group you mean the Angels?

Caesar: Yes. We've got strict discipline. You just can't say, well alright I want to be an Angel, you just can't get in like that.

Thor: Now we're saving up for us own place, but nobody will give us a chance to get us own place.

Neptune: We'll have hundreds of pounds, but as now over year, us total sum we've got £600 or more, but we won't be able to get a place, because they'll look at us when we go and say can we rent such and such a place, they'll look at us won't they, and say no.

Joan: But you haven't tried.

Thor: Ah, well, we haven't got the money, we haven't got the backing yet, but listen, we don't want some youth club leader to read this in the paper and say you can have this club, and he runs that club. We want Caesar, we want to run it ourselves. We ran our meetings successfully, we can run this club successfully. It's a club in its own right, but it isn't a youth club. We do what we want to when we want to do it, and we don't want anybody running our club only ourselves. We want to run ourselves, we want a place what we can run.

Neptune: They think there will be fight after fight. I mean we've had a party down here, us own party, a Christmas party. We went upstairs. We served us own beer, there were just us there. We had a complete night, you can ask them behind bar, there weren't a bit of trouble. We paid for everything, there were one glass broke and we paid for that glass. We paid for everything that we had — in advance. And there weren't a bit of trouble, that's right isn't it?

Thor: That's right.

Neptune: We all had a really good night and everybody was invited. We had best party that anybody could have and there weren't a bit of trouble.

Colin: That's because you were responsible for it.

Thor: If you go to a place they think OH you'll be smashing glasses up, they'll be smashing place up, they'll be smashing tables and everything, they'll be having orgies.

The Hun: They'll be having orgies, drug taking.

Colin: Yes.

Thor: But we had a really good night.

Caesar: You see, Angels, every Angel that joins is tret* as an adult. He isn't tret as a kid, I mean a youth club leader has a suit on and he looks down on them.

Joan: Not all of them.

Caesar: Oh, but they do! Take a young lad and whatever Mr Smith† says, he does.

Neptune: Joan doesn't.

Caesar: I can get closer to a young lad than any leader can. Joan is good, yes.

Joan: It *isn't* good, Caesar, it's good for kids of 13 and 14, but it isn't good for this age group, is it, to have a suit on and tell you that you mustn't come in with studs on your shoes and you mustn't have studs on your jacket.

* tret=treated
† the local youth leader

That's treating you as children.

Neptune: You know bowling alley in town, new bowling alley, well if you go with a leather jacket on or long hair you can't go in. That were first thing. People like that, they tell us what to wear. We wear what we want to wear, I mean it doesn't matter if we look like IT off Herman Monster Show. I mean we're wearing what we want to wear.

Joan: Yes.

Thor: Aren't we, I mean we're wearing us own thing. I mean I can go out dressed up every night if I wanted to, but I'd rather go out like this. It just so happens that I've got bird with me tonight.

Joan: Well, why are you dressed up like this when you're out with a bird?

Tor: Because I don't want her to ber ashamed of me.

Joan: Well, why should she be ashamed of you, are you ashamed of yourself?

Thor: She isn't ashamed of me, she doesn't say anything. I mean if I went out in a pair of underpants she wouldn't say nothing but I mean if your husband went out in clothes like this we're wearing now, you wouldn't like it, would you? You would disrespect him. You wouldn't like it, would you? Not every night would you?

Joan: No. No.

Thor: I mean everybody likes a change don't they?

Colin: Do you always wear these clothes?

Caesar: No, I sometimes go out dressed up.

The Hun: I always dress like this.

Colin: Do you always dress like that?

Caesar: Well, because when I go out . . .

Thor: I don't know how many suits he's got but he doesn't wear them.

The Hun: Me? Well, I like me jeans, I like to dress casually you know, as I want to dress.

Colin: You don't want to dress up?

The Hun: No, no. I hate suits.

Colin: Why?

The Hun: Because I like these, and when I met my wife I was like this, so I'm always like this.

4. Doomed Children

This article was published on the front page of the fifth issue of *Staveley Now* in the autumn of 1971. It was written by Pam Fry, Joan Turner, Muriel Easton, Adrian Cauldwell and myself. It is included here as an example of the close link-up between the newspaper group and various community action campaigns in the district. It is a monument to local government departmentalism, bureaucracy, incompetence, and apparent indifference. For helping to research and write it, I was disciplined by the Divisional Education Officer and accused of disloyalty to colleagues.

*

The new Norbriggs Primary School opened on September 6th. It is sited just behind Norbriggs House where Norbriggs Road joins the A619. The 1968 road census shows approximately 650 vehicles per hour use this road but since then the motorway has been opened at Barlborough so the traffic will no doubt have increased substantially.

There will be 270 children between the ages of three and eight coming to the school, from Staveley by bus, from Staveley on foot and from Mastin Moor. They will ALL have to use the crossing.

From Staveley By Bus
The bus leaves the Market Place at 8.50 a.m. and will drop the children outside James' Nurseries on the opposite side of the road from the school.

From Staveley On Foot
Children walking from the town centre and Lowgates will have to cross the road or sometimes walk on the road because of the absence of a pavement.

From Mastin Moor
Children with or without their mothers will come down the hill, the opposite side of the road from the school, and so will have to cross the road to school.

All these children will have to cross the main A619 on a blind corner at the bottom of a steep hill where there is no speed restriction. Visibility for traffic coming down the hill is 120 ft. and the braking distance for a lorry travelling at 40 m.p.h. is 300 ft. Traffic going up the hill is building up speed for the climb. 'It's the only fast stretch of road in Staveley,' said a local police inspector.

For the first two or three weeks the police say there will be a police patrol and a traffic warden and the teachers will help. BUT after that these children will be in the charge of a 70-year-old traffic warden!

County Councillor Mrs Platts says she 'realises the problem' and has tried with no success at county level. She also says Staveley UDC has tried with the same results.

The School Managers are very worried about the problem and have tried to find a solution to no avail.

Mrs Platts says: 'It's up to you (the parents) to bring pressure to bear, and pressure can be brought to bear . . . we're here to support you I can assure you of that.'

A local police inspector says that it is a very bad crossing place and the police are concerned about the safety of the children but could do nothing more about it apart from erecting flashing patrol lights forty yards either side of the crossing. They have applied for a speed restriction of 40 m.p.h.

Bus from Staveley
The bus drops our children at James' Nurseries on the wrong side of the road; then turns up Norbriggs Road to take the Woodthorpe children to school. We have written to the Education Department, i e. Mrs Skinner, and the bus company, asking why our children can't be dropped outside the school gates on Norbriggs Road when the bus passes this point.

We called a meeting of the parents because after exhaustive communications with the Education Department, Road Safety Committee, Highways Department, the police and the school governors, we could get no effective action although each department expressed sympathy.

Councillor Wickins, Mrs Platts and Mr Fairs all attended this meeting.

Mr Wickins said that he had suggested to County Council that there should be a uniform speed limit of 40 m.p.h. on the road. The latest reply was 'all the County Council roads are in fact being

being investigated and plans being approved, when no doubt this road, although not suggested, would come under the same restriction.' He suggested that there were other things we could do, e.g. zebra crossings.

Mr Fair made the point that up to six months ago Staveley was allocated only three pedestrian crossings. The regulations have now changed and we can probably get four.

Ideas from the floor were:

(1)   Subway — impossible because of mining subsidence and the danger of flooding.

(2)   A footbridge over the road — vetoed by the Highway Officer (Matlock) because
      (a)   all the allocation of money for Staveley Highways has been spent, and
      (b)   the existing conditions didn't warrant one.

(3)   A barrier round the pavement edge to the school gates — Mrs Platts agreed to take the 'excellent suggestion' forward to County.

(4)   Cross Now type of traffic lights — Councillor Wickins agreed to get in touch with the Staveley Surveyor and ask him to contact the County Surveyor, who controls the Highways, with the suggestion and say that it is public opinion that this should be done.

(5)   As the traffic wardens start at 8.30 a.m. and the restrictions don't come into force until 9 a.m. it was suggested that these two ladies were brought down to the crossing until the other recommendations were approved.

(6)   Why can't the bus take children round the corner to the school gates? — the bus company say they 'have checked with police, and the traffic warden previously employed at Mastin Moor Primary School to see children across the A619 trunk road will as from the commencement of the autumn term be employed at Norbriggs to ensure the safety of the children crossing the road at that point, to the new primary school at Norbriggs. Under the circumstances I cannot see there is any need for us to re-route the school bus which we are providing for this requirement.'

The parents decided on the following action and signed a petition to that effect.

(1)   Temporary traffic lights immediately installed.

(2)   Permanent traffic lights installed as soon as possible.

(3)   A substantial barrier should be erected around the road from the crossing point to the school gates.

(4)   The crossing should be police controlled and not by one traffic warden.

(5)   The school bus should take the children into the school gates.

One would think the safety of 270 YOUNG children would have been considered before the actual opening of the school. It seems inconceivable that planning authorities should neglect so vital a point.

All other schools in the area have adequate bus services depositing children almost at the school gates and yet none are on the main road.

While this is a marvellous school, modern in all aspects and in a very pretty setting, its location with regard to road safety is disastrous!

MUST A CHILD BE KILLED BEFORE SOME AUTHORITY ACCEPTS RESPONSIBILITY?

WE BELIEVE THE RESPONSIBILITY LIES WITH THE DERBYSHIRE COUNTY COUNCIL.

Why wait. It may be YOUR CHILD.

Pam Fry, Joan Turner, Muriel Easton,
Adrian Cauldwell and Colin Kirkwood.

5. Thoughts About UCS

This article also appeared in the fifth issue of *Staveley Now*. Until then, I had operated a self-denying ordinance within the group, as far as writing was concerned. I saw my role as that of encourager and facilitator of initiatives taken by other members, or — at very most — interviewing people with a significant angle on life that might otherwise be ignored. The work-in at the UCS (Upper Clyde Shipbuilders) provided an opportunity to discuss themes which I felt were of pressing importance to people in Staveley and elsewhere. It was an opportunity I couldn't resist.

*

The occupation of the Clydeside shipyards by the men who work in them was big news. The telly and the papers were full of it for a couple of weeks. Then it began to cool down. Events were repeating themselves — somebody flew to London, somebody else flew to London; a big march, another big march. . .

The media men swung their binoculars away from the Clyde in search of new action, new instant heroes.

News is the opium of the masses
Because, basically, their job is to keep YOU, the viewer, in front of your set, or swing you over to *their* paper.

Not to let you see right into what's happening.

News is superficial. It distorts real-life situations. A few exciting shots — a burning factory, an anguished mother — that's enough to keep you where they want you.

The lives behind the news
On the Clyde men working in a traditional heavy industry (it could have been coal or steel) were *threatened with loss of their jobs.*

They feared it meant long-term unemployment so they took action — they took control of their place of work.

What did they want to achieve?

(1) 'The right to work'. The papers and the telly went to town on

this idea — it appeals to your feelings of indignation and pity. Who could object to people actually wanting to work!

But the real point was that these men *didn't want to be out of work*, because to be out of work in this country means poverty: unemployment and supplementary benefits add up to a very thin style of life.

It means loss of self-respect. Who wants to be on the scrapheap?

(2) 'To save shipbuilding on the Clyde and stop the rot in the Scottish economy.' The media men know that viewers like to hear such words as 'save' and 'stop the rot'. It makes you feel patriotic and self-pitying.

Workers' control

(3) 'Workers' control.' This is the real message from Clydeside. But the media didn't spend much time on it. It hasn't got much 'human interest'.

In the yards, workers' control has been limited: they took over the gates, decided who was to get in and who wasn't; they inspected the company's accounts, including the advance order book, so that their policy would be finally realistic; they said they'd pay the wages of men made redundant out of contributions from the wages of those still employed, so that the yards could work on and seek new orders.

Not much, really. You could even say it wasn't workers' control, but shop stewards' control.

A picture of the future

The take-over will probably fail in its aim to stop redundancies. A lot of men will be slung out over the next eighteen months.

And the idea of workers' control will fade off the screen once the Government's solution is put into action. The shop stewards will be back where they belong, if they're not made redundant too.

So why write about it? Why talk about it?

Because in its own small way it's a picture of the future.

Jimmy Reid

The 70,000 people who marched to Glasgow Green (a park in the midst of the worst housing conditions in Europe) didn't go to hear the big names — Vic Feather, Dan McGarvey, Anthony Wedgewood Benn. They went to hear Jimmy Reid, a local shop steward.

This is what workers' control is about. People controlling the situations they're in, not being controlled by 'the authorities'.

Industry and Government

Here is what it could mean:

In industry, workers in a firm would control 'management' decisions — what to make, what materials to use, where to get them, who to employ; hours and conditions of work; the actual process of work — the order and speed of doing things, the methods, what machines and tools to use, who does what; wages and rates; communication and co-ordination would be separated from command, and thus these changes would end autocratic control *and* industrial disputes.

In government, people would not delegate the right to make decisions to their elected representatives (who in turn delegate day-to-day running of the important affairs of life to officials or experts). The officials would be controlled by the people living in the areas affected by their plans, by those on the receiving end. New forms of self-government such as street and neighbourhood meetings would grow up. The act of delegation would be carefully controlled. Its purpose would be to co-ordinate the interests of different areas, not to hand over control.

People's control now

What makes the Upper Clyde message so pressing is that people's control, *real democracy*, is needed now. Not just within the present work situations, but through all the actions and aims of our society.

Organised injustice

We are told that if ordinary people tried to control life, there would be chaos. We need order, so we ought to leave it in the capable hands of those running the show now.

Imagine a long row of people. A man with a gun shouts 'Next'. The one at the head of the row marches across to a wall. Bang! 'Next!' 'Next!'

That's well ordered. But is it right? A situation full of injustice and inhumanity can be very well ordered.

This is so with our society. We should judge not only how well it is organised, but also the sort of lives people have in it, the control, the creativity or lack of it, the sort of relationships there are, the uses made of our abilities and of natural resources.

Life in our society

Here are some opinions. If you think they're not true write in and argue.

(a) Ninety per cent of people in Staveley, given the choice (or enough money), wouldn't do the job they're doing now. They do it largely because they have to. They need the money.

(b) You must have seen this somewhere. Far more days' production are lost due to industrial accidents than are lost due to strikes. Did you ever notice the distortion of human values in that statement? Industrial accidents are bad *because they lead to loss of production!*

Would there be so many 'industrial accidents' if working people had full control over the conditions of their work?

(c) You cut your lawn perhaps once a week in the summer. It takes, say, 45 minutes. Why do so many of us buy mowers which sit unused for most of the time, when it would be more sensible to buy one among a group? Is this a good use of human energy, producing too many lawnmowers?

Is it a good use of natural resources?

How about washing machines?

Are our priorities right, in what we produce? Do we need hydrogen bombs? Concorde?

(d) Everything in the shops has got a wrapper with bright colours and images to attract you to it. Necessary? How much human energy and paper goes into making all the wrappers and packages? Is it interesting work, or is it boring?

(e) How many other products as well as cars have built-in obsolescence? Would it not be better to build fewer cars more solidly and improve maintenance and servicing?

(f) A special question for office workers. Is your work really necessary? Does it help production, distribution and communication? How much is pure bureaucracy? How much is recording whose main purpose is to *prevent fiddling*? I'd guess that hundreds of thousands of people in Britain do hours of boring work checking that nobody else is doing the firm out of money.

What sort of society do we live in if this kind of work is necessary?

Authority
I could add to this list. So could you. It is important because it builds up a case against the kind of society we live in, and therefore against those who control it.

The control is not in the hands of ordinary people but in the hands of 'the authorities' — officials, managers, chairmen, councillors — people who keep their facts close to their chests like cards, who talk in a language difficult to understand, which is meant to mystify people, and make them feel small.

One last word — *authority*. Its basic Latin meaning is to originate. An *author* is a lucky man. He not only does the work, he controls it. He forms it. He plans it.

In our society, the *forming* is separated from the *performing*, the planning from doing. The power figures make the decisions and the ordinary people do the donkey work.

6. Hunger March

This is the story of two men, Laurence and Wilf Filsell, both members of Staveley Disabled Group. They were unskilled workers and experienced long periods of unemployment before the war. Laurence took part in the York Hunger March, which passed through Staveley en route to London. The interview was published in *Staveley Now* no. 7, along with a photo of Laurence and Wilf.

*

Memories/Work

Colin: The subject of our discussion is the hunger march of 1932. We're going to look at it as a part of Laurence and Wilf's lives. (To Laurence): What age were you when you left school?

Laurence: Fourteen.

Colin: What year was that?

Laurence: About 1924.

Colin: Did you know much about the first world war?

Laurence: I was born in 1911. I can remember when the fire was lit on the Mount. It was before the houses were there. It was lit by Mr Pym Smith. I remember when the Liberals got in at Staveley. Stanley Baldwin was PM. Me father kept the Markham Hall then, you know, caretaker of Markham Hall.

Colin: When you left school, what did you do first of all?

Laurence: I went down Ireland pit.

Colin: What were the hours of work?

Laurence: Six until two, and some days we went down the pit and had to come up, because there was no work. Some weeks you had to go down six days to get three days in.

I Got Stopped

Colin: How long were you in the pit?

Laurence: Seven years.

Colin: And why did you leave?

Laurence: I got stopped.

Colin: You were made redundant?

Laurence: No, I just got stopped, there was no redundancy then.

Colin: What notice did you get?

Laurence: A week.

Colin: Did you get any payment?

Laurence: No.

Colin: What was the Labour Exchange pay in those days?

Laurence: Fourteen shillings a week.

Colin: Where were you living at that time?

Laurence: On Lime Avenue.

Colin: Did you live there as well Wilf?

Wilf: Yes.

Colin: This was your father's home was it?

Wilf: Yes.

Colin: How many others?

Wilf: There were eight in the family, five boys and three girls.

Colin: Who was the eldest?

Wilf: Laurence was the eldest boy. I was next to t'youngest.

Colin: What is the difference in age between you two?

Wilf: I am 53 this October, and Laurence is 60.

Colin: So when he was stopped — you were only a lad of 14.

Wilf: Yes, I had just started down Markham Pit, and I used to go on nights, and then get sent up, if there were no work, and I used to have to wait until next morning for transport.

Colin: Can I ask a question about 'getting sent up'? You actually had to go underground to find out if there was any work?

Wilf: That's right, you see there were some weeks they let you work two days, then let you sign on at the Labour Exchange, then send for you to do you out of your LE money, see, you had to sign three days to draw anything.

Colin (to Laurence): What was your father's job?

Laurence: Furnace worker at Staveley works.

Colin: Was he on short time?

Laurence: No, he was on full time, but then he got stopped, when they put the cupolas up — they were self-feeders to the furnaces. Those who were in Staveley Company's houses, they kept them on, but those who weren't, they finished them.

Welcome to Staveley

Colin: So there were several of you in the family unemployed! What was your source of income?

Laurence: Just the dole. Well, my father had to keep us. If I wanted to get any money I had to leave home. I stayed at home, and that's why I got no money from the Labour Exchange.

Colin: And in fact you were 23 — not a dependent child?

Laurence: We went on the hunger march to protest against this, against the means test.

Colin: And who organised the march?

Laurence: The National Unemployed Workers — Mick Kane and John Kane were the organisers at Staveley.

Colin: Did the march start from Staveley?

Laurence: No, it started from York and Jarrow, York marchers went one road, and Jarrow marchers went other road. York came through Staveley.

Wilf: We were school lads and we went to Hawthorne Hill down Hartington, to meet them with home-made 'welcome' flags, on poles, four of us, Dennis Kane, Joe McMahon, me and me brother Jack. We led them to the Salvation Army Hall where they had a meal, before setting off for Chesterfield.

En Route

Colin: What route did you take to Chesterfield, Laurence?

Laurence: We went down Wheeldon Mill, Whittington Moor, and into Chesterfield, to Bradbury Hall.

Colin: How many Staveley men joined the march?

Laurence: About six.

Colin: Were they all unemployed?

Laurence: Yes.

Colin: How many of them can you remember?

Laurence: Arthur Bax, John Tate, Pat Kane, Mick Kane, and myself. We stayed at Bradbury Hall for the night, until Sunday morning.

Colin: When did you start in the morning?

Laurence: About nine o'clock.

Colin: When did you stop?

Laurence: We would do about ten miles then have a 20-minute break. Two used to bike ahead and get cups of tea ready — advance party, and we'd have our sandwiches. Then when we pulled in at night at Alfreton, we had a meat tea — meat and salad that is.

Colin: Where did the money come from?

Laurence: I suppose it came out of the march money, you see we collected on the way. We sold *Daily Workers* and we had collecting tins.

Colin: What else did you get?

Laurence: We got shoes and socks in Staveley, from John and W. Hodson.

Colin: Did you buy them yourselves?
Laurence: No, the march did.
Colin: So first you went to Alfreton.
Laurence: Yes, then Alfreton to Nottingham to Loughborough. Loughborough to Leicester, on to Market Harborough, Kettering and Bedford where we had a rest day. We had a meeting at night. The blackshirts came in, Oswald Mosley's blackshirts, and tried to break it up. They didn't really break it up, but it finished, and there was lots of shouting.
Colin: Was there any fighting?
Laurence: No. From there we went on to Luton then London.
Colin: How many days did it take you?
Laurence: Ten days, with one rest day.

A Watering Can of Tea
Colin: Where did you stay in London?
Laurence: At Willesden. We had a mile to walk. We used to get up about 7 a.m. and the minister used to bring us a tin of biscuits and a watering-can of tea in the morning.
Colin: So you stayed in a church hall? What was his attitude to you? Did he agree with the march?
Laurence: Yes — he was a very nice chap.
Colin: Was anybody hostile to you?
Laurence: Nobody was hostile. One night the police who were outside brought us a box of Woodbines, which used to cost 8/4d a box.
Colin: How many were in the box?
Laurence: 100 packets of five. We used to get cigarettes supplied, ten a day.

The House of Commons
Colin: How many were on the march — roughly?
Laurence: I'd say about 400, four to five hundred.
Colin: And did they all complete it?
Laurence: One chap had to stop at Market Harborough to have his feet seen to for two days, then he continued by train and caught us up.

Colin: How long did you stay in London?
Laurence: About four days.
Colin: What did you do?
Laurence: We met the Jarrow marchers in Hyde Park, and had meetings there, and in Trafalgar Square on Sunday. And then we went to the House o'Commons. First we got to Whitehall, and got split up by the bobbies, you're not allowed to march down Whitehall. So some got into the House 'Commons and some didn't. The lobby was full, see.

Things Went On Just the Same
Colin: Do you think the march had any effect? Did the government take any notice of the march?
Laurence: No, I don't think they did. They just sat it out, and said go back.
Colin: Was the march in the papers, what did they say about it?
Laurence: I can't remember now, it's a long while back. They didn't get much out of it. Things went on just the same, till 1936 time. Then things started turning round, just before t'war see.
Colin: Wilf, you being at home still, what did you think, did you follow it in the papers?
Wilf: I think they did a good job, but they didn't get anything out of it at all. My brothers had to leave home, for me dad to get some dole, and I had to go out to work to keep 'em.
Colin: When did you go down Markham?
Wilf: About 1933.
Colin: And how long did you stop there?
Wilf: About five years, then I finished and went on the railway.
Colin: You chose to leave?
Wilf: Yes, I didn't like it, I went on the railway. I started as a cleaner. I had 16 years on the railway.
Colin: What did you think of it, looking back on it?
Wilf: I enjoyed it at first. I was firing at Barrow Hill Depot. We used to go all

over, we used to go lodging to Kettering and Wellingborough, Stockport, Buxton.

Building Trade/Billiard Hall

Colin (to Laurence): What happened after the period when you were unemployed?

Laurence: I went into the building trade and worked on Staveley Regal, across from the church — that's what's now the bingo hall. Then I worked on Britannic offices. I worked at Sheffield, Fulwood. Earlier I worked for A. F. Whites at Chesterfield.

Colin: And what sort of hours were you working then?

Laurence: Well, when I worked at Sheffield first, we had to catch the five to six train in the morning, and got back into Staveley at twenty past six at night and I used to get one and tuppence an hour carrying then, carrying bricks on head-boards.

Colin: And did you get any higher rates for overtime?

Laurence: No overtime. You used to have to knock off at five to catch this train and if it snowed or rained, you got knocked off, the buzzer used to go.

Colin: And you didn't get paid?

Laurence: No. It was an eight-hour day. In them days you weren't allowed a break for tea. Eight until twelve, the buzzer used to go, at half past twelve until five.

Colin: What did you do in the evenings when you got home from work?

Laurence: We didn't do anything much ... we used to go into the billiard hall.

Colin: Where was that?

Laurence: Where the new square is, the new shopping square, at the top of old New Street. We didn't get a lot of spending money then you know, we used to get half a crown a week spending money.

Seeping-in

Colin: Where were you living then?

Laurence: I was still at home living with my parents. I lived across from the church, in the old Rectory yard, No. 7. No, we lived at Smith's Row first, then the Rectory, and then the Poplars — in the row at the back of Peabody's.

Colin (to Wilf): Were you still at home then?

Wilf: No, I was away. I got married in 1940.

Colin: What do you think about the society you have lived in?

Wilf: I think we're coming back to the old days if we are not careful.

Laurence: We're better off today.

Wilf: Yes, we're better off, but we're gradually coming back to unemployment — it's seeping in very fast.

The Same Standard or A Living Wage

Wilf: It's bound to happen. It showed you on television last night those old-aged pensioners at Southend. More for the old-aged pensioners, I mean to say they're in need of it. For the cost of living.

Laurence: Butter's gone up again, it's all wrong this cost of living, everybody ought to be on the same standard.

Colin: Do you mean everybody ought to get the same amount of money?

Laurence: I do.

Colin (to Wilf): What do you think Wilf?

Wilf: You can't get the same amount of money, because you've got different sorts of work. I mean everybody's not doing the same job, are they? My idea is that everybody should get a living wage, where they can afford to have the same table. A reasonable good living, and a bit of money left for pleasure. Then everybody gets paid on their merit. If a man goes to night school and studies he should be paid on his merit, and for studying and getting where he is.

Colin: Do you think people in this society have got a living wage?

Wilf: Some haven't. But they're better

off now than in the means test days. There are these that are chronic sick.
Laurence: But they are a bit better now, aren't they?
Wilf: There are some that are getting a bit of a rise, but the cost of living is going up for them. It is going up faster than their rises. Nobody considers the chronic sick and disabled, and those who are off work for £5 per week. They've got to go to the same market.

7. Traffic and Corporation Plans For This Area

As community workers on the Barrowfield Project in the east end of Glasgow, Gerri and I lived in Janefield Street, and had the project office in our flat. Janefield Street is a long straight road running between a cemetery and the back of Celtic football park. Young families lived in a few council houses at either end. There were high levels of unemployment and chronic ill-health among residents. Janefield Street was also used by drivers to avoid the traffic lights at Parkhead Cross, and by a local garage to test car brakes. In the spring of '72 a small boy was knocked down and received serious internal injuries: it was the second time he'd been hit by a vehicle. We learned that this was a common occurrence, and that a child had been killed the previous year.

Feeling was running high among residents, but they didn't know what to do about the problem. Local councillors were approached, but were unhelpful. A meeting was held and we decided to keep our kids off school and blockade the road with prams, bikes and anything else we could find. We informed the press and — once the action was under way — the police and a councillor.

A dramatic confrontation occurred. The headmistress of the primary school appeared on the scene and furiously lectured the mothers for keeping their children off school. She seemed more concerned about that than the injury to the child. The mothers held their ground. A queue of vehicles built up, and some drivers got frustrated. One car mounted the pavement and tried to get past the barricade. It was stopped physically by mothers and children throwing themselves against it. He reversed along the pavement, turned, and drove off in the opposite direction.

The councillor arrived in his good suit, and seeing the number of people involved, and the representatives of the press, made a fulsome statement endorsing the parents' demand for the closure of the street, as if it had been his own idea. The police promised early consideration of the demands if the parents would remove the barricade. The parents agreed to dismantle it, but warned that they would repeat the action if their demands were not met. Within weeks a row of bollards was in place, and the road closed to all except emergency traffic.

The following leaflet was circulated in an attempt to build on the victory and widen the residents' knowledge of, and interest in, the development plans for the east end which were about to be imposed.

Barrowfield Community School
From conversations with mothers in Barrowfield, Gerri and I
became aware of the fact that many children at the local secondary
schools were either excluded or else 'dogging it' regularly. Gerri had
already visited the free school at Scotland Road in Liverpool. Shortly
after the Janefield Street incident we were approached by a lecturer
and some trainee teachers at Jordanhill College of Education who
were interested in the possibility of starting a similar school in
Glasgow. We made the introductions and hosted the meetings
between some Barrowfield parents and the Jordanhill group. Out of
this dialogue, the Barrowfield Community School was born.

TRAFFIC AND CORPORATION PLANS FOR THIS AREA

Our kids get knocked down regularly in Janefield St. , Stamford St. ,
Gallowgate , London Road , and so on....The authorities have known
about this for years , but presumably working-class kids are expendable....
They've done nothing till now. They'll do nothing till they're <u>forced</u>.

TRAFFIC DANGER TO CHILDREN IS ONLY ONE OF THE PROBLEMS.
WE MAY HAVE WON THIS FIGHT IN JANEFIELD STREET....BUT THE BATTLE
        ✳ ✳ ✳ ✳ ✳ ✳   HAS JUST BEGUN
THE CORPORATION SAY THEY WANT TO IMPROVE THINGS. BUT THEIR <u>PLANS</u>
          ARE ONLY GOING TO MAKE THINGS WORSE

* GALLOWGATE is to be an <u>express motorway</u>
* LONDON ROAD is to be an <u>express motorway</u>
* FIELDEN STREET is to be an <u>expressway</u>
* AND THERE ARE NO PLANS for shops...doctors' surgeries...no amenities at all .
  Existing shops will come down. Nearest shops will be at Brigton   Cross,
                       Parkhead Cross , and Duke Street......
* THIS MEANS that Janefield and Barrowfield will be made into A GHETTO.....

      CUT OFF BY MOTORWAYS FROM THE OUTSIDE WORLD

WE DEMAND

...........a public meeting in Mile-end Ward, with the planning dept.,
        and local councillors and - if he can be found -
        our M.P., Sir Myer Galpern .
        WE MUST BE ASSURED OF THE FUTURE SAFETY OF THE PUBLIC
        IN THIS WARD.

        THE PLANS MUST BE FOR THE GOOD OF THE PEOPLE -
                NOT JUST IN THE INTEREST OF TRAFFIC AND INDUSTRY
...........WE DEMAND: shops, a shopping centre, more doctors' surgeries,
                Better Police protection, and far more play spaces
                and play facilities for children of <u>all</u> ages
...........WE DEMAND that if Camlachie Community Centre must come down,
               it should be replaced <u>in the same area</u>
...........WE DEMAND that O.A.P.s should have their own premises.

...........WE DEMAND work for our teenagers.

8. Higher Rents and Government Lies

In 1972, the Conservative government introduced Housing Finance Acts designed to increase the rent and rate contributions to local authority housing accounts, and to decrease the contribution made by central government in the form of subsidies. In the private sector, the aim was to achieve an increase in rentals through decontrol. The pill was sweetened by the introduction of means-tested rent rebates and allowances.

Major campaigns against rent increases were organised by local authorities, trade union bodies, and tenants' associations. As an active member of Castlemilk Tenants' Association, I was a delegate to the Glasgow Council of Tenants and also attended the meetings of the Scottish Council of Tenants, on whose behalf I edited and produced *Scottish Tenant*, a newspaper which ran for three issues from April 1973 until February 1974. It consisted of reports from tenants' associations and rents action committees throughout Scotland, analysis of the Housing (Financial Provisions) (Scotland) Act, 1972, and subsequent housing white papers, and a miscellany of historical articles, information, poems, photos, and cartoons.

Higher Rents and Government Lies appeared as the centre page spread in the first issue of *Scottish Tenant*. It was a polemical attempt to explain housing finance, the provisions of the Act, and their likely effects on rent and rate levels, in simple language, from a tenant's point of view.

*

The truth about the Housing (Financial Provisions) (Scotland) Act, 1972

People and Houses

A family has to balance its spending against its income. Income from wages and family allowances. Spending on food, rent, clothes, fares, etc. Many families don't get enough to buy what they need. So they borrow the money, or get it on HP, and pay it off.

A council, a corporation, the SSHA, a new town — any public body which builds houses to rent — is like a family, with income *from* houses, and spending *on* houses. This is written down in the Housing Account.

Like families, they can't afford to buy their houses straight off, so they borrow from moneylenders and pay it off gradually — over forty or sixty years.

Before the new Act, they got their income from rents, rates, and government subsidies. And they spent it on repairing the houses, administration, and paying back the moneylenders.

Most of their income came from rent. Most of the spending went on paying the moneylenders. This won't change. If a council house costs £5,000 to build, the authority pays back nearly £30,000 to the moneylender. That's where most of your rent goes.

The Tories say Housing Finance needs reformed. So it does. We shouldn't have to pay the moneylender six times the cost of the house. But the Tories don't mention this at all — because they *are* the moneylenders!

Part One: Government Subsidies
Before the new Act, part of the income to the Housing Accounts was Government Subsidies, which came from the taxes we all pay. The richer you are, the more income tax you pay. So the subsidies were a Robin Hood touch. The government was giving back to the people some of what the rich had stolen from them.

The Tories didn't like this. They wanted the landowners, the moneylenders, the businessmen to keep their ill-gotten gains. So this year, Chancellor Barbour gave them £300 million in tax cuts. At a time when the incomes of working people were frozen by Tory law, Tory law gave Ted Heath (salary £23,000 per year) £8 extra per week to take home.

Cutting taxes means cutting government spending. The Tories had already cut free specs, school milk, prescriptions, etc. Now they've stopped Government Subsidies to the Housing Accounts. This means — HIGHER RENTS.

Decoy Ducks
The Tories are military chaps. And with all their money they can afford to employ some of these very clever publicity chaps (also Tories). They decided to use decoy ducks to fool the tenants. We all know what decoy ducks are for — to draw the enemy's attention away from the main target.

The main decoys they've used to conceal the HIGHER RENTS are: (1) six fancy new subsidies, and (2) the new rent rebate scheme.

The New Subsidies
The first one is just a fancy name for money the government still owes local authorities.

The second one is for increased spending on houses. Sounds great. But there's a catch. An authority has to make a contribution from the rates. And this subsidy drops year by year till it disappears. The rates contribution goes up each year. Get it? Higher rents, and higher rates as well.

The third subsidy. If an authority puts up its rents so high that they're £39 per house each year higher than the rents of every other authority in Scotland — then they get the third one. Again, there's a rates contribution — pushing rates up higher still.

The fourth (Rent Rebate) subsidy — see Part 2.

The fifth (Rent Allowance) subsidy — see Part 5.

The sixth (Slum Clearance) subsidy doesn't cover the cost of buying the *land* the slums are standing on, thus leaving the land profiteers (Tories) to demand huge prices for it.

Part 2: Rent Rebates and Allowances

A maniac with a gun is about to shoot you. Before he fires, he says he's going to send tons of beautiful flowers to your funeral — roses, daffodils, every flower under the sun. He thinks he can persuade you that *you actually want to be shot.*

This is how the Tories have tried to use the rent rebate scheme. Adverts and statements appear in the papers and on TV telling us how the rebate scheme will help the low paid, etc. Their purpose is to draw attention away from the fact that rents are to go up and up and up.

The Tories are calculating moneymakers who aim to get richer at the expense of the tenants. To disguise their real nature, they wear *masks* of human kindness, dripping with concern for the old, the poor, the deprived. They want us to forget the fact that they and their class are the *cause* of poverty and deprivation. They are devils with human masks.

The rebate scheme is for council, new town, and SSHA tenants. The allowance scheme is for private tenants. In both, if a tenant gets a reduction of the increased rent, it is paid by the local authority. The money comes from the rates, and from government subsidies, which will drop each year. This pushes up the rates.

The main idea is the Needs Allowance. Ted Heath 'needs' a new yacht costing £40,000. But the Scottish tenants are told that their weekly needs are £10.50 (raised by £3.50 from 28 April) for a single person; £14.75 for a married couple; plus £2.75 for each child.

What needs do these amounts include? The cost of an annual family holiday? The cost of enough fuel to keep the house warm in winter? The cost of plenty of good food? The cost of enough warm clothing? The cost of furniture and bedding? The cost of entertainment and leisure activities (like yachting)? The Tories' needs include all these, naturally.

It is not a needs allowance at all. It is a Survival Allowance. That's all we have a right to in Tory eyes — survival. And remember the hundreds of old folk who *die* every year for lack of money to buy enough food, clothes, and fuel. The Tories are *very concerned*. Some people will pay no rent at all under the Act, they drool. True, but they will be nearly dying of cold or nearly starving already.

Most families will have to pay the full increase, or the best part of it. Of the few who get big rebates, only a tiny minority will pay the same rent as before or less. The Act does not change the hardships they are already suffering to qualify for big rebates.

As the poet William Blake wrote:

> Charity would be no more,
> if we did not make somebody poor.

Part 3: Housing Accounts
Each local authority will have four Housing accounts:
      (1) The Housing Revenue Account
      (2) The Rent Rebate Account
      (3) The Rent Allowance Account
      (4) The Slum Clearance Account

Part 4: Rules for Raising Rents
Higher rents to be called Standard Rents. Rents to go up every year in October. Average increase each year to be 50p per week (£26 per year). So, if you're a Glasgow Corporation tenant and your rent in March this year was £1.75 a week — *not* including rates — here's how your rent will go up:

March 1973	£1.75	
April 1973	£2.50	
October 1973	£3.00	
October 1974	£3.50	DOUBLE
October 1975	£4.00	
October 1976	£4.50	
October 1977	£5.00	
October 1978	£5.50	MORE THAN TREBLE

Part 5: Huge Rents for Private Tenants
Many privately rented houses whose rents have been reasonable till now are to be decontrolled. For some it happened on 1st January 1973. For others it's 1st January 1974. For others, 1st January 1975.

This means the landlord can put up the rent as high as he likes. The

tenant can appeal to an official called the Rent Officer, whose job is
to rubber-stamp the increase.

Suppose a tenant was paying £100 a year. His house is decontrolled. The landlord says the new rent he wants is £300 per year.
The Rent Officer may agree. Or he may put it up to, let's say, £320.
Or he may say: you can only have £285. Whatever way it goes, the
increase is huge. And the rent won't be too far from what the
landlord says he wants.

So the Tory Government Ministers are saying to the Tory
landlords: FIX YOUR OWN JACKPOT, CHAPS. YOU WIN
EVERY TIME.

Part 6: Housing Associations
The Tories like housing associations because they charge high rents.
They have to make their housing accounts balance without any
contribution from the rates, and with little help from the
government. The Higher Rents Act offers them new subsidies. Their
rents will go up of course.

Part 7
Part 7 is a ragbag of threats and dirty tricks. It aims to make sure
there are no loopholes. It tells local councillors what punishments lie
in store for them if they don't do just what they're told.

If a local authority won't operate the Act, the Secretary of State
can fine it, fine individual councillors, ban them from being elected
counillors, take over the running of housing in their area, etc.

It is clear that the Secretary of State is the headmaster, the boss, the
dictator, and the local authorities (our councillors) are the pupils, the
workers, the slaves, who must do what he says or else.

When we choose our councillors, are we electing them to do what
we tell them — or what the government tells them? If it's what the
government tells them, then local democracy is a sham.

9. White Papers

The Housing (Financial Provisions) (Scotland) Act 1972 was followed by the publication of two White Papers, setting out the longer-term objectives of central government in relation firstly to housing finance and the management of rented accommodation, and secondly to the improvement of older housing in the private sector. The aim of this article, published in the second issue of *Scottish Tenant* in September 1973, was to make these ideas accessible to tenants by explaining them clearly in ordinary language.

*

The government has issued two White Papers on their future plans for housing. One is called *Homes for People* and the other *Towards Better Homes*.

Here's a good example of how *Homes for People* reads: 'Most people in Scotland no longer need, or wish, to regard a low rent as the main criterion for an acceptable house.' No new policies are needed, we're told. The local authorities are to blame for all the housing problems tenants suffer.

It's true that many local authorities are bad landlords — and some councillors try to pour cold water on tenants' complaints. But the real reason we get poor quality housing services is lack of cash. The best part of our rent goes straight to the moneylender, leaving too little for the jobs that should be done.

Homes for People ignores this. It dangles some seductive ideas before our eyes: more 'professional' housing management, one tenant representative on the housing committee, a land hoarding charge for speculators. . .

The government wants more houses to be built for sale, and less council house building. They tell us building societies don't make profits, which will amuse anybody who invests money in building societies for interest. Councils should sell their houses.

The SSHA is to build houses to rent to oil-boom workers in the north-east. Their rents will be much higher than local authority rents.

The bait of house improvement and environmental improvement is dangled — we can be sure only a few areas will get it. Reaching the rotten core of the White Paper, we learn that 190,000 Scottish houses are substandard — after all these years.

Towards Better Homes concentrates on these older houses lacking basic amenities. Its first proposal is mixed treatment — demolition, or improvement where possible. This is a good proposal.

Housing Action Areas will replace the present treatment areas. Local authorities would have greater powers in such areas. For example, they could force owners to improve their houses. Improvement grants will be bigger, and will be available for repairs only, at the council's discretion. If owners refused to improve, the council could buy the houses from them. But the government wants these houses resold.

The council would have to rehouse people made homeless in these Action Areas. The government float the idea of giving councils the right to order owners of grant-improved houses to continue to let them. This shows up the limitations of the scheme, and its real aim, for the council could not stop the owners raising rents sky-high, or intimidating working-class tenants to leave, and give way to the better off.

10. Unpleasant Face of Capitalism at Inchinnan

The third number of *Scottish Tenant* appeared in February 1974, at the time of the miners' strike and the first general election of that year, called by Edward Heath on the issue of who runs the country. Where previously we had focused mainly on the public sector, this time the impact of the Housing Finance Act on tenants in the private sector was highlighted. 'Unpleasant Face of Capitalism at Inchinnan' appeared as the lead story on the front page because it demonstrated so clearly the aim of the Act in practice. It had the additional advantage of portraying the chairman of the Scottish Special Housing Association engaged in a successful attempt to obtain an increase in the rents of tied houses.

*

Fans of W. A. Gordon Muir, Tory-appointed chairman of the Scottish Special Housing Association, will be pleased to hear of his continuing interest in the welfare of working-class families.

His most recent efforts are on behalf of the tenants of 108 houses at Inchinnan, Renfrewshire, owned by the India Tyre Company, a subsidiary of the Dunlop Rubber Company which gave £21,000 to Tory Party funds in 1972.

Walled in

Built by the company for its workers in 1930, with the aid of a government grant, the houses are walled in on two sides by factories, on the third side an industrial estate is being built, and along the fourth side runs the main road. There are no social amenities, no shops, and the bus service is poor.

Carbon emitted by the factory blackens the walls and the washings, and infiltrates into the houses themselves. A device at the factory designed to reduce this health hazard has never worked effectively since it was installed.

Primitive

Internally, the houses are primitive. There is only one electric point in the entire house. A dozen houses have been rewired — but only out of necessity, say the tenants. The window frames are rotting. The plumbing is deteriorating. A minimal plumbing repair service is provided, in that tenants can get the services of the factory plumber.

A large number of tenants have put in new bathroom suites themselves — bath, toilet bowl, washhand basin — and for this the firm has made a maximum grant of £14.

Until 1957 rents were fixed. The missive tenants signed stated that the houses were 'tied' — if you left the job, you had to leave the house. After 1957, no reference was made in the missive to the tied nature of the houses, but informally the rule still applied.

After 1957 new tenants paid higher rents. Women who were widowed would have to sign a new missive — at a new, increased rent. Or they were 'asked' to move from their three-apartment into a two-apartment — and pay a higher rent than before.

Landlords' Charter

Not satisfied with its efforts over the years as a socially conscious landlord, the firm decided to apply for an increase in the rents under the terms of that landlords' charter — the Housing (Financial Provisions) (Scotland) Act, 1972.

In September 1973, every tenant received a letter from the rent officer informing them that the firm of Murray and Muir, chartered surveyors, acting for the India Tyre Company, had applied for a fair rent to be fixed, and that the rent officers would be coming round to assess the houses. In the course of the next month every house was visited.

Each tenant then received a letter saying that an *informal* meeting would be held on the 8th November at 73 Smithhill Street, Paisley. On that day, the committee of the India Gardens Tenants' Association attended, along with their lawyer, Mr Hamilton, and Bill Towill, secretary of the Scottish Council of Tenants. The tenants' lawyer advised his clients to say nothing.

Also in attendance were three rent officers, Mr Grant, personnel manager of the India Tyre Company, and W. A. Gordon Muir on behalf of the company.

Comparing the houses with those owned by the Western Heritable Investment Co., at King's Park, Hillington, and Penilee, Mr Muir put forward the company's proposals:

For the four-apartment houses (present rents between £3.70 per month and £1.50 per week) the landlord wanted £400 per year (increases of between 500-900 per cent).

For the three-apartment houses (present rents between 56p per week and £1.06 per week) the company proposed a rent of £200 per year (a 400-600 per cent increase).

And for the two-apartment houses, whose present rents stand at between 34p and 97p per week, the company was asking for £150 a year (an increase of 300-800 per cent). (Rent figures given above do *not* include rates.)

Like the Prime Minister inviting TUC leaders to discuss with him how best to nobble the trade union movement, Mr Muir then proposed that the tenants might like to suggest what a fair rent should be. The landlord, he complained, was the only party putting forward a figure. The tenants' lawyer said they were not in a position to suggest a figure. The tenants themselves were still under the impression that this was an 'informal' meeting.

Then the question of conditions and tenure was raised. The houses were tied houses, the tenants' lawyer pointed out. Mr Muir fielded that one neatly: I can inform, he said, turning to Mr Grant the personnel manager, that the company is willing to forego the tied nature of the houses. Correct? That is correct, affirmed Mr Grant.

Registered letter

Next day an employee who was leaving the company went to pay his rent. It was refused. He went again. It was again refused. The tenants' committee told him to send it by registered letter. A month later receipt of the letter was acknowledged, and he was told he could come and pay again. But he got nothing in writing about the houses being untied.

'We are doing everything possible to improve the houses,' said Mr Grant, claiming that two maintenance men were employed for joinery work. (The tenants had never seen them. But within the last few weeks, three joiners have appeared and have told the tenants they will be around for a year.)

It was decided that the rent officer would suggest a figure for a fair rent to both parties.

Early in December, each tenant got a letter from the rent officer, informing them of the new rents. The 'informal' meeting, it turned out, was official.

For the four-apartment houses the landlord was to get £250 instead of £400. For the three-apartments, £180 instead of £200. And for the two-apartments, £140 instead of £150.

These increases range from 280-800 per cent. As we warned in the first issue of *Scottish Tenant* last April, the landlord may not get all he wants — but he gets the best part of it. Fix your own jackpot is the name of the game.

Appeal

The tenants can appeal, of course . . . the tenants of the India Tyre
Co. at Inchinnan were given until 28th December to lodge appeals,
and this they have done. At time of going to press, their appeal has
not yet been heard. Meanwhile the company has informed
(threatened?) them that it is coming to rewire the houses. The
tenants' lawyer has advised them to refuse access unless they get a
guarantee that the houses will be left as they were. They also have a
right to compensation.

But in this context a possibly temporary interest in house
improvement on the landlord's part can be seen as a public relations
exercise to ensure that the rents are raised. Anybody laying bets on
the tenants to win their appeal? Whose law? What kind of justice?
Good old Gordon Muir, the tenants' champion!

11. Secret Weapons Misfire

'Secret Weapons Misfire', also published in the third and final issue of *Scottish Tenant*, analysed the evidence about the provision of rent rebates and allowances, revealing the extent of poverty among council tenants.

*

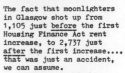

SECRET WEAPONS MISFIRE

In January, Mr Gordon Campbell, Secretary of State for Scotland, published figures for the number of tenants getting rent rebates and allowances.

His aim was to show how good the Tory Housing Finance Act was, and that really, every home should have one.

But his secret weapon has misfired.

Poor Relief

The figures reveal that more than a third of Glasgow's council tenants — one family in three — is so poor that even the Tories have been forced to hand out POOR RELIEF in the form of rent rebates.

And the rebates aren't small. They're HUGE.

The average rebate in Glasgow is £69 a year. That's over half the rent.

In Clydebank, the average rebate is £47 a year —again more than half the rent.

And in Edinburgh — where half the council tenants are on rebates — the average rebate is a staggering £107 per year — ⅔rds of a year's rent.

All in, nearly a quarter of a million Scottish families in public houses are getting rent rebates.

Why so many rebates, and why are they so high ?

Because so many household incomes are so low.

Don't be deceived by their "concerned" public face — the Tories have created mass poverty by their policies, and Gordon Campbell has let the cat out of the bag by publishing these figures.

But there is worse to come. Nearly a quarter — 37,000 — of Glasgow's council tenants are so near the breadline that they are paying no rent at all. Most of them are on social security. They used to get a rent allowance. Now they pay no rent at all — and get no rent allowance. So they're no better off.

Mr Campbell would undoubtedly be delighted if he could wake up one fine morning and announce — to a starving population — that all of Glasgow's council tenants were now paying no rent at all. The fairness of The Housing Finance Act would then be beyond dispute

Smokescreen

January's announcement is only part of Mr. Campbell's campaign to drag a dirty smokescreen of confusion over the real facts about people and housing in Scotland.

Ten days later, he sent his other secret weapon, Teddy Taylor, down to Paisley to explain that the increase in moonlight flittings had nothing to do with the Housing Finance Act.

Teddy's theory is that it's all because families are unable to cope in a new house. Now we know.

The fact that moonlighters in Glasgow shot up from 1,105 just before the first Housing Finance Act rent increase, to 2,737 just after the first increase.... that was just an accident, we can assume.

Common Market

In fact, the increase in moonlighters is the result of increased poverty caused by the whole range of government policies: rent and rates increases, the legislation to raise prices and profits while holding down wage increases, government approved increases in gas and electricity bills, Common Market entry which has forced food prices up — don't forget that it was the same Teddy Taylor who said a few months ago that price increases had been much higher in countries which had recently joined the Common Market, than in those countries which had stayed out...And the refusal to raise pensions to an adequate level, the refusal to legislate for a minimum wage, the refusal to give real equality in women's wages, the deliberate attempts to put more and more people out of work (lame ducks, 3 day weeks, public spending cuts — all these are fancy names for GOVERNMENT-MANUFACTURED UNEMPLOYMENT).

Decoy

Finally, we said last year that the Tories were using the rebate scheme as a decoy to take attention away from the fact that for the majority of people rents would go up and up.

Campbell and Taylor have proved us right. Nowhere in the announcement does it say that the great majority of tenants are having to pay the full rent increase. And the figure of those receiving rent rebates conceals another important fact — that many of those who are getting a rebate still end up paying more than before.

There are lies, damned lies, and statistics.......or should we say: carefully selected and presented statistics.

Cheaper sweets is all the Tories have got for these kids

12. No Papering Over the Cracks, Please!

In December 1972 we moved to Castlemilk, a big local authority housing scheme on the southern outskirts of Glasgow, where we lived for four years. Gerri worked as Reporter to Children's Panels and I was at home bringing up the kids and looking after the house. We were active in various organisations: the newspaper *Castlemilk Today*, the tenants' association, the Rents Action Committee, steering committees for Community Councils, and a campaign of mobilisation around the issue of broken lifts in the row of tower blocks called the Mitchellhill High Five. I was also an active member of the Communist Party, which I admired and preferred to the Labour Party, though I disagreed with democratic centralism.

As in Staveley, Gerri and I acted as catalysts in the paper group, supporting various initiatives, with a special emphasis on showing members how to do page-design and letrasetting. I did most of the typing and usually co-ordinated the selling of the paper, a considerable task since it came out monthly and sold up towards the 2,000 mark.

Castlemilk Today's orientation was pluralist. It would print, uncensored, contributions from any individual and any local organisation. This was a source of tension, particularly when the Baptist minister launched an attack on the Soviet Union's lack of religious and political freedom, and a resident hit back with a ferocious assault on minsters of religion entitled 'They shall not work, cos business is good'. This crisis prefigured a gradual process in the scheme of splitting into factions, which can roughly be characterised as radical-autonomist, moderate-centralist, and conservative. The paper itself became increasingly a platform for the radical-autonomist faction, and lost the support of several local institutions, though it should be stressed that this was not a development that paper group members intended to bring about.

As in Staveley, I operated a self-denying ordinance, except where I felt it was important to name and explore a key theme. The following letter, appearing in the second issue, identified such a theme, the danger of blinkered localism.

*

Dear Castlemilk Today,
  Congratulations on your first issue. I like the way local
organisations publicise their activities in your paper.
  I hope it will be a fearless, campaigning newspaper, drawing
attention to our real conditions and problems.
  No papering over the cracks, please!
  One critical comment, if I may. I think there is a danger of being
blinkered — of seeing problems only in local terms.
  Take litter, for example. Your front-page story exposes the
problem *locally,* and makes good suggestions for improvements.
  But do the *causes* lie in Castlemilk?
  You didn't mention the cuts in spending by local authorities the
last government ordered. Those cuts affected the way local councils
budgeted — so they cut the amount of money available for cleansing
among other things.
  You didn't mention the high rates of interest the Corporation
have to pay on money they borrow to build our houses, schools,
swimming pools, etc.
  Every month we dish out huge sums of money to the factor in rent
and rates. But most of it goes straight into the hands of the
moneylenders — very little goes to pay for the services we need.
  Did your readers know that 'work study' is being carried out in
many departments, *including cleansing,* to cut down the number of
men doing the work?
  Of course, the result will be that even less work gets done.
  Did you know that cleansing workers are so badly paid that folk
won't take the job? And the same goes for many other jobs with the
Corporation.
  Because they just look at it *locally,* a lot of folk think we have only
ourselves to blame for the litter problem.
  We all know we should get a grip and stop throwing away
cigarette papers and crisp packets. And we'll have to stop *our* kids
breaking bottles for fun.
  But what sort of example are we set?
  What about official litter?
  Who was it left that mess all along the new path from Ardencraig
Road to Mitchellhill Primary School, especially the bit near the
school entrance? It wasn't the kids, *or* the parents.
  Which big building firm left their rubbish lying for years in the
field sloping west from Downcraig Road? Wimpey? Bovis? John
Laing?
  Guess who abandoned dangerous empty houses, nissen huts, gun
emplacements, and other military rubbish, on the island of Hoy in
the Orkneys? The Admiralty or the War Office?

The big fish swim off scot free.

Yet the government and the Corporation have the cheek to run expensive advertising campaigns — with our money — telling us to CLEAN UP GLASGOW and KEEP BRITAIN TIDY.

Isn't it about time the people had a bit more control over government — central and local — in this so-called democracy of ours?

If *Castlemilk Today* becomes the true voice of the people of the area, it will help us to increase that control.

Yours sincerely,

Colin Kirkwood.

13. Vandalism!

The paper group was stuck for a front page story for the fifth issue of *Castlemilk Today*, and I was prevailed upon by a couple of fellow members to write something about vandalism. Vandalism and casual violence was something I felt strongly about. I took a very different line from the radical left, who tended to explain it away, or even justify it. For me, the underlying themes were authority and responsibility.

*

Vandalism has become a habit. Watch a woman and her child standing at the bus stop. The boy finishes his crisps and drops the packet absentmindedly. His mammy takes the cellophane wrapper and silver paper off ten Embassy tipped and lets them fall. . .

Three seven-year-old boys have salvaged some bottles from the bins. They stand them in a row. Take aim with their crossbows and — hey, stop that! Don't do that, boys — somebody'll cut themselves — a dog could cut its foot! They look at each other, and laugh, and take aim again. . .

Switch off the light and get into bed. You're drifting off to sleep when shouts followed by creaking and wrenching sounds startle you, from outside the window. You get your clothes on and go out to find that three drunk fifteen-year-olds have ripped down a stretch of your garden fence. . .

Life used to be a lot more orderly. At home the father's word was law. At church the priest or minister laid down the line to his listening flock. At school 'the golden rule was silence'. In the factory 'the worker cringed when the boss-man thundered'.

In every part of life, unquestioning obedience to authority was the order of the day.

Now the old authoritarian order is crumbling. But nothing yet has taken its place. We're in a moral vacuum, a sort of in-between time.

Living standards
Since World War Two our living standards have been rising, we consume more — but have we got a better life?

We watch hours of violent American TV programmes, we buy cheap clothes that wear out in no time, we smoke and drink more than ever before.

The system is turning us all into consumers. And the worst effects can be seen in our children. It's not so much that they've got nothing to do: it's that they don't *know* what to do — except watch telly, eat sweets, smoke, hang about . . . and every now and then their frustration bursts out in some form of violence. A casual, bored vandalism is spreading all over the place.

There are those who would like to see the old world of authority brought back. Their 'solutions' are simple.

Bring back the birch. Bring back the rope. Shoot the strikers.

Don't be tempted by these simple 'solutions'. The people who put them forward don't want to make *our* lives better.

They want to put the clock back to the nineteenth century, when the ruling class was cock of the midden, and everybody else knew their place.

But we can't just say vandalism is a symptom of our sick society, and then sit back and do nothing. We'll have to do something about vandalism NOW.

Responsible
Parents should be responsible for their children. It's no good saying 'I can't control them when they're outside the house'.

We should teach our children — and ourselves — to keep things pleasant and clean and tidy inside *and* outside the house.

Have we stopped making our children tidy up their toys after they've played with them? Do we let them fling their clothes down in a heap instead of putting them away? Do we get them to help clear the table and wash up after a meal?

Or are we just letting them be consumers — and doing all the tidying up after them? Then we're helping to make them vandals.

If they aren't expected to be responsible *inside*, how can we expect them to be responsible *outside*?

If we see a bunch of lads wrecking a fence, or smashing bottles — do we just watch passively as if it's a TV show?

Anybody who does that kind of damage should have to clear it up, repair it, or pay for it. They *shouldn't* be jailed or birched — that sort of treatment just breeds criminals.

We should have our own Children's Panel in Castlemilk, consisting of active interested local people on a rota.

Tidying up
They should be able to order offenders to make good the damage

they've done, or do some useful tidying up work if that's not possible.

In some cases, they should be able to *fine* the vandal or his parents, or make them pay for the damage — up to fixed limits.

The child should see it's not the police, nor the courts, but the community in which he lives that is dealing with him.

These suggestions wouldn't *solve* the underlying problems. There are no easy solutions.

14. People and Housing

The editor of *Scottish Marxist*, the theoretical journal of the Scottish Committee of the Communist Party, invited me to contribute an article on housing to his autumn 1974 issue. I saw it as an opportunity to do three things: to get an empirical, historical and analytical overview of housing in Scotland, and particularly in Glasgow; to discuss the *experience* of council housing; and lastly, to look at tenants' organisation and action. The significance of the experiential dimension was clear to me. I was surprised, therefore, though perhaps I should not have been, when the essay was printed with that section omitted. Here it is restored. Reading it all now, what strikes me is the extent to which I had already moved away from mainstream Labour movement thinking about housing, but hadn't yet drawn the obvious conclusion: that local authority house-building for rent was a disaster, and that what people really needed was to own and control their own homes.

✳

I

The State and Housing

The State first began to show an interest in housing in the middle of the nineteenth century. Early legislation established the State's right to demolish unsatisfactory houses, to control the quality of the building, and to improve sanitation. But *building* and *ownership* were still in private hands.

In 1915, working-class action in Glasgow forced the government to freeze rents. As a result, letting houses became less profitable. So the volume of private house-building for rent declined.

But more houses were needed. The State was forced to intervene. The 1919 Housing Act for the first time empowered local authorities to build houses for those 'in need'. The local authorities were to get subsidies for houses built, in order to bring rents below the free market level. In the fifty-five years since 1919, major Housing and Rent Acts have been a regular feature of Central Government activity. In the thirties the emphasis was on slum clearance, and local authorities acquired their statutory duty to rehouse those made homeless by slum clearance.

In the war years, enemy action cleared the slums faster than the state had planned for, throwing the post-war emphasis onto a massive rebuilding programme to ease overcrowding. Subsidies have been given, taken away, reduced, increased, or redirected, depending on which government was in power, and which 'solution' or emphasis was in vogue. In general, the provision of high-density (i.e. multi-storey or tenement style) housing has attracted most subsidy.

In the private sector, throughout this half-century of municipal housing, hundreds of thousands of semi-detached houses have been built, mostly for owner-occupation, and mainly in England. The other main private sector category is euphemistically known as 'older housing' — those terraced rows in England, and those tenements in Scotland, which have so far escaped slum clearance, and which are variously owned, rented furnished or unfurnished, sub-let, or rental purchased. Attention began to be paid to this latter category in the 1950s when grants for conversion or improvement were introduced. In 1969, an Act giving local authorities power to declare general improvement areas swung the focus from the individual dwelling to the neighbourhood, from the individual owner to the local authority. In 1974, a new Act has been passed enabling local authorities to designate housing action areas, with greater powers of purchase and compulsion.

The above brief outline of general housing trends since 1919 conceals more than it reveals. It is given as a background to a closer look at housing in Glasgow, at the experience of living in municipal housing, and at tenants' organisation and action. One contentious point should be mentioned. The fact that working-class action forced state intervention doesn't mean that municipal housing is socialist, or even a social service. The state intervened when the building industry became unable to make profits from housing. The state's role was to manage the housing market in the interests of the landowners, the financial institutions and the building industry. Council housing is basically state capitalism, not municipal socialism.

II

HOUSING IN GLASGOW

2.1 Corporation Policies and Proposals

(1) In 1958 there were 327,100 houses in the city, of which 147,300 were below an acceptable sanitary standard.

(2)   During the period 1960-72, 48,800 municipal (i.e. Corporation and SSHA) houses and 2,300 private houses were built. Over the same period, 75,200 houses were closed or demolished.

(3)   Over the same period 29,500 families were rehoused outwith the city under the Overspill Scheme.

(4)   At May 1973, there were 292,500 houses in the city, of which 69,500 were below the tolerable standard. Of the total stock 59 per cent of the houses were in the public sector and 41 per cent were in the private sector.

(5)   At May 1973, Corporation and SSHA plans for the future were as follows: a building programme for 14,600 municipal houses, and 2,800 private houses (1,300 to be formed by sub-division); and a rehabilitation programme which will produce 1,900 tolerable houses in Approved Treatment Areas. This gives a total of 19,300 new or improved houses.

(6)   The city's population in 1972 was 861,898. Assuming that it will fall to between 700,000 and 750,000 by 1981, the Corporation Planning Department estimates that there will still be a shortfall of between 17,700 and 26,700 tolerable houses. They propose to eliminate this shortfall by rehabilitating 15,300 tenement houses, building 7,200 new council houses, and 1,100 new private houses — all this as an *addition* to the 1973 programme.

(7)   The Scottish Development Department, in a circular to local authorities, referring to the 190,000 houses in Scotland below the tolerable standard, stated: 'Most if not all of these are houses which could have been classed as unfit *fifty* years ago.' Glasgow's 69,500 sub-tolerable houses come within this category.

(8)   In Glasgow in 1973, one house in four had no hot water tap. One house in three had no bath. One house in six did not have exclusive use of a WC.

(*Sources:* Planning Policy Report on Housing, 1974;
the Scottish Development Department; Shelter Report 1973)

2.2 Overcrowding

(1)   One person per room is regarded as 'a reasonable maximum level of occupation'. In 1961, 40 per cent of households in Glasgow were living at more than one person per room. In 1971, 29 per cent of households were living at more than one person per room.

        . . . there is still a significant proportion of the city's population living in overcrowded conditions. Overcrowding

is . . . now apparent in the peripheral Corporation estates,
particularly Easterhouse.

(2)   A multi-storey block is a block of over five storeys serviced by
a lift. Of the 36,762 houses built by Glasgow Corporation
between 1960 and 1972, 21,909 — or nearly two-thirds —
were in multi-storey blocks. Of these, 18,201 were in blocks
over sixteen storeys high. There are now 231 multi-storey
blocks of Corporation housing in Glasgow. On 1960 there
were three.

(3)   Percentages of houses having between one and three rooms (i.e.
small houses, not large houses):

Glasgow	Scotland	Britain
45.9%	27.9%	11.8%

(4)   Percentages of houses in buildings containing more than one
house:

Glasgow	Scotland	Britain
88.7%	51.7%	14.4%

(*Sources:* Planning Policy Report, 1974; Areas of Need Report, 1972)

2.3 Housing Management 'Problems'

(1)   The Department of Health and Social Security has refused to
make arrangements for direct payment of rent by tenants on
Social Security, should they desire it. The DHSS say it would
cost too much. No comment.

(2)   Glasgow Corporation Housing Management Committee has
so far failed to make facilities available for the payment of rents
at Post Offices on a weekly basis.
   These two steps would, together, drastically reduce the
number of court actions, absconsions, evictions, and bad
debts.

(3)   Some housing management 'problems':

Court Actions	15,390	17,325	18,863	23,058	21,170	19,626
Absconded Tenants	1,105	1,056	1,108	1,574	1,895	2,737
Evictions	195	212	254	328	403	574
Bad Debts Written Off	£53,251	£54,189	£62,662	£78,983	£107,087	£166,206
Year	1967	1968	1969	1970	1971	1972

(4)   Rent arrears before and after implementation of the first rent increase under the Housing Finance Act.

	28.11.72 (before)	28.5.73 (after)
Total Arrears	£541,877	£856,494
No. of Tenants in arrears	29,571	40,232
	(20% of all tenants)	(27% of all tenants)

2.4 Multiple Deprivation

In 1972, the Planning Department's report, entitled 'Areas of Need', attempted to analyse and quantify the intensity of deprivation in the city, by adding together 'scores' achieved by different areas of the city under such headings as 'age structure', 'unemployment', 'household size', 'housing conditions' etc. The results were mapped and it was discovered that those areas with the worst 'scores' covered one-third of the total area of the city.

'Many of the Corporation's post-1919 housing schemes feature in the highest levels of multiple deprivation.'

'Despite the great changes achieved by the clearance of the worst physical conditions, little progress has been made in general environmental improvement, or in the provision of adequate social and community facilities . . . a vast amount of investment will be required for rehabilitation in the widest sense of the word.'

(*Source:* Areas of Need Report)

2.5 Housing in Glasgow: summary and conclusions

It is clear from the preceding statistical information that municipal housing has not *solved* Glasgow's housing problem. It has merely recreated it, changed its form — adding horrific new features and dimensions. It has been a leisurely process of clearance and overspill, spun out over sixty-five years to keep the demolition, building, and building supply firms in contracts. Glasgow's overspill has resembled the effect of dropping a stone in a pond. Circular ripples spread out, wider and wider, till they reach the bank.

The first great circle was built outside the old built-up area, between 1919 and the war.

The second circle was the post-war peripheral schemes.

The third was the new towns.

The fourth circle as yet exists only in the minds of the planners. But, you might say, the Planning Policy Report on Housing explicitly *rejects* further overspill, because it creams off the skilled workers and economically active age groups. So it does. But the report *also*

allows for a population decline of between 100,000 and 150,000 by
1981. Where are these people going to go?

For the answer consult the West Central Scotland Plan, or the
Scottish Council for Development and Industry's strategic guidelines
for Scotland. Both allow for substantial population decreases in
Glasgow, and substantial population *increases* in North
Lanarkshire, North and Central Ayrshire, Dunbartonshire and
Stirlingshire. Will Glasgow reach the coast by 1984? The answer
may be yes.

Since 1960 the process of clearance and rehousing has been
speeded up, but the 'solution' has become correspondingly more
exploitative: nearly two-thirds of the houses built since then have
been in multi-storey blocks, those standing stones of the space age,
three-dimensional concrete nets full of human sprats.

The inhabitants of the new Anderston and the new Laurieston
may think they've got 'rerr hooses'. So they have — inside. But these
are high site-density developments, to use the planners' jargon, and
they will not stay 'rerr' for long. In the last decade, too, the shortage
of land has become more acute. The Planning Department, with the
connivance of successive Secretaries of State, has been
surreptitiously re-zoning bits of green belt. Easterhouse is still
seeping outwards. Around 1966, Castlemilk suddenly staggered up
the Cathkin Braes when five blocks nineteen storeys high were stuck
up to delight the eye.

Some further comment on the multiple character of overcrowding
may be appropriate here. Too many people per house is only the
obvious form, and in this respect municipal housing has perpetuated
overcrowding by building so many houses of between one and three
apartments, and so few of four, five or more. Inability to pay the
higher rents demanded for larger houses has also inhibited families
from transferring out of overcrowded conditions. In our own close in
Castlemilk, three out of eight families are living at more than one
person per room, and two of the rest were overcrowded till their
children left home recently. Friends a few closes along were living at
two persons per room till two years ago. In the other direction a
family of six we know are still in their three-apartment house —
again a 2:1 ratio. *If we were all to apply tomorrow for houses
matching our needs, the Corporation would be unable to meet more
than a tiny proportion of the demand.*

Overcrowding is also created by small rooms, which reduce the
range of activities possible indoors, forcing children onto the streets
and back-courts.

Another index of overcrowding is the number of people or
dwellings per acre of land. Citywide statistics, which include land

stocked with detached and semi-detached houses, conceal the realities. Even statistics for a whole scheme can be distortive, because they average out widely varying neighbourhood densities.

Those who design and approve scheme layouts are well aware that when they pack dwellings into one patch in order to produce an open-space feeling in another, they are helping to create and exacerbate social problems. It is where the houses are crammed in like peaches in a tin, in general, that most of acts of violence and vandalism occur, the most impoverished, under-skilled, harried and damaged families find themselves housed, and the housing stock deteriorates most rapidly.

Finally, the Areas of Need Report indicates that there are few areas in Glasgow which do not have substantial deficiencies in the provision of land for primary and secondary schools, and open space.

Overcrowding in Glasgow is multiple. It is structural. No amount of tinkering will make it go away.

III

The experience of council housing

Council housing is instantly recognisable. Passing from what is known as a residential area into a scheme is like going from the first-class part of a ship down to the steerage end.

It is difficult to avoid a feeling of entering a trap. Beauty of proportion, in the relations of height, length and depth, in the shape and positioning of windows and entrances, beauty of surface or of materials, beauty in the layout of streets, in the relationship of buildings to the contours of the land, to natural growth, the sense of a human scale — all of which human beings have been capable of recognising and creating for thousands of years — these are rarely to be found in council schemes.

In their place is uniformity, long rows of houses of regulation size, aggressively plain, spiritually empty: that emptiness that the Italian film-maker Antonioni sees in the most prestigious contemporary architecture. Houses and houses and houses, surrounded either by sites which have never been properly cleared, littered with rubble, or by mud seeded with grass, the topsoil long since flogged by the builder, or by those useless, mocking little triangles and strips of planners' green, worn at the edges, which look neat and bright on a drawing board, or from an aeroplane.

It is often asserted that the most recent council housing is of a much higher quality. It is true that rooms are getting a little bigger, there are more electric points, better kitchens and bathrooms, more attractive exteriors, more grass — but the built-in overcrowding, the pack-'em-in mentality, the uniformity, the giantism of scale, are still there unaltered.

The people who live in council houses are at once complaintive and resigned. They moan habitually about the size of the kitchen, the walk to the shops, the poor quality of repair work, the cracks in the sink, the neighbours, the damp, the kids, the drains, the overflowing bins, and on and on, with every justification.

And increasingly they retreat, many of them, within their own four walls, like prisoners, spectators half-helpless half-indifferent. There is a withdrawal from much feeling of interest in or responsibility for the external environment — the street, the pavement, the backcourt, the gardens, the worn-out open spaces, all increasingly abandoned to the kids. (And what is happening to the kids is another story worth pursuing.)

In part, this withdrawal into one's shell is a response to the overcrowding, the lack of privacy, but in a deeper sense it is perhaps not unlike a body's rejection of a heart transplant. It is a human rejection of a dehumanising external environment, particularly where high-density city housing is concerned.

Tenants of the peripheral schemes will tell you how when they first moved in twenty-odd years ago, they divided up the backcourts and made a plot for every family in the stair. But this hopeful attempt at a creative relationship with the environment *outside* the cell faded away.

This rejection or progressive withdrawal from the external environment may be one (though only one) cause of the rapid deterioration of council housing stock, the growth of vandalism, and the growing quantity of litter and other rubbish dumped by residents of all ages.

How many streets of council housing in Glasgow can be said to constitute environments which have not been rejected by the occupants? Relatively few. Carntynehall Road, Mosspark Boulevard. In such rare cases the people have been able to extend their sense of what is theirs outwards, they have come into some kind of creative relationship with their immediate surroundings. Both these streets are wide, the houses are semi-detached and set well apart, with back and front doors and gardens.

It is certainly true that most of Glasgow's tenants are dissatisfied with their environment, and many with their houses too. It is a reasonable guess that most of them yearn for one of those nice semis with their private entrances and gardens, even if they can't tell one end of a spade from the other.

IV

Tenants' Action and Organisation

Not all tenants retreat into their cell or shell. In more and more areas tenants' associations, housing action groups, local newspapers and summer playschemes are forming, bringing together those seeking to break out of their impotence.

These groups vary widely in their membership, in how they see themselves, in their activities.

(1) Barrowfield

Barrowfield Tenants' Association covers an area of only 500 or 600 houses. It meets weekly in Camlachie Community Centre. Attendance averages around 40 — almost all women, including all the office-bearers (though last year they elected a man as secretary). The main meat of the evening is when tenants give in their complaints about repairs they have applied for but which have not been done. These are written down and a weekly list of them sent to the factor. The Housing Management Department is not popular in the area. A representative attends only occasionally and strictly only on invitation.

A large proportion of Barrowfield Tenants' Association are unemployed or on Social Security. The employed and the skilled workers are in a minority. Complaints are followed by a bingo session, with tea and biscuits, a chat, and an hour or so's escape from the house and kids. Other activities are by way of being an underserviced community's self-service — parties for the kids, treats for the old folks, trips to the seaside for the members. The key activists are deeply involved in a wide range of other activities: discos, playgroups, mothers' groups, adventure playground, planning action group, and so on.

(2) Castlemilk

In complete contrast is Castlemilk Tenants' Association, covering around 9,000 houses. It meets monthly in Castlemilk Community Centre, with a normal attendance of about 30 — again mostly women. But traditionally the key offices are held by men — though in the last two years a woman has been elected chairman. (This pattern, of women on the floor and men on the platform, is repeated in many tenants' associations in the city.) Relationships between Castlemilk Tenants' Association and the local housing manager are very cordial. He attends all their meetings and records complaints personally. Most of those who attend are employed, and skilled or semi-skilled, and there is a substantial proportion of older folk.

Castlemilk Tenants' Association has less social involvement than
Barrowfield — though women's nights have recently been started.
Castlemilk Tenants' Association put months of solid work into the
recent rents campaign. It was the backbone of the local rents action
committee which sought to create a broad front of local social,
political and religious organisations in the scheme. CTA's most
recent initiatives are aimed at setting up local area tenants'
associations within the scheme, still linked to the CTA, which
will gradually change into a forum for communication between
the local associations, concerning itself with Castlemilk as a total
community.

First meetings held in two local areas of the scheme have thrown
up housing, cleansing, police and parks department issues. A
significant result has been that the Parks Department has begun
holding site meetings at neighbourhood level with interested tenants,
to find out what play and recreational facilities are wanted. An
official went on record as saying tenants should have a say in what
facilities they get and where they are sited — a modest but real
improvement in local authority attitudes. Tangible results so far
include the clearing and levelling off of several sites that had been left
unfinished by the builders.

(3) Direct Action

Not all tenants' action takes place through tenants' associations. In
Janefield Street, Parkhead, in 1972, unorganised council tenants
took direct action — blocking the road with prams, bikes and people
— and succeeded in having the street permanently closed to through
traffic. The action arose out of anger at a serious incident to a four-
year-old boy. Community workers and an activist from the Mile-end
Ward Committee, aware that direct action alone does not lead to
sustained involvement or increased understanding unless it is
followed up, used the accident and the campaign to raise planning
issues affecting the area. Comprehensive redevelopment plans had
condemned the area to be cut off on four sides by fast modern roads,
and to be deprived of neighbourhood shops and pubs.

The Planning Department responded to the agitation with a parry:
they asserted there was no demand from tenants of existing shops for
new premises to be provided. They suggested the activists undertake
a survey. The completed survey demonstrated that there *was* a
substantial demand. A planning action group was formed which
drew local activists into close contact with the planners and other
officials. The group has secured important concessions — local
shops *are* to be provided — but this can be seen as a means whereby
the planners have gained local acquiescence in their key proposals,

the four major roads. Undoubtedly involvement in the group has been an educative experience for local activists, but opinion is divided among them as to whether it has been worthwhile in terms of end results.

An example of successful action in the private sector occurred in 1971/72 in four streets of tenement houses at Gairbraid Avenue in Maryhill. The occupants — tenants and owner occupiers — were told their houses were a Housing Treatment Area. They took it to mean that their houses would be improved. It turned out they were in for demolition. A committee was formed which fought a good campaign, using both press and TV to publicise their cause, and at one stage occupying Clive House with prams. The main issue became rehousing, with the Housing Management Department trying to get them to accept poor quality offers. One old man, forty-six years in his house, was told he didn't have a long enough tenancy to qualify for rehousing in Maryhill! In face of the campaign, the tactic used was to rehouse the most troublesome activists first — a move which they countered by journeying back to Gairbraid from their new homes regularly and continuing to play their part.

Tenants' associations and other forms of housing action are of enormous importance. They assert the right of the consumers to control and improve the service they get. The implications of that are wide.

They can also *involve* more and more people in co-operative democratic action, starting from the point of their grouses. There is a natural danger, especially in organisations of those who are without power, that the organisation can become a plug stopping more involvement, rather than a tap turning it on — a result of the need for status and position on the part of the most devoted activists.

It is for this reason that it seems to me important to encourage the widest range of experiment, in size of area covered by tenants' organisation, in forms of organisation, and in type of activity. And, above all, to encourage decision-making and even meetings themselves to be characterised by open discussion, without hierarchies of status or opinion, with more experienced hands giving newer members their head in trying new ideas, rather than keeping development within rigid forms.

Brecht's words make a good motto:

> You can spot those in the limelight,
> Those in darkness you can't see.

V

The Tenant/Owner-Occupier Division
The tenant/owner-occupier division is one of the key splitting devices

in Britain. The comparison that springs to mind is with the Catholic/
Protestant division in Northern Ireland. Just as in Ireland, capital
gave better jobs, income and housing to the Protestant workers, thus
dividing them from their Catholic fellows, so in mainland Britain
and pre-eminently in England, capital gave the better housing to the
owner-occupiers, dividing them from the council tenants.

Of course, most owner-occupiers are, in one sense, really tenants.
They don't own a house, just a mortgage. If they default on the
repayments, the lender can secure the sale of the house to repay the
loan, and the owners find themselves in the same position as tenants
evicted for non-payment of rent: on the street. But in important
respects, owner-occupiers, particularly the owners of houses with
their own gardens, are privileged. They are not so overcrowded.
They feel the houses are theirs: they can look after them, and
improve them, outside as well as in, exactly as they wish, and they
have their garden, integrating themselves and their houses with the
land in a real sense. Their private space extends outside their four
walls.

In contrast, tenants feel the houses are not theirs. They have the
doubtful privilege of getting their repairs done for them — seldom
done well, and often not done at all. They are forbidden to decorate
the exterior of their homes, and in the case of tenants of multi-storey
or tenement houses, their private space does not extend beyond the
inside of the front door: the outside can be kicked, scraped or spray-
painted by invisible hands.

Finally, owner-occupiers are easily persuaded that they are
subsidising council tenants through their rates. They see themselves
as responsible, caring for land and property, self-sufficient, paying
their way: and they see council tenants as feckless, indifferent or
destructive towards the environment, subsidised and worthless: just
like the proddy sees the papes.

VI

Conclusion

For all the vast differences, it is interesting to compare Scotland with
China, and Glasgow with Shanghai. With a population of ten million
before the revolution, Shanghai was one of exploding cities of the
third world, with an endless influx of refugees from China's decaying
rural society. Glasgow is not quite like that. Her refugees came from
the West of Ireland and the Highlands a hundred years ago. Her
population is in decline and the bulk of our rural society is not so
much decaying as under-used.

The blurb for a recent conference on Scotland land use, sponsored by the *Glasgow Herald* and chaired by our very own tartan emperor, Sir Hugh Fraser, assigned to the largest part of our country the function of recreation — including tourism, second homes, hunting, shooting and fishing.

Shanghai has stopped growing since the Chinese revolution. It has been stopped, first, by the regeneration of China's rural economy, reversing the flight of people from the land; second, by a rejection of the assumption that development and big cities are two sides of a coin. Imperialism created concentrations of population and industry on the Chinese coast. The Chinese aim in the long-term is to disperse these concentrations. A combination of family planning, the decentralisation of development, the involvement of people in running the services that affect their lives, a network of street and neighbourhood committees, and the emigration of educated young people to the countryside has made it possible for the population of Shanghai to decline at a rate of 100,000 per year.

Scotland is not China. But the parallels are clear enough. Our housing problem, as we call it, will never be solved within the boundaries of our old cities with their lack of land, nor by their endless expansion. In Scotland, too, capitalism has created imbalances of industry and population, and, with minor adjustments, intends to keep it that way. The solution to the housing problem lies in the channelling of enterprise, and the planned reduction of our cities, on the one hand, and the ecologically sane development and repopulation of those vast tracts of land owned by a handful of rich people, on the other.

15. Community, Community, there's nothing like Community

This piece was written for the summer 1974 issue of the Bulletin of Family Service Units, at a time when the jobs page of every newspaper and magazine in Britain seemed to be full of 'community' posts.

Perhaps I should add that Family Service Units are small, community-based teams of social workers working intensively with troubled families. The Castlemilk Unit was low profile, sensitively led and very effective. One of the first acts of Strathclyde Regional Council was to withdraw funding from the FSU and install a Social Work office in the scheme, at vast expense.

*

The whole subject is totally confused.

Community Development is the government or local council paying community workers (usually young graduates) to help 'disadvantaged' people get organised to help themselves.

Community Action is people themselves getting together, getting organised, to fight for improvements in conditions and services.

Community Service used to be called Voluntary Work. 'Concerned' people helping people in need — usually on an individual basis.

Then there's community work itself, an umbrella word presumably, then community buses, community shops, community schools, community-based this, that and the next thing. There used to be community singing, but it hasn't been revived *yet.*

And at the top of the heap, cock of the midden, the signpost to everywhere: THE COMMUNITY.

I don't like the word myself, and never have done. It reeks of papering over the cracks. It reminds me of a rich Chesterfield company director's wife saying to a meeting of miners' wives in Duckmanton: 'After all, we're all workers, aren't we?'

But it's all the rage. Why? Well the first thing to make clear is that the 'community' trend isn't in fact *one* trend at all. It's several. It contains contradictions. You got in the mid-'60s young revolutionary or radical people going and living in working-class areas and encouraging folk to take up and fight/work together on local issues — play space, traffic danger, landlord crooks, police, schools, etc. Even within this there were at least two strands: the activist as charismatic leader/director, and catalytic enabler/ encourager, and often no doubt a mixture of both.

At the same time you were getting those nasty demos about Vietnam and suchlike. Meanwhile nice chaps from good schools had been getting a community service scene going — papering old ladies' walls and digging gardens, in between bouts of fast driving.

Before that you had President Kennedy's Peace Corps. So Harold thought he'd better do something to channel the enthusiasm of these politically motivated young idealists, so he summoned Anthony Steen to the Palace to set up Young Volunteer Force (YVF) with a government grant and all-party backing — as in Ulster. There was also VSO, CSV, and Task Force.

Lots of young graduates and others joined these organisations. Some of them tried to do community development or community action instead of community service. So the high-ups juggled the names a bit and 'legalised' community action but the unwritten rule was — no trouble, or you're out. Meanwhile it was spreading like wildfire through government departments, national institutes, local authority departments. There were Home Office Community Development Projects, Community Health, Community Involvement. Community workers were being appointed all over the place. So the revolutionaries started calling themselves neighbourhood agitators instead. The system countered by advertising for neighbourhood workers. Okay, I'll take the money.

Not forgetting, of course, the late Arthur Skeffington and People and Planning. I want to say quite seriously (in parenthesis) that *People and Planning* was quite a progressive report (which was why the Tories didn't implement it). Progressive not so much because of its specific proposals, but because it does hesitantly and partially express the idea that real democracy is a participatory thing, people working things out, not being pauperised or upstaged by experts.

So why, in a nutshell, this Gaderene rush into 'Community'? Because consciously or unconsciously or something between the two, it seemed to many people in various positions in government and other institutions the antidote to all this alienation, apathy, and *increasingly* hostility that was and still is being encountered among the 'clients'. A dose of 'community' was prescribed across the board.

The Tories of course saw it differently — as a means of reducing government spending and thus taxation. Get the buggers to do it themselves — care of the old, the sick, the mentally ill, ambulances for the disabled — all in, by, and for the community! It's so participative and democratic (and cheap)! This view is of course only a shade away from the 'scrap social security and welfare state mollycoddling, bring back the birch and the rope, let 'em learn to stand on their own feet' syndrome. The Tories also see it as an antidote to trade union militancy. Get them into local issues and they'll soon be lost in a fog, cutting each other's throats.

So it's a complex thing — even when you're involved in it. I've observed or taken part in various sorts of 'it' in the last four years. I've gone back to a place that was community worked and seen what was left. The sad truth is, after two years, precious little. Disillusionment. Disintegration. A step or two up a career ladder for some. Most of the folk who were involved are still where they were. They haven't developed further. What *has* kept going has become part of the local order, institutionalised.

It is hard to say this. I want to make it clear that I don't reject or write off community work, though I reject most of the official enthusiasm for it. But it seems clear that on its own, community action will not, cannot, change the man, woman, and child-eating society we live in. You cannot sustain islands of light in seas of darkness. They get swamped, sooner or later. I want to leave you, however, with a sense not of uselessness, but of *conditional* hope. Community action is important because it is helping to introduce into the working-class movement, imperfectly no doubt, the idea and practice of really democratic participation of people, open-mindedly working things out together, on a small scale, at a local level. This over against the leader/led mentality, the large-scale organisation, the militaristic marshalling of human units.

That would be important in itself, but there is a greater potential that has not yet been realised or practised to any great extent so far as I am aware. That is the combining of community action at local level, involving more and more people, with non-sectarian working-class adult education — whether organised and funded by working-class organisation, or wholly or partly by the state. So far it has happened more on the trade union front. An example is the free day-release classes the Derbyshire and Yorkshire NUM, the NCB, and Sheffield University Extra-Mural Department organise for miners. These have been an important factor in increasing militancy in the last few years, which is why the NCB, I understand, now wants them stopped. How much individual human development — and thus social and political development — could be reaped by classes in basic English, in reading and writing, in local authority housing finance and management, in planning procedures, and so on —

classes to be geared to the needs of those involved in tenants' associations, newspaper groups, political parties, action groups, etc. Community action, like trade union action, can only take a person's development so far. Even more than trade union action, it is likely *on its own* to drop them back into a cynical and inactive state, or else freeze them at the level of working-class bureaucrats. On the other hand, although local authority departments and the services they provide are the tentacles of the capitalist state, they are also potential bridgeheads for the working class — however much this idea may seem to have been discredited by the Labour Party's role in the last fifty years. I am not thinking of the election of councillors, but the opportunities, given widespread community action and working-class education, for getting more and more local authority employees to act and think as public *servants*. Hasten the day when pupils, parents and teachers get together, agree on their demands, and march on the town hall in sufficient numbers to realise them.

16. Community Democracy

Community Democracy was written for Gordon Brown's *Red Paper on Scotland* (1975), the first book to be published by Edinburgh University Student Publications Board. Re-reading it now I am oppressed by two feelings. First, that I really got bogged down in the data, the meticulously recorded evidence of the structure and activities of seventeen tenants' associations and other popular organisations rooted in various localities of Glasgow in 1974. I know it can be justified, then as now, as a painstaking attempt to inform anybody who might be interested about what was actually happening. But it is only in the section on the reform of local government that I give my own analysis a chance to come through. I can claim to have prophesied accurately the bureaucracy and confusion that would result, particularly in Strathclyde.

The other feeling is one of rage. How transparently people in working-class areas were *patronised* by the whole shoddy package of community development and community councils! It fairly reeks of colonial condescension, with the punters as bantu and the local government structures as district administration. The only difference was that the colour of the faces was the same. How closely the notion of areas of multiple deprivation, or areas of priority treatment, resembles the reality of apartheid's black townships. But the most depressing thing of all was this: *it was accepted*, because people were struggling to live meaningfully and with dignity in bleak circumstances which they thought were normal.

*

Popular Organisations
I am keen to anchor this article firmly in the reality it presumes to interpret. So the first and largest section of it will consist of a series of thumbnail sketches of Glasgow tenants' associations, community newspapers, action groups, and so on.

It will not be a comprehensive survey, rather a selection aiming to show the range and variety of what is happening. The reasons for confining it to Glasgow are: my own Scottish experience lies there; the role of the local authority can be well documented; the city's crop of local action is rich; and time has been very short. No greater-Glasgow chauvinism is intended.

Yoker and District Tenants' Association meets monthly in the Corporation's Spiers Hall. Between 20 and 30 attend, mostly women. Tenants' complaints about repairs applied for but not done are taken by the Secretary to the local Housing Manager. Unlike the previous factor, he listens to the tenants' views: for example, they can veto house allocations.

Secretary Mrs McCulloch feels strongly about 'anti-social people getting put in by the Welfare. These people have to be helped, but they're not just dumping them in here. We've got a bit here . . . that's the area they plump them in . . . we feel we're getting more than our share.' But she approves of the factor 'allowing people to get their children in when they get married . . . their parents are able to supervise them, we're building up a community.'

Interlocking with the TA is the Yoker Youth Movement. Councillor Perry, the clergy, and the Police Community Involvement Department have been involved. Weekly activities include a youth club, disco, swimming lessons, and a dancing class. There is an intense conflict between the local activists and the paid leaders. Originally six local people were running the club on their own, with badminton, table tennis, billiards and Lego. They accepted an offer of help from the FE Department and got nine part-time youth leaders.

Mrs McCulloch says 'they just more or less go round watching the kids playing . . . running about wild'. The local women 'canny get daein' any bloody thing'. She doesn't think there should be free expression with that number of kids. She's the driving force, she agrees — but insists she doesn't dominate. For example, TA members heard the Social Work Department were going to take over Spiers Hall. They didn't want that — the hall is right in the middle of their street, and many of them are on social security. 'Why should we walk through the street — everybody would know our business.' They insisted she get up a petition against it.

The View from Gorbals and Govanhill is Glasgow's oldest community newspaper, founded in 1968 by the Gorbals Group (an interdenominational group of Christian ministers and voluntary workers). It tended then to be written by group members, the MP, and other experts. (From early on, though, Hutchesontown TA was contributing its own regular article.) The aim was to focus on housing conditions and give people information about redevelopment. The paper came out monthly, and was sold in pubs, shops, and by teams of children.

In 1971, after editing *The View* for a year, Bill Williams suggested that it should be reorganised on the basis of local organisations contributing articles, and agreeing to sell a quota of copies. A meeting of Hutchestown TA, schools, churches, the ward committee, and the adventure playground endorsed this suggestion. Now, articles are handed in on the third Monday of the month for typing, and representatives of each organisation come along on the Wednesday evening to do their own layout. Each group folds its own papers. At present around 1,500 are sold each month, more than half of them through organisations.

Last year the Corporation Social Work Department bought a reconditioned varityper for use by *The View* and other community papers in Glasgow. This improves the appearance, but the typing has to be paid for, so most papers are not yet using it. Another application has been made for the Corporation to pay the typist. Recently there has been an increased flow of Corporation advertising to *The View* and other papers, which helps to increase the size and cover production costs.

Hutchesontown Tenants' Association, started in 1968, covers the new Gorbals, including both SSHA and Corporation tenants. Around 50 attend the monthly meeting in a school. It tends to be mainly older women, though there is a mixture of other age groups, and some men. There has been an influx of younger folk recently — young folk only come to meetings when they've a problem, says chairman Roddy Kerr. The committee of sixteen members meets weekly, with an average attendance of between eight and twelve. This is the hub of the TA, Roddy says. If you haven't got a big committee, you heap a terrific amount of work on a few officials. In HTA, different people are prominent in different activities. At the monthly meeting a councillor answers questions about Corporation matters. Complaints about repairs are sent to the factor — and if they're still not done, to a councillor.

There's an annual sports day, weekly swimming club for kids, a monthly dance, lots of ladies' nights and bus runs. The TA has achieved a lot: toilets in the arcade, a community centre, local post offices, telephone kiosks — mostly by hard pressure on councillors. In the case of traffic risk to children in the old Rutherglen Road, the usual channels failed. The tenants went out and demonstrated in the street. A compromise was fixed up. After nine months they demonstrated again, and the road was permanently closed to through traffic, in spite of opposition from police and fire brigade.

Two issues currently preoccupy TA member Jimmy Forsyth. One is that Corporation tenants in the scheme are now getting their TV aerials rent free while SSHA tenants like him still have to pay. The other is the smoke and smell from the nearby distillery.

Govanhill and District Residents' Association meets monthly in Dixon Halls, with an average attendance of 20 — mostly council tenants, with a few private tenants and owner-occupiers. They are predominantly older women, with a recent influx of some younger people. Complaints are taken and passed on to the appropriate departments. Councillors and officials are not usually invited to meetings. GRA sends a delegation to see them when necessary. Delegations report back at the next meeting.

Parts of Govanhill, like Robson Street, have now got local TAs and don't come to GRA meetings. President Bill Towill blames the community workers for this. He does not agree that having smaller TAs helps to involve more people. 'It gets them into their own wee narrow question — divorces them from issues affecting everybody else.... If the issue gets settled, that's them quiet again . . . whereas if you get them into one body, you give them a permanent interest in coming.'

GRA doesn't work by direct action. You go to one level, and if you get no satisfaction, you go to the next level up. Bill says he tends to dominate GRA meetings, because of his wide involvement in the tenants' and trade union movements. 'The folk on the floor of the meeting don't know how local government works, they're looking for advice.' He thinks TAs are inclined to be parochial. Politics should be brought in. But TAs shouldn't be the same as trade unions. They're different organisations, because there are everyday issues arising that affect women. 'Women'll come if you advertise on problems. But trade union branch life is dead.'

Govanhill Action Group started in May 1973 in protest against proposals to demolish 1,200 tenement houses to make room for an expressway. Corporation officials said most of the houses were 'done' anyway — only 85 of them could be considered 'long-life' — and arranged a public exhibition of the proposals.

Delegates from local organisations and interested individuals formed the action group after demonstrating outside the exhibition. The committee of about twelve meets once a month. They are now dealing also with housing problems — members have helped to set up local TAs (Calder Square, Annandale Square), also the Govanhill Housing Association, which will buy houses, improve them, and let them out.

The group's counter-proposal on the line of the expressway would route it not through the houses but through land owned by Templeton's Carpet Factory. Templeton's have threatened to close their factory (employing 1,500) if this is done. This alternative had not been put before the public at the exhibition because of private representations from Templeton's. The Action Group has the people of Govanhill behind it, says Davy McCracken, the chairman. They get a turnout of hundreds when they hold a meeting. Half the committee are women. There's a good age-mix — several in their thirties, one 25-year-old.

Closely associated with the Action Group is *The Working Party*, consisting of one delegate from every local organisation, plus officials from Corporation departments. It discusses the problems of Govanhill. The local delegates say what they would like to see happening. The Working Party has decided to look for premises in the area, to be rented by the Corporation for them — something like a biggish shop, to be an information centre, a meeting place for local organisations, a place to meet officials from the housing improvement section, to get free legal advice, etc. *The View* would be based there, so would the community workers. Davy McCracken feels it's a good idea to have lots of different, independent organisations — but then get them all to come together in the Action Group and be represented on the Working Party. 'A Community Council would be a follow-on from what we're doing.'

Gairbraid Treatment Area Group formed in 1971 in two blocks of tenements in Maryhill, earmarked for demolition. At a meeting the residents elected a committee of ten, which over the next year took action on issues like burst pipes and vandalism, and organised a playgroup, bingo, and nights out at the Maryhill TUC Club.

The rehousing policies of the Housing Management Department became the main focus. Some of the houses offered to families were in a terrible state and far from Maryhill. So whenever a family got an offer, someone from the committee went to see it with them. Several older tenants were threatened by officials at the house letting section at Clive House if they refused an offer. So it was decided that pensioners would be accompanied there by committee members.

The BBC made a film publicising their campaign. The result was that the next set of offers were all new houses, in Maryhill. Whenever the offers started to get worse, the group organised a new demo — culminating in April 1972 when they occupied the stairway and house-letting section at Clive House with mothers, prams and kids. The Housing Management tried to disembowel the Action Group by rehousing most of the key activists early on. But they overcame this move by coming back regularly to continue to play their part.

Eileen Thompson is suspicious of Community Councils and the Corporation's current overtures to the tenants. Participation doesn't go far enough. There should be an obligation on the local authority not only to note people's views but to *act* on them. Local people should control local planning.

Possilpark Tenants' Association meets monthly in Hawthorn Primary School. It covers an area of poor quality pre-war council houses. Normal meetings attract 160 people, mostly women, but a good lot of men. About a fifth are pensioners, the rest mostly middle aged. Tea and a cake are served at the meeting. The committee is very active and consists of two young men, two young women, and three older folk. The president takes repairs complaints to the factor. The Association helps those who get into rent arrears — but not 'anti-social' tenants — and helps people get rent and rates rebates. They organise bus runs and a big Christmas party.

The main thing just now is the Environment Improvement Project. The houses have been sandblasted. The old palings, ashpits and drying greens are being removed, and the backcourts are being landscaped with new drying greens, chutes for children, kickabouts for toddlers, and bricked-in refuse containers. The backs are to be lit up by searchlights. A new park has been created, with football pitches, changing rooms, sports facilities, rows of trees. The TA complained about the siting of the new bins and got them moved. The one backcourt completed so far is really beautiful. The committee wonder — is this just a showpiece?

There is a problem with one contractor whose men are breaking and stealing materials and blaming it on 'the vandals'. President John Mullen says there are only a few vandals — it's the contractor and his men who are doing most of the damage. However, they decided to read out the names of several vandals at a recent TA meeting. John has been told to 'leave community councils to the councillors'.

Garthamlock Tenants' Association has been going since the scheme was built eighteen years ago. Average attendance at this year's monthly meetings was 60. The thirteen-strong committee meets weekly and is extended to include anyone becoming active in the community. Each member covers one or two streets for membership.

The environmental subcommittee was active in Facelift Garthamlock (1972) — they ran anti-litter campaigns, worked on restoring the old Provan Hall, and planted trees in gardens. For the first time, Corporation departments were drawn into closer contact with the community and they were forced to co-operate with each other.

The Association helps problem families. They're not hostile to them, except when Housing Management bring in too many.

A community survey is being put out with questions on transfers, repairs, facilities wanted, part-time education, unemployment, buses, etc. 'We hope . . . [it] . . . will give us an accurate picture . . . use the answers given to press the authorities for support in our fight to improve our community.' 'We've got to improve the environment, so's the good tenants will stay,' says secretary Freddy Anderson.

The TA's very own hall is nearing completion. It is licensed, with main hall, stage, lounge, kitchen, committee rooms, toilets. It is being built with a £40,000 loan from Scottish and Newcastle Breweries, to be repaid over twelve years. They hope the hall will bring the community together on a non-sectarian basis for the first time in Garthamlock. They plan to have dancing, bingo, a women's night, OAPs in the afternoons, someone to take complaints always there, etc. Long-term aim — to extend it into a really big community centre run by the TA.

The East End Rents Action Committee was created in 1973 after the Corporation had given in to the threats of the Secretary of State and agreed to put up the rents. The driving force was Garthamlock TA and the aim was to create a broad movement of local organisations to encourage tenants not to pay the increases, and to draw attention to the social problems caused by the Housing Finance Act.

A local minister became chairman and active support was given by Councillor Edgerton, TAs in Queenslie, Ruchazie, Craigend, Lochend, and the White Panthers, a group of revolutionary young folk. They picketed the factor's office for several weeks, collected over 1,000 signatures not to pay the increase, held a march from Craigend to Easterhouse shopping centre, sold copies of *Scottish Tenant*, and ran a 'problems' surgery. They failed to bring about mass rent-withholding but created a lot of sympathy and gave many people a better grasp of how local authority activities are financed and the underlying causes of the East End's multiple social, economic and environmental problems.

Barrowfield Tenants' Association covers a small area of about 500 immediately pre- and post-war houses of low quality in the inner East End — yet it has an average attendance of 40/50 at its weekly meetings in Camlachie Community Centre. Complaints about repairs not done are written down and a list sent to the local factor, who writes back stating what action has been taken. The Housing Management Department is not popular in the scheme, and officials attend TA meetings rarely and strictly on invitation only.

The scheme is used as a dumping ground for problem families. A lot of TA members are on Social Security or do not have full-time jobs. The TA is attended almost exclusively by women of all ages and is possibly unique in having a very capable all-female committee (until last year, when one man came on as secretary). After business, they have tea and biscuits and play a few games of bingo. Trips are organised, and parties, treats and gifts for children and pensioners. Separate from the TA but run by some of its active members are the playgroup and discos. There is also a mothers' group, and this summer a Barrowfield Festival was held.

Mile-end Planning Action Group draws some of its members from Barrowfield, and others from nearby streets. It grew out of events in Janefield Street, a long straight road running behind Celtic football

park, which was used by motorists to bypass the traffic lights at
Parkhead Cross, and by Croft's Garage to test car brakes.

Several children had been hit by vehicles, and after the last
incident, in 1972, the mothers and their children, with help from
Barrowfield TA, blocked the street. They said it should be closed to
through traffic. The police said it was impossible. One councillor
dragged his feet. The other two supported the tenants' case. They
blocked the street again in the evening, and after several months'
delay, they won.

Community workers and the secretary of the ward committee
used the incident to draw attention to the Comprehensive
Redevelopment Plans affecting the area. All local shops and pubs
were demolished and not replaced. The area was to be cut off on all
four sides by fast modern roads. Later a planning action group was
formed, bringing together activists and officials. The case for local
shops was quickly conceded, but the road plans are unchanged. At
least one local member of the group wonders if they are not just being
gently coaxed into accepting the planners' proposals.

Barrowfield Community School. In June 1972 contact was made
through community workers between some lecturers and students at
Jordanhill College of Education and some members of Barrowfield
Tenants' Association. Truancy and other school problems were
discussed, also the idea of a 'free' or community-run school. After
further contacts, trained teacher Brian Addison, along with a
handful of parents and some of their children, began to feel their way
towards putting the idea into practice.

Eventually, in May 1973, Barrowfield Community School started
up in Christ Church Hall. In September they moved to a flat in St
Marnock Street, with six pupils, one full-time and five part-time
teachers. Long-term aim is to build up to perhaps four full-time
teachers and a maximum of 40 kids.

> One must deal with the *causes* of school refusal, truancy,
> and early leaving . . . If schools are perceived as irrelevant
> institutions by pupils and parents, it is that point at which we
> have to start. It is useless to simply try . . . stricter punishments
> . . . We have tried to provide a school which is perceived as
> neither alien or irrelevant by those we wish to benefit from it.
>
> We have accepted the way children in Barrowfield speak,
> the values they hold, and the kind of behaviour they evidence
> . . . We have our own values and convictions . . . The ensuing
> dialogue we consider an integral part of the educational
> process.
>
> We believe it is pretty important that teachers live in the
> community. . .

The single most important difference between our school
and others . . . is the commitment of the parents.

Child A, for example, may spend Monday working in a
restaurant, Tuesday in the school on follow-up work in
marketing, economics, and other aspects of the catering trade.
Some time on Tuesday there will be an hour or two for close
individual tuition perhaps in mathematics or reading. . . . On
Wednesday there will be work with the rest of the group on a
community project, interviewing the firemen about their
strike, for example, or talking to local tenants about the area
and its problems. Wednesday afternoon may be spent in the
local Corporation nursery working with pre-school children
. . . on Thursday morning there is work for O-level history, in
the afternoon perhaps creative writing or more maths. . . .

We have seen a change . . . [the six children] are more
confident, more articulate, more sensitive, and more
knowledgeable . . . more responsible. . . This is a school that
belongs to its pupils and they enjoy it.

Castlemilk Tenants' Association has been going for twenty years,
since the scheme was built. It covers nearly 10,000 houses. About 30
attend the monthly meetings in Castlemilk Community Centre,
almost all women, mainly middle aged or elderly. Very few are
unemployed or on Social Security. Some of the few men who attend
occupy key positions on the committee, but last year a woman was
elected chairman. Informal extended committee meetings take place
after the meeting in the coffee bar.

The TA gets on well with the local housing manager, who attends
all meetings and takes note of complaints about repairs and other
problems. Secretary Ian Towill feels this relationship of friendly
service on the factor's part is very valuable. On the other hand some
women say they're afraid to speak while the factor is there and that
it puts people off coming. This difference of opinion is characteristic
of the dialectic between men and women on the committee — the
women pushing for a bigger social side, the men emphasising the
fight for better services.

Recently they have been working towards setting up local area
TAs, still linked to the central organisation. Monthly meetings have
been held in two areas, with attendances around 30, raising issues
like vandalism, lack of beat policemen, litter collection, lifts, play
facilities, etc. Two site meetings between tenants of multi-storey flats
and Parks Department officials have resulted, bins have been
doubled up, and collection improved, several rubble-strewn areas
have been half-landscaped, and kickabouts provided. 'We feel you

should have some say in what facilities you get and where they go,' said Mr Mann of the Parks Department. In one of these areas, a new independent association has been formed. In the other a local area committee of the TA has been set up. More local meetings are planned, possibly in co-operation with the Housing Manager.

Castlemilk Rents Action Committee was set up in autumn 1972, to develop support for Glasgow Corporation's refusal to implement the Housing Finance Act. The driving force was Castlemilk TA, the aim to create a united front of local political, social and religious organisations. The TA, the Communist Party, the Labour Party, the Labour Party Young Socialists, and the Co-op Women's Guild were represented, also the district committee of the NUR, Govan Shipbuilders and Sterne's shop stewards, with occasional support from Councillors Fitch and Manson.

When the Corporation gave in, they held a 500-strong protest meeting and called for the increase to be withheld. For six months they kept up a campaign of leafletting, street meetings with loudspeakers, sales of *Scottish Tenant*, and a two-month picket of the factor's office. The campaign failed to create mass rent withholding, but it put the issue right into the centre of people's minds and showed the possibilities there are in the idea of co-ordinated local action.

Castlemilk Today is Glasgow's newest community paper, starting in March this year. Two years ago a local minister and other concerned outsiders started Castlemilk Press, with the minister as editor. It didn't get the practical involvement of enough local people or organisations, the tendency was for contentious material to be edited out, and a substantial debt built up.

A handful of activists from the old paper have been joined by about a dozen new ones, all living in the scheme, mostly young and middle-aged women. Two successful dances were held to clear the debt. Contact was made with *The View* and flowing from that it was decided to base the paper on local organisations, which would undertake to contribute monthly reports and sell a quota of papers.

The paper group itself is autonomous — its members are not delegates. It is an open, democratic group, with no editor, meeting weekly and deciding all policy matters, collecting reports from organisations, writing articles, encouraging others to write, doing interviews, editing, typing, laying-out, letrasetting, folding and selling the paper. Net sales have grown from 1,500 to 2,200 in four issues/months; 400 of these are sold by the group, the rest by organisations and newsagents. The paper is planning a meeting of all organisations in the scheme to discuss the setting up of a community council.

Scottish Tenant first came out in 1973. Three issues have appeared so far. Sales have dropped from 6,000 to 4,000, mainly through tenants' associations, shop stewards' committees and trade union branch and district committees. Three-quarters of all sales are in Glasgow.

It is the paper of the Scottish Council of Tenants and has contained reports from local TAs and RACs, campaigning/informing articles on the Housing Finance Act and government White Papers, the law affecting private tenants, bits of working-class history, contributions by councillors, poems, stories, jokes, cartoons, etc. It is an attempt to create communication between local organisations in different areas, to link in with work situations and the trade unions, to inform activisits on issues of interest to them, in general to create a wider perspective than that afforded by local involvement alone. At the moment it is being reorganised to base it more firmly on local TAs, so that it will become their paper in a practical participative sense.

The Local Authority

In this and following sections, the aim is to focus on the role of the local authority, central government and private capital in relation to the grass roots activity we have been looking at.

Far from merely *responding* to the development of local action, the state is actually *stimulating* it.

First, the local authority. In a document dated October 1973, Glasgow's Chief Constable, Housing Manager, Depute Director of Education and Depute Director of Social Work outline the involvement of their departments in Community Development.

The Chief Constable set up a Community Involvement Department late in 1971. Duties were to include liaison with the Social Work Department regarding juveniles, operation of police warning schemes, crime prevention propaganda, race relations, fostering community activities, contact with youth, TAs, churches, schools, and fostering of police recruitment. One chief superintendent, one superintendent, seven inspectors, 21 sergeants, 14 constables and eight clerkesses were assigned to this work. Activities have included helping to set up a tenants' association in Broomloan Road, giving children athletic training, and an involvement in Contact Govan, where all old people living alone in the area have been identified and volunteer wardens keep a friendly eye on them: 'the department have fitted chains in a number of their houses.'

The Housing Manager feels his department should be the 'instigator of amenity and environmental improvements . . . the agent to work out with tenants what is required to make their houses and surroundings more acceptable . . .'. 'While the authority can provide the necessary financial and labour resources . . . such work will be abortive . . . without consulting the tenants. . . . Tenants must be given the opportunity to manage their own affairs . . . through the activities of tenants' or residents' associations. . . .'

'This . . . can best be achieved by the employment of full-time Community Development Officers. . . ' He has encouraged regular meetings between TAs and district office staff. He has organised 'meetings with tenants to bring into being residents' associations . . . in Easterhouse . . . it is proposed to introduce similar ideas in Garthamlock, Drumchapel, Castlemilk, Pollock. . . .'

'What is invariably lacking in housing areas is leadership and initiative.' Implementation of his proposals is 'fundamentally essential if housing areas are to be saved from further blight and degeneration'.

The Depute Director of Education outlines the various forms of support given to voluntary organisations — grant to pay the salary of an unattached youth worker in Blackhill . . . £80,000 a year spent on paying activity leaders in voluntary youth organisations, £85,000 a year for their premises and equipment.

The most recent initiative is the appointment of Neighbourhood Development Officers — people are looking for 'a wider range of leisure opportunities and have more leisure time'. They will be based in schools in 'a new housing development, an old neighbourhood which is being upgraded, a neighbourhood in a housing estate which has for long been unresponsive to attempts to enrich the quality of life in it'. They will 'get to know a large number of residents, identify the potential leaders, encourage residents to organise their own leisure time pursuits, make best use of existing facilities and make good deficiencies as far as possible.'

The Depute Director of Social Work writes that 'the employment of community workers has been left to various voluntary organisations which have been grant-aided' — YVFF in Mile-End, Park Ward Residents' Council, Lochend Neighbourhood Project, Assist, St Andrew's Advice Centre, Gorbals Govanhill Fieldwork Unit, the Glendale Centre, the Community Relations Council.

Clearly the local authority's departmental hierarchies have been thoroughly soaked in the ideology of 'community', the language of which is intermingling with their specialist jargon and class prejudices to produce some very odd results.

How do Labour councillors see it?

Councillor Rev. Geoff Shaw, chairman of the new Strathclyde Region, interviewed in *The View*, December 1973:

> The whole movement towards public involvement in decision-making and making information available to the

public is a fairly new movement — probably within the last ten
years. . .
    I hope that community councils will be seen as a focus for
the community . . . possibly they will serve as the middle man
between the different departments and the people at local
level. . .
    Glasgow Corporation . . . put a lot of representation to the
Government . . . that the Community Councils must be
stronger, that the District Authority must be *made* to provide
the resources. . . .

Geoff Shaw has been quoted elsewhere as saying that each
Community Council should get an annual grant of £10,000 from its
district council.

Councillor Ronald Young of Greenock reported in *Glasgow
News* (16.12.72): 'The political role of the local government officer,
the accountability concept, political responsibility of the elected
representatives, are all part of a pseudo-democratic smokescreen
which can be dispelled by the fresh wind from local grass-roots
organisations.'

In the same report, Councillor John Hoey of Livingston: 'Participation is a waste of time. What we need is a Cultural Revolution. . .
We must attack the basic social structure, instead of taking toothless
bites at the local authority.'

Private Capital
It is also interesting to note the involvement of private capital in
funding many community projects, usually through a variety of
trusts, but in a number of instances by direct grant. Obviously many
entrepreneurs see community activity as an antidote to trade union
activity, and as a means of reducing government spending on social
services.

Small-scale enterprise is the well-spring of capitalism, and it is
significant to see it latching on to hints flung up by community
activity. Two new commercial newspapers have been started by city
landlord Joe Mulholland alongside existing community papers —
West End News alongside *Glasgow News* and *South Side News*
alongside *The View*.

South Side News has used *View* stories and contacts without any
acknowledgement, or getting in touch with the paper itself. It also
refused to print a letter from *The View* concerning a serious
inaccuracy in one of the reports, or to apologise.

Under the banner *Welcome to YOUR Paper*, the first issue of
South Side News told its readers that it would . . . 'Help to further

your involvement in the community . . . we believe that this local community that is dear to us all will find itself with a new identity and voice . . . it is our earnest wish to serve you in the years ahead.' The real face of community capitalism coming into focus?

Reform of Local Government

Reform of local government in Scotland, as in England, can be seen as part of the long-term trend towards centralisation, through the creation of larger and larger units.

The Tory Government's White Paper of 1971 hardly bothered to justify the changes, contenting itself with assertions that 'many authorities are too small'; 'demands on local government will increase . . . this means that local authorities will have to be larger . . .'; 'the regional authorities . . . will enjoy substantial advantages through economies of scale'. This was accompanied by bland expressions of concern about the danger of local government becoming remote from the individual — that would be overcome by administrative decentralisation. More sugar for the pill was provided by promises that central government control over local authorities would be eased, more financial responsibility would be devolved, and so on. (This was shortly before they took away the power of local authorties to fix the rents of council houses.)

Another theme is connected with the growing influence of the concept of integrated regional planning. In part, this represents an awareness of the inadequacy of the present system of watertight compartments — housing, parks, education, etc., often not communicating satisfactorily at committee, senior management, or service outlet levels, or operating on the basis of conflicting diagnoses and priorities, or even duplicating provision.

The reform represents a victory for the planners, with the old departments demoted to the level of service administrators, under a top level of policy planning. Strathclyde's new Chief Executive lays it on the line in his advert for a Director of Policy Planning (*Glasgow Herald*, 17th July 1974): 'The successful applicant . . . will work closely with the Chief Executive . . . in policy formulation. He will head a small inter-disciplinary team, the "Policy Planning Unit". . . All plans which involve the commitment of resources (will be) routed through the Policy Planning Unit . . . for presentation to the Policy and Resources Committee.'

Clearly, the bureaucracy is going to get bigger. Instead, for example, of an education department with a hierarchy of director, deputy and assistant directors and central office staffs, squatting like an idol on top of the hierarchies within the individual service-providing institutions (schools and colleges), we are now going to have a policy planning unit, on top of a regional directorate, on top of a bunch of decentralised directorates (probably at the level of the old authorities contained within the new region), on top of the hierarchies in the service-providing institutions.

The lines of communication multiply, as do the number of top jobs. The machinery will absorb more and more money simply to maintain itself in existence — more salaries, more offices, more clerical staff, more equipment, so that even with substantial rates increases, given the present rate of inflation it seems possible that the real output of services in quantitative and qualitative terms will fall. Elected representatives will be sucked more and more into the entrails of the machinery as the committee structure proliferates, and be less available to the people. Confusion will develop about who runs which service.

As for local control and local co-ordination of services — which to the humble human unit are the real problem — well, the truth is that there is no practical provision in the Act for local control and local co-ordination of local government services.

James Kellas (*Glasgow News*, March 1972): 'The Scottish Office is at the root of the local government paradox in Scotland. . . . The local government reforms fragment Scotland and leave the Scottish Office well clear of democratic controls. No region in Scotland has the financial means to resist central authority. It is time . . . that the whitewash about local democracy was put in its true perspective.'

Community Councils

It is in the context of the real nature of local government reform that we should consider the cautious and ambiguous provisions for the establishment of Community Councils contained in part 4 of the Act.

The key paragraphs read as follows:

In addition to any other purpose which a community council may pursue, the general purpose of a community council shall be to ascertain, co-ordinate, and express to the local authorities for its area, and to public authorities, the views of the community which it represents, in relation to matters for which those authorities are responsible, and to take such action in the interests of that community as appears to it to be expedient.

Regional, islands and district councils may make such contributions as they think fit towards the expenses of community councils within their areas, may make loans to those councils, and may, at the request of such community councils, provide them with staff, services, accommodation, furniture, vehicles, and equipment, on such terms as to payment or otherwise as may be agreed between the councils concerned.

The following timetable is laid down: the district council announces that it is going to frame a scheme for community councils. The public has eight weeks to make suggestions about their areas and composition.

After considering these suggestions, the district sends the scheme, plus objections, to the Secretary of State. He approves it, or holds a local enquiry, or refers it back to the district for further consideration. When they are approved the proposals are exhibited in each area to be affected. At least twenty electors in each area must then apply in writing for a community council to be set up. Within six weeks elections or other voting arrangements must be organised.

Finally, the district has powers, from time to time, to review its scheme and propose amendments. If these are opposed the matter goes to the Secretary of State.

The major unanswered questions are:

> What size of areas? Local neighbourhoods? School catchment areas? District wards? Regional divisions? Constituencies? The township — 'where I come from' — Castlemilk, Govan, Saltcoats, Wester Hailes?
>
> Are community councils to be the single channel of communication with the authorities, supplanting existing organisations like TAs, and limiting their right to access and information?
>
> Are the members of community councils to be elected by popular vote? On a party ticket or not? Or are some to be elected and some to be delegates? Or all to be delegates?
>
> Are district and region obliged to provide the community council with information on request — any information? Are community councils obliged to provide district and region with information on request?

The Scottish Development Department's discussion document on *Community Councils: Some Alternatives for Community Council Schemes in Scotland* (HMSO, 1974), published in January 1975, attempts to grapple with some of these problems, 'with a view to contributing towards as full and informed a public debate as possible, while the schemes are being drawn up. It does not lay down the law on the ideal patterns for any area (the document states) but offers a large range of possibilities which may be helpful in making a choice locally' (para. 1.4). The 'guidelines' state that 'community councils will not be a third tier of local government with legally defined duties and responsibilities' (para. 1.7).

It is suggested that flexibility in size and organisation depending on community demand would be acceptable, but that 'there may well be disadvantages for councils which are beyond the range of thirty members' (paras. 1.9 and 4.7). The document suggests that 'there are three main possibilities for the composition of a community council: entirely of directly elected individual members, entirely of representatives of local organisations, or a proportion of both. The council may wish to co-opt other members for a specific purpose. While some might maintain that only the first type (and possibly the third if directly elected members were in a majority) were truly representative, all three may be regarded as genuine options in that they all ensure, in different ways, that the community as a whole is represented' (paras. 4.7 and 4.8). On the flow of information required and requested from district and regional government, the document suggests only that 'Much of this information will be fed to community councils through contacts with regional, islands and district councillors and officials and through written reports' (para. 6.5).

It is clear that, although they won't provide any statutory services, community councils are a part of the state machinery. Ultimate power to set them up, or not, and to decide their structure, rests with the Secretary of State, through the District Council. Power to give or withhold money lies with the district.

Nevertheless, subject to these limitations, the Community Council has an independent existence. It can do whatever it wants. It need not, therefore, adopt a subservient posture towards the authorities.

Conclusions

I have tried to keep comment to a minimum throughout this article, because I believe the reader must do his own interpretation. These matters have been under-discussed, and no good cause is served by providing instant opinions. The projection of rigid, dogmatic analyses, and closed-minded hostility to other views, has disfigured the left for fifty years. It is time we made serious efforts to overcome it.

But it would be cheating not to say what I think. The following comments are offered, therefore, in an open-minded and tentative spirit.

Open, democratic TAs, residents' associations, action groups, and other similar organisations — that is to say, people voluntarily coming together at local level and organising to improve conditions and services, and to provide self-services — these are the growth points for participative democracy.

This is in spite of their reactionary features — the tendency for the platform to dominate the floor, men to dominate women, the old to dominate the young, the danger of a subservient or client relationship with the local authority. It is romantic to imagine that the self-organisation of people at the bottom of the heap in capitalist society will not reproduce many of the features of that society.

We should recognise and work to encourage their democratic co-operative features — sharing out of decision-making, encouraging people to express themselves sometimes at the expense of the orderliness of the agenda, trying new suggestions by new people, a conscious attempt by the key experienced activists to see their job as facilitating the development of younger, newer, less confident people, rather than hogging the interesting jobs, and so on.

I am for complete independence of these organisations from the local authority. Of course they will seek for concessions, improvements, rights — but not as part of a deal giving them policing or minor administrative functions. They should resist incorporation into the machinery.

I recognise the force of Bill Towill's arguments against neighbourhood TAs but don't agree with him that big TAs are what's needed. People must be free to choose the size of the area their organisation covers. The way to overcome the problems of isolation and parochialism is to encourage regular meetings between TAs in adjacent areas, to discuss common problems and services, and to co-ordinate campaigns.

We should encourage visits between TAs in widely separate areas too. As long as they remain in isolation, they tend to develop distorted views of the causes of their problems, and the system can easily deal with them by occasional concessions. It is no great strain for capitalism to do up the backcourts in Possilpark. What needs to happen now is that every TA in the city goes up there and sees for themselves — and start demanding the same for their backcourts.

I also believe it to be important to emphasise the idea of well-publicised direct action, if and when the usual channels fail. Otherwise a TA is accepting its powerlessness to change things when the system does not accede to their polite requests.

The importance of the appearance of community newspapers can hardly be overemphasised. Again, the relationship with the local authority must be one of independence — every concession, every grant of resources, must be welcomed and more pressed for, without any compromising deals. Glasgow Corporation's record on this has been very good in recent months.

A word about what I have called self-servicing activities. Many politically conscious activists are uneasy about this: they feel it is a trap. The local authority should be providing the services and we should be pressing to get them improved. I agree with that, in a sense.

But in another sense it misses the point. Take playgroups. It's a great thing that mothers in Barrowfield, Govanhill, and so on are running their own playgroups — and fighting to get one of *them* as supervisor, not someone the PPA foists on them. The fact that the (very welcome) new nursery schools now opening are run by trained experts, with mothers excluded — that's a step backwards.

What we should demand is that ordinary working people get more and more control over such resources at local service-output level.

The same applies to Barrowfield's Community School. The education authority should be pressed to provide the resources, but not attempt to remodel the school on hierarchical, bureaucratic lines. Control should rest at local level with those involved — teachers, parents, pupils.

Some socialists may look askance at the direction these comments are taking. Am I suggesting that local authority departmental and service structures be dismantled?

I am not making any such sweeping proposal. What I'm saying is that, just as nationalisation is not socialisation, so the social services are not *socialist* services. For them to become that, we will have to overcome the alienating and exploitive characteristics of the present patterns of provision and consumption. This will be a gradual, experimental process. Some experiments will be dead-ends. Some, like housing associations, can, I think, be shown to be reactionary.

Those of us who have worked as local authority officers know from our own experience that the present system of organising services could not be more wasteful, inefficient and undemocratic. The democratisation of public services is not something to be deferred till 'after the revolution'. It is part of the revolution, and we should be starting now.

Community Councils should not replace or down-value TAs, RAs, action groups, community papers, nor colonise them. They should not be elected — that will merely bring so-called representative democracy (which in practice means the dictatorship of the officials, with the ill-informed acquiescence of the elected representatives) into the local arena. The party-ticket electoral charade could set the development of participative democracy back years.

Imagine what might happen in a Labour area, under Labour District and Regional Councils. The Community Council would consist of Labour Party folk who would be under pressure to push the line that district and regional policies were great, don't rock the boat, don't demand too much all at once. The Community Council would become a tame organ of social control, an individual complaints-servicing agency, and a dependence-on-big-brother complex could develop at local level.

In urban areas, Community Councils should cover townships of various sizes, big enough to contain a fair number of TAs, political parties, churches, OAP organisations, etc. They should not be forced to fit neatly into administrative boundaries.

The council should consist of one delegate from each organisation, chosen annually by vote at a well-publicised meeting of members of each organisation. No individual could be delegated by more than one organisation, and no one could be a CC member more than once in five years.

The purpose of these safeguards would be to ensure that local activists did not become dazzled by the status of being a council member and begin to drop their involvement in their own organisation. There is already evidence of activists turning their attention away from their TA towards participation in the formation of proto-Community Councils.

As well as delegates, interested members of the public should be allowed to take part in council meetings, but not vote. Local authority officials should not be members nor have standing invitations. The council should be free to invite them or not, when it wishes. Sending a delegate should be a voluntary act on the part of local organisations. The councils should not be a single channel of communication with the authorities.

The councils should not be dependent on the district for resources. The provision of resources and services to the councils should be a statutory duty of the district. The Community Council should be empowered to require any information other than bona fide confidential information, from district, region, and central government.

Community Councils might decide to encourage local organisations to report their activities, assist organisations in difficulties, help organisations to expand their activities, provide them with a base, storage and other office facilities, set up working parties, campaign committees, new organisations of various kinds. One organisation I very much hope many Community Councils will sponsor is a committee to organise non-sectarian working-class adult education in their area.

The reader will by now be pretty clear about the kind of role I envisage for Community Councils. Based on thriving independent organisations, and particularly TAs of which we need to see a whole new crop, it would be a voluntary democratic co-ordinating body, independent from the authorities and, in fact, a counter-power against their power, a means, in short, of breeding and feeding popular participative democracy.

Thanks to the following people who patiently answered all my questions: Isa McCulloch, Eileen and Hugh Thompson, Barbara Holmes, Molly Johnstone, Freddy Anderson (and other members of Garthamlock Tenants' Association), Bill Towill, Jimmy Forsyth, Roddy Kerr, Davy McCracken, John Mullen and Ian Towill.

17.   Whose Community Councils?

A Biased View of Developments in Glasgow

This traces the implementation of the community councils section of the local government reforms. It examines the initiatives taken, the forms of popular involvement and the tensions arising in one part of Glasgow. In retrospect, I am struck by the resemblance between the divisive effects of this development and that of community councils in the black townships of South Africa.

It was written in November 1975 and is previously unpublished

*

They say it was pressure from the border burghs that led to the inclusion of Community Councils in the Scottish Local Government Reform package. Appalled by the prospect of their local democracy getting swallowed up in monstrous districts and an elephantine region, they appealed for the creation of some means whereby smaller-scale communities could assert themselves.

That a rearguard action by the existing authorities in a privileged rural enclave should have triggered off our new 'councils of democracy'[1] is enough to make even the innocent suspicious. For those who already cynically questioned the nature of the democracy hitherto experienced at any rate by the vast majority of common or urban Scots, it becomes doubly important to look past the trigger and see who is holding the gun, and why.

Corporate Participation

Community Councils are being set up by the state. It is necessary to say that bluntly, early, and often. Like other forms of corporate participation, or incorporation (such as the elected representative component of local government itself, such as lay magistrates, school managers and governors in England, children's panels in Scotland, and now also health, schools, and college councils), they have multiple and contradictory roots. It will not be possible in this article to trace these roots at length, but merely to note them, in the context of describing and analysing concrete developments.

Motives
We therefore identify, briefly, some major motives for the establishment of Community Councils. (1) To provide an antidote, or compensation, for the massive increase in scale, and decrease in number, of the new authorities. (2) To give the new authorities local 'ears', making them more sensitive to the grass roots, better informed. (3) To reduce dependency on the state, and reduce government expenditure to the social services, by encouraging people to do it themselves. (4) To encourage participation in government by the governed, and move towards a participatory democracy. (5) To do something about the mounting tide of inarticulate consumer discontent, expressed in the growth of crimes of violence, vandalism, family troubles, excessive drinking, football hooliganism, etc. (6) To counter the trend towards the creation of autonomous local popular organisations.

Key Features
Let us continue our mental scene-setting by recalling the key features of the reorganisation. These are: massive increases in scale; the introduction of corporate planning, defined by the director of one of the new Glasgow District departments as 'people talking to each other rather than not', and resulting in the appearance of a new top management level of policy planning and resource allocation, above the service departments; the major services to the region, with decentralised divisional administration; local environmental services to the districts; a large drop in the number of councillors, and in practice a substantial diminution of the role of the rank and file elected representative — 'hardly any meetings' is a recurring complaint.

That part of the Act[2] which lays down the rules for the establishment of Community Councils has been elucidated with great skill in documents published by the Scottish Council of Social Service, the Scottish Development Department, and the Strathclyde Area Survey of the University of Strathclyde.[3] Its provisions are therefore likely to be familiar to most readers. We need to bear in mind the following points when considering how the cheque is cashing out: (1) the main specified job of a Community Council is to find out what people in its area, as consumers of various public services, feel about these services, and to pass their views to the appropriate public authority; (2) a Community Council can take action on behalf of its community, and do anything else it sees fit; (3) a procedure of consultation is spelled out, by means of which people can put forward ideas about how Community Councils should be organised in their area; (4) the District Council has to take note of what people say, but is not bound to reflect their views in its scheme; (5) the ultimate decision on each district's scheme lies with the Secretary of State, who also has default powers and power subsequently to change an already established scheme; (6) the new authorities may, if they wish, give or lend resources to Community Councils.

District Council

When the new authorities took over in May 1975, things were already happening on the Community Councils front in Glasgow. The District Council had set up a subcommittee to handle the matter, and this subcommittee had developed a liaison with the Strathclyde Area Survey, as a result of which a Community Councils Information Centre, staffed by five postgraduate research workers, was opened in the city centre. Bodies like the Planning Exchange and Glasgow Council for Voluntary Service had already been providing speakers and information for public meetings on Community Councils. They now intensified their activity. The city's Community Education Service, in collaboration with GCVS, made two video-tapes in which activists from tenants' and residents' associations, matched by an equal number of members of Community Centre Advisory Committees, formed a studio audience to listen and put pre-arranged questions to prominent experts. The experts were enthusiastic, authoritative, and vague (where they were not actually ill-informed). The studio audience, some of whom succeeded in making substantial critical points, nevertheless failed to dent the overall impression of enthusiasm, sweetness and light. Subsequent editing, and the addition of a monologue by an apparently somnolent councillor, did not improve matters.

Soft Sell

These tapes were shown at meetings in many localities, organised by the Community Education Service, or by local groups. In the opinion of the present writer, there was in all this a desire on the part of some of those in authority to stimulate a genuine debate about Community Councils among local people, but this was matched and distorted by a tendency to point up the positive features, to idealise Community Councils, and in effect to engage in a soft sell.

Meanwhile, contradictory noises were coming from the ruling Labour Party. Some leading figures saw the Community Councils component of the legislation as its moral core, its most desirable feature. Others made no bones, in private, about their hostility to

anything that might turn into a stick to beat the authorities with. At
local level, some party activists feared the take-over of Community
Councils by politically motivated troublemakers, while others saw in
the legislation their chance to smash and replace existing
communist-influenced tenants' associations.

In some parts of the city existing organisations (such as the
Springburn Association) had already started thinking about the kind
of Community Council they wanted to see — even to the extent of
drafting constitutions. Spurred on by the animateurs of the
Community Education Department, GCVS, and the Planning
Exchange, other local organisations began to organise public
meetings, motivated by fear for their own position vis-a-vis these
new state-favoured organisations, and a concomitant determination
not to be squeezed out.

Steering Committees

Quietly but effectively, the word was put about that *steering
committees* were the order of the day. Suddenly everyone knew you
had to set up a steering committee. It was disruptive to ask why. The
fact that there was nothing in the Act about steering committees that,
arguably, even, they conflicted with the spirit of the Act, was
irrelevant. The word had come down, and that was that.

Throughout the city meetings were held. Publicity was in general
of the bureaucratic centralist variety, though use of Radio Clyde
announcements was an imaginative touch. In general, the first public
meeting was followed up by a meeting of delegates from existing
organisations (sports groups, community centres, churches, tenants'
associations, etc.) which proceeded, more or less rapidly, to form
themselves into committees with elected officials and members. With
the hierarchical pattern of 'platform' and 'floor' thus early
embedded, these steering committees went on to discuss how a
Community Council or Councils should be organised in their area.
Invariably they became obsessed with purely technical matters like
area, to the exclusion of what the purpose of a Community Council
was, how it related to people's problems, etc. There was more than
a hint of urgency in the air. It was widely believed — wrongly — that
finalised proposals had to be in the hands of the District Council by
the end of September (in fact the first consultation period was fixed
to run from the 28th September till 22nd November), and this
became, in the hands of those key activists who had got spun into this
frenzy of activity, a decisive argument with which to rebut the
complaint that the mass of people had no chance to take part in the
discussion. Meanwhile, out in the houses and buses, the shipyards
and industrial estates, the betting shops and shopping centres, the

vast majority of the population knew little and cared less about this grand new dispensation of democracy.

Castlemilk

In Castlemilk, a giant post-war housing scheme on the southern edge of the city, about 30 people, mostly key activists in existing voluntary organisations, attended a meeting in the Community Centre at which the video-tapes were shown. A brief talk by a GCVS speaker was followed by a discussion in the round at which the beginnings of a process of vying for prominence among existing activists could be perceived, peppered with complaints about apathy, in the context of Community Councils being presented as the greatest thing since sliced bread. The present writer protested against what he saw as soft sell. Another member of the audience, Mary Miller, made the prophetic comment that there was a danger of Community Councils being just for the top people of Castlemilk.

Warnings like this went unheeded. The local tenants' association, an active body with a core of good devoted people, clearly feeling itself threatened and determined to meet the threat head on by getting right in there, called a series of meetings of delegates from existing vol orgs, in line with the citywide pattern. This built up to a crucial meeting at which the main item on the agenda was the election of office-bearers and members of the steering committee. It is now a matter of dispute whether or not this meeting was to be open to the public or for delegates only. The TA, at any rate, believed it was the latter. When they heard it had been given out in one of the local Catholic churches that as many people as possible from parochial organisations should attend the meeting, TA activists hurriedly consulted each other and decided to get as many of their own members there as they could.

As a result, the meeting was very much an affair of antagonistic camps, struggling for control. The TA ended up with three of their members either office-bearers or on the committee, although it had previously been decided that no group could have more than one. The Catholic church too got more than what might be considered a fair share. It was later pointed out that one of the effects of the power struggle had been that no one from the Protestant churches was on the committee at all.

Out of this atmosphere of threat and inter-group rivalry, a fundamentally hierarchical structure had emerged, wholly divorced from the knowledge or involvement of the mass of residents.

A Fresh Start

At this stage, Eddie Graham, a delegate from the Mitchellhill High

Five Association, having made ineffective protests against the direction things were taking, began to propose to fellow-members of his own organisation and other friends, that a fresh start should be made, in a smaller area, on a completely different basis.

This proposal met, initially, with a cool response. However, Eddie persisted and succeeded in convincing several people of the worth-whileness of another go. The character of this second approach was determined at the outset by the experience Eddie and others had had of the central steering committee, and by the view, most forcefully argued by Andrew Parker, that it had to be on a participative, non-manipulative basis, and that participation was fundamentally at war with hierarchy. (There has been a history in Castlemilk in the last couple of years of people trying to organise on a participative basis — to some extent in the TA itself, more clearly in the community newspaper *Castlemilk Today*, and in a most thoroughgoing fashion in the Jeely Piece Clubs, two groups of mothers running summer playschemes.)

The Horseshoe
A rapidly growing core of activists threw themselves into the task of creating what later called itself the Horseshoe steering committee.[4] They leafletted and postered the whole area themselves, knocking on doors explaining what a Community Council could be like, and asking people for their views. Meetings were held with seating in the round. A different chairperson and minute secretary were chosen at the start of each meeting by those who came. There was a commitment not to become a small group or clique acting on behalf of the rest, not to do things for people, but to go out to those not yet involved and encourage them to do things for themselves. Authority lay with all those at the meeting, not with anyone delegated to a specific function.

They soon realised that discussing Community Councils in the abstract was a task most people would be unlikely to interest themselves in. The meeting therefore decided to choose a problem experienced by a large number of people and tackle it with them, to see if in that process a lot of people might think about whether or not they wanted a Community Council, and if so, what kind. Two problems in fact were chosen.

The first was presented by two teenagers who wanted to start a rock group. They were looking for somewhere to practice, had approached the Community Centre, and been knocked back. The meeting decided to send a number of delegates with the lads to speak to the warden. This time they were given the use of a suitable room for practice on a Sunday afternoon.

The Lifts

The main problem chosen was the malfunctioning of the lifts in the Mitchellhill flats, five blocks each nineteen storeys high. Those already involved knocked all the doors in each block, explaining that an open-air meeting was being held about the lifts. A delegation went to learn to use a video camera at the Third Eye Centre[5] (a skill which they decided not to use on this occasion). Another delegation went to consult a lawyer and interview the head of the section of the Housing Management Department responsible for lifts. Two local photographers agreed to record the open-air meeting.

About 200 people gathered on the grass behind the flats on a bright Sunday afternoon. A speaker from the steering committee explained why they had called the meeting, and what the steering committee was. The Housing Management Department's view of the problem was reported. Then anyone who wished was invited to speak through the microphone about their experience and views on the lifts problems.

Exhibition

The meeting then broke up into informal groups discussing the problem at length. These discussions were tape-recorded. It was decided to hold a press conference and exhibition about the lifts. The exhibition[6] consisted of photos of people at the open-air meeting, cartoons, drawings and writings by children, and a large number of wall-posters containing excerpts from the tape recordings written in big letters with magic markers. Collections of items were grouped under various themes: 'The Debate about Vandalism', 'The District Council and Us', 'The Causes of the Problem', 'The Sick', etc.

At this stage, divisions of opinion developed among those active in the steering committee about how to tackle the problem, how things had been decided so far, and where to go from there. There were also divisions of opinion amongst those living in the flats. Some who had been active in the apparently moribund Mitchellhill High Five Association resented the intrusion of the steering committee. Many of the same people also argued that you could not have an effective organisation without a committee and office-bearers. Others expected the steering committee to do it for them. Most people blamed the rest for their apathy. There was a 'communist' scare. It was widely felt that the steering committee was just a talking shop.

In the midst of this welter of criticism and self-criticism, the steering committee encouraged the blocks to organise themselves, with steering committee support, to take up the campaign to get the lift service improved. Only one block, the worst affected, did so, and many people living in that block have also become active in the steering committee. Although the lifts problem is not yet solved, maintenance work has increased, and the maintenance contract has been taken away from one firm and given to another.

Drafting Proposals
The steering committee turned again to the task of discussing and drafting proposals for setting up a Community Council in the Horeshoe area. Again, they tried to tackle it participatively. An outline was prepared as a basis for discussion, (a) stating the task, (b) spelling out how a Community Council might be organised if based on participative principles, and (c) how others had proposed it should be organised.

A public meeting then went through this outline, amending, deleting, and adding bits on. The meeting was tape-recorded and a team delegated to write up the amended draft, adding a potted history of the steering committee's work. Another meeting made final amendments and shared out the work of typing, duplicating, stapling and distributing 2,500 copies of the six-page leaflet to every house in the area. This leaflet invited everyone to a meeting to decide final proposals, and the final meeting — less well attended than most of the others — thrashed out principles and practical details and sent them off to the District Council.

Official Circles
The activity of the Horseshoe steering committee has been greeted with less than wholehearted enthusiasm in official and would-be official circles.

The central steering committee have argued that HSC was not official, that an organisation with neither secretary nor chairman could not be contacted, that steering committees were not allowed to take up issues, that this person was an anarchist, that one a nutcase, and so on. At city level, in a radio discussion, reference was made to political activists penetrating community councils which were said to be non-political. When the HSC's application to the district for a standard — very modest — grant of cash to cover the expenses incurred in its work came up for consideration, the two local councillors professed to know nothing about it, and the matter was deferred. It turned out that the subcommittee had earlier decided that a steering committee is bona fide only if recognised by the local councillors.

Whose Community Councils?
It seems appropriate to close this biased[7] view on the note on which it opened, which many of those in authority might describe as

cynical. The reader is left to decide who is cynical and who is not. Whose Community Councils are they? Does the state *really* want people to stand up and say what they feel, do things for themselves and organise participatively? Or does it want to create a new hierarchical layer between the local authorities and the people, a sponge into which key activists will be sucked, seduced by the chance of becoming top people, to justify the ways of God to men?

1 The title given to a series of discussions on Community, Schools, and Health Councils, organised by the University of Glasgow Extra-Mural Department, autumn 1975.
2 Part 4, Sections 51-55, pp. 27-30, of the Local Government (Scotland) Act 1973.
3 Topic 2 (Scottish Council of Social Service), Community Councils (Scottish Development Department), Planning for Community Councils (Strathclyde Area Survey).
4 The Horseshoe is the name given locally to the area of housing within the scheme, bounded by Castlemilk Drive and part of Ardencraig Road.
5 An Arts Centre in Sauchiehall Street, Glasgow.
6 The exhibition went on show at St Martin's Church Hall, Grange Secondary School, and Castlemilk Community Centre.
7 The use of the word 'biased' here and in the subtitle of this article is suggested by HSC member John Cooper, who argues that we should not be ashamed of our bias.

Extracts from

18.   What is Community Development really about?

From October 1975 till September 1976 I studied for a master degree in adult education and community development at the Department of Educational Studies at Edinburgh University. This gave me opportunities to step back and reflect on the fieldwork and voluntary action I had been involved in, and do some reading. During the year I wrote a series of papers on aspects of education and community of which the first was *Whose Community Councils?* It was followed by *What is Community Development really about?* which was subtitled: an enquiry into Community Development as a policy of Governments in British colonial and ex-colonial Africa, focusing on Botswana. Two excerpts from this paper are reproduced here. The scope of the enquiry was subsequently widened, resulting in a later booklet called *Community Development and Popular Participation*, which is reproduced on page 167.

*

> I sit on a man's back, choking him, and making him carry me, and yet assure myself and others that I am very sorry for him and wish to ease his lot by any means possible, except getting off his back.
>
> Leo Tolstoy

Personal Experience of Community Development in Britain as a point of departure for this paper
I first met up with Community Development late in 1969 in the person of David Johnston. David had been in India doing VSO. On his return he joined the Young Volunteer Force Foundation (YVFF), set up just a few months previously by the Prime Minister, Harold Wilson, with all-party backing, to encourage Community Service by young people. It is worth slipping in for the fun of it that the first Director of YVFF was Anthony Steen, an entrepreneurial young man

with what he called an outsize conscience. Steen had developed a
Community Service organisation (Task Force) as a school student —
papering old ladies' walls, tidying up gardens, visiting hospitals, and
so on, in between bouts of fast driving. He was — and presumably
still is — charming, voluble, charismatic, a self-publicist with a flair
for fund-raising. His relationships with fieldwork, and his responses
to the trend away from Community Service towards Community
Development and later Community Action on the part of YVFF field
staff, were less surefooted. It was said (probably by himself) that he
was simultaneously a member of Battersea Labour Party and
Chelsea Tory Party, and whatever the truth of that, it is certain that
in 1974 he resigned as Director of YVFF to enter the House of
Commons in a safe Tory seat.

Back to David Johnston. What fascinated me about David (and
about Community Development, for he seemed to epitomise it) was
his upper middle-class background — his parents owned and ran a
private school — his enthusiasm, energy, warmth, informality and,
above all, his concern. That recurs in everything I remember about
him — the things he said or wrote, how he was with people. 'To share
concerns and stimulate action.' 'One is terribly concerned.' He
exuded concern. And it was genuine concern. It is not too difficult to
place David in the political spectrum as it was in Britain then. He was
a liberal, left-wing Tory of the Edward Boyle type. He regarded
many socialists as hypocrites because their lifestyle or means clashed
with their views or ends.

This is not the place to examine my own political position then,
nor to go into details of our Derbyshire experiences. It is enough to
say that I was employed as an Area Principal for Adult Education in
north-east Derbyshire. Circumstances brought David and myself
together, and we co-operated on a number of projects. One contrast
between us is relevant here so I will describe it briefly. This is the
contrast in our political attitude to work in the area. I was
fundamentally aiming to get people to say what their experience was
really like and organise themselves to take control of their lives. This
meant, potentially, an antagonistic relationship with 'authority' if it
stood in their way — headmasters, housing managers, bus
companies, education committees, and so on. David was out of
sympathy with this position, though he shared the wish to see people
come alive and do things for themselves. At a very early stage, he had
been making contacts in a council housing scheme called Inkersall.
Nothing was happening, he told me, but there were some
tremendous people up there, and 'it *could* hum'. The humming of
council housing schemes, however, I quickly realised, would ideally
for David harmonise with the humming of local authority depart-

ments. David and other YVFF workers based in Chesterfield mostly sought to inform councillors, senior officials, and field workers, whether at urban district or county council level, of the kind of projects they were involved in at grass-roots level. Indeed often these projects were chosen and developed very much on the basis of such liaison. Co-operative activity by ordinary people, that is to say, was seen as consonant with the activity by local government, and receiving the support of local government either in the form of simple approval, cash grants, direct field worker involvement, or response on the part of a local authority department to a need revealed by a specific project.

In fact — and this is important when we come to consider the real nature of Community Development — it could not have been otherwise. YVFF was funded by central government, plus whatever cash Antony Steen could drum up from businessmen or independent trusts, and — crucially — by the local authority. If a local authority invited YVFF to set up a project in their area, the financial arrangement was based on contributions by both YVFF and the authority — the latter's contribution being increased (and YVFF's decreased) with the passage of years as the project was localised. If an authority was unhappy about what YVFF was doing, they could decide to withdraw financial backing, thus whipping the stool from under YVFF's bottom. Something very like this nearly happened in Derbyshire just before David and I arrived. A YVFF worker sent to Staveley to case the joint and indicate areas of possible activity, produced a radical report quoting from various local people. In particular she accused one of the local secondary schools of a lack of concern (that word again!) for their early leavers. YVFF HQ, ever conscious of the need for publicity, published the report nationally. The headmaster of the school chanced to pick up a copy in the local library, and went noisily through the roof. Concern all round. YVFF was told to behave or get out. The hapless girl who wrote the offending report was withdrawn. And it was David who came to take her place. Clearly, therefore, his role as defined by the employing agency and its funders, and as internalised (willingly or not) by himself, was certainly not to encourage the local population to storm heaven.

Community Development of the YVFF variety seems designed, in theory at any rate, to secure some of the benefits of revolution without struggle or antagonism — that is, without revolution. These benefits are: mass enthusiasm, mass participation, mass organisation, free labour, popularly subscribed funds. It is impossible not to conclude that the creators of these policies had one eye at least on Soviet and Chinese experience — the mass movement for literacy in the Soviet Union in the twenties: the incredible communal efforts of peasants and soldiers in Chinese rural development.

But of course CD is NOT revolution. It is a policy of rulers, whether colonial or post-colonial. For all its concern with economic growth, it generally presents no challenge to the pattern of economic power, the base. Its breadth, however, its ambiguity, enables it to incorporate in its service, often at field-worker level, a liberal radical, idealist, anti-capitalist tendency which is invaluable to CD for the enthusiasm its transmits, the popular involvement it breeds, but which is powerless to implement its radicalism effectively because of its marginality, its isolation, its lack of control of the citadels of power. Sometimes the official literature itself reflects this radicalism, as in the UN expert's statement on agrarian reform: 'Where land tenure is so inequitable as to destroy hope and incentive for the masses . . . CD may make a start in educating and organising the tenants and landless workers, but can do little to bring economic improvement until the economic base is changed.'

CD that is to say works on the existing base. It does not challenge it. It merely holds out to the masses the opportunity of participating in development on that basis.

This point is taken further by Peter Kuenstler in a letter to Peter Wass: 'CD, like all social programmes, takes its whole flavour and direction from the general ideology and socio-political philosophy of the country . . . (CD) was originally sponsored by administrators who wanted basically to conserve a stable situation.'

Community Development in Botswana
In Botswana, in the 1930s and early '40s, there was an exceptionally committed Director of Education, H. J. E. Dumbrell, who really believed in the development of Africans and made energetic efforts to encourage it. He set up schools for adults where they 'will be taught things they think will be of real value to them.'[1] He sought the assistance of the Departments of Agriculture, Medical Services, and Veterinary Services. These schools rapidly became very popular. Dumbrell also initiated or supported educational use of radio, library facilities, a newspaper project, and a mass adult literacy scheme. However imaginative and committed, Dumbrell was on his own, and on his retirement most of his projects were discontinued.

The extent to which departmental policy in the colonial era was very much a matter of either tradition or the predilection of the departmental official concerned is demonstrated by the way in which Mass Education and Social Welfare developed in Bechuanaland from 1947-61. The officer appointed was called Leech, and he was a keen scout. As a result, the entire work of the department over this period (except when Leech was directed to undertake additional tasks) had to do with building and supporting the scout and guide movements in Bechuanaland.

On Leech's retirement, the post of Social Welfare Officer was taken temporarily in 1960-61 by Mrs B. E. Coppens whose predilection was for urban social work. The whole focus swung from scouting to welfare. Peter Wass describes the nature and underlying assumptions of the social work undertaken: '. . . at the workers' compound at the Colonial Development Corporation abattoir at Lobatse . . . the appalling conditions . . . had been allowed to develop and worsen. The basic design was unsuited for satisfactory family life; the living blocks, which each contained four crowded household units, were in tight closely packed lines. There was no fencing to indicate the extent of individual family plots: and the space immediately surrounding the blocks was supposed to be communal responsibility. But since there was no sense of such responsibility, the area abounded in rubbish of all kinds, presenting both an eyesore and a threat to health. Toilet and ablution blocks were scattered throughout the compound and these likewise suffered from misuse and lack of proper maintenance. As if such conditions were not bad enough, there was in addition an open drain running through the middle of the compound carrying the effluent from the abattoir, which finally debauched into Loch MacGregor just below the compound fence. It was not unknown for toddlers to fall into this drain.'

Wass goes on: 'Despite the effrontery of such living conditions, the officials sought to find improvements through *welfare* . . . the construction of a hall which was used as a church and for recreation.'

Mrs Coppens then applied her energies to investigating the condition of native Africans in the Tatitown area of Francistown. She noted the lack of water points, latrines and health facilities. There were open effluent drains causing stagnant troughs in which mosquitos bred. There were no market facilities for those selling fresh produce, and no arrangements for refuse disposal. Having noted all this, she decided that 'the primary and most urgent need is the provision of leisure-time activities . . . a sports field, a canteen, an open-air cinema, a tea garden'. Specifically to keep the youth from 'lounging on pavements in the European shopping centre' and to prevent them from becoming juvenile delinquents, she recommended dramatic societies and kite-flying clubs! Comment is surely superfluous.

Mrs Coppens was followed as Social Welfare Officer by Peter Wass, who rapidly became uneasy with his inheritance. It is important to remember here that it was only one year previously, in 1960, that the Bechuanaland authorities had gone over from administrating the status quo to a 'development' orientation.

Under Wass, the department began to branch out from the social work of Mrs Coppens and the scouting of Mr Leech, though neither of these aspects were scrapped, experimenting first with providing community centres in 'deprived' African urban areas, after consultation with locals. Some of them became popular and well used, others stayed half-empty. One social welfare worker started discussion groups on social and economic issues, and did some work with 'unattached' young people. Casework continued as part of the work load. Wass, meanwhile, was sent on a one-year CD course at Swansea, and on his return drew up a plan for the future development of the department, with four aspects: mobile cinema work; social welfare; youth work (i.e. scouts and guides); and CD in rural areas 'to foster community understanding of local problems, leading to community projects in the field of agriculture, health, education, and other self-help activities such as dam-building, road-making and improved housing'.

In parallel with this an initiative was taken outside the Social Welfare Department by Guy Clutton Brock who through direct contact with the Resident Commissioner (head of the colonial administration) sought to effect changes in the administration's policy on rural development, to swing it away from help to individual farmers, towards a co-operative approach to improving the village economy by creating producers' co-operatives, co-operative stores, and providing finance for buying villagers' cattle in time of difficulty. This was to be backed up by establishing village clinics and community centres. This clearly is an example of the kind of radical, idealist, enthusiastic proposal with which CD records are studded. That the scheme failed in practice was due, according to Peter Wass, to a 'certain naivety with regard to existing social, economic and political pressures'. It would, I believe, be more accurate to say that such schemes are mostly doomed to fail (if they ever get off the drawing board) because they are always promoted as tiny islands of co-operative light in seas of free-market darkness.

Approval was finally granted for the establishment by the Social Welfare Department of a pilot CD project, and the provision of CD training facilities in Bechuanaland. In 1964 six CD assistants were appointed and sent off to Tanganyika for training. In their absence, plans were developed for the pilot projects. Four of these assistants shortly found themselves despatched to various villages, there to commence CD.

One such CDA, Alfoncina Nyatshano, was sent to the village of Bokaa (in Kgateleng District) with a population of 1,838. Bokaa was chosen because the people of the district were seen as receptive to change, the chief was well educated, young and progressive, and he and his councillors, the District Commissioner, and the headman of the village itself, favoured the experiment. CD was therefore undertaken as a policy of the colonial administration with the approval of the tribal and district authorities.

Alfoncina first of all got to know the local situation and language, and simultaneously explained what CD was about, emphasising the co-ordination and co-operation of people, their organisations, tribal authorities and government. The first activity she got involved in was adult literacy work, for which there was a lot of enthusiasm. Her hard work in this field earned her the respect of the people of the area. The next thing to form was a women's group, which immediately began to flourish — producing household goods like table mats and baskets. Wass describes Alfoncina's role as 'drawing out the latent ability and creativity of individual women and using them for the benefit of the group as a whole'. All products belonged to the club, and the money it made from its activities in the first year — R100 — was a very substantial capital sum by local standards. The next development was a youth club, then a Red Cross group, which started a welfare clinic. The next and climactic stage was the development of the Bokaa Village Development Committee (though who initiated it and how it was created and grew is not described by Wass) which seems to have been seen as a comprehensive local development agency if we examine its own list of aims:

1. Seeing to the development of the village.
2. Discussing its problems.
3. Making development plans and seeing them fulfilled.
4. Creating co-ordination between the activities of various departments.
5. Asking for assistance from district specialists.
6. Applying for help and advice from the CD Department if necessary.
7. Organising local training for VDC members and office-bearers.
8. Arranging a programme of local projects according to their importance.
9. Explaining education for adults and children.
10. Developing the economy of the village — handicrafts, co-operative societies, etc.
11. Encouraging better housing in the village; and
12. Encouraging better methods of farming using scientific methods.

A pause for consideration seems appropriate here. The evidence to hand does not make it clear whether or not — or to what extent — the mass of people participated willingly and with understanding in these developments, whether for example they saw the Bokaa VDC as theirs, something they could take part in, influence, control, or as set in power over them. But let us assume for the moment the best interpretation — that this was a real popular movement, liberating and mobilising many people — how then are we to interpret it? I would argue that *in itself* we can see it as nothing but good. It has some of the characteristics of a popular mobilisation, but not the dimension of struggle, nor equal or common or co-operative ownership and use of resources. Whatever enthusiastic co-operative features are *added*, the local economic base is left unchanged and unchallenged (and we know from other evidence that rural resources in Botswana are very unequally distributed) and the national and international economic system is also the same (and we know its effect on rural areas from other evidence). Further, it is the political arm of this very economic system, in the form of the colonial administration, which is stimulating and creating this co-operative enthusiastic local movement. It is for this reason that I advance the view that CD is to be seen as attempting to secure the benefits of a revolution without actually having one. Some of the less attractive features of CD itself will come into clearer focus in recounting the next phase of its development in Bechuanaland.

The next major phase of CD in Bechuanaland developed in response to a crisis. 1965 was the country's fourth successive year of drought. Crops failed entirely. One sixth of the national cattle herd died of starvation. Only massive famine relief by the World Food Programme and the UK government averted large-scale loss of life. By November 1965 it had become clear that crops would fail again the following year. The WFP expects countries receiving emergency feeding to prepare schemes of social and economic benefit as a quid pro quo. The Bechuanaland administration was concerned at the demoralising effect of dependency on the people — and at the same time conscious of the encouraging effects of the CD pilot projects the previous year (e.g. Bokaa). A decision was therefore taken to link emergency feeding with a nationwide CD scheme, based on compulsion if necessary. The plan was for lists of local development projects in all drought-affected areas to be drawn up and implemented by local labour. The workers would receive WFP rations. The scheme was named Ipelegeng — carry yourself. It was also known as Food for Work.

It is easy to be critical of the Ipelegeng project from a western vantage point. The situation was a crisis, and had to be met with rapid effective organisation. The scheme was drafted, approved and disseminated by the centre, imposed from the top down. Native leadership — at national, regional, district and local levels — was incorporated by the government into the task of explaining the scheme to the masses and procuring their participation. There was some grumbling, but the people really had no choice — to work, or to starve — and Peter Wass states that 'in the event there was remarkably little opposition locally to the new scheme, and considerable energy was displayed in working out viable projects'. A criticism that could be levelled at the planning of the scheme was that the task of organising implementation was given to district famine relief committees. What this meant in effect was that the mass of people were not only giving their labour compulsorily, but were not involved in the choosing of projects and priorities or organising the task. For this reason it could be argued that Ipelegeng should not be seen as CD at all, unless you regard CD as free forced labour, full stop. The fact is, however, that from then on in Botswana, Ipelegeng — carry yourself — was the name used for CD.

However we interpret it, Ipelegeng resulted in an impressive number of finished projects: 163 classrooms; 195 teachers' quarters; 88 dams or weirs; 324 acres of land destumped; 19 medical clinics; 24 acres afforested; 147 other buildings; and 662 miles of new or repaired roads. It was, Wass observes proudly, 'no mean contribution to Botswana's development effort . . . a major contribution to the rural infrastructure'. He notes the 'tremendous public enthusiasm for more school buildings' and that '25 per cent of all material used in fifteen months of the Ipelegeng programme was contributed by communities themselves'. Finally, he sees the effect of the scheme on MPs, ministers, senior departmental officials, and community leaders — Ipelegeng had 'given an effective demonstration of the potential for local development based on village participation'. To put it more crudely, it showed them the advantages accruing to the national thrust towards economic development from large amounts of free forced labour.

Naomi Mitchison, in an article in the CD Journal of January 1967,[2] attacks the Ipelegeng programme as one element in the colonialist orientation: 'The forces of law and order used the existing African institutions for their own ends, often twisting them, as in the policy of indirect rule when the powers of Emirs, chiefs, or whatever the traditional rulers might be called, were increased as against the people and counsellors by whom they were originally held in check. This was done for the greater convenience of white rule. Then taxation forced the people into the money economy, near the bottom of which most of them now live. . .'

She talks of the 'mess' made by the white man: 'Even without the extra complication of colonists taking the land, white law and order, trade, and religion disrupted the old patterns and customs which were designed to keep the group together.' 'How,' she asks 'is the mess to be cleared up? By CD? Not on your life.'

Then she swings round to the food-for-work scheme: 'There is a famine relief scheme — Ipelegeng — in Botswana. This is "considered extremely valuable . . . as it is transforming the attitudes of tens of thousands of people from one of wanting to get things from the government, to one of doing things on a self-help basis". . . How nice. . . Ipelegeng is run almost entirely by white administrators, some in the civil service, some VSO etc. Africans will gradually be brought in, once they are indoctrinated in white ways of community thinking. . . But are people's attitudes transformed? . . I don't think so. They realise they have got to work or they won't get food.'

And a final shaft: 'I would say to CD-ers, watch what you are being used for, and if you are being used for breaking other people's patterns and institutions of order and work and communications, don't do it.'

References
1 Community Development in Botswana, with special reference to the evolution of policy and organisation, 1947-70, Peter Wass, unpublished PhD thesis, Edinburgh University, 1972.
2 Community Development Journal, January 1967.

19. Some Problems of Marxism

Explored in relation to the theory and practice of education

I joined the Communist Party in 1972 and resigned four years later. Leaving was a painful decision which made me feel politically homeless. Not only did I like the communists for their warmth, steadfastness, responsibility, practical caring and clarity of analysis: they were the *only* politicians for whom I felt any respect at all! But I realised, shortly after joining, that the gulf between the dominant ideological position within the party and my own was enormous. The party was centralist, statist, and economic-determinist, with a strong authoritarian streak. The Soviet Union was admired and defended, whatever public gestures might periodically have to be made about 'mistakes'. In the end, there seemed to be no alternative but to struggle inadequately to define one's own stance. *Some Problems of Marxism* was one of the series of such attempts made during 1975-76. It was also my first encounter with the work of Paulo Freire, which was a source of relief, because he seemed to have wrestled with the same dilemmas and found a way through them.

While discovering Freire mitigated the sense of loss I experienced on leaving the party, it did not dissolve it altogether. The loss was reinforced by our decision to leave Castlemilk in 1976 after nearly four years, which felt like an admission of failure and at a deeper level an act of betrayal of those we left behind. Although I was determined to fight for my ideas about adult education, creativity and popular self-organisation, and found some good friends in Edinburgh who shared my views, I was dismayed by the trendy left-wing scene in the capital, both in its revolutionary and its reformist manifestations. The last three years of the decade were, for me, years of personal unhappiness and alienation which I was unable to resolve. The turning point came in the autumn of 1979, after the referendum, and after completing *Community Development and Popular Participation*. Realising I had struggled as far as I could on my own, I followed some good advice from Janet Hassan and began a personal analysis with Alan Harrow at the Scottish Institute of Human Relations. Gradually the exploration which Alan's help made possible revealed to me the interplay of inner and outer reality, in myself and my personal relationships, in others, and in the wider society. The missing pieces of the jigsaw had been there all along, but I needed help to find them. The sense of alienation diminished, and a new period of collaboration began.

But all this is jumping ahead. The original version of *Some Problems of Marxism* was a 20,000-word exposition and critique of the main concepts of Marxism, Soviet and Maoist views on education, and the ideas of Freire. For reasons of space, the expository pasages have been removed, leaving the analysis. The references in the original version are included in the bibliography at the back of the book.

MANSIE CONSIDERS THE SEA IN THE MANNER OF
HUGH MACDIARMID

The sea, I think, is lazy,
It just obeys the moon
—All the same I remember what Engels said:
'Freedom is the consciousness of necessity'.

Ian Hamilton Finlay

from *The Dancers Inherit the Party*,
Migrant Press, 1962

... the characteristic of the human species is its repeatedly
demonstrated capacity for transcending what is merely
given, what is purely determined.

Joao da Veiga Coutinho

(from his preface to Paulo Freire's
Cultural Action for Freedom, 1972)

Thus we profess the doctrine of the total responsibility of
the individual for his deeds and the amorality of the
historical process ... it is not true that our philosophy of
history decides our main choices in life. They are
determined by our moral sense. We are not communists
because we recognise communism to be a historical
necessity. We are communists because we stand on the
side of the oppressed against the oppressors ... when we
have to accompany our theories with an act of *practical*
choice, then we act out of moral motives, not theoretical
concerns ... the most convincing theory is unable to
make us lift our little finger.

Leszek Kolakowski

Marxism and Beyond, 1971

The process of men's orientation in the world involves
not just the association of sense images. It involves,
above all, thought-language; that is, the possibility of the
act of knowing through his praxis, by which man
transforms reality . . . this process of orientation in the
world can be understood neither as a purely subjective
event, nor as an objective or mechanistic one, but only as
an event in which subjectivity and objectivity are united.
Orientation in the world . . . places the question of the
purposes of action at the level of critical perception of
reality . . . there is both a historical and a value dimension.

Paulo Freire

Cultural Action for Freedom, 1972

*

Introductory

I had planned to investigate a number of themes which might
develop an interconnectedness that could be expressed as a general
thesis. I gradually formed the view that there is in Marxism an underdevelopment and a distortion of the ethical dimension, resulting
from unresolved ambiguities in dialectical materialism, and that
Freire's work can be seen as an attempt to enter into a radical
dialogue with Marxism, and restore to it, or create for it, the
humanist ethical dimension it lacks.

On the rules for pupils in Soviet schools

Whatever we may think of these as moral values, three points are
worth noting. First, the futuristic orientation: the goal, the purpose,
the end, is seen as in the future, not in the present. The present is a
means to the end of the future. Second, the authoritarianism: these
virtues are to be inculcated. Third, the determinism: people come to
have certain behavioural features and virtues by moulding.

On Soviet educational psychology

We note at the outset that human nature, the given, is seen as a foundation on which to build, and that mental processes 'depend on what is done, the purpose, the character, and the structure of the activity'. Who decides the purpose, character, and structure of the activity? Clearly not the human being in question. Already the door is opened to authoritarianism. The human being is seen as a given with a variety of potentials, which can be formed by those in authority for whatever ideological and practical purposes they have in mind.

On the formation of ideas in the mind by association

Two points are worth making straight away. One is that this view leads to a conception of human beings as passive and moulded; not as creative, investigative, choice-making subjects. Second, it opens the door to authoritarian forming of people by someone or some group who regard themselves as superior. Embedded here, therefore, is another theme we shall develop: the dichotomy between shaper and shaped.

On dialectical materialism in education

Authoritarianism and determinism, therefore, seem to characterise both Pavlov's and Simon's views of education, based on a physiology and psychology supposedly dialectical materialist, but when we begin to consider the obsession with conditioned reflexes and their practical application, not really so very different from the mechanical materialism they both reject.

On the process of skill and concept formation in Soviet education

Now it would be silly to deny the importance to education of this step-by-step breakdown of basic concept and skill formation. What is to be challenged, though, is generalising it throughout education, the implication that this is all education is about. To generalise these useful insights as a method and point of departure for all education is to institutionalise a concept of human beings as moulded into all skills, concepts, values, attitudes and behaviour by someone or some group who are above the rest — who find out what methods work, what the values are, and what skills and information are needed.

On lesson-planning in Soviet schools

From the implications of a key fact about how human consciousness relates to its environment, Soviet educational psychology shades off into what can be done with this fact by benevolent despots. This is the point to be hammered home, not to let go of. If human mental processes are formed in activity, by active interpenetration with the environment, then a crucial issue becomes: who shapes the activity, who decides the information, attitudes, values and skills to be learned? If some people do this — the psychologists, the educators, the party, the leaders — then of course *their* creativity, *their* moral responsibility, is being exercised, but on the basis of suppressing and stunting the creativity and responsibility of those being done unto. This conception of education will stunt and distort people's creativity, their critical questioning, their ability to compare, analyse, make new links and make their own judgements.

On Makarenko's concept of collectives

This is imposed co-operation. It is group think. The solidarity and communality of these groups is (a) created by those in authority and (b) used by those in authority. It is therefore a distorted communality whose purpose is social control. But it bears a resemblance to an authentic communality based on the human need for groups, and on the recognition on the part of each participant of the autonomy and interdependence of each member. The fundamental question posed by the Soviet method of imposing and using collectivity is: does it produce genuine co-operation, trust, openness, sharing, mutual aid and support — or does it produce overt playing along, fear, orthodoxy, suppression of originality and initiative? The theme that begins to come into focus here is that the individualism-versus-collectivism polarity promoted in the West for anti-communist purposes is a false dichotomy. The real antagonism is between, on the one hand, the co-operative inter-dependence of subjects which does not suppress individual creativity and moral responsibility, but supports it, and on the other hand, coercion either by the predatory individual or group (capitalist individualism) or by the elite controlling and subordinating individuals and collectives (Marxist-Leninist collectivism).

On Robert Owen and New Lanark

The Robert Owen position leads to the dividing of society into two parts, one of which is superior to the rest. It implies that certain men, such as David Dale and Robert Owen, can rise above circumstances in god-like fashion, and form the circumstances of others for their own good. This is benevolent despotism, the theft of the creative, critical, choosing roles from the mass of people, and the concentration of them in the hands of a few. This is what pervades Soviet and Marxist education in general: the party and the educators place themselves in the Robert Owen position vis-a-vis the mass of people whom they intend to benefit by improving their circumstances and upbringing.

On Marx and Engels

Marx and Engels themselves are ambiguous as between authoritarianism and libertarianism, determinism and freedom.

On the relationship of means and ends

Marxists frequently fail to distinguish between means-to-ends and ends-in-themselves. The motive for failing to make the distinction is that, in the last analysis, they tend to see everything as means-to-ends, and therefore have a vested interest in not perceiving the distinction.

On Markusevich's account of polytechnical education

It is laden with authority. It is thoroughly generalised: there are no loopholes. Each proposition is determinist. The model is: X is a necessary condition of Y. To get to Y, you must go through X. X produces Y. We could call it production-line determinism. Since such-and-such a process is asserted to be the only way to produce such-and-such a product, choice is pre-empted. Each proposition also dichotomises means and ends. What is being done now is being done to produce something else later, and the value lies in the later, in the product. But we can ask: does the later, the end, ever come, or are we, trapped in the now, doomed forever to labour towards a later end? The present will always be only the means. Here is another let-in for authoritarianism. Over what human beings do now there looms the god, the professor, the party, the state, which, having arrived at an overview, having worked out what needs to be done to achieve progress for all, imposes its prescriptions firmly. Thus the overview, the ability to generalise, to project, to have intentions, has been expropriated from the people by the authorities. This, regrettably, is what Marxism seems to mean in practice in the Soviet Union. It is difficult to believe that Marx would have endorsed it.

On Maurice Levitas's account of knowledge and freedom

Our knowledge can only amount, then, to an awareness of the shape of general trends, and our freedom to collective action which is in tune with them. This is a pitifully locked, determinist position, which denies or tends towards denying the historical action of human beings. We can entirely agree that in our analysis of any culture we must try to see what is dying and what is emergent, but that does not tie our hands or anaesthetise our moral faculty. It is people who make trends wither and flourish, and if they do not will a certain trend, they can struggle to change it.

On generalising

What Marx and Engels were doing was studying the evolution and internal dynamics of human society, much as Darwin studied the evolution of species. Now this is an essentially generalising activity — not, of course, that Darwin and Marx were uninterested in individual flowers or individual human beings. But the tendency is to see individual plants or human beings as mere members of the species. One is interested in general trends, in shared features, and one does not focus, generally speaking, on the particular, individual, experiencing, living and working human being, but rather on the major typical collectivities of them.

On the subordination of experience

To recap, the search for an overview leads to an overemphasis on behaviour and an underemphasis on experience; thence to the subordination of experience to behaviour; and finally to a point where, though consciousness is not denied, it is seen as a medium through which the correct typical behaviour is learned. If this hypothesis is accepted, it gives us part of an explanation of the inbuilt drift in all mainstream Marxist analysis towards determinism and authoritarianism.

On progress

The concept of progress also contains an inbuilt bias towards determinism. Marx and Engels' concept of history is progressive: 'in spite of all seeming accidentality, of all temporary retrogression'. The development from tribal society to feudal, from feudal to capitalist, from capitalist to socialist, and from socialist to communist, is progressive. This is a grand-scale, highly generalised conception of stage-by-stage development in time, from lower to higher. It led Marx and Engels to make some curious moral-historical judgements. If a state, for example, fell into the hands of an iron despotism with a ruthlessly centralising tendency, Marx and Engels might well pronounce it to be progressive if it led to development of the forces of production, achieving, let us say, higher technology, or greater mobility and concentration of labour or capital. What Marx and Engels demonstrate in this kind of sport is a blunting of the moral sense in the here-and-now, a tendency to hitch their morality to their long-term-progressive view of history. By a similar ideological process it was possible for some communists to see the rise of the Nazis in Germany as not so very dreadful because it was 'our turn next'.

There are several distinct points to be made about the idea of progress:

(1) It can lead to regarding certain developments as inevitable, stage B arising inevitably out of stage A. This devalues the moral conscience and historicity of persons.

(2) It tends to subordinate means to ends and the particular to the general. This leads some people, on the rebound from Stalinism, to adopt a position of hostility to generalities, or to argue that we must be concerned only with the short term, with the praxis of people in the present. I do not believe that it is a solution to the dichotomising of means and ends, and the subordination of means to ends, to rebound to a position of concern only for present ends. To pose present ends as sufficient is to attempt to ignore the time dimension, our intentionality and ability to project, which are fundamental to our humanity. What we have to do is to develop an unambiguously *moral* understanding of the complex relationship between means and ends. We must reject the placing of value, of ends, only in the future. Men and women always live in the present, in the point of transition, the point of focus, the process of becoming. Therefore, some at least of our ends must lie in the present. What we do now should be an end-in-itself in the present unless there is a very convincing moral reason why it cannot be so. Our creativity and our morality should be expressed and bear fruit in the present. But neither should we seek to arrest or spatialise the present, to deny its transitional temporal quality, our intentionality, our

projectivity. As well as living, creating, relating and evaluating now, we also, as a part of those processes, set ourselves projects or goals that will be realised in the future, that are not one whit less meaningful, less ends-in-themselves.

(3) Progress also contains the idea of approval. It implies that the moves from tribalism to feudalism, feudalism to capitalism, and so on, are not just stages of development. Each is seen as in some sense better than the last, or at the very least leading to a desired final stage. The same is true of the developments in technology which are held to underlie these social transformations. They are thought of as technological progress: the higher the better. The same view is applied to historical events. After the UCS campaign, or the rents campaign, or the miners' strike, party members are assured that things are now on a higher plane, we have reached a new level, comrade. Marxism is dyed in this attitude.

On the drive for an overview

The themes of base and superstructure, authoritarianism and determinism, progress, the subordination of present to future, means to ends, and the particular to the general, are of course interrelated. Let's look again at the generalising habit, the drive for an overview, which I have argued is a key (and let me say also, a desirable) component of Marxist analysis. It does nevertheless contain the danger of adopting a god-like posture. The very word 'overview' expresses this. It is only a shade away from the idea of central control. The macro level is the natural habitat of that dangerous species, the Great Marxist Overviewer. The micro level is subordinate, part of the greater whole, not autonomous. The Overviewers are not interested in individuals, in small groups, small communities, individual work-places, except as they form parts of larger totalities. This leads to centralism, to large-scale organisation, to concentration of power, to the subordination of individuals, small groups, localities, and work-places, to their being directed, marshalled, regimented into accepting the line, believing that the party is always right, saying correct things to win approval and position, uncritically implementing the policy locally. A ghastly distortion of humanity and communality!

On ideas, values and choices

One does not need to be an idealist to see that ideas, values and choices have a curious freedom, as well as a rootedness. An idea, that is, a concept, an abstraction, a generalisation, grows out of human consideration of/activity among particulars, either particulars directly experienced or mediated. There is also the insemination, in this process, of previously-forged ideas, interacting with those particulars in human consciousness, in the generation of the new concept; and the idea thus created, with these roots, becomes free in a certain quite specific *material* sense. It takes off from that particular context, journeys in time and space, and can land in many space-time contexts and interact with other ideas and particulars, in other consciousnesses. Consciousness and language are central to this process. The crude economic-determinist notion of the relation between base and superstructure forgets: (a) that it is people who make the base; (b) that ideas and values travel in space and time as outlined above and can influence the thinking and acting of people in other contexts; and (c) that people's critical reflection on reality can lead them to decide to try and bring about change, or at least to bear witness to a different point of view, at any time, whatever the conditions. The conditions alone do not determine the outcome.

On technological progressivism and giantism

Some of the implications of this are worth pursuing. Economic determinism, combined with progressivism and giantism, leads some people to believe that all technological developments are desirable. They trap us into the view that if a new, large-scale, more efficient (in input-output terms) technology is developed, we must have it. If we believe, on the contrary, that we are free to select among available technologies according to our values, our needs, and our conceptions of what is human, then we can make different choices from those which might otherwise appear to be inevitable.

Specifically in Scotland, economic determinism, progressivism, and giantism have led not only central government but also the labour movement to believe that the form of development appropriate to the Highlands is large-scale coastal petro-chemical complexes in a few areas. And the same labour movement attacks any choiceful view of technology as a romantic yearning for a pre-industrial age. Yet increasingly, pressure is coming from the very scientists and technologists who make the innovations to regard technological development and choice as a moral and ecological issue.

When Strathclyde Regional Council asked the public to comment on two alternative structures for schools councils, one large-scale and one smaller-scale, the STUC made representations in favour of the large-scale alternative.

Our social world is polluted with false dichotomies, each of whose poles drives the other further in the opposite direction. Pundits of higher and larger technologies are polarised against anarchists with green fingers. Authoritarian teachers are polarised against advocates of laissez-faire. Universalists are polarised against particularists.

On particularistic speech

Here we are again, face to face with the addiction to the general, the universal, which leads Marxists to think in large-scale terms and in terms of authoritarian control from the top down. It also expresses their conception of human beings, whom they only see to their satisfaction when they see them in generalities. Thus they inhibit, bind up, lock in, subordinate people's own experiences and feelings, their language, their potential for self-management, all that would rock the boat of general trends and centralised strategic management.

Not only does this imply an impoverished view of the person and the small group of co-operators, it also implies an impoverished view of particulars. It confuses being bogged down in particulars with sensitivity to particulars. Particularity is exclusively seen by Levitas as associated with synpraxis and the restricted code. It is only there to be transcended, it is only of value when seen as part of a large-scale process viewed from empyrean heights. The implications of this for persons, for their appreciation of particulars, for sensitive and creative interpersonal and group relations, are unacceptable. Human relations, perception, sensitivity, creativity and responsibility are by implication stigmatised as anarchic and ungeneralised (unless they can be suitably incorporated and managed). This is a fundamental issue about the spiritual character of most versions of Marxism. No wonder so many poets and novelists have run foul of the Soviet party and state machine: they represent values which simply do not figure in most Marxist conceptions of what being human is all about.

On particularity and universality in education

Do we have to reject the child's experience, language, locality, parents, the culture in which he or she is immersed? The child needs to understand his or her own context, to investigate it, and to criticise it; but in order to do so, needs access to information and concepts that come from way beyond the locality. It is not a matter of compromise between two poles. It is a matter of how we regard human beings, and how we see the relation of the particular and the general.

Marxist universalism tends to see particulars much in the same way as Plato sees the actual things of this world, as pale, secondary reflections of ideal forms, except that, in Marxism, the ideal forms are the general trends. And in a real politik sense they are right. There *are* real social structures which transcend and control not only individuals, groups, localities and workplaces, but even regions, nations and continents: cartels, states, multi-national firms, international military alliances. Here we are touching on another reason for the drive towards an overview. Marx and Engels saw that the ruling classes have developed large-scale organisations for achieving an overview and maintaining control. They saw the need for the oppressed to develop an alternative overview, and a countervailing power. The moral issue is: who does it, how, and using what means?

To refuse to seek an overview, to refuse to connect and relate and see developments both in small-scale and large-scale contexts, is to stick your head in the sand. That is what some community workers encourage people to do. It poses a problem for those who recognise the need to communicate and organise across boundaries, but who do not wish to start from the universal insight or the large-scale structure. We say that we want people to be self-determining, to start from where they are, to work it out for themselves, and *then* they'll move on to link up and create wider connections. Sometimes they don't get to that stage. Perhaps we have to devise with people forms of education and activity which integrate the two from the start.

20. Adult Education and the Concept of Community

In the autumn of 1976 I joined the WEA in south-east Scotland as Tutor Organiser. I had hoped that this might be an opportunity to implement some of the new thinking that I had been developing. However, initially it turned out differently. The District Committee wanted to concentrate on the growing field of trade union education, using the TUC's centrally-produced curricula on Health and Safety and Basic Shop Steward training. As the district's only Tutor Organiser, I also had some responsibility for the large existing programme of liberal arts studies in Edinburgh, and for work with the branches in Fife. It was several years before the committee became convinced of the case for a reappraisal of its policy. In the meantime, in the summer of 1977, I wrote *Adult Education and the Concept of Community*, summarising some of the conclusions I had reached the previous year, with particular reference to the new community education scene. An edited version of this article was published in *Adult Education*, the journal of the National Institute of Adult Education, in September 1978.

*

I

I write as an adult education practitioner, a field worker with an interest in theory. It is my belief that in British adult education, for the most part, theory and practice are divorced. Practitioners are out in the field, taken up with teaching (if they are lucky), organising, and administrating the provision. They come up against theory either on in-service training courses or when they seek to obtain professional qualifications by full or part-time study. They feel a complex of inferiority, deference, resentment, and occasionally contempt, for theorists.

Most theorists, on the other hand, live and work in academic worlds remote from those of field-work practice. Much British adult education theory is bland, latinate, unilluminating. For insight and regeneration of the world of practice, it substitutes obfuscatory abstracts of, and rationales for, the existing patterns of practice. This state of affairs will not change until practitioners realise that theory

is their province too, not the possession of abstracted theoreticians
— that they must develop a critical stance towards the patterns of
practice they inherit.

Recent articles in *Adult Education* by Brian Stewart, J. A. Simpson
and K. H. Lawson, each represent a serious attempt to come to grips
with some of the real issues implicit in the current debate. Some raw
nerves are exposed. This is a measure of the extent to which
innovation in the field has challenged theoretical shibboleths. I find
their contributions stimulating, even where I don't agree with them.
If at times they adopt a superior tone, at least they are not bland. But
it is significant that not one of them is at present a field work
practitioner. One is a senior administrator with a local authority,
another an academic theorist, and the third an ex-HMI, now heading
a European *animation* project. Yet they are discussing the
assumptions, the ideology, the terminology of innovative adult
education, which has been and is being carried out by field workers.
It is important therefore, that those same field workers enter the
debate — and at a conceptual and theoretical level, not merely with
accounts of their practice.

My first assumption, then, is that we need an interaction of theory
and practice in practitioners, in the course of their work, and in
dialogue with those they work with. The second is the need to
discover and evaluate the ideologies underlying existing patterns of
practice in all adult education (and not only in that area dubbed
community education).

Ideology is embodied, embedded, in practice in various ways: it is
embodied in the structures of organisations and institutions; in the
social relationships between such institutions and 'their' publics or
target populations: in their existing patterns of practice; and,
crucially and pervasively, in words.

In a short article we cannot hope to study each of these dimensions
of adult education. I therefore propose to concentrate on the last:
ideology in adult education as embodied in some of the language
used by adult educators.

Let us list some of the keywords of adult education, its ideological
load-bearing words: *needs, identifying the needs, meeting the needs,
provision, service, opportunities, the professional, the public, the
consumer*. Most writing on adult education — even where it calls for
new development, or criticises the status quo — uses these keywords.
Linden West, for example, summons us to a

> search for structures of provision which can adequately respond to
> human need (*Adult Education*, vol. 49, no. 1).

and describes a strategy for a new approach as involving identification of all the needs, co-ordination of all the available opportunities, and

> the presentation to the public of the range of such opportunities as a
> coherent service.

To those of us who have worked closely with community workers or social workers, this analysis has a familiar ring. It recalls the Seebohm Report (in England and Wales), the Kilbrandon Report (in Scotland), and the subsequent structural integration of the separate social work services into a new holistic service, an integrated provision. It is a structural analysis which proposes structural alterations, but it leaves the keywords of the existing ideology unchallenged and unchanged.

When we turn to K. H. Lawson's attempt to winkle out the underlying ideology of community education, we find a curiously uncritical — or else positively conservative — stance with regard to the ideology of traditional adult education. He sees Brian Stewart's suggestions simply as proposing a sort of extension to the existing consumer service:

> to make adult education more appealing and more readily available
> to those people who are not attracted to traditional provision. (*Adult
> Education*, Vo. 50, no. 1)

Referring to Keith Jackson's proposals, he comments:

> the audience may be new, what is offered may be in a new format.

The words 'audience', 'offered', and 'format' all imply a consumer ideology of adult education. He speaks later of

> the value assumptions underlying the plans for educational provision
> for the working class, for the 'disadvantaged', and in the interest of
> 'communities'.

which he sees as

> attempts to make education more significant.

— completely overlooking, apparently, his own value assumption embodied in the phrase 'provision for'.

Lawson believes that he can identify in statements by Jackson and Tom Lovett a key ideological feature of community education as a 'a practical instrumentalism'. I think he has got it wrong. Many recent innovative forms of adult education take as their starting point matters of immediate interest or concern to participants. They need not, however, remain locked in practical particularity, but can and often do branch out into matters of general significance and multiple interconnectedness. Lawson's apparent contempt for the practical ties in with his assumption elsewhere that skills and training have nothing to do with the cognitive, with education. I feel he is revealing a sort of *snobbisme*, a belief common among many that working people don't or can't think, and that practical work processes are divorced from thought. I am reminded of a passage in *The Ragged Trousered Philanthropists*, where Robert Tressell takes indignant issue with this kind of attitude.

I agree with Lawson's insistence on the importance of discovering the values implicit in any approach to education, but we must insist that he applies the same kind of vigour to his own position. What are the values he is asserting and defending? On this question I find him vague. He contrasts the alleged practical instrumentalism of community education with

> more traditional conceptions of education as a worthwhile thing for its own sake or at best directed to more distant and more nebulous goals

and again, later:

> the more traditional role of general cultural diffusion and personal development through studies on a broad perspective.

This is incredibly vague. A rose is a rose is a rose. Traditional adult education is here implicitly posed as an abstract essence to be defended. What is this essence? What is this rose that we are assured is a rose, this valuable culture that is to be diffused? Who makes it? For whom is it important?

I hope Mr Lawson will give us a clearer statement of his own values in the pages of *Adult Education*, so that those who have been involved in innovative adult education can evaluate his stance. By innovative adult education I mean, for example, women's studies, trade union studies, local newspapers, parents' discussion of, and involvement in, their children's education, participatory education taking off from issues like play, roads, housing, community councils, vandalism race, oral history, the writing of poetry, short stories, and reminiscences, by people who have learned through the processes of traditional school education that they are incapable of such creativity. (The list could go on.)

Frequently in his article, in spite of repeated protestations that every practice is value-based or value-laden, Mr Lawson seems to be harking back to a familiar stance — that he is both the arbiter of the values of others, and at the same time somehow above the field of contending values. We are constantly warned of the values and biases present in community education, as if the warner's own stance were at one and the same time value-free *and* right. Traditional adult education is up there on a pedestal, part of the structure of reality, God-given not people-made, and — like the wild wooders from *Toad of Toad Hall* — in rush these nasty community educators with their biases and concealed values. What bad form!

To pivot our theory and practice of adult education so exclusively around the concept of needs is, I wish to argue, distortive. A human being consists not only of needs, but also of aspirations, interests, preoccupations, consciousness, conscience, creative potential. A human being is a whole, sovereign, capable being — and also a *social* being. To excerpt needs from the whole human beings whose needs they are is paternalistic and exploitative. It drives a wedge between them and their needs. Meeting the needs is an alienated and alienating way of relating to people. It implies two sides. Those with the needs, mindless incompetents, on the one hand, and the need-meeters on the other, perceptive, enquiring, responsible, able to take a broad view and make prescriptions. There is a striking parallel with Marx's criticism of Robert Owen and the moulding conception of education, in which one part of the human race, superior to the other part, creates the right conditions for the development of the rest, for their own good.

The prime need, as the late Derek Morrell, theorist of the Home Office CDP, said to a gathering of child care officers in 1968, is to be treated as wholes, as integers, and not as collections of needs.

Instead of concentrating on what people need, we should concentrate on their interests, on what they think about their lives, their situations. This implies for the adult educator not the role of provision to meet needs, but dialogue to discover and pursue interests and concerns. It is for this reason that some so-called community educators take off from practical problems, not because of any narrow commitment to a practical instrumentalism.

The centrality of needs in Mr Lawson's ideology of adult education anchors the other keywords: provision, service, consumer and, above all, professional. Professionalism is theft — the theft of creativity, of co-operative responsibility from those who are supposedly being served with dollops of various public services. It is a concept embodied in most British public services, so it is unreasonable to blame adult education for it. But we might reasonably hope that in adult education — of all services, that one in which people participate voluntarily — we could make moves to overcome it. Some alternative keywords for discussion might be: *creativity, co-operative use and control of resources, responsibility, voluntarism, dialogue, full-timer, people.*

II

With regard to the words community and community education, I find myself in agreement with Mr Lawson on many points, though from a different stance. The first question we have to answer is where the concept of community comes from, both historically and in the present context. The answers are surprising. Community has strange bedfellows. May I say at the outset that over eight years of educational involvement in working-class localities, some of it paid, some of it unpaid, all of it deriving from a value-laden (and always developing) political commitment, I have never happily used the term community to denote where I was or what I was up to. Community is a soggy, spongy concept. It absorbs so many different liquids. It even dissolves into them.

There is a profound, spontaneous desire for what we might call organic community among people of all classes in Britain. The word community is popular, because through it people can express this yearning for social wholeness, a mutuality and interrelatedness, as opposed to the alienated, fragmented, antagonistic social world of daily experience. Linked with this desire for warm relatedness is a desire for stability.

Analysing the activities, attitudes, language and style of a group of Hell's Angels, I have argued elsewhere that

> The group is a small world of voluntary equals recognising and valuing each other in a world which does not recognise or value them. It thus embodies a solution, their solution, to one of the deepest needs or aspirations of human beings. . . It is this (sense of organic community) at every level — from local up to national and world levels — that (Hell's Angels) find missing and yearn for. It is this which the stories and imagery of Hitler and the Third Reich embody (for them).
>
> (Community Work and Adult Education in Staveley, unpublished MSc dissertation, Edinburgh University, 1976)

This longing to experience and create in the world an organic interrelatedness has a retrospective dimension to it. There is a longing for the warm family of the past, literally and metaphorically. This generates, in many forms and fields, the myth of prior community — for instance, the belief that there was a tremendous sense of community in the old slums with their extended families, which vision is contrasted with the present experience of life in post-war council housing estates and high-rise blocks. Memories of prior community are strong, and inflatable, often eclipsing those of hardship or struggle.

The myth of prior community has been a feature of epochs other than our own. It was strong in the thinking of nineteenth-century communitarians, who looked wistfully from their industrial slough of despond back towards the feudal village, for their vision of the whole community of whole persons. This medieval community incorporated everybody, willy-nilly. Everybody was in for life, and in a fixed station. There was a hierarchy of statuses, with little status mobility or geographical mobility. It was static, orderly, rooted and controlled by one seat of authority. The community dominated the individual.

This is a reactionary sense of community, though one with its roots in the emotional and social needs of all of us. Most readers of *Adult Education* probably share my doubt that human beings were whole in feudal society. I personally prefer Marx's position, if I understand it correctly, of trying to integrate authentic free individuality with co-operative egalitarian community. The point I am trying to establish here is simply that the desire for community is and always has been fundamental and deep-rooted, and that in some of its manifestations, at any rate, it is intertwined with very hierarchical, even coercive, conceptions of social order. Here, for example, is one such manifestation, which I came across recently, written on a school blackboard in Fife.

THE SCHOOL COMMUNITY

RECTOR

Depute
Rector

Senior
Assistant Rector

Assistant
Rector

Principal Teachers
(subject)

Principal Teachers
(guidance)

Assistant Principal Teachers
(subject)

TEACHERS

PUPILS

Another such manifestation, taken from a very different social context, is the nazi use of the concept of community. The nazis used the phrase 'the people's community' very intensively, linking it with the idea of 'all Germans together'. People were urged to put the community interest before self-interest. Hitler wooed the churches in language which chimed with their own. He called for 'a strong inner community to face the problems of the nation'. The theme of community was pumped out in every area of life — schools, sport, youth movement. The nazis succeeded in generating feelings of hope, enthusiasm, togetherness — in short, what we call community spirit.

One example of this nazi 'community development' is particularly relevant: the creation in the Third Reich of a labour movement (very different from our own). For a fortnight each year, rich industrialists, managers, and shop-floor workers went to live in barracks, working together at manual jobs, getting the same food, clothes, treatment and status. The aim was to generate a feeling of community spirit among them. Then they went back to their normal houses and jobs (ITV programme entitled 'Hitler's Germany').

What these examples show clearly is that often the term community is deployed to unite people of different statuses and classes, and to conceal conflicts of interest. Such community both ignores and is used to conceal the structural roots of antagonism. It may claim to break down divisions — for example, those of class, race, or religion — but in reality it does the opposite. Its unity is skin-deep, paper-thin, a plaster for existing stratifications.

This concept of community is one of the key unifying concepts in British culture. It is used and appealed to at regular intervals by national leaders, and mediated by the press and television. Under its umbrella, the lion lies down with the lamb, the miner with Mrs Thatcher, the office cleaner with the company director.

Community as used in this way is a reactionary concept. However, it is also used by radicals to denote a different kind of relatedness — co-operative, egalitarian. It is for this reason I have argued that it is a soggy word, not so much a concept as a field of contending ideologies, an ambiguous battleground. Among Christians, again, the term community is employed by radical and reactionary alike. For both, it carries a heavy ideological charge, relating to the idea of people being *members of one body* — the body of Christ. Then there are the related concepts of the community parish, the community minister, participation, outreach, and so on. Use of these terms by Christians, however, does not always helps us to differentiate between those who take a liberatory stance and those who take an authoritarian stance.

In identifying some of the reactionary associations of the word community, I have underplayed its use by radicals. Briefly, we can point here to its use by those in the Labour Party, the Liberal Party, and even some left-wing Conservatives, who wish to move towards participatory democracy in many areas of life. This has resulted in a whole host of familiar developments: the Home Office CDP, YVFF, Community Politics, Community Action, and so on. At one point, two or three years ago, the word community used as an adjective ran like wildfire through most government departments, leading to a proliferation of 'community' posts being advertised. Community has come to connote, in some usages, wider popular involvement, an anti-bureaucratic stance, even the right of people to control their own local life-situations. Like its bedfellow, participation, the term itself makes no distinctions between tokenism and more authentic forms of control.

I would like to conclude by mentioning briefly the historical origin of the term community education. How many of those who use it, or argue the pros and cons of the animal, realise that its origin is colonial? The concept of community education was developed by white educational theorists and administrators concerned with the education of black Africans. Features of the concept were notion of relevance, the emphasis on locality, and on popular (native) culture and organisation. In Kenya, for instance, spearthrowing and tribal dancing were introduced to the curriculum for the sake of relevance. Some of the white proponents of community education in Africa were liberal, even radical. Others were reactionary, and the most distasteful form that community education has taken is Bantu Education in South Africa. Since its earliest days, militant Africans have suspected and rejected community education as second rate, designed to train servants, clerks, operatives. They have campaigned not for relevance but for control. An account of the history of white initiatives and black responses in the field of education during the present century might be a useful article for a future issue of *Adult Education*, for the light it throws on our current debate on community education.

21. The Community Worker as Politiciser of the Deprived

This review appeared in the Journal of the Scottish Institute of Adult Education in 1978. The author of *The Community Worker as Politiciser of the Deprived* (Scottish Community Education Centre, Edinburgh), Charlie McConnell, was for several years a lecturer in community education at Dundee College of Education (now Northern College). Charlie was one of a number of non-Scots active in the field of adult and community education in Scotland during the 1970s and '80s. Typically senior managers, trainers or aspirant politicians, many of them preached a cure-all rhetoric of community development of varying quality. The fact that community development was an imperialist policy evolved in the late-colonial period and that several of us had been questioning the value of bringing it home, was ignored or somehow accommodated. It took me till the early 1980s to accept that there was a neo-colonialist dimension to our experience, and that this time *we* were the natives. Several factors combined to delay that recognition. One was the constant noise of the trendy left, which was both distracting and confusing. Another was the complication that many of the non-Scots were decent, competent and supportive of innovative developments in the field. A third was the behaviour of us Scots ourselves: aggressively oppositional, or manoeuvring for personal advantage, or cautious, conservative, grey-suited, authority-dominated and fearful of change, or viciously punitive, or demonstrating feelings of inferiority by taking refuge in silence, if not deeply withdrawn. Finally, as I now realise, facing up to the reality of colonisation is humiliating and is therefore resisted.

It seems to me now that silence and avoidance only serve to perpetuate the problem. A frank avowal of these perceptions is not to be confused with anti-English sentiment. At a personal level I have benefited enormously from my relationships with English people, and do not wish to lose the opportunity for similar connections in the future. At a more general level I recognise that it is often Scots who appoint non-Scots to senior positions in our own country, and conversely the more imaginative incomers who sometimes hold out for the able Scottish candidate. But to end on that note would be a liberal cop-out. Sooner or later we must face up to the psychological impact of having so many non-Scots or anglified Scots in leading positions. It makes the majority of us feel inferior and incompetent. The principled way to proceed would be to agree a national recruitment policy for appointments at all levels. An overall proportion of, say, 75 per cent Scots to 25 per cent non-Scots would maintain our proud commitment to internationalism, retain the benefit of outside perspectives, and help rebuild our confidence in our ability to run our own affairs. To ensure that we don't revert to a misogynist patriarchy, I would favour the adoption of a policy of appointing 50 per cent women and 50 per cent men at all levels and in all sectors. These broad grain proposals are intended as a contribution to a continuing debate, which cannot be conducted exclusively at the level of numerical guidelines because it is about the kind of nationalism and internationalism we want, in a worldwide sense. I am against chauvinistic-militaristic nationalism and in favour of pacific-collaborative nationalism. I am against the over-development of supra-national institutions, and in favour of the further development of collaboration and exchange between families, communities, institutions and peoples. Not *e pluribus unum*, but *inter plures communicatio*.

*

The title of this book is something of a misnomer. It is not a study of the community worker as politiciser, but a rapid tour of the literature that has grown up around community development, social welfare, radical education, politics, and ideology. The author has set himself the task of uncovering and clarifying the ideas embodied in the work of many theorists and practitioners active in these fields. He tackles the job with confidence and in an orderly fashion. An enormous amount of reading appears to have been done — no fewer than 385 references are given. Herein lies one of the book's weaknesses. To survey such a wide range of material in a mere 136 pages of text entails the risk of over-summary, over-generalisation, and hitting things to make them fit. The author does not always avoid these pitfalls and, connectedly, the book is not securely anchored in a critical analysis of community work practice.

Mr McConnell starts off by examining a number of definitions of ideology, and opts for one which, I think, tends to dichotomise ideas from social practice, and downgrades practice to the level of mere implementation of previously worked-out ideas. We are then presented with models of the three main ideologies said to be at work in contemporary British society. Their key features are listed. The three ideologies are: the liberal pluralist; the democratic socialist; and the Marxist. I personally find these three unsatisfactory as general categories. To define the dominant ideology in Britain as liberal pluralism may be fashionable, but it devalues both liberalism and pluralism. In summarising the features of the democratic socialist and Marxist models, Mr McConnell seriously distorts reality. How many Marxists subscribe to *both* existentialist ethics *and* scientific socialism? The two are at daggers drawn, yet in this account they figure as compatibles. Among the features of the democratic socialist model, he includes equality, freedom, and fellowship. Tawney, certainly — but the Webbs? Can we square these features with the paternalistic Owenite tradition? And does individual fulfilment and responsibility not figure in the Marxist tradition at all?

The three ideological models offered conceal rather than reveal important breakthroughs and convergences that have been happening in recent years — for example, between the radical Christian tradition and elements of Marxism in the work of Paulo Freire. Freire's work cuts across the boundaries of the three models presented. So does the women's liberation movement.

In his chapter on deprivation, the author knows his ground better. He attacks the simple equation of deprivation with material poverty. His analysis of the term 'power' is very useful, as is his discussion of the cycle of deprivation and the culture of poverty theories. His exploration of the role of the professional, the concept of 'the public interest', and the varying attitudes of professionals at different levels in departmental hierarchies towards the public, is full of insight. As Mr McConnell notes: 'the higher up the hierarchy . . . the greater the likelihood of identifying solutions to problems in terms of the conventional practice of one's organisation' — a comment adult educationists should take to heart.

The remainder of the book looks specifically at Community Development. Nothing is said about the colonial origins of Community Development and Community Education — a serious omission. The concept of participatory democracy is discussed, but the problems encountered by community workers, outreach adult educators, and community groups, in seeking to implement this concept in the context of the provision-mentality prevailing at higher levels, and among elected representatives, are not confronted. There is a tendency to identify community work with education — in fact, regrettably, the educational element in community work is under-developed, and likewise most adult education still holds aloof from community work, in spite of Alexander's call for a community development approach.

Mr McConnell's examination of the false dichotomy between the 'directive' and the 'non-directive' approaches is stimulating, as is his attack on attempts to impose values by stealth. In his final chapter, entitled Case Studies, he holds back from a close-up look at what has happened in particular Community Development projects, and concentrates instead on further analysis of governmental policies towards 'the poor', and on statistics. There is indeed a tendency throughout to equate the empirically verifiable with statistics. What about direct perception by participants? Not enough of this finds its way into the book.

Nevertheless, Mr McConnell's book is worth reading, and contains valuable insights. It is a worthy attempt to develop an overview in a relatively new and still expanding field.

22. Master of their own Destiny

The review also appeared in a 1978 issue of the *Journal of the Scottish Institute of Adult Education*. Apart from the inherent interest of the comparison between the work of Moses Coady and Paulo Freire, what is significant is the declaration of the relevance of Freire's ideas to the Scottish situation. I had already decided to take steps aimed at widening the interest in Freire's ideas and their application. The first of these was a Pedagogy of the Oppressed reading group, which met in our flat and was attended by some of my students on the postgraduate Diploma and MSc courses in Community Education at Edinburgh University. Three members of this first reading group were later to become involved in the Adult Learning Project (ALP), an attempt to implement Freire's ideas in Scotland, which began two years later.

*

The work of Paulo Freire poses so many challenges for Scottish adult education. He denies that education is neutral. He denies that it is about compartmentalised subjects. He rejects the cafeteria approach. He rejects the concept of education as the transmission of information and skills. And he rejects the domination of the teacher, whether autocratic or managerial. The voice of Jesus in the land of John Knox and Willie Ross!

Although a few senior figures and many young field workers in the adult education world hold Freire's ideas and methodology in high esteem, very little work has been done on how his ideas might apply in an advanced society like ours. The paper under review is an attempt by a Canadian adult educator, Anne Kathleen Armstrong, to compare Freire's work in Brazil in the 1950s and '60s with that of Father Moses Coady in Nova Scotia in the 1920s and '30s. She argues that, although separated by time and geography, these two

---

A review of *A comparison of the thought of Coady and Freire* by Anne Kathleen Armstrong (Occasional paper number 13, published by the Centre for Continuing Education, The University of British Columbia, Vancouver, Canada).

societies have in common *poverty, control from outside, and an absence of co-operative initiative and direction from within.*

Where Freire describes the Brazilian peasants as oppressed, submerged in reality, Coady speaks of the fisherfolk of Nova Scotia as little men who have lost the will and capacity to act on their own. In Coady's picture, an element of blame attaches to the poor. They have, he says, become slaves becuse they have not taken the steps or expended the effort.

In spite of this significant difference in diagnosis, the solution proposed by both men is the same: transformation of the situation by the poor themselves. Their critiques of the existing education system are close but not identical. For Freire it is the banking system, where facts and attitudes are deposited in the poor by the rulers. For Coady it is like the upward social mobility we are familiar with in our own country: '. . . it is the trapdoor that enables (the bright and vigorous) to go into the so-called higher professions . . . essentially a skimming process. . . .' Against this process, both pose another kind of education: for Freire, education for liberation; and for Coady, education for mobilisation. Reflection and action are united for the task, in Freire's case, of transforming society in an unspecified way, and in Coady's for the achievement of economic control by the poor through the development of co-operatives for the production, marketing and distribution of their goods, through credit unions, through housing co-operatives and through participation in trade unions.

The differences between the two sharpen when we consider two main areas of concern: initial contacts with people as prospective students; and the educator's attitudes to emerging popular leaders.

Freire's approach to the people of an area is described in his 'Pedagogy of the Oppressed'. It is a slow, painstaking process in which a complex picture of the political, social and economic situation is built up, integrated with a picture of the people's consciousness of it. It is from the outset a process in which popular involvement is sought, and at no stage is an attempt made to impose a single 'correct' analysis.

Coady has no time for such subtleties. He starts with a big public meeting, at which '. . . is exploded intellectual dynamite . . . in a kind of intellectual bombing operation. It must shatter the mind-sets of people . . . blast these minds into some real thinking.'

Both Coady and Freire are concerned that emerging popular leaders should not develop away from their fellows. Freire opposes the education of popular leaders in isolation, on the grounds that such education will merely make the leaders more efficient at manipulating their members, more likely to become upwardly mobile. Coady on the other hand believes leadership training to be essential. Which of them is right? Should we not be asking the same question about shop steward training, and about skills courses for community activists?

Anne Kathleen Armstrong's brief and clear paper is a welcome addition to the literature on Freire. The comparison with Coady and Nova Scotia illuminates the work of both — and also some of the questions currently preoccupying us in Auld Scotia.

23. Some Key Words in the Social Services

Shortly after we moved to Edinburgh, Gordon Brown persuaded me that the best home for the ideas about popular self-organisation and anti-paternalism which I had been propounding was the Labour Party. I was familiar with the reality of Labour both in England and Scotland, and had considerable reservations, but feelings of political isolation, and personal regard for Gordon, who had just been adopted as Labour candidate for the Edinburgh South constituency, combined to overcome these.

I raised at branch meetings the view that the party should stimulate popular self-organisation, and met with the usual paternalistic or Fabian resistance. However, there was sufficient support from working-class members of the branch living in the Prestonfield housing scheme to go ahead. We responded to dissatisfaction with the house modernisation programme in the scheme by conducting a complete door-to-door survey of the faults people were complaining about. The evidence was compiled as a report and used by Gordon to get publicity through the *Evening News*, by Brian Wilson in *Seven Days*, and by Sadie Rooney and myself to encourage people in Prestonfield to form a Tenants' and Residents' Association, which they did.

I realised that what we were doing was being tolerated as a marginal diversion by most party members and had no impact on their fundamental orientation, which was to act as powerful tribunes who would get things done for the local plebs. I also realised that, however much he cared for people, that was Gordon's orientation too. I was determined not to give up without a fight. Keir Hardie House had established a Social Services Working Party under Gordon's convenership and I accepted his invitation to join it. I was aware of the danger that we might become preoccupied with structures, and levels of service delivery, and that matters of fundamental orientation might be taken for granted. So when we were asked to submit papers I decided to write about the key assumptions underlying the social services provided by the state. That was how *Some Key Words in the Social Services* came to be produced, in March 1978. It did not go down very well. Neither Gordon nor other members of the group showed any interest in tackling Labour's paternalism. At the next meeting, Kay Carmichael, the guest speaker, spoke enthusiastically in favour of my analysis, but once again there was no response from other colleagues.

It dawned on me that the problem was not bad habit, or lack of understanding. The case could not have been explained more clearly.

Fundamentally, Labour *did not want* to depart from paternalism, because that was the source of its support. To put it crudely, they wanted the Scottish people to stay in the position of dependent children, so that they could go on being the parents who provided public services for them, thus buying their allegiance and their votes. The Labour Party and I parted political company shortly afterwards.

*

The British state social services are based on an ideology whose main key words are:

> needs
> identifying needs
> meeting needs
> client
> professional/ism
> service
> provision
> welfare.

These key words, and the attitudes and practices rooted in them, interlock and form a single system of social relationships and power over resources which can be found, with variations, in any one social service. Taken together these services make up the welfare state.

A note on each word

needs: a need is an aspect or part of a person. People, however, consist not only of single needs, but of many needs, not only of many needs, but of abilities, creativity, aspirations, consciousness, conscience, nor are they collections of many aspects, bags of needs and abilities, but whole persons, integral, sovereign over themselves, autonomous. Further, people exist not only as separate individuals, but as social beings, interdepending and co-operating. To focus exclusively or mainly on needs is multiply exploitative. It separates that need from the other needs and abilities of the individual; it invades and seeks to invalidate the individual's integrity and autonomy; and it isolates the individual from authentic co-operation with others, and from the socio-economic context.

identifying needs: identifying needs means first that the need is not known, or not clearly known, or in dispute. This implies that the process of provision which follows the identification of needs is based on a narrowing of focus, an exclusivity — an identified need (or needs) is the problem to be tackled. Any interconnection with other needs, abilities, social co-operation, or the social context, tends therefore to be excluded. Also excluded by the same assumption is any subsequent play or roving of the intellect of either client or professional over the need in relation to other needs, abilities, etc. The field/scope of action and interconnection is drastically narrowed in advance. The concept of identifying needs thus carries further the process described above under need — the atomising and isolating process. It also begins a new process: the introduction of two poles; the person with the need (to be identified and met), and the person who will identify and meet the need. The first is implicitly passive, the second active; the first known, the second a knower; the first incapable, the second capable; the first being helped, the second helping; the first receiving, the second providing.

meeting the needs: meeting the needs consolidates and carries further this latter trend. It now clearly posits two sides: the needy, on the one hand, helpless incompetents, and on the other hand the need-meeters, superior, perceptive, intelligent, able to take an overview, make prescriptions, or guide towards solutions. The concept of meeting needs also confirms that the need-meeters *give* to the needy, who *receive*. The need-meeters *know* others, and *act* on and for them, while the needy *are known* and are *acted upon*. The passive object role of the client is coming into focus.

We are reminded of Karl Marx's criticism of Robert Owen and Owen's paternal, moulding attitude to the human objects of his benevolence at New Lanark. (Owen's New Lanark is one of the models underlying British social welfare, and also underlying some Labour conceptions of the socialist commonwealth.) Owen provided adequate housing, jobs, environment, education, moral guidance, welfare. Marx said it implied two sides: the benevolent figure who knows what's good for them and provides it; and the objects or recipients or clients or pawns of this process. Not for them to analyse, understand, to arrive at values, purposes and projects, and to implement them.

client: client is the term for this isolated human object, this recipient, this useless bag of needs. Client sovereignty, like consumer sovereignty, is a myth. The client is controlled and contained by the imperial values and acts of the provider, the professional.

professional: the professional by contrast is the one who knows and acts on the client. The professional is able to perceive, to find out, to weigh up, to judge, and finally to prescribe (gently) for the client. An important qualification: the rank-and-file professional at the point of service delivery is defined in the interlocking set of key words as having these powerful roles. In one sense s/he has them, but in another sense s/he does not, because real control of him/her rests with (a) the laws defining his/her tasks and judges' interpretation of these laws; (b) the controlling bureaucracy — team leaders, area officers, service directors, trainers; and (c) with the ideology embodied in and shaping the whole service.

professionalism: professionalism is the ideology that shapes and controls the professional, developed and communicated by training institutions, professional associations, and the hierarchies within the individual service departments. Its main feature is a justification of control of the service by the professional and not the client or the public, on the grounds of the professional's training. It is a superior form of trade or craft chauvinism.

service: service is what the professional does to the client. The implication is that the professional is the servant of the client. The reality of the relationship, however, is that the public servant, the professional, is the *master* of the client. Public service claims in its rhetoric to enable. In fact, it disables. This is not surprising since it *sees* people in terms of disabilities — needs, lacks, incompetence, problems.

provision: provision is another term for what professionals do to clients, except that it often has a more general all-encompassing sense, and is based on a different metaphor — a more honest metaphor too. The metaphor here is with the perception and action of the Miltonic God-the-Father, the creator and provider, the knower, who judges all his creatures. Provision by the area team, by the institution, by the local authority, by central government, is based on this metaphor. Authority creates and provides, clients receive and use (and *abuse* — like Adam and Eve, who were therefore expelled from the garden: the client as 'fallen').

welfare: welfare is those aspects of the human being catered for by such provision — or that is the rhetoric — the irony is that very frequently little, or an insufficiency, is provided. What is *in effect* provided is a dose of control, disability and dependency. This is because to provide for people's *welfare* on the model implicit in this set of key words, kills, denies, excludes *individual and communal human creativity*.

In sum, British social welfare, whether in housing, social work, education, income maintenance, or health, divides society into two parts, the doers and the done-unto. The clients' ability to know and act, their individual and social wholeness, their human creativity, is systematically suppressed and denied.

There has been an almost total convergence of Tory and Labour conceptions of social welfare, with some differences of emphasis. The Labour conception goes back to Owen and New Lanark. The Owen concept has not, however, been fully implemented in Britain

— it would have been if Labour had had its way, but the Tories have exercised important moderating and diversifying influences. (The Soviet Union is an example of a society where the Owenite conception has been most thoroughly implemented.)

The origins of the Tory conceptions of social welfare are to be found in Victorian social welfare: the poor are seen as the causes of their poverty. They are evil, degenerate, depraved, sunk in squalor through their own lack of moral fibre. Helping them only creates dependency. 'Down with the poor!' (Rhodes Boyson) aptly sums up this view. There are two possible sources of hope for them: one is to pull yourself up by your bootstraps, get up and go, stand on your own two feet, do it yourself, show initiative, enterprise. This is Samuel Smiles. The other is *saving the children*, the argument being that while the adults are to blame and should be left to sink or swim, we cannot really blame the children, but should seek to excerpt them from the degenerate social context and in social welfare institutions like schools teach them the good social habits and skills with which they can escape from the morass. Among some Tories, the concern which flows towards the children is extended also towards the adults.

These two traditions — the Labour/Owenite and the Tory/do it yourself/save the children — have converged and only differences of emphasis remain. Here for example is Richard Crossman in 1970 talking about CDP. It could just as easily be Keith Joseph:

> particularly in the black spots of our industrial areas, there are groups of underprivileged people who suffer from so many, often interrelated, social handicaps that they hardly know where to turn. . . It is not just a matter of helping to get these people back on their feet by gearing up the social services for them in a fully co-ordinated way, but of helping them to stand on their own in the future by their own efforts without having to rely on external support.

What is common to both views, and characterises the amalgamated view, is that the poor are the cause of their own poverty, and that therefore the solution lies in the *treatment* of the poor. The treatment, when analysed, breaks down into state stimulation of:

> better behaviour by the poor,
> improved services to the poor,
> more individual and communal self-help by the poor.

Buttressing this view, and this prescription, are two other key words: *deprivation* and *disadvantage*.

The word *deprivation* suggests not having something necessary for well-being, or having had this something taken away. It focuses on the person or group deprived. It does not focus on how they got like that. They are deprived, but the word doesn't make us think about who or what process deprived them. It does not point up the relatedness of the state of deprivation to the process of being deprived, or the subjects or agents of that process.

The same is true of the word *disadvantaged*. It does not draw attention to the process or people who render the disadvantaged disadvantaged. It focuses instead on the state of disadvantage.

A further characteristic of both words is that they imply some kind of thing or content whose absence renders the deprived deprived, and the disadvantaged disadvantaged. They imply that the process could be reversed by restoring this content: the deprived undeprived, the disadvantaged readvantaged, by appropriate restoration or provision. The deprived and the disadvantaged will be the passive recipients. The bad state is to have not, and the good state is to have.

I want to argue that for a humanist socialist approach to social service, these two words are entirely inappropriate. Instead we should use concepts which state social situations not in isolation, but in relation to causes and contexts, and which link social questions to economic and political questions. In my view, two appropriate concepts are *exploitation* and *marginalisation*.

Exploitation suggests not merely that the exploited don't *have* something, but that what they make, or part of it, is taken away from them unjustly. It states the fact of exploitation in relation to the process of exploitation. The exploited unlike the deprived are not human beings considered in isolation, out of relation. The word exploitation, unlike the word deprivation, is not evasive, neutral, or omissive about causes. Finally, in exploitation, the good state is making and using something you need. The bad state is making it and having it or a part of it taken away from you by someone who did not make it.

The term exploitation seems appropriate particularly with reference to that section of the population who are in employment, but on low wages.

The weakness of the term is that it emphasises economic values but underplays the whole question of choice, creativity, and control.

Marginalisation is the term I think we should use for all those who are denied any *valued* creative role in society: the long-term unemployed, the so-called unemployables, the new unemployed, young people in schools, the disabled, pensioners, and women at home. The humanist socialist solution, however, is not to create jobs (i.e. any old jobs, in which they would simply move from being marginalised to being exploited) but to involve both the marginalised and the exploited in the process of identifying and

making the things they need. That would imply, in Scotland, a programme of development with the ongoing involvement of all the
people, plus a mass programme of education for genuine participation.

This brings me to two final general considerations:

1. It seems to me that Labour must make a decisive, open and
sincere break from the paternalism of the Owenite conception.
Therefore it must recover from the Tories the concept of do-it-
yourself, stand on your own two feet, enterprise, initiative — which
should be a socialist, not a capitalist, value. To do this we need to
attack the Tory jugular, which is this: that the Tories, while
preaching self-help, do-it-yourself, do so *in the context of continuing
to exploit*. They say — *you* do it yourself, *we* keep the major
resources, *we* keep the capital.

> I am sitting on a man's back, choking him and making him
> carry me, and yet assure myself and others that I am very sorry
> for him and wish to ease his lot by any means possible, except
> getting off his back.
>
> (Leo Tolstoy)

2. A final key word: *participation*. Participation of the Keith
Joseph variety — i.e. you participate, we keep the capital. In other
words, you participate in your own exploitation or marginalisation.
You are incorporated into the system as it is at present — in our case,
the capitalist system. This is false or bogus participation, exposed
most succinctly by the Austrian socialist Ernst Fischer, at the time of
the Soviet invasion of Czechoslovakia:

> there can be no agreement between the wound and the knife.

This *bogus* participation has been all the rage in Britain in the last
ten years: community service, CDPs, children's panels, tenant
management of housing schemes, housing associations, school,
health, and Community Councils, Community Development (a
policy of white colonialists towards black natives). Down at the
grass-roots level, most attempts to achieve genuine participation
have been repulsed — by paternalistic Labour councillors, repressive
Tory councillors, and bureaucratic officials.

But *genuine participation* is surely our goal: the authentic
participation of people with each other, co-operation, this is the core
of socialism. That is what we are struggling for. Not participation
with authority where authority lays down all the rules and defines
the scope and character of the joint activity, but participation of
people with each other, to decide their values, the purposes, their
projects, and then to implement them. Social services which were
socialist services would *serve* this process in practice.

A good example is the Jeely Piece Clubs in Castlemilk. Here groups of working-class women get together and plan and implement themselves summer play activities for their children. They achieve a high degree of involvement of parents and the clubs are popular with the children. The people themselves make and implement all the decisions. They ask the Social Work and Education Departments for support services — use of schools, playing fields, grants of money to buy equipment and pay some workers. This is a new role for the public servants in these departments, and they play it grudgingly and with a bad grace. This is the direction for Labour in Scotland. We must go out and encourage people to take control of their own lives, and involve ourselves consistently in practice with them and develop supporting policies at all levels of scale.

I have not gone into the theory and origins of community development, something I feel the group should do. I have not gone into the philosophy of the Social Work Scotland Act: you will remember we agreed that someone else should be found to do that. We need to confront the fundamental questions of direction and ideology before looking at specific sectors of state activity. The Act heralded the integration of the separate services into a holistic service. Generic social work is the key concept. But its real effect, in my view, is a bureaucratic structural integration, part of the general development of corporate state apparatus, in turn part of the corporatist, centralist, multi-national drift of our whole society. I do not think in practice it has taken us in a socialist direction. It is true that Kilbrandon (Social Work) in theory moved the focus from the needs of the individual to the family, the group, and the community. But it *still* excerpted these 'deprived' groups from the larger socio-economic context. In the practice of social work departments, needs continue to be atomised. Clients continue to be excluded from control over their own lives. Their creativity and responsibility doesn't figure. The professional still rules (in spite of the radicalism of many field workers and academics). Social welfare is still dichotomised from economic and political questions. The poor are still the problem. The attempt at participation (through the children's panel system) has meant a recrudescence of middle-class voluntarism, no matter how sincere (and it is almost always wholly sincere). Where 'the community' as panel members, family members, and offenders, have participated in decision-making, they are participating in the system which identifies the offender (now the 'child in need of care') as the problem. Treatment rather than punishment is the watchword, but substantially the disposals remain the same.

In conclusion, genuine participation remains to be won. Will Labour in Scotland grasp the thistle? It will have to transform itself.

24. Community Development and Popular Participation

This paper represents the culmination of my long-term project to find the answers to the question: what is Community Development really about? It was delivered at the Scottish Council of Social Service Community Development Summer School at Hamilton, in August 1979.

*

I want to start by quoting a conversation which took place in India in the 1950s, between a Senior Administrator on the Indian Community Development Programme and a village-level worker. I am not good at imitating voices, so try to imagine two quite different accents and attitudes, one upper class and self-confident, the other lower class, deferent, making a valiant effort to use the academic jargon of Community Development (CD). The administrator speaks first:

> *How long have you been here?*
> Four months, sir.
> *What have you been doing?*
> Collecting data.
> *What about?*
> Felt needs, sir.
> *What do you mean by felt needs?*
> Mass approach method, sir.
> *Mass approach method?*
> Yes, psychological approach, sir.[1]

As an ex-CD field worker on an inner-city project in Scotland in the early 1970s, I identify with the rural field worker and resent the interrogative arrogance of the administrator. It is tempting to abandon — or never to start — the attempt to *understand* CD and to settle instead for uncritical parroting of the received phrases: felt needs, stimulation of self-help, development of local leadership, and so on. Ever since I first came in contact with CD I have had this urge to find the answer to the question: what is CD really about? Ten years later, after a fair amount of practice and a lot of reading, I think I know some of the answers.

We have to start by going back to the position of negroes in the southern states of the USA after the Civil War.[2] The negroes had been freed, they were no longer slaves, but they were still in the worst jobs, the worst conditions, at the lowest cultural level, and subject to intense prejudice and discrimination on the part of southern whites. The question was, what direction would black aspirations now take? In the field of education, the first development after the Civil War was the attempt to develop institutions for the *literary* education of blacks. They didn't flourish, and towards the end of the nineteenth century an alternative view began to grow, that the blacks' best interests would be served by *industrial* education. The concept of industrial education is linked particularly with the name of a negro educator, Booker T. Washington, who ran a college in Alabama called the Tuskegee Institute for Adult and Juvenile Education. It had an all-black staff, and offered blacks an education to fit them for life mainly in the rural areas of the south. Here is Booker T. Washington talking about the curriculum:

> We wanted to teach the students how to bathe, how to care for their teeth and clothing. We wanted to teach them what to eat, and how to eat it properly, and how to care for their rooms. Aside from this, we wanted to give them such a practical knowledge of some one industry, together with the spirit of industry, thrift and economy, that they would be sure of knowing how to make a living after they had left us. We wanted to teach them to study actual things instead of mere books alone.[3]

For Washington, this view of education was explicitly linked with a political perspective:

> The wisest among my race understand that the agitation for social equality is extremist folly.[2]

He did, of course, want to better the lot of negroes, but he envisaged it as a gradual process, not as a struggle against the whites.

Washington's views did not go unchallenged. In 1903 another negro, W. E. B. DuBois, attacked the assumptions of industrial education as education to fit in with the white-dominated system, education for subordination. He did not reject industrial education out of hand, but objected to the implication of conciliating the whites by promoting it as a way of life for all negroes. DuBois stressed the importance of literary education, leading to access for negroes to institutions of higher education, as the indispensable means of achieving equality. He wrote:

> Mr Washington represents, in Negro thought, the old attitude of adjustment and submission. His doctrine has tended to make the whites, north and south, shift the burden of the negro problem to the negroes' shoulders and stand aside as critical and rather pessimistic spectators.[2]

In this early clash between Washington and DuBois we see prefigured some of the debates and conflicts which have taken place over CD and over relevance in education both in colonial Africa and in Britain.

It would be a mistake, though, to see Booker Washington simply as an Uncle Tom. He and DuBois did co-operate to some extent. They were both committed to the advancement of negroes and they both objected to the kind of education offered to negroes by whites in the USA.

Booker Washington saw industrial education as appropriate for all non-whites. Even as early as 1905 he was keen that these ideas should be applied in Africa. Tuskegee became known in Africa, both to black militants and to colonial administrators and missionaries, and seems to have been regarded as a sort of beacon, almost a Mecca. The black Africans saw, not the northern white philanthropists' money behind Tuskegee, but the black president and the all-black staff. Tuskegee to them was an island of black pride and solidarity. One African nationalist argued in favour of a Tuskegee-type education on the grounds that it would ensure that Africans valued their traditional culture and built on it, whereas Africans educated in the white system would learn European culture and neglect their own. There was a need to develop a pride in things African as against an uncritical fascination with things western. (Arguments paralleling this have been used in Britain in the last fifteen years, by radicals, in favour of community education, and have been countered by other radicals using DuBois-style arguments.)

Before shifting our attention to Africa, however, we need to consider a decisive turn of events in the USA. In 1915 Booker Washington died, and his mantle fell on the shoulders of a white Welsh immigrant to the USA, Thomas Jesse Jones. Under the influence of Jones, Washington's black self-activity in educational matters, however non-antagonistic, was transformed into a dependent activity, more and more controlled by white philanthropy. Jones held a cluster of key ideas which it is important for us to grasp, because they are, in fact, though not in name, the core ideas of

CD. Jones was opposed to the idea of racial antagonism, or antagonism of any sort. There was, for him, no such thing as racial discrimination or oppression. There were simply 'natural difficulties'. He saw each race — white, negro, Indian, and so on — as going through a gradual process of evolution, with various phases or stages. This he called race progress. Some races were further evolved than others. From this point of view, phrases like social equality, or negro independence, were just unrealistic. In his 'sociology' of race, each race was described as having a neutral set of characteristics. One race might, for example, have less height, greater ill-health, earlier death, and a higher rate of infant mortality. These were simply the characteristics of the race at that stage of development, and implied nothing about its relationship with other races. Jones believed that the 'correct' presentation of the facts about racial differences would go a long way towards easing racial tensions. It would put a stop to:

> unrealistic ambitions in Negroes and Indians . . . (and) enlist white altruism for the lower races.[2]

Since there was nothing to be gained for the blacks by antagonising the whites, Jones discouraged the use of terms implying criticism of whites — words like lynching, discrimination, rights, etc. Instead, he emphasised *co-operation*, the search for *agreement*, and *unity* through *compromise*. Kenneth King writes:

> He mastered a technique for use in conflict situations, the main element of which was avoidance of the real issues.[2]

Jones' educational theory flowed from his racial theory. He stressed rural needs and rural betterment, the stimulation of the local community and the encouragement of industrial and domestic education.

> The underlying principle . . . is the adaptation of educational activities . . . to the needs of the pupil and the community.[2]

The notion of 'adaptation to the needs of the community' is a familiar one in CD literature. Some questions arising from it are: which needs? Who decides the needs? Jones defined the negroes' educational needs for them as a knowledge of sanitation, health training, improved housing, and industrial and agricultural skills. Subjects like Latin, French, philosophy, were not 'needed'. Kenneth King comments that Jones' principle of adaptation to the needs of the community:

> conceals a basically reactionary principle: the educational diet

(of the Negro) was to be limited and defined by the most pressing needs of the backward rural communities.[2]

Jones became a powerful figure in the USA, coming to be seen as the expert on negro education. He was given the task of reporting on the provision of negro education, and in particular on the institutions, such as Tuskegee, run by negroes themselves. In his report he shows great distrust of independent negro activity and antagonism towards literary and higher education for negroes. He consistently counterposes 'traditional forms of education' and 'adaptation to the needs . . .', and, when he is reporting on individual schools, he recommends in almost every case that there be added to their curriculum the theory and practice of gardening.

DuBois attacked Jones on two counts. First, that he was stifling the real freedom of the negro colleges by making them more dependent on white philanthropy; and, secondly, for his emphasis on a rural way of life. He wrote:

> for any coloured man to take his family to the country districts of Georgia in order to grow and develop and secure an education and uplift would be idiotic.[2]

Let us leave the USA suspended in mid-air for a moment and turn our attention to Africa. During the second half of the nineteenth century, the colonisation of Africa by Britain and other European powers was proceeding. I want now to look briefly at the response of the native Africans to the colonialists' offer of education .

In any African colony, the white settlers were present in three main guises: as colonial administrators, as missionaries, and as traders/ entrepreneurs. In the early years of colonisation, up till the 1920s, the colonial administrations in general had little to do with education, which they left to the missionaries. According to Terence Ranger,[4] while developments took different forms in different African societies, a broad pattern of African response to the offer of mission education can be discerned.[4] An initial period of suspicion was followed by a period of enthusiastic welcome. This enthusiasm was soon accompanied by criticism as the Africans found that the education offered did not meet their needs and aspirations as they saw them. This criticism built up steadily and had become fully articulated in most societies by the 1920s, amounting to what Ranger calls an 'educational rebellion'.

In the first decade of the twentieth century, for instance, the Lozi of North-west Rhodesia were pressing for education without a commitment to Christianity, and more and better education in English and technical subjects. In 1907 the Secretary of State for Native Affairs in the area wrote:

They have long been disillusioned with the teaching of the
missionaries, which is confined to the bible, singing and a
smattering of imperfect English.[4]

At a later stage, however, African critics fought against too much
technical and vocational education, seeing it as a method of
maintaining European supremacy by placing Africans in inferior
trades. The Africans recognised education as the power-house of
European civilisation and rapidly came to want it as a means of
gaining the power of the Europeans. But they wanted education in
full measure, not by half measure. Ranger summarises their demands
as follows:

> What African critics were demanding was modernisation
> under African control; the presentation to Africans of the full
> range of western education without conditions and the
> freedom to select and make use . . .[4]

Their dissatisfaction with the education offered to them by the
missions led to various forms of action by Africans to obtain the kind
of education they wanted. First, they tried to get direct control of the
mission schools, and, when that strategy failed, they pressed the
colonial governments to set up schools, or to take over the mission
schools, arguing that the taxes they paid should be used to provide
education. When this strategy was sabotaged by government
inaction, or by the development of a closer partnership between the
government and the missions, many Africans turned to the creation
of independent schools, generally associated with independent (that
is, African-controlled) church movements. Such schools began to
spread rapidly during the First World War, and continued to spread
subsequently.

In summary, then, the early years of this century saw the
beginnings of a struggle for control of their own education and the
right to define their own educational needs by Africans, particularly
in East Africa. This early struggle can be seen as a precursor to and
progenitor of the struggle for political independence.

It was this native educational dissatisfaction and agitation, as well
as external factors such as the First World War and the Russian
Revolution, which caused the missionary societies and the colonial
educationalists to begin to rethink their educational policies and to
look around for a new model. L. J. Lewis writes:

> when the war came to an end in 1918, the European colonising
> powers were exhausted and their confidence in their own way
> of life was undermined. Furthermore, new concepts of national

self-determination forced governments to reconsider their colonial policies.[5]

The model which came to their attention was Tuskegee. While the directors of missionary societies and senior colonial administrators were scratching their heads about how best to meet the educational needs of their 'backward' and unruly African natives, Thomas Jesse Jones (now educational director of the Phelps Stokes Fund, one of the white philanthropic agencies concerned with the education of negroes in the USA) was busy in Europe helping the US government to pacify unrest among the negro soldiers in the US Army. As soon as the war ended, Jones began pressing the officers of the Phelps Stokes Fund to undertake a survey of the educational needs of African negroes. High-level connections were established between the Fund and the missionary and colonial interests across the Atlantic and, as a result, two Commissions funded by the Phelps Stokes Foundation and led by Thomas Jesse Jones made extensive tours of west, central, east, and south Africa, the first in 1920-1, the second in 1924. (It provides an interesting side light on the Commissions that they contained one — and only one — negro member, the Reverend Robert Aggrey, who shared Jones' views about race.)

The reports of the Phelps Stokes Commissions make interesting reading. As we might expect, they reflect the values of their director. No mention is made of the independent schools movement, or of the right of Africans to define their own educational needs. African discontent is referred to in terms one might use to describe a hyperactive child:

> (in) the notable awakening of the African people . . . certain elements of restlessness extend rather widely . . . their state of mind is susceptible of guidance either towards constructive improvement of the present situation or towards futile and even destructive restlessness harmful to their own welfare.[5]

Jones' belief that conflicting interests can always be reconciled shines through from the start:

> the first responsibility of the Commission has been to eliminate aims that are obviously antagonistic to the best interests of the natives and of the colony and to harmonise those aims that are natural, reasonable, and desirable in the development of Africa and Africans.

> the education and civilisation of the Africans requires the co-operation of governments, missions, commercial and industrial concerns, and the native people. There is some

evidence of misunderstandings and even antagonisms. Fortunately, most of the antagonisms are due to a lack of acquaintance with each other on the part of the several groups.[5]

The Commissioners do make radical criticisms of colonial educational practice — at times the voice might be that of DuBois rather than Jones:

> No greater injustice can be committed against a people than to deprive them of their own language.

> Why should the African youth sing 'The British Grenadiers' and 'The Marseillaise' and despise the music of his own people? Why should the history and geography of Europe and America receive more attention than that of Africa itself?

And note this completely frank statement:

> economic requirements of ruling groups have hitherto determined education's aims.

The colonial governments, they explain, want education to produce clerical workers and skilled road surveyors. The traders want clerks. The settlers want labourers.

> Some desire to assist the natives to realise their full capacities as human beings. Others have thought of them as economic assets to be exploited.[5]

What then are the Phelps Stokes recommendations for the education of Africans? The central principle, of course, is 'adaptation to the needs of the community', by which is meant needs related to living in mainly rural settings and to manual work. School has responsibilities to the community. There must be genuine participation by the native people. Different educational agencies should co-ordinate their work. Education should extend into the realms of health, agriculture, home economics, etc. There should be mass education, as well as training for native leadership and the native language should be used where possible.

The publication of these reports marked a major stage in the emergence, or development, of CD, although, of course, the term 'community development' did not yet exist. Let us now turn our attention to the response of the British colonial office, and colonial administrators in Africa, to the Phelps Stokes spirit.

The response at top policy-making level was immediate. The publication of the second Phelps Stokes Report was followed quickly by the publication in 1925 of a Colonial Office White Paper on *Education Policy in British Tropical Africa*. It defines the aim of education as the 'advancement of the community as a whole'. There should be concern for adult education as well as the education of children. There should be co-ordination of the activities of different government departments, and co-operation between official and non-official bodies. There was a concern for morals, and a concern that education should not produce an unsettling, disintegrating effect. The White Paper emphasised respect for local culture and the need to build on traditional forms of social organisation. There was a need to improve agriculture, develop native industries, improve health, train people in the management of their own affairs, and inculcate ideas of citizenship and service, in order to create able and trustworthy native leaders.[6]

Over the next ten years little was done to implement this new educational orientation. In 1935, a *Memorandum on the Education of African Communities* reiterated and further developed the Phelps Stokes idea of community education. It called for the integration of school and community, for a team approach among government departments, for the education of the mass of people. An increased emphasis was laid on obtaining the consent and support of the people — African self-help, initiative and responsibility were to be the driving force.

It is clear, however, that these policies were not being urged out of pure altruism. *An Economic Survey of the Colonial Empire*[6] had been carried out, concerned with agricultural production and marketing in the colonies in order to meet *world* needs (my italics). It also investigated the relationship between the health of the labour force and economic development, with particular attention paid to nutrition and disease. The new policy of community education was linked in the minds of colonial policy-makers with exploiting the natural resources of Africa, which required a healthy labour force.

Still little was done to implement these policies. Evidently those who held the purse strings were not yet sufficiently convinced of the return to be obtained from sinking good money in African human resource development.

Then came the Second World War and, with it, a change in the orientation of Britain towards its colonies. Firstly, Britain needed more raw materials and food. Secondly, it needed soldiers. Thirdly, it needed to communicate with native Africans in order to convince them of the need to mobilise these human and natural resources against a distant enemy. The advantages of mass literacy become obvious. A committee was set up 'to consider the best approach to the problem of mass literacy and adult education . . . in the more backward territories'. Its 1943 report, entitled *Mass Education in African Society*,[6] emphasises the need for mass literacy and makes reference to the popular movement for literacy that had taken place in the Soviet Union. Mass education was taken to mean schools for children, adult literacy, fundamental adult education, and 'the ensuing local community projects'. Mass education was not only a matter of fitting people out with skills and knowledge, but would encourage them to participate actively in understanding and controlling the socio-economic changes taking place around them.

The colonial orientation was changing. From basically administrating the status quo, with the strongest emphasis on maintaining law and order, it was becoming one of concern for the social, economic and political development of the colonies. For the first time Britain offered the colonial governments money to help them mount mass education programmes. The 1943 report also proposes a method: the *project* or campaign method of team work, with specified limited objectives, applicable to particular communities. Each campaign was to be preceded by a survey of the community. And a new type of official would be needed, a mass education officer, who would be on the spot, in charge of these combined operations, and not flying a desk in some distant central office. This official would work non-directively. For mass education was to be a people's movement. The Africans themselves were to be the main agents of change.

One other characteristic of the change of orientation must be emphasised. The Colonial Secretary in 1943 described his job as being 'to guide the colonial peoples along the road to self-government'. There is an implicit belief that the Africans were not yet capable of self-government and that one of the aims of mass education, with its emphasis on active participation in local projects, was to help Africans get practical experience of managing their own affairs.

Pausing and summarising for a moment, we note how this cluster of ideas — which is still not called CD — is becoming more elaborate. It is opening out like a flower. We see specific new features appearing, such as the project, the community survey, and the non-directive local worker.

By 1947 the Committee on Education in the colonies was trying to define more precisely what mass education was. It emphasised that a new department of government was not needed. Instead, existing departments should adopt this new technique designed to 'release the latent energy and enthusiasm of the people themselves'. In the same year the Colonial Office held a conference on Local Government in Africa, and it was agreed that:

the key to more rapid progress in the dependent territories lay in the stimulation of initiative on the part of the people themselves.[6]

How to bring this about was to be decided at a conference the following year and it was from this conference that a document was published, entitled *The Encouragement of Initiative in African Society*,[6] which finally adopted the term 'community development'. The terms 'mass education' and 'community development' were to be interchangeable and were defined as:

> a movement designed to promote better living for the whole community, with the active participation and if possible on the initiative of the community, but if this initiative is not forthcoming spontaneously, by the use of techniques for arousing and stimulating it in order to secure its active and enthusiastic response to the movement. CD embraces all forms of betterment. It includes the whole range of development activities in the district, whether these are undertaken by government or unofficial bodies; in the field of agriculture by securing the adoption of better methods of soil conservation, better methods of farming and better care of livestock; in the field of health by promoting better sanitation and water supplies, proper measures of hygiene, infant and maternity welfare; in the field of education by spreading literacy and adult education as well as by the extension and improvement of schools for children. CD must make use of the co-operative movement and must be put into effect in the closest association with local government bodies.[6]

It would be wrong to complete this picture of the emergence of CD as a policy of Britain as a colonial power without making brief reference to the continuation of a trend we discussed earlier; that is, the distrust felt for community education, 'relevance', mass education and community development by militant African nationalists. They consistently attacked these policies, since they were associated with persistent white refusal to meet African educational aspirations. What these aspirations were has already been indicated. The following quotations from Jomo Kenyatta (writing in 1929) are worth noting:

> Busy yourselves with education. . . . But do not think that the education I refer to is that which we are given a lick of. No, it is a methodical education to open out a man's head.

and:

for the Kikuyu have immediate need of men like these: 1. The
Kikuyu Lawyer, 2. The Kikuyu Teacher, 3. The Kikuyu
Doctor.[4]

In the context of these aspirations, community education with its
'relevance', spear-throwing, tribal dancing, and the wearing of
traditional clothing instead of school uniform, was like taking coals
to Newcastle. The Reverend Ndabaningi Sithole puts it like this:

> to us education meant reading books, writing and talking
> English, and doing arithmetic. . . . At our homes we had done
> a lot of ploughing, planting, weeding and harvesting . . . we
> knew how to do these things.[4]

That African suspicion of relevance and CD is not without justification is suggested by this comment by the Governor of Kenya in his
1951 report on CD, which describes its purpose as:

> to direct their energies to constructive ends rather than to the
> political platform.[4]

Community Development quickly caught on and spread through
the British African territories. India, which became independent in
1947, adopted a national CD programme. The ideas travelled to
other Third World countries and soon the United Nations was
heavily involved. It may be useful to quote the other major 'classical'
definition of CD, produced by a UN group of experts, mainly from
Third World countries, in 1963:

> the term CD has come into international usage to connote the
> processes by which the efforts of people themselves are united
> with those of governmental authorities to improve the
> economic, social and cultural conditions of communities, to
> integrate these communities into the life of the nation, and to
> enable them to contribute fully to national progress. This
> complex of processes is, therefore, made up of two essential
> elements: the participation by people themselves in efforts to
> improve their level of living, with as much reliance as possible
> on their own initiative; and the provision of technical and other
> services in ways which encourage initiative, self-help and
> mutual help and make these more effective.

I now want to make a qualitative shift in direction and consider
some radical comments on colonial and post-colonial CD in the
Third World context.

First, a short paper by Gerrit Huizer. Huizer worked as a CD field
worker in Central America and, while he accepts the value of CD,

he stresses the need to link it with larger development measures such as agrarian reform. Huizer describes his experiences on a CD project in El Salvador. Although it involved activities based on the actual felt needs of the peasants — for a better road, and for sanitary drinking water — they did not respond. Huizer tried to find out why. Among the reasons he discovered were, first, distrust: the villagers believed the water project would benefit not them but the big local landowner. Secondly, there was resentment: the villagers would have to give their labour free, whereas the officials who were encouraging them were getting big salaries. Thirdly, they felt that government agents were treating them not as responsible citizens, whose collaboration was being sought, but as inferior beings who were being told what to do. As a result of these factors, the peasants withdrew into silence and did not take part in the project.[8]

Huizer's conclusion is that CD in rural contexts is made difficult if not impossible unless it is undertaken in the context of land redistribution. Where big landowners retain their dominance in such rural localities, community self-help can have only limited effect, and can even become a device for evading this central issue.

Huizer then describes two projects where, as a result of land redistribution, CD achieved a considerable transformation. He also examines a project where redistribution took place, but after an initial period of enthusiasm, morale dropped. Among factors affecting the drop in morale, he identifies neglect of the educational side of CD, and the disastrous effect of government paternalism on local popular leaders, some of whom began to dominate and even exploit their fellows.

In his conclusion, Huizer stresses the need to consider very seriously the obstacles to people's effective participation before embarking on CD projects.

Marjorie Mayo is much more scathing in her attack on colonial CD, although she falls short of rejecting it altogether. She reminds us that colonial rule was based on two principles: metropolitan self-interest and benevolent paternalism. In the early colonial period, the British showed very little concern for the education and welfare of the natives. Why then, she asks, in the 1920s and '30s, did this dramatic increase in concern occur? And she answers — for self-interested reasons. The British were anxious about the implications of self-government, both in India and Africa. The main preoccupation was that the colonies should not become communist. Therefore, they had to be prepared, trained up, for democracy on the British model. She comments, for example, on the Indian CD programme, that:

> the whole programme was quite explicitly an attempt to create

plausibly democratic institutions without serious dislocation
of the vested interests of the status quo.

and she goes on:

> an idealised and supposedly democratic version of village life,
> the Panchayat, was to be recreated, as part of this scheme to
> promote rural development without offering any explicit
> challenge to existing property or power or caste relationship.[9]

A comment from a UN evaluation team which visited India in the
late 1950s appears to confirm Mayo's case:

> despite all the efforts of the CD workers, the poor peasants
> were worse off, and the richer peasants and landowners better
> off . . . as a result of five years' CD.[9]

Up till now, Mayo is in fact developing the same argument as
Huizer. She proceeds to go one step further. After reminding us that
the colonial power needed the colonies for economic purposes — a
need which was intensified during the war, when Britain made an
arrangement to repay American war loans with raw materials from
the colonies — she argues that CD was a policy actually *designed* to
assist this process of economic exploitation: a means of obtaining
unpaid native labour for building up the infrastructure needed —
wells, dams, roads, bridges, schools, clinics, and so on.

Marxists at their most paranoid tend to see everything as a
conspiracy, designed to further the process of the exploitation of
labour by capital, *always* reducible to underlying economic
intentions or effects. This lack of recognition of complexity, of a
multiplicity of motives and purposes, sometimes undermines the
value, or certainly the credibility, of their analysis. Having said that,
Mayo's arguments about the *effect* of CD seem to me to carry some
weight. What I would question is whether CD field workers,
administrators, or theorists, intended these effects.

What is clear from the evidence we have considered, and what is
confirmed by many commentators, is that colonial CD programmes
operate on the existing economic base, the existing pattern of
economic relationships, ownership and power. It invites popular
participation on that basis and, if the existing relationships are
unjust, CD is incapable, of itself, of transforming them. Another
undeniable characteristic of CD is that it holds out to people the
opportunity of participation on a strictly limited *local* basis. It does
not invite participants to begin to develop an understanding of the
complex interconnections between their locality and the wider world

beyond. This is a point developed by the Brazilian writer Paulo Freire:

> ... In 'community development' projects, the more a region or area is broken down into local communities without the study of these communities both as totalities in themselves and as parts of another totality (the area, region, and so forth) — which in its turn is part of a still larger totality (the nation, as part of the continental totality) — the more alienation is intensified. And the more alienated people are, the easier it is to divide them and keep them divided. These focalised forms of action, by intensifying the focalised way of life of the oppressed (especially in rural areas) hamper the oppressed from perceiving reality critically and keep them isolated from the problems of oppressed people in other areas.[10]

The ground we have covered so far brings us up to the mid-1950s, the classic or golden age of CD. Before coming up to date and back home to Britain, or rather Scotland, I want to look briefly at some of the theorising done about CD in the 1950s and '60s by people who had spent many years involved in it.

First, the views of T. R. Batten, whom we might regard as the father of colonial CD, whose books are still prescribed reading on CD courses. To read his best known work, *Communities and their Development*,[1] is a pleasure. He writes simply, eschewing all jargon. He comes over as a warm and sincere person. One imagines that to know or hear about violence or exploitation would be really quite upsetting for him. For Batten, CD is simply about local development rather than national development. It is:

> a process during which people in the small community first thoroughly discuss and define their wants, and then plan and act together to satisfy them.

Its purpose is simply to make people's life better — to help them grow more food, enjoy better health, possess more goods, and adapt to changes. He is, or appears to be, wholly naive about larger economic questions. He says, for example:

> everyone, rich or poor, landowner or worker . . . has the right to share in the discussions and to help make the decisions.[1]

In other words, it is all, or it could be, one big happy family. He has very insightful comments to make about working in disorganised or factionalised communities, making sure you don't get identified with one faction. His comments here are relevant to work in many British localities. He insists that purely technical solutions are useless.

People's attitudes and feelings must be taken fully into account. This he calls the emphasis on *process* rather than goal. The criterion of success in CD, according to Batten, is that it should make people more satisfied with living where they do.

A final characteristic of Batten's view of CD is what I would call 'psychologism' — a humanist, partly true, but very partial and naive, view that problems in communities have to do with psychological states in individuals and the psychology of interpersonal relationships. A key word for Batten is *tension*. Tensions are 'good' if they lead to development, 'bad' if they lead to conflict. Such tensions as those between employers and workers, between races or between nations, are 'unpleasant'. The aim of CD is to help people reduce tensions. Thus he explains aggression in purely psychological terms. The Mau Mau movement in Kenya, for example, is explained as aggression deriving from frustration, rather than as the guerrilla activity of a national liberation movement struggling against a colonial power.

The other two writers whose work I want to consider are William and Loureide Biddle. They are Americans involved in what they call 'community dynamics' projects in depressed rural and inner city urban areas of the USA. Their book is subtitled 'the rediscovery of local initiative'.[11]

Like Batten they are attractively sincere and committed. They are Christian humanists — CD is the implementation of 'love thy neighbour' — and any suggestion that they are engaged in deliberately exploiting the disadvantaged would be absurd. They believe that 'people can be encouraged to help create a better social order'. They want people themselves to change, as well as having programmes to eliminate ignorance, poverty, bad health, bad housing and so on. They are social scientists and they believe that social scientific research and, in particular, action research, have a significant part to play in CD.

Their first assumption is that:

> each person is valuable, unique and capable of growth towards greater social sensitivity and responsibility.

In CD:

> participants are urged not to seek control over others . . . rather to share ideas, points of view, and control.

They believe that:

> when people are free of coercive pressures, and can examine a wide range of alternatives, they tend to choose the ethically better and wiser. . . .

For the Biddles, CD is holistic: it involves a collaborative effort on the part of all institutions and agencies, all professions, and all classes. They are aware of class divisions and of social injustices, but fight shy of aligning themselves exclusively with those they describe as the underprivileged. The community they seek to create must be all-inclusive. They are opposed to class struggle, and to Marxism. They see themselves as committed to American pluralism and to the Christian tradition.

They are concerned about the relationship between what they call microprocesses (of which CD is one) and macroprogrammes (grand-scale planning). They recognise that modern society is in an era of large-scale decision-making which calls upon individuals to acquiesce. As such centralised controls increase, the Biddles believe that ordinary citizens can hope for independence mainly through a reactivation of local initiative. But this local initiative cannot be effective if it relates only to local processes. It must, they argue, address itself also to the great problems, the macroprogrammes.

Some questions which arise are: how are these two to be integrated? Can they be integrated? The Biddles believe they can. Experts and bureaucrats can be helped to become more sensitive, more human. They are human beings, after all. If everyone became involved in the microprocesses of CD, they could learn to contribute to and help to guide the macroprogrammes. They seek a creative tension between large-scale programmes and small-scale communities.

However much I sympathise with their aspirations in this direction, I find the Biddles naive and well-meaning. Whether or not you think it is realistic or naive is an important question to ask yourself, because similar thinking underlies the adoption of CD ideas in Britain and specifically in Scotland in recent years (for example, the notion in local government reform that corporate management and CD are two sides of the same coin).

Let us now turn our attention to the introduction of CD in Britain, the 'bringing home' of CD.

We can point to a whole variety of contextual factors, which intertwine to form the background out of which CD emerged in the mid to late '60s in Britain.* There is, in the slightly more distant background, the colonial CD experience itself. There is, more

---

* In Scotland, community development in the rural areas was initiated in the 1960s by the Scottish Council of Social Service. The SCSS Rural Community Development Committee contained several members with experience of colonial administration in Africa, and its concept of CD in Scotland derived directly from that African experience. Writing in Community Development Journal in 1968, Muir Dickie, a member of the committee, identifies five ingredients which 'we have adopted ... as our main guides in Scotland:

immediately, the American experience of CD — overseas in the form of Peace Corps, at home in the form of the War on Poverty. There is, in Britain, the cultural upsurge starting in the '50s with rock and skiffle, culminating in the late '60s with the Beatles and the Rolling Stones. There is the resurgence of rank and file working-class militancy over wages. The erosion of whited-sepulchre puritanism, and the growth of moral laissez-faire-ism. The enormous growth of higher education, particularly in the social sciences, pointing ahead to a future problem: how to employ all these young people with college and university qualifications. The appearance of racial antagonism in some inner city areas. The growth of student militancy, Vietnam, the new left. The balance of payments crises, Britain's relatively slow rate of growth, the rediscovery of poverty. And bobbing along on the choppy seas of all this, the technological radicalism of the Labour governments, with their belief that higher technology, plus regional incentives, would mop up the remaining puddles of poverty and underdevelopment. And we could point to some of the specific reforming intentions of those governments — setting up commissions and making proposals for reforming almost every social service provided by the state, and the very apparatus of local government itself.

We can't go into any of these in detail. I want to mention briefly just two important precursors of home CD. First, the activity of committed radical Christians, people like Geoff Shaw and the

I   *Concern for the community as a whole*
    We must not be concerned with the interest of one group within the community to the exclusion of others.

II *Concern for development as a whole*
    Community Development is concerned with every sphere of community life, social, cultural, economic, health and welfare.

III *Maximum participation by the people themselves*
    The involvement of members of the community is essential — community development is WITH people not FOR people. It is most important that not only the men of the community should participate, but also the women and young people.

IV *Help from outside the community*
    Community improvement by local effort does not, in itself, amount to Community Development. Help can come from both governmental and voluntary agencies, and may take such forms as money grants, credit facilities, supply of materials and equipment, and expert advice of all kinds.

V   *A marriage of local to national interests*
    Community development involves the reconciliation of local felt needs with national policy. There must be two-way communication.[12]

Dickie goes on to say that the three main institutions involved in rural CD in Scotland were Councils of Social Service, Community Associations, and Village Halls. He regards Councils of Social Service as the main instruments. During the 1960s and early 1970s a number of rural Councils of Social Service have been formed in Scotland, mainly in the Highlands and Islands.

Gorbals Group, starting in the late '50s, going out beyond the church and seeking to serve the oppressed people of the city slums.[13] Second, the growth of autonomous community action growing out of the CND, the Committee of 100, and the new left — people like George Clarke, and John and Jan O'Malley, dissatisfied with the Labour Party, the Communist Party and the trade unions, trying to develop a new kind of political practice based not on left dogma or centralist structures, but on people getting together to take action on local issues.[14]

Let us start our investigation of the question — why apply CD to Britain in the '60s? — by listening to what those who actually applied it thought. The best-known British CD project was the Home Office CDP. In the immediate sense, CDP was the child of a Home Office working party formed in January 1968 and chaired by a senior civil servant, Derek Morrell. Morrell gave a talk to the Association of Child Care Officers in April 1968, on *Social Work and Community*. He speaks of the disintegration of community in modern society, arguing that only isolated oases of community remain. He urges his listeners to see people as integers, as wholes, and not as assemblies of needs and functions. Even in doing good, he says, we fragment people, by organising services to meet many different needs, when the prime need is to be valued for all that you are as a person. The goal of Social Work is 'to support and foster the growth of persons in community', and its target is 'those who are suffering most from the impersonal character of much of modern life'. 'The damaged and the deprived need friends . . . knowledgeable and resourceful friends.'[15]

I'd say that Derek Morrell sounds not unlike William and Loureide Biddle. Very much the sincere concerned humanist genuinely appalled by what is happening to some people. Here he is talking about one particular part of the Home Office CDP — the Hillfields project in Coventry:

> The whole project is aimed against fragmentation . . . the starting point is . . . that ours is a fragmented disintegrating society . . . depersonalisation is another problem . . . the technical juggernaut is taking over and we are no longer the masters . . . the crucial task . . . (is) . . . raising the people of Hillfields from a fatalistic dependence on the council to self-sufficiency and independence.[16]

Again it seems to me that the voice is the voice of the Biddles, or a slightly more pitying and paternalistic voice, with a humanist outlook, but one focusing resolutely on the psycho-social state of the victims rather than analysing the underlying socio-economic causes of their state.

Perhaps one ought not to overstate people's naivete. At a conference in 1969 about British and American CD, Morrell explicitly aligns himself with 'the liberal democratic process', indicating his belief that it has 'a highly creative future potential'.[16] It seems that the Home Office CDP may have been promoted partly as a bit of public relations. The Seebohm Report on the social services was about to be published. It contained recommendations for the integration of the separate social work services, a major and costly undertaking. It was felt that the government might not be able to implement its recommendations for some time to come and so, as an earnest of good intent, it was decided to launch CDP and project it as a trial run in Seebohmery.

Let us look at some of the ministerial statements made at this time, to see if they offer any further clues. Here is Richard Crossman, Secretary of State for the Social Services, speaking in 1970:

> particularly in the black spots of our industrial areas, there are groups of underprivileged people who suffer from so many, often interrelated, social handicaps, that they hardly know where to turn. It is not just a matter of helping to get these people back on their feet by gearing up the social services for them in a fully co-ordinated way, but of helping them to stand on their own in the future by their own efforts without having to rely on external support.[17]

And here, from the other side of the House, is Sir Keith Joseph:

> why is it that, in spite of long periods of full employment and relative prosperity and the improvement of community services since the Second World War, deprivation and problems of maladjustment so conspicuously exist?[16]

It might be argued that politicians' statements are not to be taken seriously, that they are just strings of elegantly phrased current clichés. So let us go behind them and look at some of the detailed papers produced about CDP by civil servants. In an annex to a Home Office document on CDP Objectives and Strategy, we find a very detailed list of what are called *indicators* to be used by researchers engaged alongside action workers in CDP teams. This list is significant because it reveals the *particular* purposes of the project in the minds of Home Office officials:

1. *Indicators of improved personal care* — including better personal hygiene, more family planning, more vaccination, reduction in illness and disease.
2. *Indicators of improved family functioning* — fewer crises, desertions, abandonments, less debt and rent arrears, less damage to housing, and more family stability.

3. *Indicators of improved child-rearing practices* — less infant mortality, neglect, ill-treatment and cruelty, fewer children taken into care.
4. *Indicators of improved education and support of young people* — more home-school co-operation, more use of school health and child guidance services, more school attendance, more achievement, more staying on after the leaving age, less delinquency, fewer court appearances, more use of juvenile libraries.
5. *Indicators of improved physical conditions in the community* — more basic amenities, better maintenance of houses, more use of house improvement grants.
6. *Indicators of increased support of the individual and the family, and of improved community functioning* — more use of clinics and libraries, fewer isolated people, more uptake of supplementary benefits by some, and less by others 'enabled by new forms to help to maintain themselves', more rent rebates, more legal aid and advice, more 'community communication and activity outside the home', more 'participation in identifying and meeting community needs', more co-operation between agencies, fewer evictions for anti-social behaviour, less 'dissatisfaction with employment', less fraud, less voluntary unemployment.

I think that these indicators can be further summarised to reveal three underlying aims or purposes of CDP, in the sense of outcomes hoped for by government. Basically these are:

1. better behaviour by the poor;
2. improved services to the poor;
3. more individual and communal self-help by the poor.

But we are still left asking why? Why this noble concern to improve the poor by using CD techniques developed in the colonies? They have, after all, been festering away for long enough. Why not leave them to get on with it?

First of all, and at a very general level, the persistence of poverty was an affront to the very idea of affluence, the notion that we'd never had it so good. The hope of Social Democratic theorists like Anthony Crosland, in the '50s, had been that poverty and indeed class differentiation would gradually fade away. That it wasn't doing so and, on the contrary, seemed to be increasing, was worrying. So everything possible had to be done to ensure that these people had opportunities to escape from the 'deadly quagmire of need and apathy' as James Callaghan called it when speaking about the Urban Programme in 1968.

Secondly, there were problems associated with the technological radicalism already referred to. British industry was under-capitalised and using out-of-date machinery. Labour was concerned to encourage owners of capital to invest in the private sector. Simultaneously they were trying to streamline, rationalise, and modernise the public sector. And they were trying to increase productivity all round. The net result was that jobs were steadily being lost throughout the 1960s. There was more poverty because there was more unemployment. And the government of Harold Wilson was helping to create it — remember the concept of shake-out? Remember the closures of the railway workshops, the cutting of the railways, the shutting down of unprofitable mines? Unemployment climbed throughout the '60s and has continued to rise through the seventies, with the prospect of much more to come.

Thirdly, there were problems of crime. Robert Carr, speaking in 1973, put this very succinctly from his own point of view:

> The urban problem is fundamental to the problems of our society and the level of crime in our society. . . . The level of crime is only the visible tip of the iceberg of social ferment lying beneath.[16]

This helps to explain why it was the Home Office — the Government department responsible for law and order — which promoted almost all the early CD schemes: Community Relations, Urban Aid, CDP, neighbourhood schemes, CCP, etc. We are entitled to ask whether the Home Office was primarily concerned with poverty itself, or with the public consequences of poverty — for example, the rise in crime and, in particular, the rise of juvenile crime. In 1967/68, the Children's Department of the Home Office, exploring the problem of juvenile delinquency, came up with a plan to attack it at its roots. Their view was that juvenile crime had to do with inadequacy, or breakdown in the family. The community was standing by and letting this happen. So the solution was to strengthen and help the family, by mobilising the community around it: 'to regenerate the old informal mechanisms of social control'. This was one of the main aims of CDP and was felt to be more desirable than the alternative solution — more police, more prisons, more powers for the police, the creation of new offences, and so on. This helps to explain the importance of projects relating to juveniles in CDP — adventure playgrounds, summer playschemes, intermediate treatment etc.

Fourthly, the Home Office was very concerned about racial tension. There had been and continued to be an influx of coloured immigrants. As unemployment grew, these people — many of whom suffered most from unemployment and poverty — became convenient scapegoats for those discontented, disappointed, often older and less skilled, native whites who remained in the run-down inner-city areas. There was inter-party agreement about what should be done — stem the tide, on the one hand, and integrate the ones who were already here, on the other. Thus the Community Relations industry began, and thus it was that several of the areas chosen to house a CDP contained a high number of immigrants.

But, in one sense, the question we've asked — why CD? — still hasn't been answered. If poverty is basically the result of a steady increase in unemployment and the decline of traditional industries, then surely what is needed is new jobs. In the USA in 1969, where the War on Poverty had already had a good run for its money, the same question was already being asked by commentators like David Brokensha and Peter Hodge.[3] CD in the USA, they said, is unlikely to succeed. What is needed is massive state intervention and investment on all fronts — housing, education, planning, jobs, police, social security, etc. Tinkering is irrelevant.

So we have to persist a bit further with our why? Did the Labour, and Tory, governments really believe that CD would solve the problem of poverty? Or were they going through motions of concern, knowing that they were just tinkering? How did they describe the problem to themselves? How did they see it? The first thing we note is their persistent attempt, as it were, to isolate the poor, to separate off poverty. They seemed determined not to see it in relation to causes, but as a separated-off thing-in-itself.

They saw it as geograpically contained — isolated pockets of poverty, areas of special need, deprived neighbourhoods. (The CCP actually said there were about ninety areas of intense urban deprivation in Britain.) They also tended to imply that the poor were, to a large extent, the cause of poverty — they were apathetic, sunk in a quagmire, unable to stand on their own two feet, didn't take the opportunities open to them. The had this theory that there was a cycle of deprivation, passed on from generation to generation — that poverty repeats itself, it breeds, it is not the effect of external factors like unemployment or low wages. The problem would be solved if the poor, with a wee bit of enabling, could break out of the cycle. This whole way of seeing enabled them to believe that big injections of money were not needed. The early CDP papers specifically rejected big injections of cash to provide decent houses, schools and jobs. Instead, having defined the problem in social-psychological terms, they proceeded to a cure which is also social-psychological. Marjorie Mayo calls it community psychotherapy. Alex Lyons, MP, Minister of State at the Home Office, speaking in 1974, confirms this:

CDPs are not a means of channelling money into areas of need. They were designed to put teams of articulate young people into areas where the population, though deprived, was inarticulate, to help these people express their own sense of grievance and to put pressure on the authority to do something about the situation.[16]

Interwoven with the reasons we have already identified, we should note one other. There was, on the part of some of the promoters of CD, a wish to initiate a movement away from the system of representative democracy towards genuine participatory democracy. Even here, though, there was on the part of some an element of cynicism. I remember in 1971 discussing with Eric Varley, MP, the idea of participatory democracy, in the context of some successful examples of community action in his constituency. He took the view that no more than 10 per cent of the population wished to participate in the local political process. Our job, he told me, was to create the opportunities for the 10 per cent, and that would be that.

The contrasts between colonial CD and home CD are fairly obvious. The first is mainly rural, the second mainly urban. The first is, to some extent, concerned with economic questions — the creation of a local infrastructure — though it skirts the really major economic questions of resource ownership and control. The second has tended, certainly till very recently, to concern itself largely with state services, 'at the point of service delivery', to use the jargon. There is very little mobilisation of people for construction activities in home CD. Colonial CD, again, puts a strong emphasis on educational dimensions — schools, adult literacy, adult education. Home CD workers would no doubt claim that their process is itself educative, but they would find it difficult to point to many specifically educational elements in their work, which tends to involve getting people organised to take some kind of action. Many colonial projects are concerned with building up craft production in villages, and with co-operatives of one sort or another. Until very recently, home CD has eschewed that sort of activity, though we can see the beginnings of it in Craigmillar Festival Society's Community Industry Project, or in the multi-purpose co-operatives that have formed in Lewis. In home CD there has been a much closer link with social work and social welfare, though a similar link had been strong in many Third World CD schemes. In other ways, also, the two converge as much as, if not more than, they diverge. They are both based on collaborative strategies between different interests and classes, and between people and governments. And they do not challenge the economic base on which they find themselves.

I want now to suggest some lessons that have been learned from home CD experience in the last twelve years or so. These are presented as personal opinions.

(1) It seems clear that CD cannot do away with poverty, because it is not able to tackle the root causes of poverty.

(2) The implication that the poor lack community and need help to create and develop it is not only insulting but also untrue. The extended family is alive and well. New community networks do become established gradually, after the disruption of slum clearance. Poor and working-class areas probably have more 'community', quantitatively and qualitatively, than lower middle-class, upper middle-class, and ruling class areas. A high level of 'community' is not of itself strong enough to overcome the continuously functioning mechanisms which generate poverty, disadvantage, degradation. (This is not to denigrate 'community'.)

(3) The poor in general do not live in poor ghettoes, but are mixed in with the blue- and white-collar working class. Community workers have consistently found themselves working with those who have jobs, and in some cases quite well-paid jobs, as well as those with low-paid jobs or none at all The attempt to separate off the poor is socially divisive.

(4) While it should not be denied that there are profound psychological problems to be found not only amongst the poor, but amongst manual workers, white-collar workers, managers, and for that matter amongst ruling élites as well, and while these problems are important and crying out for a response, emphasis on them to the exclusion of such factors as income, housing, employment, physical environment, and deep-rooted questions about the ownership and control of resources, is itself distortive and can lead to (or sometimes proceed from) a blame-the-victim posture.

(5) CD will be largely irrelevant, though well intentioned, unless and until it begins to confront the questions raised by Gerrit Huizer in relation to the El Salvador experience.

(6) While the focus on the local geographical area is important and shouldn't be thrown overboard, there is a need for deprived and oppressed groups, as well as organising locally, to communicate with and link up with similar groups in other areas and develop analyses of and responses to the problems they experience which transcend the boundaries of locality.

(7) The absence of an adult education dimension in home CD is a crippling weakness, leading to an activism controlled by the dominant values of our society.

(8) While not personally rejecting the idea of struggling for community control, I think experience has shown that we need to

look very carefully at bogus forms of it. For example, when a CD agency 'gives' money to local organisations for self-help activities, there is a real danger of this becoming a new form of paternalism.

(9) The danger of incorporation. CD theorists' resolute refusal to recognise the existence of conflicting interests in society, class antagonism, injustice in the ownership and control of resources, creates again and again the danger of the incorporation of activists and organisations of oppressed and exploited people.

(10) There is a need to undertake investigation and analysis of social problems, not in terms of atomised and depoliticised needs, but by digging into the political economy of areas and regions — finding out who the major resource owners and controllers are and what net effect they are having on the area. This kind of political economy cannot be value-free or neutral, but it is essential if CD is to have any hope of succeeding. For example, in the Western Isles, I believe that the multi-purpose co-operatives will experience great difficulties in the long run, unless the question of ownership and control of large tracts of land by people who are intent on keeping it for huntin', shootin' and fishin' is confronted. (This is where the HIDB has chickened out ever since its formation.) Ian Carter, in arguing the enormous potential of a CD strategy in the Highlands, the use of intermediate technology, of small-scale industrial processes, of co-operatives, to obtain more intensive use of underused labour and land resources, also warns:

> where CD projects typically fail is in trying to pursue CD strategy without at the same time trying to change the wider structure of inequality in the society — then the CD project becomes assimilated to the real local power interests. . . .[18]

(11) There is a need, in CD projects, to get people thinking seriously about their own values and the dominant values of our society. Otherwise the activities undertaken are undertaken on the basis of the uncritically accepted dominant values.

(12) There is a serious weakness, among some 'left' CD workers in particular, which is the belief that campaigns and activities should only be about putting pressure on public authorities to provide or release more resources. It is undoubtedly true that there *are* abilities and resources locked up in people themselves, and there is wide scope for developing activities that tap these resources and build up people's self-confidence.

(13) Another serious and characteristically 'left' danger is the attempt directly or indirectly to impose policies on people. Here the CD workers get carried away by their own fantasies, and confuse their own 'self-activity' with the 'self-activity' of the people they are

working with. Recognition of this danger doesn't at all contradict the need to help people understand large-scale, trans-local, trans-regional factors, or the need to create links with people from other areas or with struggles at the point of production.

(14) Community Action was a deliberate attempt to involve and organise women, not as opposed to men, but as opposed to the male-dominated and orientated forms of organisation at the work-place and in the traditional, centralist political parties. Community development shares this emphasis on women's involvement. What it is not, however, is a movement that is consciously part of the women's liberation movement. The implication of women's roles in community development, as local activists and as CD workers, are beginning to be explored analytically by women, and it may be in this area that some of the most significant lessons of CD experience in the last twelve years are to be learned.

Finally, the term popular participation. I believe passionately in popular participation. So does Teddy Taylor. He doesn't mean what I mean, and I don't mean what he means, but the two meanings do overlap. And it is more complicated still, because instead of two contrasting meanings, there are several.

Let's look first at the root meaning of the word participation and at some of its connotations. It's a Latin word and it means simply taking part. In normal usage, particularly in the local authority service department context, participation means getting some sort of popular involvement with the authorities on a specific project or plan. For example, if there is a traffic plan for an inner city area, the relevant department may produce a visual representation of it, write a popular account of it, and hold a public exhibition, inviting people's comments.

It very rarely happens that the plan is substantially changed as a result of people's comments, and the authority doesn't seriously expect this. In this kind of participation, the authority is dominant and primary, the local people are subordinate and secondary. It's a sort of cross between openness and consultation. This is how professionals generally use the term participation in their professional activities. Politicians are the same. Sometimes, if they have burned their fingers with participation — for example, if the people of an area have taken to the streets or the newspapers in protest against a plan — then they will retract their commitment to participation and state, more cautiously, that they favour 'limited popular participation' or some such formula.

The idea of participation, in many usages, is closely and interestingly allied with the Christian idea of the church. The church is all its members, and the word member means limb. They are all limbs of the body of Christ. This is a very beautiful and meaningful metaphor. You will note how, as in participation, the whole is of greater importance than the parts. The body of Christ is the whole, and is primary, and the individual members or limbs are the parts, and are secondary.

It is perhaps here that we find one of the problems about participation. It understates or mis-states the autonomy and apartness of the parts, and literally incorporates them into the body. This kind of participation, in community, political, and indeed, industrial arenas, is always in my view to be treated with caution, if not suspicion, because there is the grave danger of the incorporation of individuals and popular organisations.

Sir Keith Joseph's idea of participation would be that society as it is presently structured, that is to say the private ownership of the means of production (factories, machinery, land, etc.) is fundamentally okay — indeed, he would want more and more taken away from the state and put back into private ownership. So participation in society should be on that basis. *You* participate — *we* keep the capital. On that basis he would — very sincerely — believe in people playing an active and responsible part in society both in private and public life.

In the Soviet Union, on the other hand, all the major resources are owned by the state, and controlled by the machinery of the state and by the party. But they, too, believe in popular participation. In every area of life there are organisations of the people: the trade unions at work, organisations based on residence, organisations based on specialism. There are, for instance, organisations of pupils in every school class, and these organisations animate and supervise a whole range of educational and sporting activities beyond what actually goes on in the classroom. They have been described as substituting for, and organising, the informal networks of social control normally found in the peer group in the west. Some would argue that, given the powerful control of centralised organisations and party ideology over these organisations, they are embodiments of communitarian coercion rather than free participation, but they must nevertheless be counted as a form of popular participation. The aim in the Soviet Union is that there should be enough popular organisations in every area of life for everyone to get actively involved, and this active involvement is, theoretically at least, sought.[19]

Now, if we come back home to Britain, and begin to move politically to the left of Sir Keith Joseph — towards the left-wing Conservatives, the Liberals and the Social Democratic wing of the Labour Party — we shall also find an enthusiastic commitment to popular participation. It was the Liberals who invented the term 'community politics' (though it was not the Liberals who invented the practice). Politicians in this general neck of the woods are keen on popular participation, seeing it as an alternative to, and a challenge to, the development of more and more state bureaucracy.

Moving left again, we find a complex of contradictory attitudes. Many traditional left fundamentalists in the Labour Party, who are deeply paternalistic at heart, suspect popular participation as a capitalist cosmetic, a fad, something to distract people's attention from the need to increase state spending massively in the social services and in the provision of jobs. Since they believe primarily in jobs as the key, and increased spending as the means, they have little interest in the user control or user participation. They may have more interest in workers' control or industrial democracy. Here they and the TUC fight a battle of Titans with the CBI. Both sides fear participation, but, if they have to have it, it means to each something quite different. The CBI means employee share ownership, workers' suggestions, more flexible arrangements in the workplace, and worker directors — but not with the power to control major decisions. The union side fights shy of participation on these terms, which they see as leading to incorporation and emasculation. They feel forced to stick to a 'them' and 'us' orientation, which leaves them free to fight the employers economically.

The Communist Party interestingly favours popular participation and the idea of participatory democracy. The new version of their programme makes that abundantly clear.[20] Mick McGahey recently accused Maggie Thatcher of trying to make democracy a vote-in-the-ballot-box-every-five-years affair, insisted that democratic participation should go on all the time, and summoned the working class to participate in mass campaigns to force an early general election.

Where do I stand in all this? No one of the above stances is, in its entirety, the one I would adopt. I believe in genuine direct participation of people with each other (rather than with those having coercive authority over them). I tend to equate participation with co-operation, and to prefer the latter term. I believe that it should not exist just on the margins of life, but spread throughout society and involve everyone. Paulo Freire calls this 'the emergence of the people on to the stage of history' and 'fundamental democratisation'.[10, 21] I think that this process can only succeed in the context of a determined and successful challenge to exploitative concentrations of ownership and control of resources. That challenge has to be co-ordinated on a large-scale. Nevertheless, I believe that people can also generate their own resources, and that a struggle needs to be carried out against hierarchical, manipulative, cynical and coercive attitudes within popular organisations, which actually inhibit the flourishing of popular self-organisation.

I hope I have said enough to set a context for our discussions throughout the week, and that we can all sharpen our perceptions of what our own values and ideas are, and-thus get a clear sense of what we are trying to do.

References
1 *Communities and their Development*, T. R. Batten, Oxford University Press, London, 1957.
2 In the following section I draw extensively on Kenneth J. King's PhD thesis, *The American Background of the Phelps Stokes Commissions and their influence in Education in East Africa, especially in Kenya*, University of Edinburgh, 1968.
3 *Community Development: An Interpretation*, David Brokensha and Peter Hodge, Chandler Publishing Company, San Francisco, 1969.
4 *African Attempts to Control Education in East and Central Africa 1900-1939*, Terence Ranger, in *Past and Present* No. 32, 1966.
5 *The Phelps Stokes Reports on Education in Africa*, ed. L. J. Lewis, Oxford University Press, London, 1962.
6 *Community Development*, Central Office of Information Reference Pamphlet, Number 76, HMSO, London, 1966.
7 *Community Development and National Development*, United Nations, New York, 1963.
8 *Community Development, Land Reform and Political Participation*, Gerrit Huizer, 1969, in *Peasants and Peasant Societies*, ed. Teodor Shanin, Penguin, Harmondsworth, 1971.
9 *Community Development: A Radical Alternative?* Marjorie Mayo, in *Radical Social Work*, ed. Roy Bailey and Mike Brake, Edward Arnold, London, 1975.
10 *Pedagogy of the Oppressed*, Paulo Freire, Penguin, Harmondsworth, 1972.
11 *The Community Development Process: The Rediscovery of Local Initiative*, W. W. and L. J. Biddle, Holt Rinehart and Winston, New York, 1965.
12 *Community Development — Scotland*, M. A. M. Dickie, Community Development Journal, Vol. 3 No. 4, October 1968.
13 *Geoff: The Life of Geoffrey M. Shaw*, Ron Ferguson, Famedram Publishers, Gartocharn, 1979.
14 *The Politics of Community Action*, Jan O'Malley, Spokesman Books, Nottingham, 1977.
15 *Social Work and Community*, text of a talk given by Derek Morrell in April 1968.
16 Quoted in *Gilding the Ghetto*, CDP Inter-Project Editorial Team, The Russell Press, Nottingham, 1977.
17 Quoted in *New Ways of Meeting the Needs*, Colin Kirkwood, Unpublished Paper, 1976.
18 'A Socialist Strategy for the Highlands', Ian Carter in *The Red Paper on Scotland*, ed. Gordon Brown, Edinburgh University Student Publications Board, Edinburgh, 1975.
19 *Soviet Education*, Nigel Grant, University of London Press, London, 1965.
20 *The British Road to Socialism*, Communist Party of Great Britain, London, 1978.
21 *Education, The Practice of Freedom*, Paulo Freire, Writers and Readers Publishing Co-operative, London, 1974.

25. Applying Paulo Freire's ideas in Scotland

During the winter of 1978/79, under the aegis of the WEA, I ran an in-service training course introducing Freire's ideas to community education, social work, community work, and citizens' rights office staff in Lothian. Among the participants were the Community Education officers who prepared the urban aid application which succeeded in obtaining from the Scottish Office resources for the Adult Learning Project (ALP). In the autumn of 1979, as ALP got under way, I ran another course on Freire, this time aimed at the general public. The women who had set up the community-controlled Adult Learning Project, which preceded the Freire-orientated urban-aid ALP, joined to find out what Freire was all about. Both courses were heavily over-subscribed. On each of them we explored the issue of whether or not Freire's ideas were relevant to the Scottish situation, and if so, how they could be applied. This paper is a shortened version of the notes I prepared for one of the meetings of the second course, in November 1979.

*

To me, the desirability of trying to apply the ideas of Paulo Freire in a technologically advanced country, and particularly in Scotland, is self-evident. However, it is not self-evident to some other people, and specifically not to X, who has written several times to me over the last three years inviting me to justify my assumption. I want to make three points.

First, in some respects Freire's ideas are a case of 'what oft was thought, but ne'er so well expressed'. Many of us have intuitively had some of his perceptions of the traditional education system as banking and domesticating, and had hunches, glimpses, of a different kind of education based on investigation, dialogue, and people's creativity. And in partial, small-scale, particularistic ways, we've even developed and practised methods of education that embody these insights. Tom Lovett's method of making radio programmes and using them for listening/discussion groups is a good example. The point is that Freire has put it into words, and not just words that are a *description* of a particular piece of educational practice, but a conceptual, theoretical level. And he has based his theory on a vision of what education is and could be, and what people-in-the-world are and could be.

Here I am shading into my second point. Freire's vision integrates two significant intellectual and moral traditions: Christianity and Marxism/Hegelianism. Into this confluence he also draws insights from a variety of international sources: phenomenology and existentialism from Europe, the thought of Mao Tse-Tung from China, Julius Nyerere from southern Africa, Frantz Fanon and Albert Memmi from north Africa, North American anthropology, linguistics, and educational theory, the socially-applied psychoanalytic theory of Erich Fromm, the metropolis-satellite, development-underdevelopment economic theory of Andre Gunder Frank, and so on. His work is a synthesis of elements drawn from many cultures, and in that sense it is not culture-specific or culture-bound. As a moral theory, it applies anywhere, just as if somebody from Bethlehem says 'love thy neighbour as thyself', then it can apply equally in Beirut or Bonn, Recife, Hong Kong, or Manchester. It's not an argument against it to say: hey, wait a minute, this guy's not British. The question of relevance has to be assessed at the level of the content and significance of the statements, not the level of where they were made (though their original context, or environment, is part of their significance).

The third point I want to make is that Freire has a specific view of the relationship between theory and practice: that theory has no significance unless it is embodied in practice. Joao da Veiga Coutinho, introducing Freire's thought, describes it as a *situated thought*, growing out of reflection and action in a specific Third World situation. Freire himself argues that you cannot simply take an idea or practice from one context and transplant it into another. It won't *take*. He's not denying that it can have relevance elsewhere, he's saying that it has to be translated into the terms, forms, values and relations which constitute the reality of that other environment. He refers to this process as 'sociological reduction'. I must confess that I'm not really sure what that means. What I take it to imply is that the ideas and approaches Freire articulates in his own situation have to be re-invented, rediscovered, by people reflecting and acting in *their* situations, rather than just imitated. Merely to imitate them would be a sort of exemplarism, uncritically following a dominant model. If we were to do that, we would be participating in a process rather like the one Freire calls cultural invasion, the imposition of ideas and practices on a people and their culture by a dominating power from outside.

But he is not arguing for cultural insularity. As we've seen already, he draws insights from all corners of the world and uses them to illuminate his own Brazilian situation in its global context. And he has had the opportunity to apply these ideas, suitably reinvented, in collaboration with people in Chile and several African countries.

I feel that (a) we don't yet know how to apply Freire's ideas systematically in our own situations, because we haven't yet tried; (b) it's worth trying; (c) perhaps the *ideas* themselves could be followed fairly closely, translated and adapted as our reflections on our own situations suggest; and finally (d) it is the *situations* and the *themes* that are likely to be different.

To give a few examples: the Brazilian situation of peasants on a latifundium, dominated by the god-like power of the landowner, is not replicated in our situations. Freire refers to the impersonality of oppression in first world situations. Joao da Veiga Coutinho refers to the countries of the affluent first world as 'overconsuming and overmanaged'. Another commentator suggests that, in North America, 'the psychic boundaries between oppressors and oppressed are fuzzy'. A major theme for us in the so-called developed world, drinking the light from our TV screens and gobbling down our daily papers, is the theme of communication as dialogue versus communication as imposition. Another major theme is technological change as involving real human growth and development or as mere modernisation, leading to intensified alienation. Another difference relates to the theme of the culture of silence which we discussed last week. If Brazilian peasants are submerged in their reality and respond with a literal silence, then it could be argued that we are submerged in noise, a barrage of messages, a sea of rebounding and resounding instructions all round us. Are we 'silent', or are we indulging in 'mere talk, mere blah', or are we reflecting and seeking to act upon our situations?

Let me run quickly through an outline of a possible approach to applying Freire's ideas here in Scotland. It is not the only approach, just one that strikes me as possible. We take a region which has a good radical Labour or Nationalist administration, by which I mean one whose leaders are neither corrupt nor irredeemably paternalistic in their outlook. Within the adult or community education section of the education department, there are, either at senior or middle management level, people who are willing to admit frankly that they are dissatisfied with the patterns of fieldwork practice they have inherited, and wish to move, carefully and realistically, on the basis of sober reflection on the present situation, with obtainable resources, in dialogue with politicians, resource allocators, field workers, and people living and working in an area, towards a dialogical educational practice. A geographical area is identified, preferably one large enough to have a multiple function, that is, not just an area of housing, but containing also a number of productive enterprises employing significant numbers of people, an area containing a majority of manual workers, skilled, semi-skilled and unskilled, a minority of unemployed, a minority of middle-class people in professional jobs, an area which is a significant part of the total economy of the region.

A team of workers are employed, and before they get started they take part in a dialogical process of orientation and training in the approach envisaged. Their next task is to find out about the life of the area from sources other than the people who live and work there. They approach, for example, the planning department of the local university or college and ask what research studies have been carried out focusing on or including that area, about employment, industrial development, housing, health, population profile and trends, traffic, play, education and so on. Similar approaches may be made to other departments — economics, social policy, sociology, community medicine, education, linguistics, literature, etc. Where possible, copies of these reports are obtained, read and discussed by team members, and retained for subsequent use by people in the area.

The same academics are told of the intentions of the project, and if they are sympathetic may be invited to become involved in various capacities at later stages. Parallel approaches to those outlined above are made to various local and central government bodies with responsibilities relating to aspects of life in the area. Again, the material is read, discussed and retained, and subsequent involvement may be suggested.

The next stage is to make contact with people in the area itself, explaining the intention of the project and inviting people to take part. These contacts are initial, tentative, exploratory, part of the process of getting to know the people and the place. They should be wide ranging and representative in the pictorial sense, that is, attempts should be made to contact people in all the local groups and situations. It is important to contact Catholics as well as Protestants, workers as well as residents, immigrant and mobile groups as well as long-term resident 'natives', male and female, old and young, high and low paid, skilled and unskilled, unionised and non-unionised, people in their homes, shopping centres, community centres, playgroups, churches, pubs, the bingo, the bookies, and in local organisations of all kinds. In this process, the workers should be guided by the situations and organisations people are actually in, not the ones they think they ought to be in.

Two new things start to happen as soon as the workers go into the area. First, they are no longer finding out on their own: they are meeting and having discussions with the folk who live and work there, and need to be frank about their intentions. Second, their intentions are no longer the only intentions, and their investigations are no longer the only investigations. The appropriate orientation and method is dialogue, both at the level of general purposes and of specific focused investigations. They must admit that they are in an unknown, experimental situation, feeling their way. The appropriate attitudes are a willingness to expect the unexpected, openness, confidence and optimism, tempered with a realistic awareness of the limitations of their own competence. There is a belief that things are possible, rather than not possible. As people make the decision to participate in the work, the team of co-investigators expands and will continue to expand.

The contacts made lead to a public meeting or a series of public meetings, which lead in turn to a systematic investigation by the expanded team into the life of the area, identifying its main features, its contradictions and difficulties, not in an intrusive way, not in a sloganising way, not in a resigned 'that's life' way, not in an academic 'people as objects of interest' way, but so as to identify and explore, empathically, the significant situations in people's lives, with a view to naming themes.

Those who have read it will have realised by now that I am following through the process outlined by Paulo Freire in chapter three of *Pedagogy of the Oppressed*. Since you can do that for youselves, I'm going to stop there and turn my attention to offering some speculation to help clarify what Freire means by situations, themes and contradictions, and what these might be in the lives of people living and working in Scotland.

One area the group co-investigators might find concerns people in play: if, for example, the area is very overcrowded and there is little open space, they might find situations in which rather old-fashioned play equipment provided by a local authority has been vandalised. Or it may, on the other hand, turn out to be very suitable. Kids may get their adventure by breaking into disused warehouses. The smaller children may play in side streets, or not be allowed to play at all. There may have been traffic accidents to children. The police may bemoan the breakdown in the authority of parents and teachers. The challenge for the investigators at this stage is to try to discover the whole complex in all its aspects, rather than focus too narrowly on specific dimensions, or get seduced into premature analysis.

As the investigation proceeds, housing may emerge as an important area, throwing up, for example, themes of women's isolation in the home, or the different roles played by men and women. Again, the temptation will be to start offering diagnoses or proposing solutions, but the task at this stage is to help identify the situations in their complexity, as they are perceived by the people in them.

Another significant area may be work and unemployment. Themes which may emerge here include the satisfaction which may (or may not) be obtained from the exercise of skill, the absorption, and social contacts, and how work involvements hinge with home/ family involvement, which again may vary for men and women. Relationships between people and their situation, and between people and people, may emerge as crucial, particularly for example when they are unemployed or retired and have lost the contacts work gives.

A major theme may turn out to be control and lack of control, in personal life, at work, and in relation to the environment and the public services. The themes of power and bureaucracy are likely to be around in one form or another.

A question which such a project may have to confront at an early stage is people's motivation for participation. Is it a need to overcome alienation, or become less isolated, a desire for meaningful co-operation with others, or a desire for education for its own sake or as a means to other ends? This question of motivation is likely to be related to the difficulties and pressing purposes participants identify during the course of the investigation. A variety of motives for involvement is likely to be revealed.

Finally, we come to the task of codifying or representing the significant situations, contradictions, and themes. Most people in Britain are literate, although the extent of limited literacy is much greater than is generally supposed. Need codifications be pictures? What advantages and disadvantages accrue from the use of photographs and videotapes? What other media can be used? What *styles* are appropriate in making codifications? A representational style where situations can be instantly recognised? Could collage or juxtaposition of images or situations be used? Could we use statements by experts, or extracts from books? These are all questions which will confront the team as they consider and try to organise the material produced by their investigations.

26. Education — for life?

This review article was published in *Continuing Education,* the journal of the National Extension College, Cambridge, in March 1980. Its theme is the radicalism at the top which was such a feature of British adult education in the late 1970s, a radicalism preoccupied with large-scale structures and policies, with a lofty disdain for practice.

Something remarkable has happened to British adult education in the last ten years. In a period of national self-doubt and international decline, adult education has become self-confident, indeed aggressive. The only other national institution showing a sea-change of similar nature is the trade union movement. I think there is a connection between these two phenomena, but superficially at least they are very different. After all, the trade union movement is a long-standing — or long-sleeping — part of our national life. It has had half the working population in membership for decades. And its structures and workings are Victorian, to go no further back.

Adult education, on the other hand, can claim no more than a marginal impact on the lives of about 5 per cent of the adult population. It is relatively recent in origin. It has hardly any money. Indeed, to call it a national institution as I have done above is stretching the meaning of the phrase. It consists of (or subsists on) the margins of bigger institutions, in the form of extra-mural departments of universities, evening classes and TOPS schemes in FE Colleges, and vulnerable subsections of local authority education departments. These parasitical fragments, along with a curious radical/nostalgic organisation called the WEA, and a dynamic 'outfit' called the Open University, together (but they don't come very close together) make up British adult education.

Review of *World Yearbook of Education 1979: Recurrent Education and Lifelong Learning,* Tom Schuller and Jacquetta Megarry (eds.) (Kogan Page/ Nichols) and *Education and the Challenge of Change,* Ray Flude and Allen Parrott (Open University Press).

And this unlikely Cinderella comes to the Ball, demands the biggest slice of the cake, yells 'roll over Beethoven' at the mainstream education system, and ignores the fact that midnight has struck not once but several times. Will she go home, or is she here to stay?

This new self-assertiveness characterises the *whole* of adult education, not just a radical fringe. The outspokenness of field workers in a turbulent period is to be expected. What is less expected is the sound of more urbane and better-tailored voices — not, certainly, arguing for a radical redistribution of wealth and power (indeed frequently and deliberately disclaiming any connection between adult education and such purposes, in order not to alarm resource allocators) — demanding the implementation of the Russell and Alexander Reports, insisting that national councils of adult and continuing, or community, education be established and given money to spend, pressing the case of the adult literacy project, and more recently of the adult basic education project, pushing for political education, and so on.

And now these reasonable voices are seriously proposing the restructuring — if not transformation — of the British education system on the basis of the concept of recurrent, or lifelong, or continuing, education, involving a redistribution of national educational investment as between the compulsory education of children — the front-end model they call it — and the education and training of adults throughout their lives.

What is going on? What will be the outcome of all the noise and all the pressure? The two books under review can be seen — or rather heard — both as moments of the clamour, as symptoms, and also as attempts to clarify and explain, as diagnosis.

They are very different books. The *World Yearbook* is a revival of an education annual of long standing which ceased publication in 1974. It is significant that the theme of Recurrent Education and Lifelong Learning should have been chosen for the first year of the relaunch, and equally significant that the person chosen to edit such a volume, Tom Schuller, should be Director of the Centre for Research in Industrial Democracy and Participation at the University of Glasgow — again the link between adult education and the trade union movement.

The *Yearbook*'s centre of gravity is very much British/Western European, with ten contributions from the UK, three from Scandinavia and four from other Western European countries, two from North America, and one each from Australia and Tanzania. The quality of the contributions varies widely. A problem with collections of essays is that often the reader develops a feeling of disappointment as one author after another picks up and toys with his or her theme, only to put it down soon after the exploration has started. Tom Schuller's own contribution, 'The Democratisation of Work', shows a sharp grasp of the theme at a general level, but he does not have the space or time to take us very far into consideration of, for instance, the vital questions of what a curriculum for education for industrial democracy would consist of; how should it be arrived at; who will be the students (trade union representatives, or any workers who are interested); should industrial democracy take participatory or representative forms; and so on. The *Yearbook* is only able to whet our appetite for exploring such themes as these.

A valuable contrast with Western European experience is given by Marjorie Mbilinyi's essay on 'Lifelong Basic Education Reform in Tanzania'. More than any other contributor she opens up the contradictory nature of basic education, and in particular she attacks the notion of a low-cost education aimed at fitting out the worker with what are called 'minimum essential skills'.

For those interested in the demographic and technological factors which, it is argued, underlie the pressure for recurrent education, Jarl Bengtsson's essay 'The work/leisure/education life cycle' is very useful, and Tom Stonier's McLuhanesque hymn to electronic information technologies and the post-industrial economy is full-blooded and stimulating. I disagree with his perspective, but it is good to have it spelt out so clearly. Naomi McIntosh makes a lucid case for a system of educational credits for adults, in the course of describing some of the requirements for an effective continuing education system. The contributions from North America frankly bored me, and the Scandinavian contributions were disappointing. Much of the *Yearbook* is well worth reading, but its authors have an unfortunate tendency to operate at too general a level. The overview is so wide that the microtexture of social reality tends to become invisible. There is too little here about adults learning and teaching, and why that is important.

Ray Flude and Allen Parrott offer something quite different. Their collective voice is exclusively British — indeed, to a Scot, recognisably English. They present themselves, proudly, as pragmatists, they are hostile to theory about recurrent education — 'a concern of detached academics and non-resident eurocrats'. They are 'not concerned with utopias and revolutions'. And yet they are proposing a restructuring (adaptation without trauma they call it) of the British education system, based on the idea of recurrent education, and incorporating the compulsory school system.

Education and the Challenge of Change is a lively and challenging book. It deserves to be read and responded to. There is energy and enthusiasm in it, and it confronts some of the problems of effecting a transition from the present system to a recurrent system (should that be desirable) in a way that the *Yearbook* does not. It has, for instance, a good brief critique of compulsory schooling, and of the public examination system. Where I disagree with Flude and Parrott is in their belief that a recurrent education system would somehow not have to carry out the nasty selection and failure-manufacturing tasks that schools do at present. It would have to do just the same job to more people, more often, and I am not at all convinced, from a radical humanist point of view, that an extension of certification from adolescence to the grave is a good idea. There are so many things to be excited by in this book that it seems carping to complain about other things. But it's that sort of book. The authors are right to want to bring education and training closer together, but they seem unconcerned about the dangers involved. The aims must be to humanise training, and to open the way to the highest quality of education for those working men and women who are currently denied it, *not* to get education any further embroiled in the process of allocating unequal rewards.

What is so characteristically English about this work is a certain *magical* utopianism, or perhaps I should say, a certain po-faced Dickensian moralism. Here we have a couple of self-confessed hard-headed pragmatists arguing, for example, that 'all jobs should be designed with human dignity in mind'. Try telling that to Sir Michael Edwardes, or Sir Keith Joseph. Unless a transformation along these lines occurs very soon, then the system of recurrent education (should it be instituted sooner) must perforce serve the needs of a social system that does *not* design jobs with human dignity in mind. By all means let us press for a dramatic expansion of adult education; by all means let us take our chalk and blackboards — and our flipcharts and our VCRs — into the workplace and concern ourselves with the actual activities and processes and systems and relationships and contexts in which people are daily entangled. But let it be adult education for humanisation, for meaningful participation in society as whole human beings, and not as the automatic motors of fractional operations.

In conclusion, I see a danger in trying to ameliorate a destructive system of compulsory education for children by proposing a system of education extending throughout the whole of life with unending opportunities for certification — and failure. Do we want *that* sort of education looming over us for good?

27. Statement About The Key

I joined the Campaign for a Scottish Assembly in the spring of 1980, and was an active member over the next two years. The main task at that stage was to rally the Scottish people after the demoralising setback of the 1979 referendum. We realised that the words and images used had to symbolise renewal and potency. It was at a CSA meeting in Cannonball House, in the course of a discussion involving Iain Glen and others, that the image of the key was first proposed. It was adopted as the symbol of the Campaign, in juxtaposition with an image of the Assembly building (then surrounded with barbed wire and under police guard).

I prepared the following statement and read it on behalf of the Campaign outside the locked gates of the Assembly, beside a huge brass-coloured key made by students at the College of Art. That was on 1st March 1981, exactly two years after the debâcle.

Taking part in the Campaign had been like crossing a bridge. The warmth of the welcome, the openness of the discussion, the sense of joining in an effort to take responsibility, in which common ground was sought, differences respected, and narrow self-interest absent, contrasted with the unprincipled manoeuvrings of the Labour Party. Later that year I completed the transition and joined the SNP.

*

This is the key to unlock the door of the Scottish Assembly building.

The key stands for the power of the ordinary people of Scotland. Not the power to dominate, but the power to work together, to create and renew, and to take responsibility for our lives and our country.

The Campaign for an Assembly can become the key to open the prison in which the creativity of the Scottish people is stifled. The key to humanisation in a dehumanising situation. The key to the future, in a present becoming daily more like the past.

We call on the Scottish people to reach out their hands, turn the key in the lock, and open the door. Let us begin the process of thinking and acting together to create the kind of society we want.

28. *from* Adult Education and the Unemployed

In 1979, the District Committee of the WEA in South-East Scotland adopted a policy called New Directions, which involved a decision to redeploy some of their existing resources. As Tutor Organiser for Lothian I was asked to develop writers' workshops, and approaches to educational work with unemployed people and women with young children. The work with unemployed people began early in 1981, and still continues. It was written up by myself, Sally Griffiths, and our co-tutors, and published in 1984 as *Adult Education and the Unemployed*. Relevant chapters are included here.

*

Initial investigation and the pilot course

with Sally Griffiths

We decided that a sound way to discover the educational needs of unemployed people would be to start by conducting personal interviews with as many of them as possible. Although we would seek a certain amount of useful factual information (such as job histories, or the days of the week that would be most convenient for studying), our main purpose would be, first, to elicit and record what interviewees thought and felt about some of the main experiences of their lives, and second, to identify their study wishes.

An approach was devised using prompt questions. Thirty-one interviews were carried out, mostly in Edinburgh, during March and April 1981. Of the thirty-one interviewees, fifteen were men and sixteen were women. Each interview lasted between one and two hours, and took place, with one exception, in the interviewee's home.

In order to help those embarking on a similar task, the full text of the Background Notes for Interviewers is included as an appendix. We do not suggest others should copy our approach uncritically, but it provides something to push off against, in the process of arriving at a method appropriate to other circumstances.

More precise targetting of our work was a feature of the WEA's New Directions policy. In the unemployed we had already chosen a broad target group, but we wished to discriminate further still. We intended to make contact especially, but not exclusively, with the long-term unemployed, the unskilled and semi-skilled, women, and those who had left school at the first opportunity. We hoped, thus, to reverse the *apparently* natural tendency of Adult Education to drift up-market.

The Scottish Adult Basic Education Unit was approached for financial support. At the same time, Edinburgh University Settlement also approached SABEU for money to undertake work with the unemployed. It made sense for the Settlement and the WEA to join forces and from then on the project was a collaborative one.

As the texts of the interviews came in, it became clear that it would not be possible to digest the findings straight away. This task was deferred to the summer. In the meantime, a small team from the WEA, the Settlement and SABEU read the interviews and began to consider how best to create a programme for the pilot course. Prospective tutors were also involved at this stage. It is clear in retrospect that the outline curriculum and educational approach subsequently devised were a shunting together of different views and traditions, rather than an integration which, at that stage, given the shortage of time, would have been difficult to achieve.

An analysis was made of the interviewees' study interests which revealed the following information:

- Far and away the highest demand was for writing, reading, spelling, grammar, punctuation, and English; this group of study interests was wide-ranging, from basic language skills to creative writing, reading Shakespeare, and going to the theatre.

- After writing and reading, the greatest interests were in maths, arithmetic and welfare rights.

- After these basic concerns with language, number and income, came political, social and economic interests.

- Then came minority interests: psychology and relationships, Scottish themes (history, literature, culture), women's studies, history, philosophy, science and technology, running a business.

- Finally, there was a long list of interests expressed by only one or two people.

A lot of time was spent trying to group the study interests in various combinations, as if that was how a curriculum based on interests or wishes could be built. We have since realised that the study interests expressed by those interviewed cannot be taken as a final prescription but as a guide to broad zones of felt need or curiosity. Interests and felt needs *alone* do not give us the key to curriculum building. They have to be looked at *through* the main (personal and subjective) parts of the interviews. They have to be interpreted in the light of the experiences and responses, the whole lives, of the participants.

Furthermore, these two elements — study interests and life experiences — need to be illuminated by a third: the perspectives of the investigators and prospective tutors themselves. This process should yield a considered assessment of the educational wishes, needs and possibilities thrown up by the investigation.

After much consultation and discussion, it fell to the WEA Tutor Organiser to put together a package. Two things were required. First, an outline curriculum and structure to the day (it had already been made clear that we were offering a one day per week course, lasting roughly from 9.30 am till 3.30 pm). Second, an orientation to characterise and unite the course components.

The outline curriculum arrived at divided the day into three parts, giving participants choices in the first two, as follows:

9.30-11.00 am		11.30 am-1.00 pm		2.00-3.30 pm
Tackling Problems		Brush Up Your		One topic per week:
or	TEA BREAK	Skills: writing,	LUNCH BREAK	Health
Politics and		reading, number		Running a small
Sociology				business/
or		Writers' and		community
Human Relations		Readers' Workshop		enterprise
or				Unemployment
Women's Studies		Scottish Studies		Welfare
				Rights
				Trade Unions

The course would last five weeks.

The second requirement concerned what was contained within this outline, that is the content and approach to be adopted by tutors and organisers. A pre-course briefing session for tutors was held, and the following points were made. First, that the outline curriculum had been based on the interviews and that the educational approach to be adopted was also to be based on the idea of responding to the concerns identified in the interviews. The concerns of the course students would, of course, be the same, since places on the pilot course were offered only to interviewees. For this reason the tutors were all asked to read the interviews. Second, it was stressed that the students were not to be given long lectures or treated as empty vessels, and that it was important to draw out and further explore their experiences and opinions. The third point, on the other hand, recognised that it was not desirable to negate or deny the tutors' knowledge, and important to respond to the students' wish for new knowledge. Finally, attention was drawn to the battered self-confidence of the unemployed students. The individual tutors and the course as a whole had the task of confidence-building, of affirming the students as people, valuing their perceptions, stimulating their creativity. A balance had to be struck and an integration reached between these and the search for new knowledge.

Despite the evolving nature of the courses for unemployed people since the pilot course, our views about the educational approach have not changed.

Of the thirty-one interviewees, fifteen accepted a place on the pilot course (see Appendix 3). The social composition of the course membership can be studied on page 240. Those interviewees who joined the course are marked with an asterisk.

Friday was identified as the best day for a course to be attended by unemployed people and ever since, there has been an all-day course on a Friday. Similarly, the pilot course, like all the subsequent courses, took place in Riddle's Court Adult Education Centre, owned by Lothian Regional Council, situated in the middle of Edinburgh. This is a suite of rooms of various sizes, on several floors, which are pleasantly decorated, with comfortable chairs, and usually fairly warm. There is also a coffee bar area, and there is little traffic noise or other interruption to distract participants. The physical context of adult education is crucial. The Riddle's Court centre has made a major contribution to the success of the Unemployed Courses.

Assessment of pilot course

At the outset, some consideration was given to the question of assessment. Two representatives from Lothian Regional Council's Community Education Department agreed to act as external assessors, but due to pressure of work were unable to carry out this commitment. Course tutors were invited to make a written, personal assessment and to attend and contribute to a tutors' assessment session. The principle of responding to student concerns and experiences had an obvious implication in relation to assessment, namely that the most important assessment of all would come from the students themselves.

In all three forms of assessment sought, the stated aim was the same: to assess the quality of the educational and social experiences of the students on the course, in order to make the next course better, and in a wider sense, to develop an approach to education for unemployed people. After the pilot course, we no longer sought an external assessment. The process of taking into account students' recorded comments when planning future courses has become the principal mechanism for development in curriculum and approach, from course to course, over the last three years. Tutors have continued to meet to exchange ideas, share problems, and discuss proposals for change in the light of students' and their own observations.

On the pilot course, students were asked to attend an extra meeting to tell us what they thought of the course. Their comments can be summarised as follows:

- They expressed strong views about teaching and learning methods. They wanted to learn new things, but they also wanted to express their opinions and explore their own problems. Some expressed a desire for therapy. One student was appreciative of one approach: 'Whatever we were saying was very important to the tutor, as important as what he was saying to us.'

- They readily and easily got satisfaction from participation in small groups, where they felt secure. They often felt afraid in larger groups, but this fear could be mitigated, perhaps even dissolved, if the tutor of a large group led it in such a way as to enable everyone's participation, and prevent hogging of the air-waves by individuals; or if they felt they were learning a lot.

- The afternoon sessions, focusing on one topic a week, with an introductory talk by a speaker followed by discussion, were almost universally disliked. There were criticisms of organisation, content, and teaching method.

- Overall, they positively enjoyed the experience. Their interest had been aroused. 'It opens your scope up.' They had had good social experiences in small groups and at the tea and lunch breaks. They wanted to go on.

- Most were frustrated about having such a wide choice because some of the subjects they wanted to do clashed. A few wanted a taste of everything.

- It was felt to be a good thing that people came from a lot of different localities.

How did students feel about coming on the course, and why had they come? They answered as follows:

— to learn purely for the pleasure of learning
— to mix with people the same as myself
— to get solutions to personal problems
— for something to do
— to learn
— for re-education
— I lack confidence; it's not easy to say something in public
— I was nervous about coming on the course.

One pivotal discussion took place at the tutors' assessment of the pilot course. A suggestion was made by one tutor that the core of a course for unemployed people should consist of everyone looking at themselves and their situations, and that the educational approach to be adopted should be a problem-solving one. Another tutor made a counter-proposal which was favoured at the time and has guided our orientation since. She said the course must not go over into the area of therapy, although it will have therapeutic effects. The emphasis must remain on learning. The methods used should aim at getting the students to respond personally but not internally.

We now had the experience of the pilot course behind us, together with comments offered by the students, tutors and external assessors. The next task was to carry out a careful analysis of the interviews themselves. This was done during the summer months and written up in the form of a report whose aim was to identify some of the common experiences, concerns and themes of the interviewees. The text of this report follows.

Some unemployed adults and education

A report on thirty-one interviews with unemployed men and women carried out in Edinburgh in the first quarter of 1981, and first published by the WEA later that year.

The first and largest part summarises the comments of the interviewees in relation to some of their main life experiences. These are presented in the following order: school; family; living in peripheral housing schemes; paid work; trade unions; ill-health, accidents and medical treatment; experience of unemployment;

lack of money; depression; drink; fear of life; withdrawal from life; wish to escape; missed opportunities; hopes and aspirations; political opinions; search for work; help and support; welfare benefits; job centres and government training schemes; something to do; and adult education.

The second part presents the interviewees' study interests.

The third part summarises the other information obtained in the interviews.

The following appendices are added:
1. Briefing notes for interviewers.
2. Approach to obtaining interviewees.
3. Pilot course take-up.

I

School

None of the interviewees paints a picture of his or her school experiences as wholly satisfactory. About a third do, however, make some kind of positive comment. Five indicated that they liked primary or secondary school. Two liked both. Three say they did well at primary, and two say they did well at secondary. Several mention subjects they liked, such as woodwork, metalwork, art, technical drawing, and English.

In six cases there is gratitude towards individual teachers who paid close attention and gave real help. One 49-year-old interviewee remembers in detail the names of the three prizes he won in his last year at primary school. This was his only happy year at school, and a very good teacher figures prominently in his account of it.

One woman whose parents had separated, and who hated her foster mother, liked teachers because they were soft with her and called her 'wee yin'. Another says she needed teachers to love her. Yet another could only do well at a subject if she felt the teacher liked her.

These positive comments are outweighed by negative ones, however.

Most interviewees did not like school, or felt that the teachers did not like them, or did not pay attention to them, or concentrated on the brighter kids. Five felt that particular teachers did not like them because they were slow. Another group disliked particular teachers. One man refers to a primary school teacher who 'made my life a misery for a year' as a 'psychological hooligan'. Many were afraid in school (see the themes of violence and imposed order below). Secondary school was disliked even more than primary.

Most interviewees did badly in one or more subjects. Arithmetic and maths is the area most often mentioned (by twelve interviewees) as one where difficulties were experienced. The other problem area most frequently identified is reading and writing — including word recognition, spelling and grammar.

Examinations are often mentioned as a problem. Three specifically say they were good at class work but couldn't cope with exams. For at least three, exams were traumatic experiences. Others simply say they worried about exams, had problems with them, or weren't good at doing them. There is a hopeless and depressed tone in most of the comments about exams. There is frequent use of the words 'failed' and 'failure'.

There's a strong sense, reading the texts, of the school as a factory producing success and failure, with a lot of pain and distress as by-products. The examination system comes over as the biggest, most productive, and most dangerous machine in the factory.

Interviewees indicate a variety of responses to their bad school experiences. Five admit they did not pay attention. Five took the more drastic step of 'dogging' school, occasionally or frequently. And three, who had been evacuated, or lived in a children's home, or with foster parents, ran away altogether.

Almost all seem to have left school at the earliest opportunity. Several indicate that, as one puts it: 'you were just waiting until you could leave'. For another interviewee, the day he left school was the happiest day of his life. Another, with a more positive sense of his own dignity, 'couldn't wait to get away and be an adult and start work'.

Only two — both women — wish they could have stayed on at school. One had to leave in order to contribute to the family income. The other had more complex family pressure on her.

Another significant response to these bad experiences is to be found in how interviewees *feel* about themselves in relation to schoolwork and teachers. Many describe themselves as 'slow', 'bad', 'dunce', 'not good at', 'nervous', and one uses the phrase 'too far gone'. Several communicate a sense of defeat: 'I threw in the towel', 'I fell behind and couldn't catch up'.

A very small group describe themselves as tearaways or devils. One man uses the phrases 'horrible wee devil' and 'horrible mischievious wee beast'. There's an ambiguity here. On the one hand they are proud of themselves, they see themselves as unbroken. On the other, there's a sense that such creatures are not attractive to teachers. They feel disapproved of.

A larger group — between a fifth and a quarter of our sample — describe themselves as shy, awfy shy, shy and withdrawn, self-conscious.

Some interviewers make their own comments about how interviewees see themselves. These include: has no respect for himself, self-blame, low self-opinion, and — of one man — 'he starts out on a topic confidently enough, then falters through lack of nerve'.

Another important theme making its first appearance in the 'school' section of the interviews, is that of ill-health. Three say they were blue babies. Six interviewees mention illnesses or accidents in childhood as having kept them off school recurrently or for one significant period, and causing them to miss crucial stages in the learning of basic skills.

Nine mention the fear and/or experience of violence in school, in every case from teachers and in one case also from fellow pupils. Most of the nine mention the belt. One adds that a teacher also used his hands. One man describes getting twelve of the belt in the first four periods of secondary school, with the result that he lost interest in academic achievement and developed 'schoolitis'. An illiterate man describes getting three of the belt for leaving a written test blank. Later the teacher involved said to him: 'You should have told me you couldn't read.' Two describe headmasters as only being seen when belting or 'laying down the law'.

The theme of violence in school is linked to a wider pair of themes: imposed order and self-regulation. Awareness of these themes is shown by the interviewees in various ways. A small number have or are close to some sort of overview of school as a coercive system, in which a few adult figures of authority force a mass of children into regimented moulds, using the methods of bellringing, registration, checking up, and examination, with the belt as the main physical sanction. But these themes are more widely perceived at a particularistic level, in the form of resentment of the compulsory nature of schooling, and the lack of choice of subjects. When identifying subjects they did badly at or disliked, many interviewees *also* indicate that they objected to having to do the subject in question. When indicating the subjects they liked, they also frequently indicate that they would have preferred to spend more time on these subjects. Five actually go beyond this particularistic level of comment and say angrily that schools don't teach you the right things, what they teach has no relevance, subjects are old and outdated, there should be Modern Studies and General Studies, and that pupils should have some real authority and real choices. A very small number also objected to authoritarian teaching methods. One man describes teachers as 'ramming' and 'standing there lecturing us'. One woman adds: 'We always had to write what the teacher thought.'

Most interviewees, however, do not make such angry challenges. They just indicate they didn't like getting up to go to school, or that they felt bored or stifled while they were there, and in many cases preferred playing to working.

Family

Interviewees offer comments about their family experiences as children (referred to hereafter as childhood family), and as adults (adult family). Some young unmarried interviewees still live, as adults, in their childhood family.

In the childhood family, three out of thirty-one mention the divorce or permanent separation of their parents. This led to the interviewee living in children's homes or with foster parents. In each case the divorce caused distress to the interviewee, and the institutional and fostering arrangements did not work, in the sense of giving a new, stable, accepted family. Each of the three, as an adult, has formed a marriage or long-term relationship which has ended in divorce or permanent separation.

A total of eight (including the three mentioned above) have experienced the break-up of their own marriage or long-term relationship.

There is a theme, only made explicit in a few cases, of the search for emotional stability and security leading to marriage or the wish to marry at a very early age.

Two describe experiences of actual physical violence in the childhood family. One man indicates that 'if I got a hammering at school, I got a hammering at home'. The other is a woman whose childhood family seems to have been steeped in violent experiences and responses. She describes assaults on her by her brother, and by her on her brother. She describes a maiming assault by an outsider on her mother, in the family home. This woman also indicates a fear of rape, and of men, and on the other hand a wish or impulse to attack her fellows at work.

One woman describes actual physical violence in her adult family — 'I'm a battered wife'.

Five refer to their parents as very strict. Mothers and fathers are mentioned equally often. The mother of one interviewee was strict with her in adolescence. In another case, the mother forced her daughter to keep up certain hobby interests against her will. A father forced his son into a plumbing apprenticeship, against his will. Both parents forced one girl to continue with her studies after she left school when she would have preferred a 'year out'. And one woman describes an oppressive, duty-ridden childhood full of adult responsibilities, in which both parents were experienced as domineering.

A few indicate experiences of conflict within the adult family, which stop well short of physical violence: interviewees not getting on well with their husbands or wives; a man having conflicts with his daughter; a husband and wife — both unemployed — having arguments about the division of domestic labour, and who's the boss.

Where young adult interviewees are still living in the childhood family, such non-violent conflicts seem more numerous: a woman and her father getting on each other's nerves; a woman having an intense rivalry with and jealousy towards her brother, and to a lesser extent her sisters; and other similar examples.

Against this picture of intra-family conflict, we can set two instances of stability. A man describes his good relationship with his wife and daughters. A woman describes how well she gets on with her daughter, how much it is possible for them to talk about, and how she has always been careful not to impose her own ideas.

Among the interviewees' experiences of bringing up their own children there are several comments about children getting them down. Two women mention hyperactive children as particularly exhausting. One comments: 'I hate school holidays, I'll be glad when they've grown up.' Two women describe shouting at their children. One describes the immediate aftermath of the break-up of her first marriage:

> I found it hard to cope when I was on my own with them. I'd have taken my own life, but I knew they'd be put into homes. I took it out on them. They were battered babies in those days. I loved them but I couldn't cope.

This interviewee describes herself as having been 'saved' by her second husband. He could cope where she couldn't, and she now depends heavily on him. He for his part is investing a lot of energy and hope in helping her children with their school homework, taking them out, and encouraging them to share with others.

The theme of the need to depend on another, and to *be* for others, is taken up by several interviewees. Three women (and one man) describe being for their children and their husbands. The woman quoted above, speaking of herself and her second husband, says:

> We sacrifice our own nights out to give the kids a treat at weekends. We've no time for ourselves. We're never away from the kids.

The comment made by a young woman interviewee who has worked as a helper at a hostel for battered wives, helps to focus this theme more sharply. While her involvement at a hostel has helped to bring her out of herself, it has been a great strain, and she feels drained: 'I feel I've done my bit, and now I want something for myself.'

These people are on the horns of a serious dilemma: to be for others, or to be for self. It is a dilemma which confronts us all. But in families in straitened circumstances, it seems to cause particular anguish. One is almost forced to choose, one way or the other. Or perhaps the circumstances make the choice for you. Married women with small children in such circumstances seem often to become beings for others.

Living in large peripheral housing schemes

Two-thirds of our sample live in large peripheral housing schemes. The words they use to describe these environments are 'dull', 'bad', 'depressing', 'a place like this'. One woman describes the scheme as 'putting pressure on you'. There's a sense of being stuck in a bad place, with no chance of moving to a better one. The same woman is aware of a stigma on the area that rubs off on its residents and on their children. Two interviewees say their houses are damp. Overcrowding is mentioned by four, either overcrowding of people in houses, or houses in the area, or both. 'All those screaming kids.' There is a sense of communal lifestyle, within and between families, expressed by one interviewee as follows: 'I wouldn't like to live alone — never have.'

There's a reference to good neighbourliness. But this sense of communality coexists with a sense of isolation for individuals. Explaining his sense of solitude, one man speaks of 'being out here all day, like a housewife'.

Paid work

In this section, the dominant impression is of interviewees disliking, and sometimes hating, some or all of their jobs. There is frequent repetition of such terms as 'unsatisfying', 'unfulfilling', 'boring', 'monotonous', 'useless', 'unskilled', and 'soul-destroying'. One interviewee characterises his many experiences of paid work as 'doing things you didn't want to do'. For him, the thing was to get the job over, so as to enjoy one's leisure. Five interviewees specifically say they do not want a job of the kind they can get. There is a strong sense that failure at school has determined the kind of work one can expect, and that it won't be satisfying. This is experienced as frustrating.

One man who feels all his jobs have been far beneath his abilities describes the experience of clock-watching:

> Looking at the clock all the time, wondering when the next break is, when you're going to be finished, wishing your life away.

In three cases, initial opportunities for professional or skill training were abandoned. In two of these the interviewee has subsequently moved downwards from skilled to unskilled work. In the third case he has managed to switch from job to job in skilled, unskilled, and professional fields, amassing a total of twenty-five jobs at the age of thirty-three, with an average duration of four months.

This man's record is the most striking example of the theme of rapid change of jobs, which can be seen also in the job histories of four other male interviewees (that is, one-third of the men in the sample).

Another major theme, mentioned by nine interviewees, is the experience of conflicts at work. In one case, conflict was experienced with senior management, and in another with fellow workers. But in nearly all cases where conflict is mentioned, it is with immediate supervisors or foremen. One man describes supervision as an infringement on his freedom to get on with the job when he knows how to do it, and particularly resents the attention of supervisors who don't know what the job entails. Another speaks bitterly of the supervisor avoiding work, of strict rules applying to workers and lax ones to superiors. Most interviewees, however, simply identify the existence of the conflict and the distress they experienced in relation to it, without offering an explanation.

Only one man expresses a sense of deep alienation, of being at odds with *all* social contacts at work: senior management, supervisors and fellow workers:

> There was always a barrier. It was as if I was somewhere else. I couldn't make contact. It was as if I was some weird alien from outer space.

A counter theme to those above is that of enjoying or valuing your work. About twelve interviewees make some sort of positive comment about work (even if they also make negative comments). Seven say they want a job. Five say they enjoyed some of their jobs. Of these five, three enjoyed work because they got on well with workmates and supervisors. One simply enjoys general labouring. Another, describing the three jobs he enjoyed out of his total of fifteen, liked one because it was creative — there was a finished product, and the work involved both physical and mental effort. The second he liked because he experienced a sense of freedom doing it. In the third, he felt he had independence, could use his initiative, and was treated as an equal. Two other men mention the sense of achievement they got from work.

One woman says it's important that women should work. Another says it's important to enjoy work. A third woman likes shop work in a large store like Woolworths, because the job makes her feel important and gives her longed-for social contacts with fellow workers.

Four men make comments suggesting that work is important for what it helps you get away from, rather than any intrinsic satisfaction it may have. One is referring to personal emotional problems, and two to the sense of having nothing to do without a job. The fourth connects the loss of the esteem of his daughters with the fact of his worklessness, and feels that it would be restored if he could get a job — any job. He links esteem with money. Two others, though, indicate that money is not their primary motive for working.

Another important theme, already touched on, is that of losing or leaving jobs. Several mention leaving jobs voluntarily, following conflicts with superiors. One invented spurious medical grounds for leaving, as a cover. Another indicates that he packs in his job whenever he has a conflict with his supervisor.

One woman mentions leaving jobs involuntarily because of factors other than dissatisfaction or conflict, such as factory closure, her husband moving to another locality, and her divorce.

The young man referred to above as having enjoyed three jobs out of fifteen, was asked why he left even the jobs he enjoyed after a relatively short period. He replied that he usually felt the time had come to move on.

Seven interviewees mentioned being sacked, some several times. The reasons given include: failed skill test at work; couldn't operate a cash register; bad timekeeping; drop in personal output; accused of embezzlement; for being a Communist; on completion of his apprenticeship.

Literacy and numeracy problems relating to work figure in several comments. Two interviewees mention turning down jobs offered because they knew they couldn't cope with the counting involved. Numeracy problems seem to have been among the contributory factors in several sackings, including the case of alleged embezzlement.

One man with severe literacy difficulties states that when his illiteracy was discovered at work, no attempt was made to offer help. He was just left to get on with it. (This was a repeat of his experience at school, where his problems were contained rather than tackled, by giving him plasticine to play with, and frequently sending him down to the janitor's office to get the pencils sharpened.)

This man mentions a trick he employs which seems significant. In order to get or keep work, he makes a practice of offering to do things others won't do, such as working outside in the rain.

Finally, three interviewees mention, with intense bitterness, the sense that they are exploited in the jobs they do — that they get paid much less than the value of their labour to their employers.

Trade Unions

Only twelve interviewees made any comments about trade unions, in spite of positive prompting, indicating that trade unionism is not a major concern for those interviewed. Of the twelve, those holding unfavourable views about unions slightly outnumber those favouring unions. Negative comments about unions outweigh positive comments in a 2:1 ratio. Among the negative comments are: hostile to unions, unions hurt ordinary people, dislike left-wing influence in unions, unions not very effective, unions have got too strong, doesn't think much of union people, unions cause strikes, some people take shop stewards jobs to avoid work, spending their time supposedly on union business, stewards take the job to get perks, stewards are in with the management, people are more effective than unions.

Positive comments include: in favour of unions; was sacked for campaigning actively for his members on health and safety issues; workers need a union where the employer is the 'hire and fire' type; unions help you with your problems.

The most extended comment in favour of unions comes from a man who also makes some of the negative comments about stewards:

> the union's role is to give the workforce a chance, a fairer deal, instead of the bosses having complete power, being able to pick and choose between men, deciding who will work and who won't, and what they will do.

Cutting across the positive/negative polarity, there may be another theme, concerning shop-floor versus official trade unionism. The suspicion that some full-time officers and stewards are in with the management, avoiding work, or out for perks, taken together with the comment that people are more effective than unions, which are seen as ineffective, could be interpreted as the expression of a desire for more direct member participation in, and control over, union affairs.

Two women indicate that union membership was strongly discouraged by management in places where they worked. Two other women indicate ignorance about trade unions. The lack of response to prompts about trade unions on the part of the majority of interviewees suggests that such ignorance may be widespread.

Ill-health, accidents and medical treatment

A total of twelve interviewees indicate some kind of serious physical or mental ill-health, disability, accident at work, or failure in medical treatment, as a factor, and in some cases the main factor, in causing unemployment, or in making employment difficult to obtain.

Three indicate disabilities or diseases involving limbs. Three indicate childhood illnesses or accidents having a long-term effect on their employment prospects. Three indicate what they variously call mental or nervous breakdown, mental illness, and severe depression.

Four describe bad working conditions aggravating physical weaknesses and leading to job loss. Two of these cases involve fumes from machinery affecting sinus conditions, resulting in breathing difficulties. Another involves a man doing heavy driving who had a sequence of heart attacks and who was eventually ordered by his GP to leave the job. He has subsequently been successful in obtaining a number of job offers, which have been vetoed, no doubt wisely, by his GP. The significant contradiction here is that society is supplying this man with medical advice which prevents him from doing work that could be injurious, but is not helping him to obtain — or retrain for — work that would be more appropriate to his condition.

One other man mentions an industrial accident resulting in a serious and permanent disability.

Three indicate medical interventions which failed, making bad physical conditions worse. One of these interviewees now has a fear of hospitals.

In two cases, medical labels seem to have been applied to interviewees in a way that tends to predict the continuance of the condition labelled. The labels are 'nervous debility' and 'endogenous depression'. In both cases the interviewees have taken the labels as authoritative and permanent descriptions of themselves. Careful reading of the interview texts suggests that they both have human relations problems originating in childhood experiences. The application of these labels may not have been particularly helpful or appropriate.

The theme of human relations problems originating in or traceable through childhood experiences in the family and at school, and continuing into adulthood and the experiences of marriage, work and unemployment, is one that comes through in many of the interviews. How the needs implied by this theme could be met is a very important question.

The experience of unemployment

Some academic research suggests that unemployed people go through a definite sequence of stages in response to job loss. We did not attempt, in these interviews, to explore this area in that sort of structured way. We simply asked interviewees to say what it felt like, being unemployed.

Their comments about money, depression, drink, television, fear of life, withdrawal from life, and the wish to escape, have been taken out and are presented as separate themes.

Most of the comments about how unemployment feels are negative. Interviewees often describe feeling bored, frustrated, apathetic, powerless, alone, hopeless, impotent, very disappointed, losing heart, losing interest, having time on their hands, getting fed up, experiencing emotional strain, nagging their wives. (Unemployed women do not mention nagging their husbands.) Life has been blighted, everything seems bad, one's scope has been narrowed. The time that is now on their hands gives space for emotional and relationship problems to come out of their hidey-holes. One man says working is easier, and unemployment is more difficult. One unemployed woman, whose husband is also unemployed, points out that it puts special pressure on the man because he feels he can't provide for his wife and children. One man blames his unemployment for the break-up of his long-term relationship.

Another describes unemployment as like an illness or epidemic, hitting the family all at once. His two daughters, his son, his wife, and himself, have found themselves without jobs in the space of a year. He paints a picture of his son watching TV, reading, and taking drugs, and of his two daughters who have literacy problems:

> They sit around the house all day. They have no hobbies. They just do nothing all day and get bored.

One man feels it makes other people see you as a scrounger, and another — also with literacy problems — sees the main difficulties as having to fill in forms, and go to the DHSS and the broo.

Against this dominant picture, we can set the responses of four other interviewees. One woman does not experience *any* adverse effects as a result of being unemployed. Another is *not* bored, and does not even see herself as unemployed (though she does not have a paid job, and is bringing up children on her own). A young woman, after an initial response of lying in and watching TV, now enjoys cycling, reading, swimming and squash, and does not see herself as one of the '*really* unemployed'. Finally, one man points out that 'I can do all those things I couldn't do when I was in all those monotonous jobs'.

Lack of money

Two-thirds of the interviewees responded to a prompt which mentioned money incidentally. It's clear from their responses that lack of money is a major problem.

Four refer to worrying financial problems — rent arrears, electricity arrears, and debt. One mentions that his son is in trouble for stealing.

Three mention being unable to afford the equipment, materials, and travel involved in pursuing their hobbies.

Three say it is no longer possible to travel to visit friends or family at any distance. Three say they cannot go on holiday. Ten indicate they cannot go out to films or meet socially for a drink. Other effects of lack of money mentioned include: can't raise the cash needed to open a shop, can't get a flat of my own, can't buy decent clothes, can't afford to tax, insure and MOT the car, and can't buy things for the house.

There is a strong consensus that they do not get enough money in benefit. They need more, and feel they ought to get more. One woman, describing herself as 'trapped' by lack of cash, adds: 'More cash is the key'. There seems little room for doubt that lack of money forcibly narrows the horizons of unemployed people. One man comments:

> It amuses me when people who have money say it doesn't matter.

Two interviewees indicate that lack of money is not or has not until recently been a problem. One received a substantial sum in compensation for his industrial accident. The other got a redundancy payment, which enabled him to keep up his old lifestyle for a while. Now it is spent, and he too is feeling the pinch.

Depression

Twelve interviewees feel depressed about being unemployed. One speaks of bottling it up, another of taking it out on the kids, shouting at them, and two of seeking escape from depression through drink. Most mention other factors, as well as unemployment, as associated with the depression. One woman is depressed because she has no friends and her mother is dead. Another links her depression to the experiences of her strict duty-ridden childhood. Another woman is depressed by the state of the world — wars, terrorism, the threat of the Russians.

> Ah dinna ken why everybody cannae live in peace. Ah dinna ken whit they fight aboot.

Yet another is depressed by her lack of success in education, specifically her failure at maths. One man finds it depressing that he has no money to buy clothes. Another gets depressed thinking about life's disappointments:

> Life's just full of disappointments. I don't want to think about things — it makes me very depressed. I don't want to build up my hopes . . . I think things could have been very different if I'd stuck in at different jobs. I could have been better on in life.

One man finds his sense of impotence in relation to unemployment depressing. Another is certain that obtaining any job, however menial, would lift his depression within days. Yet another finds it depressing that all the unemployed people featured on a local radio programme, called Job Seekers, are graduates. He, in common with almost all the interviewees, has no qualifications or certificates of any kind.

Drink

Comments about drink were noted from thirteen interviewees. One never drinks, because she saw what it did to her father. Two say they can't afford it. Four say they drink a little, very occasionally. Two who used to drink heavily now drink much less.

Five — all men — say they drink a lot. Of these, one says he spends all his money on drink; another 'overdoes it — and likes it'; and two drink more now than when they were employed. One conceals his drinking from his wife, and she complains when she finds out. Three of these men make extended comments about drinking:

> With having no job and not much money, I just go out drinking
> to make up for it. . . . The less money I've got, the more I spend
> on drink.

> Somehow or other one can always afford a drink. Especially
> when you haven't got much money. It's a form of escapism.
> There's nothing I like better.

> I think there's a terrific temptation when you're unemployed
> to drink to pass the time, when you've money . . . and the
> temptation increases in relation to . . . emotional crisis . . . I
> could write a paper on the relation between unemployment,
> drink and emotional problems.

Television

Nine interviewees make noticeably brief comments about television,
as if TV were a familiar part of their lives and not worthy of special
note. One mentions preferring TV to drink. Another views
selectively, and objects to the number of American imports. The
woman suffering from severe depression, whose life experiences
come over as grim and oppressive, enjoys funny programmes.
Another woman, who has literacy and numeracy problems, and feels
bad about being slow, enjoys fast-moving programmes. Another
depressed man uses TV to escape from his depression. Two enjoy
violent programmes with hard-hitting good-guys like Starsky and
Hutch. One disapproves of violent programmes. Three say they
watch a lot of TV.

Fear of life, and withdrawal from life

These two themes are connected. The reason for distinguishing
between them is that there seems to be a fear of life at the early pre-
adult, adolescent, and young adult stages — a fear to venture out at
all. Then later, when people have ventured out and experienced
disappointment or hurt, a similar reaction of fear leads to
withdrawal.

Fear of life

It is striking that the theme of early fear of life is identified only by
women — eight out of our total of sixteen women interviewees. This
is not to say that the theme is not significant for the men, but they
don't mention it.

They speak of having been, or still being, afraid to go to the youth
club or to the community centre.

> I've never been to a youth club or a club in town. I've never had
> a boyfriend.

It seems to be a fear of doing something themselves. They want to watch others, but remain on the brink themselves, afraid to take the plunge. They fear exposure. They mention this fear in connection with such activities as skating, ski-ing, swimming, dancing, and taking part in adult education. They actually reject opportunities to take part which present themselves. One speaks of wanting to go back to where her mother lives, back to security. They offer explanations and rationalisations:

I'd like to dance, but I'm afraid to.

I can't be bothered with dancing, I'm too tired.

There seems to be a sexual dimension — several examples given involve boys, a brother, and the possibility of boyfriends.

One woman explains her feelings on this theme as follows — she is talking about the possibility of taking part in the WEA course for unemployed workers which has been mentioned by the interviewer:

I don't like to commit myself. I would like to watch and listen, without having to speak. I get so panicky if I feel I've got to say something.

Later, the same woman adds:

Unless I'm sure I can do something, I don't even try.

Another has experienced a very particular version of this fear, or perhaps, in her case, of early withdrawal. She was the victim of a traffic accident as a young child, which occurred when her brother was in charge of her, and from then on she says that she withdrew from any activity when it began to get too difficult for her. There is at least a hint that at a deep level the accident provided a pretext for withdrawing from participation in life.

Another connected, but distinct, fear of exposure mentioned, which has a special characteristic of concealment, is shame about one's illiteracy. It has to be hidden from the outside world.

Withdrawal from life

The response of withdrawal from life, which seems to occur at a later stage, after an initial period of exposure or even of wholehearted participation, is expressed by two men and one woman, but can be sensed as a significant theme for other interviewees though not mentioned by them. It is linked with job loss, with the failure of the search for work, with cumulative disappointment, and with not having enough money. It is a response of giving up, of not trying any more, of feeling unable to try. Life is reduced, in range of activities and in geographical scope. One interviewee's repertoire of activities has been narrowed down to reading, sleeping, going to the supermarket once a week, with some half-hearted attempts (rebuffed by his wife) to participate in the housework. Another interviewee who at various times in the past used to go walking and dancing, watched stockcar racing, bowled, played snooker, went out for a drink, to the pictures, and to variety shows, has now drastically narrowed down his range of activities. He looks back hopelessly to the good times that are gone.

The wish to escape

The theme of wishing to escape is expressed explicitly by seven interviewees, and can be sensed in the texts of other interviews. What is being escaped from, the real or imagined means, and the desired destination, vary.

One man feels his own life, and that of his wife, have been blighted by the loss of his job, the threat to his wife's job, and their failure to realise their long-term aspiration of finding work as a cook-and-gardener team. His fantasy is to go abroad and make a fresh start:

> I want to leave Britain because I just don't see any future here. This country is finished ... I can't have any ambitions with the way this country is. . . . We would like to better ourselves, take a definite line with our lives, but we can't do it.

Three others share this wish to escape, by emigrating to Italy, America, or Australia.

Two younger interviewees are discontented with the dullness of daily life, and with the restrictions of small town culture. One fantasises a transition from disco to reggae, to be achieved by moving from her small town to Aberdeen. The other has tried various means of escape: dope, drink, parties, games, dogs, horses, and jobs. None of them work, so he tries to escape again.

Missed opportunities

To read the texts of these interviews is to explore the dark side of our equal opportunity society. The opportunity to succeed implies the opportunity to fail. Here are opportunities lost, missed, bungled, thrown away, and even opportunities rejected. The seven interviewees who identify this theme contemplate their lost chances with nostalgia, and wry self-blame. A few feel hopeless: 'Oh it's too late.'

Hopes and aspirations

But in most cases hope has not been abandoned. Twenty-one interviewees identify one or more aspirations. Most often mentioned (nine times) is the desire for a job, but only three want any old job. The other six specify that they are after 'a job with satisfaction', 'a job that really interests me', 'a worthwhile job'. Several link this desire for a meaningful job with a wish for an adequate income, and dignity. One wants to be a teacher.

Next most frequently mentioned, by five interviewees, is the desire to write books, to be a professional writer, or to help produce a local newspaper. One woman, brought up by a series of foster parents, plans to write the story of her life, and has chosen the title already: *Queen o' the Orphans*.

Next comes the wish to travel, or to have holidays, especially abroad. One woman would like to have the first holiday of her life, and to be able to take her children camping. Two want to start their own business. Other aspirations mentioned are: to understand myself, to get out of here (peripheral housing scheme), to be able to buy things for the house, to have children, to 'have the best of both worlds' (explained as intelligent conversation at work and freedom to read at home), to go to plays, to get Maggie out, to get a good standard of education, to save a bit, to achieve something, to find something I really believe in, to broadcast my own music live and have it published, to get a course to make me good at maths.

Most of these aspirations are narrowly self-orientated. A few identify their own interests with those of their children, as in the case of this woman:

> I hope to have a good life with my bairns. To have holidays. To bring them up with a lot more happiness than I've had in my life. I hope they'll achieve more than I've ever done. I hope that education will pay dividends.

One man expresses his aspirations, for himself and everyone else, in the form of his ideal vision of socialism:

> In socialism every man should have the opportunity of doing what he's best at.

Political opinions

Eight interviewees made comments about national and world politics. There is no strong trend in these views, except perhaps a sense of grudge against society for being unfair to the unemployed, giving them no chance to play a meaningful part. One man demands:

I want to know why they're not doing anything about helping the unemployed.

Several feel that the country is going to the dogs. One doesn't trust politicians. Another feels politicians are like children. Another doesn't understand politics and therefore doesn't vote. Three blame Mrs Thatcher and her government.

She's earning such good money, she's nae time for the unemployed.

One supports her: 'somebody had to do it'. The same man believes there is a lot of waste of materials in our factories and on our construction sites. Another believes that a lot of the money collected in local rates is squandered. A woman fears the Russians and their navy, while a man 'loves and admires' the Soviet Union, which he describes as 'the Mother of Socialism'. Two want to see Scotland independent, and one — a refugee from Chile — is exasperated by the British working class which she sees as liking the monarchy, bought off with wages, houses, and cars, and lacking in political consciousness.

The search for work

The interviewers were not asked to prompt responses about the search for work, but nine interviewees offered comments about it. Three mention putting a great deal of effort into the search. Three speak of giving up after a while because you're getting nowhere. What's the point of going to the Job Centre when there are ten people after each vacancy? One man has been offered several jobs, only to have each vetoed by his GP on medical grounds. Another man has got close to a job offer but failed an eyesight test. One has been offered jobs in the demolition trade, which is all he's qualified for, but he turns them down because they're dirty and beneath his aspirations. Sometimes he does work on the side, to top up his benefit. Two women, refugees from Chile and Uganda, described experiences of racial discrimination in their job search, and one of them also mentions anti-communism. Finally, one woman finds that if you mention you have children, it puts potential employers off.

Help and support

The theme of help and support — the need for it, the lack of it, getting it, and attempting to give it — threads its way through at least twelve interviews. It is an unprompted theme, with complex implications, and needs a lot more exploration.

The sense of needing help comes across strongly. Help is felt to be needed in relation to spelling, reading, and maths difficulties, in relation to nervousness, illness, and understanding oneself and one's problems. The need for help is, in some cases, also resented and resisted. One man, recognising that he is now looking for help from others, nevertheless dislikes being put in that position, and blames the system.

There is also a sense that help is either not forthcoming or else that there is not enough of it. Parents in several cases are described as not having been supportive, or supportive enough, in childhood.

There is a theme of trying to help and failing. One woman, herself in multiple difficulties, describes trying unsuccessfully to support a colleague in a bad way at work. An unemployed man and his wife have tried unsuccessfully to help their unemployed daughters with their literacy problems.

There is a theme of women as supporters, looking after sick husbands, fathers, and children. One man who is ill speaks of his wife — also ill — as:

Keeping the whole thing together — she's been very good.

There's a theme of ineffective, inappropriate or even damaging help, for instance where one interviewee's mother insisted throughout her childhood that her nervousness was not as serious as in fact it was. Several examples are given of disabling medical help.

One woman found group therapy at a local hospital very helpful. Another got a lot of support from her aunt. One man has been amazed by the moral and material support he has had from friends during his period of unemployment. Several interviewees speak with gratitude of the help given by particular school teachers, literacy tutors and Citizens Rights workers.

More often, however, the public institutions in which interviewees find themselves — school, Job Centre, work situations, etc. — are found to be unhelpful. They often seem to be experienced as predicting continued failure on the part of the interviewee, even as punishing past failure, rather than helping them to get to the roots of their problems and put things right.

Four interviewees describe the sense of embarrassment and exposure involved where help is offered or given in public situations under the gaze of their peers.

It is important to add to this section another theme that one is aware of in reading the interviews. It must be difficult in some cases to be effectively helpful, or even sympathetic. A few interviewees come over as far gone, pathetic, unattractive. One is reminded of the comment about the significantly named Willy Loman, made by his wife, Linda, in Arthur Miller's play *Death of a Salesman:*

> Attention, attention must finally be paid to such a person.

Welfare benefits, Job Centres, and training and retraining

One interviewee comments that many people do not know what they are entitled to in welfare benefits. Given the extent of literacy problems among the thirty-one interviewees, this seems undeniable.

Another takes a militant and aggrieved view:

> They tell you on the one hand what you're entitled to, then they begrudge you and try to do you out of it.

Another interviewee, who worked for several years as a counter clerk in the DHSS, claims that management deliberately creates divisions between claimants and counter staff.

Among the five other interviewees who make comments in this area, there is a feeling that DHSS counter staff generally treat you well, but that Job Centre staff treat you badly.

One man who makes no negative statements about treatment by staff says he can read *some* of the cards in the Job Centre, but not most of them. He has now stopped bothering to go there.

Three interviewees make comments on Government Retraining or Rehabilitation Centres. These comments are negative. One describes the training as 'no good'. Another describes it as 'useless', and adds that having been to such a centre helps prevent you getting a job, because of the stigma attached. The third, a young woman whose self-opinion is very low, as a result of her school experience, comments that she 'failed again' at the Retraining Centre and adds: 'they could tell I wasn't any good'.

Three have had some experience of TOPS or PRETOPS courses. One was given a test and didn't see the point of it, so he walked out. The second was disappointed because she was not offered a job after her placement finished. And the third describes the PRETOPS course at the local college as 'bad'.

Something to do: creative hobbies, recreation, unpaid community work, and participation in voluntary associations

Most interviewees identify a need to find something to do. When they become unemployed, and their search for work fails or is abandoned, this need stands out in sharper relief.

In five cases they seem to experience difficulty in getting some activity going. These interviewees speak of lying in, hanging around, not being able to motivate themselves, or *wishing* they had something to do.

Half of the interviewees say they have got something to do. Among activities mentioned are: crochet, playing a musical instrument and making up tunes, gardening, patchwork, knitting, baking and cooking (as a hobby, not as housework), gambling, drawing and painting, writing poems and stories, repainting the house, shampooing the carpets, cycling, swimming, squash, listening to music, learning shorthand, watching TV, reading the papers, horror stories, science fiction, and Mills and Boon romances.

Two mention active church membership.

One man feels people are conned into being interested in sport. He is interested in culture and the arts, goes to lectures at the city museum, and takes part in a WEA writers' workshop, both of which he feels have opened up new horizons for him.

Five describe taking part in unpaid community work as very important and satisfying. One woman has been doing it for many years. It takes up most of her day, and she does not think of herself as unemployed. She helps with clubs for children of all ages and a lunch club for old folk. To her, the community centre is life. To another woman her voluntary work with the elderly is preferable to having a paid job. One man, the chairman of his local tenants' association, which provides lots of services in the area, comments:

> I get a lot of respect for what I do in the association.

He feels this involvement has given him something to do, and results in getting things done for everyone. He disapproves of those who take part in the work of the association out of selfish motives.

Adult education

In addition to mentioning specific study interests, which are described elsewhere in the report, eleven interviewees make comments about adult education. Several important themes can be identified in these comments.

Several interviewees draw attention to the importance of the marginal or incidental costs of participation in adult education, and the most frequently mentioned is bus fares. If you live in a housing scheme on one side of a city, and there is an otherwise suitable daily course for you in an FE College on the other side, the cost of bus fares mounts up and may be felt to be too high. Other such costs are lunches, paper and pens, and books.

Easily the most frequently identified complex of themes here derives from the interviewees' negative experiences of schooling and low regard for their abilities and past achievements. One interviewee, in response to the WEA's offer of a course based on her wishes, said she did not want to study because it sounded like school. Another describes her fear of going to night classes, where she felt the other students would know more than her. Several say they are not good in the normal class situation, and want either one-to-one tuition with a personal tutor, or a small group. Those who have experienced one-to-one tuition in the University Settlement's Literacy Programme are enthusiastic about it. One describes it as changing her life. She speaks of trying hard to please her tutor. Another indicates that her motivation is not in the pleasure of studying per se, but in the therapeutic effect of participation in the one-to-one or small group situation. One interviewee mentions the embarrassment felt in taking part in a Basic Maths class for adults.

Several indicate that they want to study purely out of interest, or for something to do.

One wishes to return to formal study with a view to obtaining qualifications.

For the interviewee who had a serious industrial accident to his back, Open University TV programmes are a great boon. He now plans to take a WEA Open University Preparatory Course.

II

Study interests (number of times mentioned)

Writing	17	Theatre/going to plays and shows	3
Reading	15	Sociology	3
Welfare Rights	11	Science	3
Maths/arithmetic	11	Scotland	3
Unemployment/recession	9	Scottish history	3
Politics	8	Family relationships	2
Social class	8	Drawing	2
Psychology	5	Technology	2
Spelling/grammar/punctuation	5	Writing and reading music	2
Economics	5	Cinema	2
Women's studies	5	How to create jobs	2
Work	5	How to cope with unemployment	2
Running a business/management	4	Typing	2
Philosophy	4	How local government works	
History	4	(rates, grants)	2
English	3	Religion	2

Study interests—contd. (number of times mentioned)

Memory	2	Art	1
Scottish literature	2	Nature Study	1
Scottish people's history	2	Biology	1
Relationships at work	1	Ecology	1
Friends and relationships	1	Health	1
Childhood	1	Anthropology	1
Good and bad feelings	1	Astronomy	1
Anxiety/guilt/tension	1	German	1
Psychoanalysis	1	Ancient Egypt	1
My family tree	1	Geography of other countries	1
Attitudes to unemployment	1	Welding	1
Trade unions	1	Stitching and sewing	1
Getting a job	1	Signwriting	1
Scottish Studies	1	Baking/cooking/confectionery	1
Scottish folk culture	1	Deaf and dumb language	1
Scottish politics	1	Filling in forms	1
Working with the handicapped	1	What to do with our money	1
How people acquire their moral		Computers	1
values	1	Immigration	1
		Country dancing	1

III

Other information

Number of interviewees: 31 (15 men, 16 women)

Ages: Range: 19-56 Average 33
Distribution:

under 20	1
20-29	15
30-39	4
40-49	8
50-59	3

Marital status:

Single 14		Cohabiting 1		Married 11
Separated 1		Divorced 4		

Children:

None	12
1-2	6
3-4	10
5+	3

Children's ages:	Range: 5 months–over 30 years	
	Distribution:	
	Child/most children aged 0-10	9
	11-20	4
	21+	5
	no indication of children's ages given	1

Telephone:	No phone or phone disconnected	18
	On telephone	13

Locality of residence:	Peripheral housing scheme	20
	Intermediate housing scheme	1
	Peripheral private housing area	1
	Intermediate private housing area	1
	Inner city private housing area	4
	Town near Edinburgh	3
	Village near Edinburgh	1

Would you like an offer of a place on the WEA course?	Yes	20
	Yes if content of interest	1
	Maybe	9
	No	0
	No indication	1

Days unable to attend:	None	11	Mon	3	Tues	5
	Wed	11	Thurs	7	Fri	2

Length of time unemployed:	Range: 2 weeks–35 years		
	Simplified breakdown:	0-6 months	8
		7 months-1 year	10
		1-2 years	3
		2-5 years	4
		over 5 years	5
		no indication	1
	Detailed breakdown:	0-1 month	1f
		1-3 months	1f 3m
		4-6 months	3m
		7-9 months	2f 3m
		10-12 months	3f 2m
		1-2 years	2f 1m
		2-5 years	1f 3m
		over 5 years	5f
		no indication	1f

Physical handicap:	Yes 8 No 23	
	Handicaps identified:	
	arthritis in hand	m
	deformed left arm	m

Physical handicap:	damage to back	m
	limited use both hands	m
	severe sinus trouble	m
	heart disease	m
	sciatica and arthritis	m
	nervous debility	f
	Handicaps identified by 1 woman out of 16	
	Handicaps identified by 7 men out of 15	

Trade unions:	Never been a member	18
	Has been a member, but not now	9
	Currently a member	4
	Is or has been a union member: men	11 out of 15
	women	2 out of 16

Unions mentioned:	T&GWU	6	AUEW	1	USDAW	1
	NUPE	1	NUM	1	NALGO	1

Community organisations: (excluding political parties)	Not a member of any	16 (6 m 10f)
	Member of one or more	15 (9m 6f)
	Organisations mentioned:	
	Community Centre Management Committee	1
	Community Centre	2
	Tenants' Association Committee	1
	Tenants' Association	?
	Community Association	2
	Handicapped Club Helper	1
	Youth Club Helper	1
	Football Committee	1
	Theatre Workshop	1
	Writers' Workshop	2
	Unemployed Workers' Association	1
	Church	2
	Housing Co-operative	1

Would a crêche be useful?	None said yes

Do you look after the children?	The 13 (6m, 7f) with children under 20 answered:		
	Yes	1 man	7 women
	No	4 men	0 women
	No indication	1 man	0 women

Summary of job histories

Sex	Age	No. of paid jobs	Average job duration (where calculable)	Last paid job	Normal work
m	33	9	11 months	Shop assistant	—
f	29	4	1 yr 11 months	Shop assistant	Shop work
f	56	1	—	University kitchen	Voluntary work
f	20	3	11½ months	Filing clerkess	—
f*	27	6	—	Waitress	
f	25	4	—	Assistant nurse	
m*	21	3	1 yr 10 months	Baker	Baker
m*	51	5	—	Milk rounds-man	Baker
m	39	7	—	Monument attendant	Storekeeping/clerical
f*	19	3	—	Drycleaners	Shop work
f*	45	0	—	Shop assistant	Shop assistant
f*	35	6	—	Typist	Secretarial
f*	25	5	—	Part-time cleaner	Unskilled work
f	40	7	—	—	Laundry/dry-cleaning/catering
m	24	?	—	Demolition	—
f	21	2	—	CSV	—
m*	50	8	—	Machine operator	—
f*	40	3	—	Shop assistant	—
f*	46	5	3 yrs 8 months	Bottling	Labouring
f	24	6	—	Machinist	—
m*	25	4	—	Storeman	—
m	26	3	—	Sign painter	Sign painting
m*	47	10	—	—	—
m	46	4+lots	—	Gardener	—
m	46	2	—	Heavy earth-moving plant driver	—
m*	49	9+	—	Tannoy tele-phone operator	Catering
f	21	5	—	—	—
m*	28	15	3 months	—	Unskilled temp
m*	22	6	11 months	—	Unskilled temp
f	28	3+	—	Bar trade	Bar trade
m	33	25	4 months	Information Centre	Community work/welfare rights

* accepted invitation to join pilot course

Some job histories

Male aged 22
Junior railman (2 years)
Labouring (6 months)
Fish processing (5 months)
Street cleaning (2½ years)
Painter (1 month)
Barman (6 weeks)

Male age 28
Apprentice grate builder (4 mths)
Apprentice butcher (1 day)
Apprentice grocer (3 months)
Changing tyres (2 months)
Lemonade vanboy (twice) (3 mths)
Message boy (6 months)
Warehouseman (4 months)
Barman (3 months)
Cooking/serving in canteen (3 mths)
Internal messenger (3 months)
Rehabilitation centre (4 months)
Storeman (2 months)
Waiter (1 week)
Cleaner (1 month)
Pre-Tops course (4 months)

Male age 33
Trainee navigation officer (8 mths)
Apprentice baker (very short period)
Army Catering Corps
Stacker in plastics factory (1 year)
Three other unskilled jobs (over
    3-year period)
Shop assistant (short period)
Government retraining scheme
    (6 weeks)

Male 39
Milkround boy
Foundry (clerical)
Timekeeper
Garage
Light Labouring
Storeman
Monument attendant

Male age 50
Baker
Apprentice store grocer
Store manager
Air Force (5 years)
Opencast coalminer
Bulldozer driver
Site agent
Assistant builder controller

Female age 19
Making cardboard crates
Woolworths (filling shelves)
Drycleaners

Female age 27
Waitress
Betting office
Factory cleaner
Nanny
Waitress (several times)

Female age 40
Apprentice printer (2 months)
Laundry (10 years)
Drycleaning
Restaurant kitchen
Restaurant under-manageress
Uniform presser
Machine operator (cleaners)

Female age 46
Bottler in lemonade factory
    (9½ years)
Laundry (1 year)
Biscuit factory (1 year)
Uniform manufacturers (machinist)
    (several years)
Bottling (dairy)

Female age 56
University kitchen (many years ago)
Plus voluntary work:
Helps with lunch club
Helps with kids and teenage clubs
Takes centre kids on outings

Appendix 1

> *Background notes and outline approach for interviewers*
> *interviewing unemployed people.*

The attached script is long and includes all the possible 'prompt' questions I could think of. I would not expect to actually say more than a third to a half of the script. The script, however, gives you a detailed idea of the sort of approach we want you to adopt. It also gives a broad framework, as follows:

1.   Introducing the interviewer, the project, and the purpose and scope of the interview.

2.   Identifying and exploring some of the interviewee's fundamental concerns in the following areas:
       School
       Work
       Family
       Social Life
       Aspirations/Hopes/Interests

3.   Identifying possible subject/thematic areas of education and gauging and exploring the interviewee's interest in them.

4.   Obtaining a few essential facts about the interviewee.

When we obtain an unemployed person's name and address and their permission for an interview, this will be followed by a brief visit by myself or Tony Graham of the University Settlement. At this visit we will confirm their willingness to be interviewed and that they fit the specifications already circulated to you. We will arrange a date, time and place of interview, which will probably be the interviewee's home. I will then ask you to undertake the interview, having first agreed with you the times of your availability. Please ensure that you turn up at the time arranged (i.e. don't arrive late). No interview should last longer than two hours. Please treat the interviewee with courtesy and respect, and not in any sense as a client. Remember — the interviewee is doing us a favour — not vice versa. Finally, we need to have your fair copy of the interview, which should be a full record, not a summary, plus any observations of your own, not later than one week after the interview, and in any case by April 10, 1981.

My name is ....
I'm from the Workers' Educational Association (WEA).
The reason we want to interview you is this:
      The WEA is concerned about the fact that there are now hundreds

of thousands of people in Scotland who are out of work, and who may be unlikely to get a job over the next period.

This applies especially to people who haven't got a trade or other qualification that might make them look attractive to an employer.

So we have decided, as a sort of experiment, to see if some of these people who are unemployed would like to spend some of their time studying. The idea is to organise a course one day a week, say from half-past nine in the morning to about four in the afternoon.

It would take place in rooms behind the WEA office in Riddle's Court, in the Lawnmarket — just across the road from Deacon Brodie's. There would be no charge for the course. The WEA, through Lothian Region, would provide tutors and lecturers, also some books and equipment, paper, and so on. You would have to pay 10p or so for tea and biscuits. You would bring your own piece, and people on the course and the tutors would eat together in the café which is part of the rooms at Riddle's Court. You would have to pay your own bus fares.

This trial course will start after Easter. It'll last for eight weeks. We're going to offer you a place on this course, and we hope you'll take up this offer. But if you don't want to — that's fair enough. We would still like to interview you, anyway.

By the way, supposing you did decide to go on the course, which days of the week would you definitely *not* be able to go?

Something I would like to emphasise really strongly is: it's not meant to be like school, or going back to school. It's not compulsory, it's not something you have to do. It's voluntary — you only do it if you want to.

Also the WEA aren't going to just decide out of their own head what you're to study. *That's the main reason for this interview.* We want to ask you what you're interested in, what sort of things concern you, worry you, what you hope for, what you'd like to know more about. What you'd like to study.

What I want to do now is this:
I've got a pen and a notebook. I'd like to ask you some questions to sort of jog your memory, get you talking about the things that really interest or concern you. I would like to write down what you say, word for word. Anything you don't want written down — just tell me. You don't need to *answer* my questions. You can talk about what you want, including things I haven't mentioned.

One last thing before we start:
I've got to make clear the things we *can't* offer you. We can't offer climbing, woodword, dressmaking, dancing — the sort of *craft* and

recreation things. They are available, as I'm sure you'll know, in community centres and sports centres. Also, we can't give you the sort of specialist training in a trade which you can get in a college.

What we can offer you is anything from reading and writing, at any level, through writers' workshops, to novels, poetry, plays, politics, economics, history, philosophy, psychology, trade unions, how to go about coping with unemployment, and doing something about it, and so on.

**We hope to find from you what you want,
and what level to pitch it at**

Note: In each area look for feelings and opinions.
Encourage the person to say what they really think.
Don't challenge any feeling or opinion expressed.
Don't ask all the questions — one or two may do.
The interviewee may launch off from one of these prompts — encourage that.
Leave plenty of time.
No hurry.

Okay, well let's get started then. There's several areas I thought you might be interested in. We could maybe start with SCHOOL. Your feelings about school, about education. How did you get on at school? What experiences did you have there? What did school make you feel about yourself? What did it make you feel about education? What did you feel about teachers? Other pupils? The headmaster? Did you ever dog school? Any subject you liked? Anyt' .ing you'd like to have studied more?

Then we could maybe move on to WORK. What sort of jobs have you had? What did you actually have to do? Did you like it? What other feelings/opinions have you got about the work you did? Was it useful? Worthwhile? Creative? Satisfying? Boring? Useless? Did you feel you were important and valued? Or just a name and number? What about your fellow workers: good mates, or bad feelings? What about your foreman, supervisor, your boss? A bully, a hard man, or weak, inconsistent, or supportive, concerned? Were you in a union? Which union was that? What did the boss think of the union? What did you think of the union? Were you actively involved or just a member? What do you feel about unions?

Gauge whether or not to raise these questions.
Gauge how far to go and when to stop.

Then there's FAMILY. What's your family set-up? By the way, *if you feel I'm prying into your personal life, just tell me you don't want to go into that.*

This interview will be treated confidentially, names will be kept separate from the detailed record of the interview.

Are you married? Single? On your own? Any kids? Living with your parents?

Does being unemployed put any sort of pressures on you, or cause any bad feeling in the family? Does it lead to rows? How do other members of the family see you? How do you see them? What do you think is the cause of these problems? What do you think can be done about them?

Is your family spread throughout the city? The country? Do you come from the area you live in? Or elsewhere?

What responsibilities have you in the family? What responsibilities do the others have? The children?

What do you spend time doing at home? Hobbies, interests? Nothing? What do you feel about TV? Any programmes you like? Dislike? Why?

Then there's the wider SOCIAL LIFE. What do you do for your social life? To relax, to see friends? Have you a local pub, a club you're a member of? Do you go swimming, golf, the bingo, the community centre? What do you do there — play darts, football training, chat, yoga, play bingo, play chess, dance, go to parties?

Are there other things that take you further afield? Such as fishing, visiting relatives, football matches?

Does being unemployed put limits on your social life? What would you do if you had a job and a bit more cash, that you find you can't do now?

What do you feel about drink — booze — alcohol? Is it a temptation to do a fair bit of drinking, as a means of escape, to relax? Or can you not afford it?

Then there's your ASPIRATIONS, your HOPES, your INTERESTS. What would you really like to do? What things do you wake up in the morning feeling: I wish I'd done that, if only I'd done this, I'd really like to do that.

What really depresses you about life/yourself, and how would you like it to be different? What do you think would lift that depression?

What things are you really interested in, keen on, would like to know more about?

Do you do much reading? What sort? Newspapers, magazines? Which? What do you like about them? Why do you read them?

I'm going to move on now, and read out a list of things, TOPICS, SUBJECTS OF STUDY. If any one of them interests you, I'd like you to interrupt me straight away, and tell me what sort of interest you might have in it.

Scotland, what it is to be Scottish, Scottish Politics, Scottish People's History, Scottish Literature.

Trade unions, shop stewards, full-time officials, the TUC, being a member of a union and taking part.

Religion, God, values for living, good and evil.

Class, social classes, studying the way people live in society, sociology, study of other societies.

Economics, the economy, employment, wages, prices, investment, capital, employers, shareholders, managers, workers.

Unemployment, its causes, political policies on unemployment, new technology, recession, how to cope with unemployment personally, the possibility of getting jobs, the possibility of creating jobs, campaigns against unemployment.

Psychology, psychoanalysis, therapy, personal relationships, family relationships, relationships at work, memory, childhood, good and bad feelings, anxiety, guilt, tension, pleasure, sex, friendship, rivalry. . . .

Work, the labour process, how it's organised, the production line, tools and machines, technology, new technology, nuclear technology, intermediate technology, what work feels like for workers, production and natural resources, ecology.

Philosophy, Philosophy of Science, Technology and its consequences, mathematics.

Politics, parties — Labour, Conservative, SNP, Communist, Liberal, Social Democrat, and so on. Political ideas. How parties are organised, what they stand for, politicians and their motives, how politics affects our life, ordinary people and politics.

Health, income, wealth, security, ownership, housing.

Writing, writing poetry, writing letters, writing memories, writing a diary, writing to relatives, writing stories, novels, punctuation, grammar, spelling.

Reading, reading newspapers, reading novels, reading romantic novels, reading poetry, plays, books.

Going to shows, going to the pictures, to plays (which ones, what do you like about them?).

Welfare rights, entitlements, social services.

Note: In each of these lists, when the interviewee says *yes* I'm interested in that, then the interviewer immediately follows up with encouraging, eliciting questions: what interest have you got in that? What do you feel about it? What's your view on it? What is it you'd like to explore further?

In each case the *aim* is to get what the interviewee really feels and thinks. Once she/he is in such a vein, the interviewer's job is to listen carefully, and write. Don't worry about asking the interviewee to wait a minute. Just say hang on, you're leaving me behind, wait till I get that down. That pause gives the interviewee another pause for thought, a chance to think more and further pursue, or qualify, thoughts.

Remember always — you are not a *News of the World* reporter — the probing is not to find out salacious details of people's private lives, but to find out what their most pressing and deepest interests and concerns are, and what they want/need to know more about.

Essential facts

Towards the end of the interview, once the interviewee has had a good innings and feels she/he has spoken about some of the things that really matter to him or her, we want you to get the following facts. When you are writing up the interview, make sure you put all these facts on a separate sheet. For the purpose of confidentiality, the fact-sheet and the interview itself will be stored separately and linked by a system of numbers.

Name:
Address:
Phone:
Age (exact or approx.):
Sex:
Married or single:
Children — Yes/No
If yes what age/s:
Does the interviewee look after the children and if so when does she/he leave them in the morning and have to be back in the afternoon:
Which days of the week interviewee can't come to course after Easter:
Would like the offer of a place on the course — Yes/no/maybe:
What was last job (if any):
What sort of work does interviewee normally get:
How long unemployed:
Which agencies is interviewee registered with e.g. DHSS, Job Centres, Careers Service, etc:
Does the interviewee have a physical handicap. If so what?
Is or was the interviewee a trade union member?
Which trade union?
Is or was interviewee a member of a Community Organisation *other* than a political party:
If so, which organisation?

Would you be able to come on the course if there was a crêche? Or would it not make any difference?
RETURN FAIR COPY OF INTERVIEW WITHIN A WEEK OF INTERVIEW. THANKS FOR YOUR VALUABLE HELP.

Appendix 2

WEA Unemployed Workers' Education Project

Interviewees

We want to interview at least thirty men and women between the ages of, say, 21 to 65 — a good mixture of ages.

They must be unemployed and without much prospect of getting a job in the next couple of years.

Ninety per cent should be unskilled or semi-skilled, and only 10 per cent having a skill or trade.

They should come from various localities of Edinburgh.

Fifty per cent men, 50 per cent women — a special effort is needed to ensure we get 50 per cent women.

No one who has previously been, or is eligible to go, to university, college or FE on a full-time grant-aided basis.

No one covered by MSC schemes (STEP etc).

They should be at various levels of literacy — from difficulties with basic reading and writing, up to fluency in reading and writing.

> Please contact: WEA
>   322 Lawnmarket
>   Edinburgh.

NB: We do not guarantee to interview people you put us in touch with. We'll choose a representative sample. Thanks for your help.

Interviewees were obtained from the following sources:
- Citizens' Rights Office (6)
- Edinburgh University Settlement Literacy Scheme (8)
- Community/Community Education Workers/ Centres (8)
- Job Centres (5)
- WEA Writers' Workshop (2)
- Suggested by interviewers (2)

In each case personal contact was made with potential interviewees, consent was sought for an interview, and a date, time, and place for interview arranged.

Interviewers were matched with interviewees on the basis of time of availability and a subjective assessment of compatability.

Appendix 3

Pilot course take-up

All thirty-one interviewees were encouraged to take up the offer of a place on the pilot course.

Fifteen did so, seven women and eight men. Of these, thirteen continued as effective students throughout. Two dropped out. One of these, a woman, wrote to say that she had become pregnant and felt very sick on the bus in from the peripheral housing scheme. She added that she found the course 'very enjoyable and interesting', and that what we were doing was 'a good thing for society'. The other drop-out was a man, whom we did not hear from. He has a very bad back as a result of an industrial injury, and finds difficulty in sitting for any length of time. It may be, also, that what we had to offer was not what he was after.

Efforts were made to follow up all those who did not take up the offer of a place. In five cases we were unsuccessful in our attempts at contact. In the remaining eleven cases, the following reasons for non-acceptance were identified:

Started a rehabilitation centre (2)

Got a job (2)

Moved house to another region or town (3)

Friday not a good day (1)

Interviewee's wife indicated that 'He's been away' (1)

One interviewee (the wife) in hospital with complications relating to pregnancy, and the other (the husband) having to be available all day for the other children (2).

Tying up loose ends

with Sally Griffiths

Following the pilot course and the publication of *Some Unemployed Adults and Education,* the WEA and Edinburgh University Settlement continued to work together. Seven further courses were held in Riddle's Court, on Fridays, lasting eight, nine or ten weeks,

depending on funding. In autumn 1983 and spring 1984 we were
able to expand the range of provision to include an open programme
of activities on Mondays. Various follow-up activities have also been
organised. A short residential course took place at Newbattle Abbey
College. Other WEA courses for unemployed people have been held
in Eyemouth, Falkirk and Stirling. Over 300 men and women have
taken part in the Lothian programme.

In 1984, Edinburgh University Settlement withdrew, and Lothian
Regional Council's Adult Basic Education Unit and Edinburgh
Walk-in Numeracy Centre are now involved in the project.

1. Funding

The costs of the initial investigation were met by a grant from the
Scottish Adult Basic Education Unit. Interviewers were paid at the
Extra-Mural rate. Tutors on the pilot course were paid by Lothian
Regional Council, at the same rate. Since then, Lothian Regional
Council has continued to pay the teaching costs of the programme.

The WEA and the University Settlement have each contributed the
time of one permanent member of staff. As well as organising all
aspects of the programme, they co-ordinate writers' and readers'
workshops, and run the coffee bar at breaks. The Riddle's Court
premises are provided free by Lothian Regional Council.

Successful appeals have been made to trade union bodies for
money to buy books, contribute towards the cost of students' bus
fares, and subsidise theatre and film visits. The most recent appeal
raised £450.

Coffee and biscuits are provided free. Publicity costs are shared by
the Settlement and the WEA.

The Scottish International Education Trust made a small grant for
the purchase of books. More recently a grant of £4,300 has been
received from the Gulbenkian Foundation, to encourage writers'
workshop publications.

2. The evolution of the curriculum

(a) The Friday course

From an initial pattern which emphasised student choice, yet by the
same token excluded options not chosen, we gradually evolved a
pattern of four key curricular components:

> Human Relations
> Writers' and Readers' Workshop
> Society and Politics Today
> Maths or Arithmetic.

These are the areas that the great majority of students on all courses have shown most interest in. On the Friday course itself, students are no longer confronted with choices.

The core group of tutors and organisers, which has stayed almost unchanged, with some new additions, since the pilot, regards the Friday course as a total package of inter-related parts. Students are encouraged to attend it all, but a small minority on every course choose to omit sections they find uncongenial.

Having identified these four key components, we attempted to timetable them all into one day. Various devices were used such as shortening breaks from 30 minutes to 15, lengthening the day by half an hour till 4.00 pm, and reducing sessions from one and a half hours to one and a quarter hours. This system operated for three courses, but was increasingly felt to be unsatisfactory by everyone.

Our dilemma was: on the one hand something had to give; on the other hand, we feared that if one key component was moved to another day, students would be unlikely to attend for it.

The dilemma was finally resolved in the autumn of 1983 by moving maths and arithmetic to Mondays as part of a new open programme.

The Friday course, with its three components of Human Relations, Writers' and Readers' Workshop, and Society and Politics Today, each lasting one and a half hours and running from 9.30-3.30, continues as the basic programme offered to new students.

(b) *Follow-up*

The idea of follow-up activities emerged early on. Students who had enjoyed the Friday course felt they were going to be dropped, and asked if they could come back for more. Funding for follow-up activities was almost non-existent, and at first all we could offer was a writers' workshop. This group flourished, recruiting members from two previous Friday courses and other unemployed people interested in writing. Their six months of work resulted in the publication of *Write Now*, in summer 1982. (*Write Now* is a popular collection of stories, poems and reminiscences.)

The size and range of the follow-up programme is affected by three factors:

(i)   the amount of part-time tutor money available

(ii) what a substantial number of students on the last course say they want — we cannot cater for tiny-minority interests

(iii) what we feel it is appropriate and possible to offer.

By the autumn of 1983 we were able to offer a more ambitious series of follow-up activities: Human Relations, Study Skills, and a writers' workshop. This led in turn to further requests for follow-up — for literature, and yet again, a writers' workshop.

A distinguishing characteristic of the follow-up programme is that it can be seen by participants either as a total package, or as separate parts.

The emergence of this full range of follow-up coincided with the expansion of the unemployed programme from one day to two, and the appearance of a new element: the open programme.

(c) *The open programme*

The idea behind the new Monday programme was that unemployed people unsure about committing themselves to the full-day course could be given the opportunity of joining separate activities. We hoped that those who began with, for example, one activity on a Monday, might be encouraged to attend the all-day Friday course next time round.

We were also aware that, for certain groups of women, a full-day commitment was impossible.

Maths and Arithmetic were moved from a Friday to a Monday. Requests for history led to the inclusion of a history project. The history tutor also made a case for Exercise, Relaxation, and Health and this was included as an experiment, with the name Body and Mind.

Although Writers' Workshops emphasising content and not style were very popular with students, there were still requests for help with spelling, punctuation and grammar. In the spring of 1983 Lothian Region's Adult Basic Education Unit offered to pay for a Creative Writing group, in response to those requests, and this was included in the Monday programme.

The existence of the open programme, alongside the follow-up programme and the Friday course, restores the element of choice, both to new students whether or not they join the Friday course, and to students who have already been through it.

The element of exclusion is minimised, because people can sign up for courses they missed, when the programme is repeated the following term.

(d) It is interesting to note that topics explored in the afternoons on the pilot course (sessions which were disliked by the students because of the way in which the topics were presented and discussed) have found their way back into the programme:

> —*unemployment* and *trade unions*, in the Society and Politics Today part of the Friday course

—*health* in the Body and Mind exercises and discussions; and
—*welfare rights* on the last day of the Friday course.
The only topic dropped entirely is running a small business.
Several sessions have been held on this theme, but at no stage have
unemployed students shown much interest in it.

(e) On the last day of the Friday course, the programme changes.
There is an information-giving session on welfare rights, at which
personal enquiries are also dealt with. Another session covers adult
education opportunities in Lothian, both full and part time,
including follow-up requests. Then there is a course assessment
session, co-ordinated by an outsider, with another outsider as
recorder. The course ends with celebratory drinks and readings of
work done by students in the Writers' and Readers' Workshop.

The Writers' and Readers' Workshop: evolving a method

The approach initially adopted drew on my experience of Tollcross
Writers' Workshop. TWW aimed at encouraging working-class
adults to write from their lives, with the emphasis on content rather
than style, and with little attention to spelling, punctuation, or
grammar. Auto-bio-graphy, or self-life-writing. All workshop
members wrote, including the WEA full-timer and volunteers who
started it, and if we couldn't write we tried to identify the blocks that
prevented us. Group members suggested the themes. A Teacher I
Hated Most, Religion and Me, A Strike I Took Part In, My Parents
Then and Now, were among the early ones. The writing was done at
home and read in the group, with discussion following each piece.
We always sat in a circle.

That was one of the main streams flowing into the Writers' and
Readers' Workshop on the Unemployed Course. But there were
other influences as well. There was an intention to have a reading
dimension, above and beyond the reading of members' own work.
Members could be asked what papers, books, or magazines they
read normally, and we could use some of that material in the group.
I also wanted to introduce them to books, poems, or plays they might
not have read, in such a way as to connect with what they wrote, or
with themes that emerged as important in discussion.

I realised that motivations for joining an Unemployed Course would differ from those for coming to a writers' workshop. People might not want to write, and basing a whole section of the course exclusively on writing might be threatening. From that point of view the readers dimension was a safety valve.

There is a cluster of characteristics of writers' workshops, which the present reader may not be aware of, and which are best described at this stage. In the course of the first year of TWW meetings, I became sharply aware of the role several of us played as careful listeners. On the surface it was a symbolic act, a show of attention and respect for the writing and the reader. Its deeper intention was equally important. By listening carefully one could identify some of the key themes or concerns of the reader, which could, if appropriate, be named and re-presented to the reader and the group, leading to further exploration, and opening in turn onto linked themes. Listening, considering, responding; associating; spotting, naming, and exploring themes, became features of the TWW process, growing within its simple framework of writing at home and reading in the group.

The management of the process was shared amongst the members, but not equally. It is possible to identify two opposite, but not antagonistic, tendencies. On the one hand there was a tendency for a co-ordinator or co-ordinators to emerge, taking a greater responsibility for the process than other members, but with limited rather than absolute right. On the other hand, there was a tendency towards each member taking responsibility for the process, to a greater or lesser extent. In the course of any one meeting it was possible to see both tendencies operating.

Listening, responding, and spotting themes — in other words, playing it by ear, but without the connotation of last-minute improvisation. Because you don't know what is going to happen, you don't plan rigidly in advance. Where TWW was concerned, after the first couple of meetings I personally didn't plan at all. Like other members, I wrote, turned up, and took it from there. But for writers' and readers' workshop meetings I usually *do* have a plan, of which some elements are used and others discarded, and which is some-times abandoned altogether. My part as co-ordinator of WRW is to be in charge, to exercise authority, deciding which leads to follow and which to leave. In leading in this way, however, I believe I am using my authority to promote the authority of each workshop member, to generate confidence and trust, to evoke contributions and responses, and develop mutuality.

A member may read a piece, or make a verbal contribution. I listen attentively. I may leave space for another member to respond. Or, if

I have spotted a theme that seems important, I may name it and invite
the speaker to take it further, turn to another member and seek her
response, throw it open to the whole group, or invite each member
in turn to contribute an experience or opinion relating to that theme.
Sometimes I ban comments on these contributions, sometimes I
invite them. Indiscriminate encouragement of negative comment can
produce an atmosphere of negation, full of heat rather than light, yet
such comments can be important as a means of disrupting sleepy
acquiescence, precipitating important opposing viewpoints, or
simply finding more pieces of the jigsaw. If it is used, it is used only
for a limited stretch of time. Allowing, yet limiting, space for the
contributions of those members who *need* to negate is a skill that
takes a while to develop.

This process — of recalling and saying, of reading and responding,
of listening and considering — creates *the possibility of
reconsidering*, or considering more deeply than before. It is a
particular kind of conversation, or dialogue, whose essence is that
those who take part are speaking from their core, and listening and
responding from their core. Speaking from your core like this seems
close to Paulo Freire's idea of saying your own word.

The content of it is the participants' reflection on their experience
of life, which can be seen as a well, and speaking from your core as
the act of drawing from the well. The terms 'experience' and
'relevance to life' are keywords from the educational debate of the
sixties and seventies, and it is important to distinguish the WRW
approach from either of the extreme poles in that debate. In WRW
the expression and celebration of experience are valued highly, but
listening and reconsidering in the light of what others say or write is
also an indispensable part of the process. At worst the expression of
experience can consist of sitting on live wires and screaming. In
giving written or spoken expression to their experiences of life,
participants are weighing, sorting, working out, struggling to
understand and evaluate, those experiences, as well as celebrating
them. The need to reconsider our experience implies the need to go
beyond it and benefit from the celebration and reconsiderations of
others. This provides us with an explanation of the value of reading
and writing in small groups, and also a justification for the use of
books and excerpts whose themes can link with personal
experiences, offering new insights, different ways of seeing and
feeling.

One final general feature of the WRW approach arises from a wish
to benefit from carry-over from one part of the course to another.
The deeper themes of life do not respect subject or professional
boundaries, so we often find ourselves writing and talking about
themes from the Human Relations and Politics sessions of the course.

J

With such a responsive method, it is impossible to point to a fixed curriculum, or even a series of stages. What we can do is follow the evolution of the method from course to course.

The pilot course began with a discussion of what we could write about. I invited members to write at home and read their work in the group. I asked what they had read and noted their interest in horror stories by Stephen King and James Herbert, Tolkein's *The Hobbit*, Famous Five books by Enid Blyton, and stories of love and adventure by Wilbur Smith and Jeffrey Jenkins. One member had read Jack Kerouac's *On the Road* and a book by Aldous Huxley.

I talked about the possibility of looking at writers like Joe Corrie, Liz Lochhead, Jimmy Boyle, George Orwell and Robert Tressell, poets like Wordsworth and Hopkins, and poets from other countries. I presented a poem about a mining disaster by Joe Corrie, and one by Peter Bott called 'Unemployment', but neither stimulated much interest. I sensed a potential antagonism to 'literature', remembered the question of motivation, and decided to home in on what members actually enjoyed. We made up a programme of reading based on expressed preference, which included *The Fog* by James Herbert and *Eagle in the Sky* by Wilbur Smith. My contributions to the list were *The Outsider* by Camus and Alan Spence's short story 'Christian Endeavour'. We bought multiple copies of these books, and members read them at home.

Our discussions on *The Outsider* and *The Fog* were lively. Several members identified with Meursault and his youthful hostility to falsity in the expression of feelings, hypocritical public morality and the boring character of normality. We discussed the sado-masochistic side of human relationships, cruelty, pleasure and the issue of death. The juxtaposition of *The Outsider* and *The Fog* was a lucky accident, since the deep themes of the two novels were connected, *The Fog* being a deliberate evocation or release of violence, evil, sexuality, a powerful disruption of normality.

The exploration of these themes led to discussion of the upsurge of violence and tension in the world, which led in turn to the theme of Peace. Other topics on which we wrote were An Important Event in Childhood, Status and Social Climbing, taking part in Violence at football matches, and the experience of using Drugs.

I put a lot into that workshop, and so did the other members. There were a lot of satisfactions. But it didn't seem right yet. The desire to write at home wasn't there as a given, as it was in TWW. Though all six members wrote once, and several wrote more often, on any one occasion there might only be two peices of writing brought in.

In the autumn of 1981 came the first full-length course, and with it a slight shift in emphasis in the WRW. Basically, it went further in the direction of becoming a readers' workshop, reflecting my anxiety to get in touch with what members *wanted*. At this stage we were running writers' and readers' workshops on three levels: basic, intermediate, and advanced. I had the last and largest group. This division reflected the alliance of the WEA with its liberal literary tradition, and the University Settlement, with its tradition of one-to-one literacy work, coming together to create a course meeting both literacy needs and literary interests.

At the start of the advanced writers' and readers' workshop, I again invited members to name books they enjoyed, and themes they would like to write about. The books mentioned were *Roots, Hatter's Castle, Tenko, The Ragged Trousered Philanthropists, 1984, Joey, The Second Son* and *Why I Am Afraid To Love*. There remained the problem of discovering how far these wants were shared. A list was made. The person introducing each book was asked to give its title, the author's name and asked to say briefly what it was about. We took a vote and came up with an order of popularity which put *1984* well out in front, with *Roots* next. *Hatter's Castle, Tenko, Joey* and *The Ragged Trousered Philanthropists* shared third place. At the same time the following themes were mentioned as worth writing about: The Experience of Hospitalisation; Experiences at the Job Centre, the DHSS and the Department of Employment; and My Happiest Journey.

Each member was given a copy of *Clock Work*, the first collection of stories and poems by members of TWW. The recognition that writing about personal experiences could be done by 'people like us', who had left school early without qualifications, was a source of confidence and a stimulus to write.

The procedure of inviting participants to name and vote on books they wished to read was repeated in the early spring course in 1982, when some of its limitations became apparent. While the autumn course had been more or less homogeneous in class terms (most members came from a manual working-class background, left school early, and had no higher education), the spring course, which was also larger in numbers, included a minority of unemployed graduates, university and college drop-outs, and others who had gone through a full six years of secondary schooling. Members of this minority were more widely read, and on the whole more self-confident. Several had feelings of cynicism, resentment, and suspicion. Are we being exploited? Are we being observed? Are we the objects of someone's research, several of them asked? Some of their themes differed from those of course members who had left school early, and this posed the problem for me as WRW co-ordinator of making space for, and harmonising, the contributions of people with different needs.

The group opted to read the following texts: Steinbeck's *Winter of Our Discontent*, Orwell's *Homage to Catalonia*, and Lawrence's *Love Among the Hay-Stacks*; Greenwood's *Love on the Dole*, Osborne's *Look Back in Anger*, Le Guin's *The Dispossessed*, an anthology, *Modern Irish Short Stories*, and Tressell's *Ragged Trousered Philanthropists*.

I invited members to read one agreed book per week, to be discussed at our next meeting, but though this led to lively discussions, it was unsuccessful because most had not read it or read only part of it, when the day came.

Co-ordinating these meetings was one of the hardest jobs I have had. We lost members from the less and more educated ends of the spectrum. We had to work through strong feelings of suspicion early on. And there was the challenge of handling the participation of one or two members with personal difficulties. It was a tribute to the efforts of those who stayed with it that trust and cohesion did grow, and there was some valuable writing and talking on such themes as abortion, class, religion, and nostalgia.

Various lessons were learned from this experience. There was too big a programme of reading. Reading a whole book for a meeting led to splintering of focus, since members were responding to different parts or themes in the same book, if they had read it, linking them with different personal experiences and creating a hornets' nest of simultaneously buzzing themes which could not all be tackled at once. Some members felt bad if they hadn't read or completed the book, thus stimulating the very feelings of hopelessness and self-blame we were trying to diminish. Mixing those who had left school early with quite a low opinion of their intellectual ability, and those who had gone on to Highers, college or university was unproductive. The group was too large.

The last lesson, and the one hardest for me to grasp, was that basing the WRW programme so much on rather haphazardly identified *wants* fuels a process in which wants become demands aimed at testing how far the tutor is authoritarian or democratic, and ultimately at negating the authority of the tutor, turning him or her into a servant. It was as if I had forgotten about the interviews we had carred out a year previously, in the course of which we had discovered common experiences, difficulties and frustrated needs, my assessment of which should have had a much greater influence on the content of the WRW programme. In my anxiety to discover members' wants, I was undermining the authority of my own knowledge.

These lessons weren't instantly obvious. I had a certain resistance to seeing them. They were perceived gradually over a period of months.

At this point Sally and I became involved in planning a short residential course for unemployed people at Newbattle Abbey College, with writers' workshop sessions as a major component. Susan Maciver planned these sessions with us, and in doing so helped to reconstruct my own approach. Susan had experience as a literacy tutor and trainer, a tutor of Women in Literature classes, and as a writers' workshop co-ordinator. The essence of her method was to use short excerpts from texts by well-known writers, illustrating a particular theme or stage of life. These excerpts were photo-copied and read in the session as a stimulus. Participants then spoke about their own experiences, and this was followed by writing done in the group. The approach clearly worked and had implications for the Unemployed Course.

One outcome was that we decided to forget about the three levels, and have instead three mixed workshops of equal size. We also abandoned for the time being the effort to tackle basic functional skills problems. By the time we came to publicise the autumn course, we had made another important decision: to exclude from the course those with Highers or A-levels and those who had been full-time college or university students. The project had begun with a clear commitment to those who had left school early, and we were now reaffirming that commitment and giving it teeth.

In the meantime, one of our follow-up groups, the Writers' Workshop and Publishing Project, whose members came from the two previous courses, had produced a book. Called *Write Now*, it reproduced in an attractive format some of the stories, poems, reminiscences and jokes written by members of the Unemployed Courses, and other unemployed people living in the city and surrounding areas. Simultaneously, Tollcross and Leith Writers' Workshops brought out *Clock Work Two*, *With Foot in Mouth* and *Multistories*.

The publication of these books gave the writers' workshop movement a renewed impetus, and gave us a new tool to use: multiple copies of texts written by people like those joining the course.

The autumn course consisted again of working-class people. On the first day each received their complimentary copy of *Write Now*. I hoped to combine some features of Susan's approach (writing in the group, and using stimulus material), features of the TWW approach (writing at home, reading and discussing in the group), and some of the methods I'd developed on previous courses (playing it by ear, association, naming and exploring themes). This workshop would therefore be a crucial transition.

As usual we arranged the seats in a circle. I talked about how a writers' workshop operated, stressing that members were just ordinary people without much experience of writing, and little hope of becoming famous authors. I invited them to look through their copies of *Write Now* and pick out any pieces they fancied. Several were read out and approving comments were made. Then I asked if each member would introduce herself or himself, giving their name, saying whether or not they did any writing, and if they had ever wanted to write. What sort of books or papers did they enjoy? I turned to the man on my immediate right, who wore a dark suit and had a lined face, with signs of depression and diffidence. Pass, I pass. Don't want to say anything. My heart hit the floor, but I managed to say that's fine, okay, and asked the woman sitting next to him. After hesitating for a moment, she took the plunge. I'd love to write, but I've got no talent, she said, explaining that she liked reading biographies and autobiogrpahies. We were off. I made a point of writing down the key things each person said, occasionally asking a question. Gradually others began to ask questions, or offer comments. Slowly we went round, with contributions like these:

> I read Wilbur Smith — escapist stuff.

> I identify with the devil.

> When I write it's not natural.

> I like comparing the book with the film.

> I've read no books since I left school . . . I write to my friends abroad. In primary school I used to write down things that came to mind.

> I like Shakespeare's Roman history plays . . . I feel my English isn't very good.

> I like the *Kon Tiki Expedition, Born Free, Expedition into the Sahara, Ice Station Zebra, Day of the Jackal.*

> I like Henry Miller. I write letters. I read as much as I can, but you need quiet, and that's difficult to find. D. H. Lawrence is the best I've ever come across.

Here the first challenge was made. In response to this man's contribution, first one woman, then another, interjected:

> Oh, I find Lawrence depressing.

Lawrence is boring. Did you see *Sons and Lovers* on the television — I can't get anything out of it!

And so on, round the group. When I had finished writing the points made by the last contributor I turned again to the man on my right, and asked if he wanted to say anything now. I'd like you to read that, he said, indicating a page in his copy of *Write Now*. Would you like to read it, I asked. No, you read it. It was a poem by Walter MacIvor, entitled 'Old Age'. The theme was loneliness and aloneness, powerfully and briefly realised. Do you want to say anything about it? No. It's very good.

What happened then was like in one of those high-excitement aeroplane accident films, when a door shoots off into space, and people and objects are sucked out the hole one after another. Without my inviting any response to this little poem, members began to contribute stories or comments from their own lives about old age, bereavement, isolation, emptiness, loss. We had stumbled, early and unexpectedly, on a theme important to members. After most of us had contributed, I intervened to name it. Look, can I stop you there, I think it is obvious that this theme of loneliness or aloneness is important to us. I'd like you to stop for a moment and think of an incident or a situation in your own life which has to do with this theme, and then write it down. There's some pens and paper here. Don't bother about spelling or punctuation or anything. Just write down what it means to you.

All of us wrote, or tried to, and everyone willing to do so read out their contribution. Some stated an experience or feeling openly. Others hinted at one, twisting and twining around it, aiming to obscure as much as to reveal. The man who introduced the poem read out a single line so bare and enigmatic that it expressed little more than the determination to reveal nothing about his evident loneliness. The woman who found Lawrence boring said she couldn't write at all.

The time was up. I invited members to have a read through *Write Now* at home, and see if there was anything else in it they liked. If anybody would like to write for the next meeting, they could write more on the theme of loneliness or aloneness, or on any other theme of their choice.

Later on we read, at home, Lawrence's short story, *The Man Who Died*, but nobody thought much of it. I invited members to bring in books, passages, and newspaper cuttings they enjoyed and would like to present to the group. We read several powerful pieces by a group member who had already contributed to a writers' workshop publication. His willingness to present, in writing, some of his own difficult experiences helped others to do the same, though it may have inhibited a few initially. Themes we wrote about included Fear of Teachers, Doctors Now and In the Past, and A Mystery in My Life. We used the first pages of Jimmy Boyle's *A Sense of Freedom*, and some short imagist/objectivist poems by Carles Reznikof, as stimulus material. And we devoted some time during the last three meetings to part-reading Tom McGrath and Jimmy Boyle's play, *The Hard Man*. It is valuable because it neither glamorises violence nor moralises about it, but realises it in an amusing way. It can be used as a dramatic codification of poverty, violence, personal responsibility, crime and punishment, and lead into discussion of the sexual, emotional, and economic division of labour between men and women.

This workshop had another significant feature. Several members had deep-seated blocks to writing, entwined with blocks about expressing some of their personal difficulties. But because they cohered early as a group, a cohesion based partly on recognising the existence of these blocks and difficulties, it was possible for most of them not to flee, or retreat into silence, but gradually to unfold. Several of the most blocked members are now contributing regularly to one of the city's writers' workshops. The woman who said she couldn't write at all has trained to be an adult literacy tutor.

Writers' and readers' workshops need to be elastic, to hold together those who want to expose their lives, and those who want to keep things tight, and need a slower process of unfolding. The crucial enabling element is the development of an atmosphere of mutual support.

The theme of blocks is one that comes up in the early stages of most workshops. I usually encourage members to discuss them, often on several occasions. As a blocked writer myself, I understand the experience from inside. Even when the internal taps are opened, some members go through agonies plucking up the courage to write from life and read to the group. It can feel like presenting yourself naked in front of mocking observers.

The following list includes most of the blocks members describe, in the terms in which they are presented:

I'm no good at spelling/writing/grammar/punctuation.

I didn't like English at school/I didn't do well at school.

I don't like what I've written/keep changing it/tear it up/destroy it.

My writing is poor quality/uninteresting/inferior to written literary English.

My experience of life is unimportant/not interesting/worthless/bad/no good.

I don't want to talk/write about my experiences.

I don't want to reveal/want to conceal/am ashamed of my experiences/needs/wishes.

I'm suspicious/are you a trick cyclist/what's going on here?

Advice sometimes given includes the following:

Don't choose words/don't revise/use the first words that come.

If you're unsure or self-doubting, write that in as part of the text, as and when you feel it.

Forget about spelling/punctuation/grammar for the time being.

It doesn't matter how little (or how much) you write.

Write straight from experience without embellishment.

If you can't write, or don't want to, then don't do it. Contribute by listening to others and commenting on their work, or by talking from your own experience. Writing may come later.

The next course, in spring 1983, was one in which I felt a whole approach formed at last, twining together the different strands. For me as co-ordinator it was the easiest of all. Responses came readily. Members opened out when they could, trusting the process, and supporting those who couldn't yet take that step. Perhaps it was too easy, missing out on some of the difficulties and blockages, and the themes they can throw up.

Here is a list of the themes, stimulus-reading and writing forms used.

Theme	Stimulus Reading	Writing Form
Earliest Memories	from *A Sense of Freedom* by Jimmy Boyle	autobiography
Teenage Experiences	*A Teenager in the 1950s* by Helen Ann Reid (from *Write Now*)	autobiography
Love	*Giro Plus Giro Equals Love* by James Houldsworth	writing in third person
Religion	'Christian Endeavour' by Alan Spence	autobiography
Visual perceptions of external situations	Imagist/Objectivist Poems by Charles Reznikoff	short poems

Theme	Stimulus Reading	Writing Form
Experience of Redundancy/Unemployment	*Unemployed* by Peter J. Bott *The Ragged Trousered Philanthropists* by Robert Tressell (read at home over several weeks)	autobiography
Women/Men Relations/ Perceptions	Six Poems from *Memo for Spring* by Liz Lochhead Three poems by men (Alasdair MacLean, Alan Brownjohn, Bertolt Brecht) 'A Woman Misunderstood' by Angie (from Edinburgh Women's Newsletter, November 1982)	
Scottish Society/ violence/men/women	*The Hard Man* by Tom McGrath and Jimmy Boyle (part-read over several meetings)	
Hell/Distress/Crisis in Mid-life	First and Third cantos of Dante's *Inferno* (translated by C. H. Sisson)	autobiographical
Say our own word/ transcribing speech	Selection from *Six Glasgow Poems, Bunnit Husslin, Unrelated Incidents* and *Ghostie Men* by Tom Leonard *A Relationship* by David Logan	autobiographical transcription of present or childhood speech

The Writers' and Readers' Workshop has grown and changed. This process can be expected to continue, though there are times when my own needs make me long for the stability of a fixed curriculum. It is an indispensable part of the course because, more than any other, it challenges participants to draw from the well of their experiences of life. This is a difficult challenge. It seems like being asked to find strength in weakness. When a person has become unemployed, and in most cases feels discarded or of little worth, their self is a very important source of strength that is left. In a radio interview to publicise one of the courses, I argued that 'they can take away your job, they can take away your income, they can take away your status, they can even take away your house — but they can't take away your experience of life, or your response to it.' A key vehicle of our response is our voice. It has to be added, however, that we cannot draw strength from the well of ourselves *on our own*. We need the attention, support and responses of others, and we need to give them our support. The Writers' and Readers' Workshop helps to build up this mutuality.

I would like to acknowledge the deep influence that Alan Harrow and Janet Hassan have had on my approach to WRW.

29. Writers' Workshops in Edinburgh

Following the WEA's policy change, a group of volunteers from the Edinburgh Industrial Branch and I decided to target the poorer streets in the Tollcross area of the city, and to explore with residents the possibility of creating what we tentatively called a Writing Workshop. That was how Tollcross Writers' Workshop was born. The movement spread rapidly throughout the central belt, leading two years later to the first Scottish Writers' Workshop Come-All-Ye at Newbattle Abbey College. This article appeared in the pages of the Edinburgh Council of Social Service Newsletter in 1982.

*

Guilds or circles of writers are to be found in most major cities and Edinburgh is no exception. These are groupings of established or aspiring writers concerned with achieving publication through the conventional outlets: commercially published newspapers, magazines or books. Such groups tend to be orientated towards success (successful publication, that is), and if they are interested in the content or process of writing, it is often with a view to improving style or learning to meet the requirements of a particular outlet. There is a sense that writing is a means to an end, rather than an end in itself. Writers who do not achieve the success of publication have their failure certificated in the form of rejection slips.

Alongside these associations, but really in contradiction to them (although it is not an aggressively asserted contradiction) is the writers' workshop movement, a young movement with a very different identity. Writers' workshops usually form in working-class or disadvantaged localities, though that is not always the case. I know of workshops currently or recently operating in Gorgie/Dalry, Tollcross, Leith, Pilton, Craigmillar, Drummond High School and Wester Hailes (which has two — a Women's Writers' Workshop and an Unemployed Writers' Workshop). There are a few others, formed not on the basis of locality, but condition, common interest, or ideological orientation, such as the feminist writers' workshop associated with the Stramullion publishing group, or the Edinburgh Unemployed Writers' Workshop.

It's important to be cautious in making generalisations about such a movement. After all, if there are differences in orientation, condition, or interest, surely each workshop will be distinctive in its purpose and its mode of practice? On the basis of my own limited experience, I would say that they probably *are* all distinctive. But I also believe they have major values in common.

Briefly, these common values are: first, the writers' workshop movement tends to encourage the involvement of anyone, not just those likely to succeed; those who left school at the earliest opportunity, who did badly at school, or did not enjoy school; those who have experienced, as adults, work situations which do not give outlets for their creativity or sense of responsibility; and those with difficulties or disadvantages of one kind or another. Second, it places great emphasis on writing about personal experiences: writing is seen as a means of exploring, expressing, recreating, celebrating and reflecting upon actual experiences the writer has had, whether good or bad. Methods and orientations vary widely, but this emphasis on personal experience is shared. Third, although personal autonomy and personal development are valued highly in the movement, they are valued in the context of the development of mutuality, support, and solidarity. In other words, the individual and the communal are not counterposed, but are seen as a proper context for each other. Again, methods vary in practice, but this is a value in common. Fourth, writing and reading to each other in the group are held to be ends or values in themselves, and not *primarily* means to publication and success. In some groups, members write at home, in solitude. In others, they write during group meetings. In every case reading to each other at meetings is the heart of the workshop's life. Fifth, although there may be an emphasis on the development of style (this varies from group to group), comments after a member has read are often concerned with the content of the experiences written about, or similar experiences other members have had. Sixth, although writing for group meetings is the norm, public readings and occasional publications by the group are regarded as desirable extensions of its work, so long as the writings of all the group members are represented. These publications range from the very finely printed (such as *Hens in the Hay*) to the cheap duplicated edition (such as Wester Hailes Women's Writers). The distinction has nothing to do with the quality of the work, but reflects an unresolved debate about whether to go for good quality publications which cost more to sell (and therefore exclude some working-class readers) or go for cheaply produced publications which cost very little and are within the financial reach of all.

Most writers' workshop meetings take the form of an actual circle. There is sometimes a co-ordinator, who plays either a minimally co-ordinating, or a teaching, or a leading role. (It varies from group to group, and from meeting to meeting.) The co-ordinator, however, also writes and reads as an ordinary member, and members share responsibility for order, attentiveness, response, mutual support, and the furtherance of the group's aims and projects.

Information about when and where writers' workshops meet can be got from the Workers' Educational Association (226 3456), the Adult Learning Project (337 3659), and Wester Hailes Education Centre Community Affairs Department (442 2201).

The following writers' workshop publications are available for sale:

Clock Work	(Tollcross Writers' Workshop, £1.00)
Clock Work Two	(Tollcross Writers' Workshop, £1.30)
With Foot in Mouth	(Jacqueline Robertson, TWW, £1.00)
Multi Stories	(Leith Writers' Workshop, 60p)
Write Now	(Edinburgh Unemployed Writers' Workshop, £1.00)
Clamjamfrey	(Wester Hailes Writers' Workshop, £1.00)
First Lines	(Wester Hailes Learning Exchange Group, 20p)
Glimpses of Childhood	(Wester Hailes Learning Exchange Group, 35p)
All Our Yesterdays	(Calders Friends & Neighbours, 20p)
Pen Pourri	(Gorgie/Dalry Writers' Workshop, 50p)

Association among writers' workshops takes the form of home and away readings or visits, the annual Come-All-Ye at Newbattle Abbey College, and informal meetings of workshop co-ordinators. Such links are in their infancy. They recognise the autonomy of each group, and represent a federative or collaborative rather than a centralising tendency.

30. Community Education Perspectives

This review article appeared in *SCAN*, the newspaper of the Scottish Community Education Council, in February 1983. It summarises the case against community education hype, and the identification of community education with community development, discussing the negative impact of these factors on the resourcing of adult education in Scotland. It confronts the practice of stewing incompatible theories and methods, and serving up the mish-mash to students on training courses. I regard this as a form of neo-colonialism, with the colonist condescendingly exhorting the natives. The 'feeding' of the common people with second-rate educational junk food fills me with the kind of savage indignation Swift expresses in his *Modest Proposal*. And I endorse — from a different perspective — MacDiarmid's position:

> Nae Marx-withoot-tears for working men
> But the fu' course insteed

＊

Community education has existed officially in Scotland for over seven years, long enough to establish a distinct identity as a mode of education. What kind of claims does it make? What is community education practice? Is there a theory of community education? Have its claims, its practice and its theories been subjected to scrutiny?

These are important questions. Dundee College of Education, and editors Laurie Bidwell and Charlie McConnell, are to be congratulated on producing a book which addresses itself to some of them. Anyone interested in the broad field now labelled community education will want to obtain a copy.

The book is in an A4 format, with an attractive cover. It uses a nice typeface and size, which makes for easy reading. It contains

---

A review of *Community Education and Community Development*, edited by Laurie Bidwell and Charlie McConnell, Dundee College of Education, 1982.

some good photographs. The proof-reading has been poor, unfortunately, and some of the contributors write atrociously, but it is usually possible to work out what they mean.

There are case studies on work with women, information and resource centres, health, the arts, community business, planning and the environment, community/primary school liaison, work in rural areas, rehabilitation of council houses, informal adult education and the fieldwork training of community workers. There is also a combative piece on community schools, a statistical overview, with some reflections on the academic training of community workers, and an attempt at a theoretical overview by one of the editors.

As a representation of fieldwork practice in community education, the book is defective in having nothing on youth work, nothing on community centre work and only one piece on adult education.

Of the individual contributions, I would pick out Richard Bryant and Barbara Holmes' paper on fieldwork placements as outstanding. John Horobin manages to make the statistics meaningful and it is interesting to note that the main victim of the community education period, in terms of enrolments at any rate, is adult education. The fall has been most dramatic in the local authority sector — a 29.8 per cent decline in enrolments between 1974/5 and 1978/9, with the WEA and the universities declining by 16.6 per cent over the same period. This period has also seen increases in membership of local authority and voluntary youth organisations, a 72 per cent increase in the number of buildings administered by regional community education departments, and a 44 per cent increase in full-time regional community education staff. This increase consists exclusively of area or field staff (generic community education workers, in the jargon), since there has been a simultaneous fall in the numbers of full-time, building-based workers, youth leaders and specialist staff employed.

These statistics pose some important questions for the regional education authorities and for the Scottish Community Education Council. Like, is adult education being run down? And what are the new community education field staff actually doing?

I want to turn to the theory and the wider claims of community education, and take issue with my friend Charlie McConnell, who contributes the first chapter of this book.

Charlie is an enthusiastic teacher and has a record of practical involvement. It pains me to attack his theoretical work, but there is no alternative. His chapter is poor and it reflects the poverty of much theoretical and promotional writing about community education.

A central feature is the making of grandiose, inflated claims for community education. It is presented as everything you would want education to be — permanent availability, freedom of choice, access for all members of the community but especially those currently excluded, relevance, feedback, etc. — an ideal.

Another feature is an all-inclusiveness, a voraciousness. Community education's ambition is to swallow everything, like an omnipotent infant. It is identified with, or said to comprise, recurrent education, *education permanente,* life-long learning, community development, social action, and the whole formal education system. This fantasy lacks focus. It lacks humility. It opens up a massive gap between the ideal and the real, between claim and performance. It also divides the education world into blacks and whites and projects all evil onto the other side. Community education is everything that is good. The school system and traditional adult education are everything that is bad.

When Charlie comes down to specifics, his accuracy is sometimes suspect. He states that Batten and Freire had a significant influence on the theory of community education in Scotland in the 1960s and '70s. Well, community education did not exist in Scotland in the '60s and Batten is a theorist of community development, but if we allow the identity of community education with community development, then maybe we could stretch a point there. His assertion about Freire is wrong. As one who has worked hard at trying to interest community education workers in Freire, I would say that his influence has been marginal.

He proceeds to assert that Freire and Batten's methodology is similar. This is not true. He refers to Freire as saying that learning could only come about through an increased awareness of one's life situation that resulted from action upon it. My understanding is that Freire does not hold that view.

Charlie then identifies community development as the methodological common denominator between informal adult education, youth work and community work. I do not accept this view, but even if it were true, he cannot have it every way. He cannot then identify Freire as one of the theorists of community development, since Freire explicitly repudiates community development.

His wish to incorporate Freire and Batten in his account gives us a clue to what is happening. In creating an all-inclusive theory of community education/community development, he is carrying his eclecticism to the point of failing to distinguish or discriminate. Gobbits from Faure, Freire, Illich, Batten, Carnegy, Alexander, the Home Office CDPs, Jackson, Lovett, Goetschius, and Mayo, are flung into the pot and stewed together. The incompatibility of some of these theories is ignored.

In outlining a model of how a community education worker operates, Charlie blends elements from the adult education process in with the community work process. But these processes are different, and nothing is gained from treating them as if they were the same.

The claims made for community education by Charlie McConnell and others are excessive. They need to be scaled down to a level at which community education field workers can operate with effectiveness. This implies more modest goals, and the skills to achieve them, which in turn requires training — in-service and pre-service — for competence. It requires a more modest and focused self-image for community education as a service and a concept.

There is a need to question the notion of a single overall community education model or approach; to discard the concept of generic community education worker; and to realise that, for the much-vaunted multiplier effect to operate, there has to be something solid there to multiply.

31. A Statement of Educational Philosophy and Objectives

The New Directions policy of 1979 represented a major step forward for the WEA, but also left us facing several different directions. Above all, it did not answer the question: who is the WEA for? To simplify a complex issue, there were two 'pure' viewpoints: one argued that the WEA should continue to provide education for anyone who sought it, the other that we should concentrate our resources on those who were educationally disadvantaged. Those of us who took the latter view favoured targetting the work in order to counteract the apparently natural tendency of adult education to drift up-market. The counter-argument was that targetting was socially and politically divisive.

In 1984 I persuaded the committee to undertake a complete review of the District's educational policy, so that we would have a clearer framework within which to work. The process lasted nearly a year. It was participative, involving consultation with students, tutors, branches, affiliated bodies, district committee members, and staff. The outcome was this document. The title is misleading insofar as it is not *primarily* concerned with matters of philosophy, though it does touch on them in various ways. It is, in fact, a Policy Statement, adopted as such in February 1985. I should make clear that, although I had the task of drafting and structuring it, and originated some of the sections, it is the District's statement and is reproduced here by kind permission of the present committee.

*

1. Who Is The WEA For?

The bulk of the resources of the District, including the time and work of the staff, should be devoted to those who are educationally disadvantaged. That is the overriding general principle, which will be specified in more detail in relation to work with particular target groups, but which is formulated in such a way as to leave the District free to do some work with those who are not educationally disadvantaged, and with other target groups identified by the District Committee from time to time. The term 'target groups' is used to help us clarify our aims and focus our work, not to divide people from each other.

Educational work will be undertaken with the target groups, within broad policy guidelines specified under each, with the proviso that there is no implication of a preference for work done exclusively with members of single target groups. In other words, the District leaves itself free to organise work with the unemployed, or the retired, for example, and equally free to organise classes and activities open to members of several target groups, or to a general mix of participants.

The target groups are *the retired and those about to retire, the unemployed, trade unionists, women, and the physically and mentally handicapped.* None of these groups has priority over the others. The District leaves itself free to make (and change) policy choices among these groups, in the light of a variety of factors, including the availability of suitable funding.

Within the broad policy, and under the general direction of the District Committee, the emphasis may vary from one part of the District to another, depending on local circumstances, local branch policies, and on the talents, wishes and needs of staff, tutors, voluntary members, students and affiliates. Since all the target groups are regarded as equally important, we should at all times and in every area of the District avoid over-identifying the WEA with any one target group.

Target Groups

(1) *The retired and those about to retire*

We should concentrate our resources on certain groups within the retired population: the educationally disadvantaged, the poorer, the immobile living in old folk's homes, those attending day centres, and those living in sheltered housing. In the field of education in retirement, work should normally take place in the localities where people live, rather than in central locations. Tutors who know the locality should be used, where possible. Subjects and themes should be chosen by students or with student participation.

In pre-retirement work, emphasis should be placed on poorer and educationally disadvantaged employees. Employers should be encouraged to send such employees on pre-retirement courses. This should not, however, lead to the exclusion of skilled or white-collar workers. Existing pre-retirement programmes should be retained, but the whole approach should be reviewed. With regard to the content, methods and staffing of existing programmes, the approach based on a series of visiting speakers runs counter to our educational philosophy of student participation in deciding what is to be studied, and during sessions. There should be more discussion and fewer visiting speakers. The aim should be changes in attitude, not only to put over information. In pre-retirement work, a flexible approach to the location of classes is required. Central and local provision both have advantages.

Both these fields (pre- and post-retirement) give great scope for all kinds of innovative WEA work, and should be expanded if possible.

(2) *The Unemployed*

The point of departure here is the feelings of shame experienced by members of this group, as if they had been branded 'unemployed'. These feelings make the experience of unemployment itself worse, and must be taken fully into account. For this reason alone it is important to go and find out what unemployed people want, to knock doors, speak to people, and listen to them. The District recognises that this labour-intensive spadework has to be done.

The bulk of our resources and time should be devoted to the long-term unemployed; to those who have had little formal education or did not like their schooling; to those with fewest educational qualifications; to the unskilled and semi-skilled; and to women. On the other hand, unemployment may come as an even greater blow to those who *have* skills and qualifications. For this reason the participation of skilled workers is to be sought and encouraged. The unemployed category is taken to include the following groups: those about to be made redundant; those experiencing voluntary and involuntary early retirement; those who are unemployed and do not register; and women who are not allowed to sign on because they paid the small stamp.

Some of this work should be aimed exclusively at unemployed people; some at a mix of target groups; and some at the general public. The unemployed should be encouraged to participate in other WEA programmes. We should establish and maintain close links with Unemployed Workers' Centres and other organisations of or concerned with unemployed people but we recognise that many unemployed people do not frequent such centres. We should not necessarily locate our educational activities for unemployed people in them.

The District will continue to allocate a substantial proportion of its existing resources and the time of its staff to this work, and will seek new resources for it.

(3) *Trade Unionists*

While noting that many of our current courses attract trade unionists
as students, the absence of a substantial programme of education for
trade union members in the District is a matter of great concern. This
District wishes to encourage such work, and identifies trade union
branches as the level for making the contacts which are likeliest to
bear fruit. However, it is recognised that it will be appropriate also
to make contacts at area, district, and regional levels.

In the District's view, much trade union education has, hitherto,
been provided at too high a level, both in the sense that it has been
aimed at stewards and reps rather than members, and in the sense
that basic educational needs have been missed. We are referring here
to very basic needs indeed, for instance the need for tuition in
language and number so that members can read and understand
their own union's rule book. The extent of problems of illiteracy and
limited literacy and numeracy within the trade union movement has
been played down. Other subject areas include the history, structure,
purpose, and concerns of the trade union movement, including
current social and political issues, and the question of new
technology. It is important always to identify what union members
actually want to study.

While there is a need for flexibility as to which groups to work
with — and the availability of finance is recognised as a crucial factor
— overall priority should be given to members of manual trade
unions. Education should be arranged in situations and at times
convenient to union members. The ideal would be to negotiate
arrangements for classes to take place during working hours without
loss of earnings, but it is recognised that classes will normally take
place outwith working hours. The problem of obtaining adequate
funding is central. Trade union bodies should be encouraged to pay
for tuition, the rent of rooms, materials, and administrative back-up.
The possibility of obtaining funding from employers should also be
explored.

One method of approach proposed involves offering an
educational package to trade union branches. Another involves visits
by voluntary members to trade union branches to inform them what
the WEA can do. Whatever methods emerge as most effective, it is
envisaged that there are roles for our existing full-time staff and for
our voluntary members. Voluntary members should be trained to
address members of trade union branches about education and the
role of the WEA. The District recognises the desirability of
appointing Trade Union or Industrial Studies Tutor Organisers.

(4) *Women*

As far as women are concerned, the bulk of our resources and time should go to the educationally disadvantaged, the unemployed, those with few or no formal qualifications, those living in socially and economically disadvantaged areas, and women's groups in working-class areas (such as miners' wives' groups).

Many women are low in self-confidence in general, and especially in the presence of men, and for this reason it is appropriate to organise initial courses for women, with women tutors. Such courses can act as a bridge for women, enabling them to participate at a later stage in mixed groups with greater confidence. It is recognised, further, that a range of courses (i.e. not just bridging or initial courses) can be organised beneficially for women. On the other hand, it is also recognised that the promotion of women's interests, and a full response to women's needs and wishes in relation to education, requires us to go beyond the provision of courses for women. In our general provision, steps should also be taken to ensure that women can participate as equal partners. We should provide crêches and push for crêches to be provided, where appropriate, and where possible.

Some of our resources should be allocated to publicising and presenting our work in women's education. This is an area in which we have pioneered new methods, and we should claim credit for them. A programme of research and response in connection with the educational needs and wishes of working-class women is one for which new resources could be sought, and to which existing staff time and resources could be reallocated.

(5) *The Physically and the Mentally Handicapped*

Work with these groups is a welcome new departure for the District. The physically handicapped and the mentally handicapped are two distinct groups, not to be lumped together as far as the provision of classes is concerned, but a major issue in relation to both is that of separate or integrated provision. It is generally desirable that both groups should be integrated with the able-bodied. This is a matter of particular importance in the case of the physically handicapped. Where the mentally handicapped are concerned, we recognise that integration poses greater problems. We are also aware that mixed provision for the able-bodied and the handicapped is impracticable as a norm for a variety of reasons.

Some attention should be paid to the provision of awareness education for the general public about the handicapped, and the attitudes of able-bodied people to them. We would regard these as bridging courses for those on the other side of the bridge.

Where possible, classes should not take place in day centres or hospitals, but in normal locations. The question of access to general provision is crucial. We should try to make all our courses accessible to the physically handicapped, where possible. Where access does exist (for example, for wheelchairs) this should be indicated prominently on our publicity material. The blind and the deaf, in particular, should have a right to bring an interpreter to classes, if they wish.

The handicapped should be treated a whole people with abilities and not as bundles of disabilities, though the disadvantages they suffer from should be taken fully into account in devising educational approaches. Many handicapped people have low morale, a poor self-image, and place little value on their own experience. One point of departure for our approach, therefore, is discussion of common features in their situation and life-experiences. As in our New Opportunities for Women courses, one aim would be to boost morale, develop greater self-confidence and, so far as possible, greater independence. Assertiveness training might also be appropriate for members of both groups.

In principle, we believe that a WEA-style approach is feasible with both groups. For example, a Living Memory Project could be attempted with elderly mentally handicapped people. Work with the handicapped should be conceived, described and carried out as education, not social work, although the statutory responsibilities of Social Work Departments and the scope for collaborating with them are recognised.

At present, lack of resources prevents us from embarking on this work on any scale. Subject to the availability of sufficient resources, direct provision of classes should be made by the District, within the framework of these guidelines.

Other Dimensions

(1) Men and Women

The provision of courses aimed at women and the current emphasis on women's educational needs and wishes, which the District fully supports, have important implications for men and for the relation-ships between men and women. Some of our resources should be applied to educational programmes exploring these implications.

(2) Emotional and Mental Distress

On many of our courses there are participants experiencing varying degrees of depression and other forms of emotional and mental distress. Some have been encouraged to attend classes by hospitals where they have been receiving treatment. Others have taken this step themselves, often as a last-ditch attempt to do something about their lives. In other instances, classes have been organised for or in conjunction with local associations for mental health.

For those on the point of breakdown, or who are suffering from severe distress, participation in a class may not be the most appropriate step. In these circumstances we should refer people to agencies where they have some chance of obtaining suitable therapy. In less severe cases, participation in our classes can be helpful and is to be encouraged. We are concerned about the increasing incidence of such distress among the population in general. It is a major feature of our times. These people should not be regarded as a separate target group: on the contrary, every effort should be made to integrate them in the whole range of our courses. Having said that, courses aimed at specific groups of distressed people are not ruled out.

2. WEA Aims and Values

Aims:

— to attract back to education people who left school at the earliest opportunity, with few or no paper qualifications, and little or no experience of further education
— to bring as many people as possible out of depression, withdrawal or social isolation
— to contribute to processes of social contact, interaction and re-integration
— to promote personal growth, and mutual support
— to restore and develop people's self-confidence and sense of their own potential
— to enable people to speak more openly and honestly
— to stimulate people's curiosity
— to re-animate people's ability to learn, to think, to study
— to develop informal yet demanding methods which enable people to express and reflect upon experience, and integrate that with the acquisition of new insights, knowledge and skills
— to enable people to take more control of their everyday lives
— to encourage more effective and informed participation in society
— to diminish alienation and the sense of personal failure, shame or guilt
— not to raise expectations too high: to hold firmly to the view that our efforts are educational and interpersonal, as are the outcomes to be anticipated
— although our aims are educational rather than political, our view

of education is not such as to abstract it from the socio-political contexts of participants' lives, nor from their concerns and purposes. No area of interest is therefore excluded, however topical or controversial. What is excluded, however, is the use of the educational situation itself for the pursuit of political objectives

— finally, to offer education and training about the WEA's structure, its antecedents, its origins, its history, its teaching and learning methods, and its values.

Values:

— we favour a personal and social view of education, rather than a narrowly utilitarian view of skills to be learned by separate individuals. Such narrow skills training may be less effective, even in a utilitarian sense, than the setting of skills development in wider personal and social learning contexts.

— we take the view that education programmes should aim to integrate inner and outer, facts and feelings, present and past, politics and human relations, knowledge and experience, information and creativity, the personal, the interpersonal and the societal.

— learning experiences in general should be seen and planned as socialising experiences. Education is not merely the acquisition of skills and knowledge.

— the idea of relevance which has become fashionable in education in the last twenty years is of dubious value. There is a danger of producing a second-class, second-rate, practicalised, localised curriculum. Our approach struggles to integrate what people say they want with what it seems to our tutors and organisers that they need. In the context of such an orientation Shakespeare's *King Lear* or the study of Chinese history can be relevant.

— we adhere to the traditional WEA view that a class of twelve students, with one tutor, contains thirteen students and thirteen tutors.

3. Educational Approaches

(1) *Devising Curricula*

The WEA favours a healthy plurality of approaches to the devising of curricula. Common to them all, however, is the maximisation of student participation at every stage. We favour initial investigation of the experiences, wishes, and needs of those for whom education programmes are intended, rather than approaches based on guesswork, personal or professional preference, fashion, habit, ideology, or the priorities set by government or industry. Equally, we favour the negotiation of curricula between tutor and students, at the outset and throughout courses of study. Questioning, listening, and responding appropriately are key features of such approaches. The WEA does not, however, rule out the use of given or preconstructed curricula based on the authority of the tutor's or tutor group's own knowledge, so long as this is not merely imposed on a class.

(2) *The Authority of the Tutor*

Although we favour student participation we do not believe in negating the authority of the tutor. The crucial question here is: what is the nature of the tutor's authority? We do not believe tutors should have dictatorial powers. The tutor's authority is not to dominate a group, nor to yield to the temptation of being a guru. On the other hand the tutor is not just a listener or group member. He or she is not just 'one of us', asking the students: what do you want to do? A good tutor has knowledge, expertise, insight, skill, and will win the respect of group members and exercise purposeful overall control of the group. The tutor uses the authority of his or her knowledge and leadership to promote the growth of students' knowledge and authority, drawing on the students' contributions as well as on his or her own. This will be reflected in the styles of relating, teaching and learning used.

(3) *The Student/Tutor Relationship*

The relations between student and tutor are interactive, supportive and democratic, on the one hand, and involve leadership, direction and structuring of activity on the other. The tutor puts members at their ease, so that they can say what they think and feel. The tutor should be able to speak the students' language. The tutor draws out the students' views and knowledge in order to build on their potential. There is an atmosphere of relaxed informality, attentiveness and rigour.

(4) *Teaching and Learning Methods*

A range of teaching and learning methods can be employed, from lectures and structured presentations to participatory group work and independent study. The overall intention is to combine the acquisition and creation of new knowledge with expression of and reflection upon personal experience.

(5) *Content*

Tutors are also employed for their knowledge or expertise in a particular area, and there should be a high quality of well-structured content in all our courses.

(6) Evaluation

Where possible, students should have well-organised personal and communal opportunities to evaluate the courses in which they have taken part, without the tutor present. The results should be fed back to the tutor or tutor group whose evaluation of their work should be informed by the comments of the students.

(7) Training, Support, and Payment of Part-time Tutors

The District acknowledges the key role of part-time tutors, and wishes to give them greater responsibility. High standards of planning, preparation, knowledge, sensitivity in handling a group, regular attendance, and commitment to the aims and values of the WEA are expected. Suitable support, supervision and training opportunities for tutors should be arranged. In general, tutors should be paid, and paid at a good rate, in recognition of the quantity and quality of work expected of them, including preparation time. Where possible, they should be paid for attendance at course planning meetings, and their travel costs should be reimbursed.

(8) Volunteer Tutors

The District cautiously welcomes (and will in some cases accept) offers to tutor on a voluntary basis, but not unconditionally. Volunteer tutors are subject to the same expectations as paid tutors.

(9) Fieldwork Training

The District regards training in adult education fieldwork methods — for voluntary members, part-time tutors, full-time staff, and placement students — as an important function which the WEA is well placed to carry out. The feasibility of expanding our present efforts in this field should be investigated, and appropriate finance sought.

4. The Role of Voluntary Members

The District reaffirms the ultimate sovereignty of students and voluntary members within the WEA. At District level they are responsible for the general content and direction of policy, including educational policy and staff remits. At District and branch levels they should receive and comment upon regular reports of all educational work, which should appear high on the relevant agendas.

There is a need for much more active recruitment and involvement of voluntary members. They should be trained and organised in branches and student groups, so that they can become working parts of the association. Regular branch meetings should be held, to which students from all branch classes and events should be invited.

Voluntary members should be encouraged to identify with and contribute to the WEA, financially and in other ways. With the current preponderance of shorter courses, students may come and go, and be lost to the association. It is recognised that, as a result, there is a danger of the WEA becoming a professional movement.

There should be training for voluntary members, which should, for instance, equip them to go to meetings of trade union branches, community organisations, to hospitals and old folk's homes, to speak effectively about the work of the WEA.

The major tasks for voluntary members are practical: to plan and organise programmes of classes and other educational events; to make and circulate publicity material; to get newspaper and radio coverage; to rent rooms; to act as class secretaries, collecting fees, taking registers, and organising course evaluation sessions, feeding the findings back to the tutor, the tutor organiser or the branch as appropriate; to serve as officers and members of branch and district committees; and generally to further the District's aim of becoming a self-generating movement of members.

5. Staff and Resources

The District recognises the high quality of the work of its staff and their commitment to the WEA and to those who are educationally disadvantaged. The District also recognises that overwork does occur, and steps should be taken to limit it as far as possible.

Each member of staff should have a remit which defines their workload as accurately as possible. They should have suitable opportunities to communicate their wishes and preferences, but it is emphasised that this is only one factor in the process of arriving at remits. The others are: the District's educational policy; the District's current priorities and emphases; the need to expand the work of the District in particular geographical areas and types of work; the need to obtain new resources; the need to build a strong voluntary movement; the wishes of our branches, students, affiliated societies, and individual members; and the talents of our staff (which are not necessarily the same as their preferences).

Decision-making in the matter of remits lies with the District Committee, and with the District Secretary acting on the District Committee's behalf. Remits should be reviewed and changed as appropriate from time to time.

The District will make every effort to obtain increased resources of suitable kinds in order to expand our educational work. Resources may be obtained from Central Government, Regional and District Authorities, Health Authorities, Trade Union bodies, Chambers of Commerce, Employers, Trusts, Community Organisations, individuals, and any other appropriate source.

The resources of the District will be applied in accordance with this statement of educational philosophy and objectives, and the District's current priorities.

The District reaffirms its policy of concentrating resources and the work and time of our staff on certain geographical areas, types of work, and target groups, as part of a strategy for growth based on developing our expertise, maximising our impact and thus attracting new resources. This strategy is based on a recognition that because our resource-base is small it has to be used carefully.

32. Vulgar Eloquence

The emergence of writers like Tom Leonard, Liz Lochhead, Agnes Owens, James Kelman, Alasdair Gray and Alan Spence is a key to how Scotland has been changing in the last twenty years. They are speaking in their own voices, and getting published in their own country. It is not the emergence of a new regional school. It's about changing the relationships between speech, writing, and publishing. There are class, gender, and national dimensions here: common to each is the reality of division, and the issue of power. It is significant that all of these writers, one way or another, have taken part in the writers' workshop movement.

Tom Leonard's *Intimate Voices, 1965-1983* appeared in 1984. This review article was published in *Cencrastus* number 20, in the spring of 1985.

*

Tom Leonard's first volume, *Poems*, was published in Dublin in 1973. We have had to wait nearly a dozen years for a comprehensive selection of his work, bringing together early material with some of the astonishing things he has done since. Only his sound poetry, his radio play, his multi-media performances, and his as-yet-uncompleted research on James Thomson are not represented in *Intimate Voices, 1965-1983* (Galloping Dog Press), joint winner of the Royal Bank/Saltire Society Award for 1984.

By a coincidence that can be invested with meaning, a similar period of time has elapsed between Liz Lochhead's *Memo for Spring* and the recent appearance of her collection, *Dreaming Frankenstein*. I think Tom and Liz are the best Scottish poets of the post-war generation. It is significant that they both hail from the west, from the urban working class, one from Lanarkshire, the other from Glasgow, one from a Protestant background, the other from a Catholic background, one female and the other male. They have helped us look and listen to ourselves, and particularly our common or urban, working-class selves, in ways that the Lallans tradition, for all its importance, has been unable to do.

Tom Leonard is above all a poet of the voice, and a poet concerned

with the *politics* of voice. That's why I chose *Vulgar Eloquence* as the
title of this review-article. Dante in his *De Vulgari Eloquentia* says he
wants to be of service to the speech of the common people, the vulgar
tongue, by which he means the various dialects of Italian. He defines
it as 'that to which children are accustomed by those who are about
them when they first begin to distinguish sounds', and 'that which we
acquire without any rule, by imitating our nurses'. Later, he
continues, a few of us acquire another *secondary* speech, by which
Dante means Latin or Classical Greek. This secondary speech can
only be acquired by much study and instruction. It is 'rather
artificial'. The vulgar tongue is nobler. It is natural to us, and it is
employed by us all.

The parallels between the regional and working class dialects of
English and the dialects of Italian, on the one hand, and school-
taught standard English and Latin or Greek, on the other, seem
obvious. To anyone brought up in the west of Scotland, where many
schoolchildren were˙ (and in varying degrees still are) taught that
their speech is not a language at all, but slang, Dante's words send
out ripples crossing some of the central concerns of Tom Leonard
throughout his work.

Tom's views on the relation of language to class are stated in his
brilliant essay 'The Locust Tree in Flower, and why it had Difficulty
Flowering in Britain', which is included in *Intimate Voices*. Here is a
string of quotes indicating some of the main lines of his analysis:

> There are basically two ways of speaking in Britain: one which
> lets the listener know that one paid for one's education, the
> other which lets the listener know that one didn't. . .

> It is this very variety of regional working-class accents which
> 'bought' education has promised to keep its pupils free from,
> and to provide them instead with a mode of pronunciation
> which ironically enough is called 'Received'. . .

> All modes of speech are valid — upper-class, middle-class,
> working-class, from whatever region; linguistic chauvinism is
> a drag. . .

> But to have created, or at least to have preserved, a particular
> mode of pronunciation on a strictly economic base, cannot but
> have very deep repercussions in a society, and in the *literature*
> of a society. . .

> Enter the inevitable assertion that the language of these

economically superior classes is *aesthetically* superior — then in the interests of 'Beauty' and 'Truth', the regional and working-class languages, whatever else they're capable of, certainly aren't capable, the shoddy little things, of great Art.

Another angle of Tom's viewpoint on language is to be found in his admiration for the work of William Carlos Williams:

> What I like about Williams is his voice. What I like about Williams is his presentation of voice as a fact, as a fact in itself and as a factor in his relationship with the world as he heard it, listened to it, spoke it. That language is not simply an instrument of possession, a means of snooping round everything that is not itself — that's what I get from Williams.

This essay, with its courageous assertions, its daring connections, its sharp sideways glance at Lallans and MacDiarmid's 'insistence on the primacy of name and category', ends with an analysis of Williams' lovely thirteen-word poem, 'The Locust Tree in Flower'. For anyone concerned with the themes of language and class, and with the transformation that has been happening in the relationship between poetry and speech, this essay is essential reading.

I am concerned to establish, and will continue to underline, the deep seriousness of Tom Leonard's work. There is a temptation for readers, audiences, and admirers to content themselves with hilarity, to kill themselves laughing and go elsewhere for reflection or analysis. It is impossible to overemphasise how much of a mistake that would be, particularly in view of the existence of a tradition of sentimental and, in the end, self-mocking working-class comics. (Incidentally, while there is anger and irony in Tom's poems, and gentleness and tenderness, there is no sentimentality, and this distinguishes his work in a transcription of Glasgow speech from that of others using the same genre.) I want to concentrate on two factors, which should properly be taken together: Tom Leonard's technical virtuosity, and the themes and insights with which he is concerned.

To start with questions of technique, let me re-emphasise that it is underpinned by fundamental values: the importance of *listening carefully* to what people say, to the meanings of word, sound, phrase, pause, emphasis and tune; the respect for *working-class speech*; the attention to *what people say for themselves,* as distinct from what is said on their behalf; and attention to *the themes embodied in speech*.

Allowing for all of these values, Tom Leonard must be accounted

a brilliant technical innovator. The signs have been there since his
earliest poems. His sense of phrase and line is unerring, as is his
savouring and use of the qualities of particular sounds, and his
musician's sense of build-up, contrast, restraint, release and
conclusion. These skills can be heard in such poems as 'Poetry' from
the series *Bunnit Husslin*:

> the pee as in pulchritude,
> oh pronounced ough
> as in bough
>
> the ee rather poised
> (pronounced ih as in wit)
> then a languid high tea . . .
>
> pause: then the coda —
> ray pronounced rih
> with the left eyebrow raised
> — what a gracious bouquet!
>
> Poetry
> Poughit.rih.
>
> That was my education
> — and nothing to do with me.

and this untitled poem from the series *Ghostie Men*:

> efturryd geenuz iz speel
> iboot whut wuz right
> nwhut wuz rang
> boot this nthat
> nthi nix thing
>
> a sayzty thi bloke
> nwhut izzit yi caw
> yir joab jimmy
>
> am a liason co-ordinator
> hi sayz oh good ah sayz
> a liason co-ordinator
>
> jist whut this erria needs
> whut way aw thi unimploymint

inaw thi bevvyin
nthi boayz runnin amock
nthi hoossyz fawnty bits
nthi wummin n tranquilisers
it last thiv sent uz
a liason co-ordinator

sumdy wia digree
in fuck knows whut
getn peyd fur no known
whut thi fuck ti day way it

Another specific feature of Tom's technical mastery illustrated by these and other poems is his use of a particular kind of transcription of speech which, so far as I know, he has invented. Various forms of transcription of popular speech have occurred in novels, plays and poems for centuries. Comedians like Stanley Baxter use it to make folk laugh. The process is one of indulging in the language transcribed, empathising with its speakers to some degree, but also subtly misrepresenting it and belittling those who use it.

Leonard's methods reflect his values. He is concerned to achieve as exact a transcription as possible of the sounds used in a particular speech/dialect/accent, by pressing into service letters and combinations of letters representing sounds that are common, or nearly common, across accent/dialect boundaries. But this simple linguistic transcription works by a dimension which has been misunderstood by at least one reviewer of his work as the introduction of puns or even metaphors. This dimension is the use, in transcriptions, of recognisable elements of other words, or even whole words, which usually have nothing in particular to do with what is being said. This creates a lexical and phonological space of anarchic hilarity, of tangential associations and noises off, around the words transcribed:

Noah's Green Izzam Cabbage Lukn

ma heed duzny
buttn upthi back yi
no, ah wuzny boarn
yisstirday.

yi no ah didny
kumupthi Clyde na
bananaboat hen,
nay flies n mee.

> doant no ma arse
> fray ma Elba?
> puhll thi uthir wan
> — its gut bellz n it!

Again we are in danger of drifting towards a vision of Tom Leonard
as merely a comic poet. His sense of the music of word, phrase and
line comes over equally in poems without the dimension of humour,
and written in English, like this:

Storm Damage

There is a stain on the ceiling above the bed.
Rainwater. A relic of last year's storm.
It is roughly circular. Darkest at the centre.
The perimeter is not clearly defined.

Eclipse. Your body moves on mine.
Your face looks down on me.
The lips are smiling. The stain
Becomes a halo round your head.

My mind goes back twelve years.
I am a child again, lying in the grass,
Staring into the sky. Eclipse.

You ask me what I'm thinking.

and this:

Placenta

Good-bye to that good woman
who fed you life through a cord
and pushed you into the world:

leave go the rope —
let the weight of her body
leave you. Let the grave

be stitched up. In nine months
the scar will be invisible.

In sum, what is remarkable about this dimension of Tom's work is his sure sense of musical form in poetry. Both Yeats and Dante would have been interested in this. I am thinking for example of Yeats' advice to younger poets to

> Scorn the sort now growing up
> All out of shape from toe to top.

or of Dante's careful attention to the number and weight of syllables. Leonard, certainly, has moved on from the traditional standard forms (regular line lengths, stanza form, rhyme scheme). But every one of his poems shows an alert, weighed and balanced sense of the shape of what is emerging.

The case for Tom Leonard's poetry as crucially important to us in Scotland now, socially, culturally, politically, is not complete until we have made some reference to the range and character of his themes. Paulo Freire, in *Pedagogy of the Oppressed*, refers to the Brazilian novelist, Guimaraes Rosa, as the investigator *par excellence* of the meaningful thematics of the inhabitants of the Brazilian hinterland, and as an example of how a writer can capture authentically the syntax of a people: the very structure of their thought. Maybe that's a wee bit over the top from a crimped, repressed, envious, kent-his-faither Scottish standpoint. Nevertheless one would like to be able to accord such recognition where it is due.

Through his attention to what people have to say, and the terms in which they say it, Tom Leonard is investigating, celebrating and reflecting upon the themes and syntax of urban working-class people in west central Scotland, particularly, but not exclusively, the men. What makes it possible for him to do it, is the depth of his identification with them. He is not speaking *for* working-class Scots, but *from* the position in which many find themselves. Hugh MacDiarmid claimed he was *of* not *for* the working class, but the evidence of his work runs counter to that claim. It is of great value and importance for quite other reasons. Leonard, on the other hand, because of his origins, his disposition and his character, identifies with working-class experience, knows it from the inside, and yet is able to distance himself from it and thus to objectify it.

His themes are violence, ranging from the violence of those in power, through pent-up repressed violence, and the fantasy of violence, to direct physical aggression against others; male/female relations, including men's attitudes to women and to sexual relations, men's responses to ideas about women's liberation, men's physical and emotional rigidity, including our inability to express feelings of love and tenderness; Catholicism and Protestantism (in the multi-media sound poem, 'My Name is Tom', not included in this selection, he identifies Catholicism with insistent dependence, and Protestantism with insistent independence); language and speech and their connections with social class and political power; urban working-class Scottish speech and its relationship to Lallans and what he describes as prescriptive Scots; education and upward social mobility; relationships between parents and children; the nature of authority, and authoritarianism, in Scottish society; the pleasure of drinking, watching football and listening to classical music. Many of these themes are, of course, multiply inter-connected. For example, the Catholic/Protestant theme meshes with the male/female, sexual and class themes.

His writing is imbued with a deep vein of irony, which is related to a pervasive sense of violence and outrage, and the presence of a sharp mind. The tone of the intimate voices of these poems sometimes verges on paranoia and rage. Each one is an intense drama, with (usually) one voice speaking direct to the microphone. The tone is of such urgency that the hearer is unlikely to switch off. As well as this sense of the listener being directly addressed, there is also a sense of the voice considering itself. There is a space around the voice in which some kind of assessment is happening. Expression and reflection seem to occur in an integrated way in the monologue: there is no sense of a calm, withdrawn detachment. On a very few occasions the sense of irony topples over into outraged bitterness as in the case of the poem beginning 'ulstir fur fucks sake'. On a few occasions, on the other hand, an abstract, endlessly analytical reflectiveness seems to take over, and the outcome can seem a bit arid (for example, the poem entitled 'breathe deep, and regular with it').

I recently asked Tom where he stood in relation to T. S. Eliot's notion of the dissociation of sensibility, and specifically the Scottish application of it attempted by Edwin Muir in *Scott and Scotland*, where Muir argues that the Scots are crippled because they think in English and feel in Scots. Tom was unsympathetic to this dichotomy: he found it unsatisfactory to speak of thinking that is not carried out in terms of feelings, and of feelings that do not involve thoughts. This response is persuasive, but I remain personally convinced that a set of deep divisions associated with this dichotomy is crucial for many Scots. Muir's formulation is bold but maybe unsatisfactory. The reader may recall Eliot's assertion that 'a thought to Donne was an experience; it modified his sensibility', whereas Tennyson and Browning 'do not feel their thought as immediately as the odour of a rose'. Tom Leonard does his thinking in terms of energetic verbal expressions of feelings and perceptions, laced with (often lacerating) personal and political comments. The fastidious 'thought' of the odour of a rose is liable to be expelled by the feeling of a fart in the face, in the Leonard *oeuvre*.

But the deep divisions are still there: Catholic/Protestant; male/female; east/west; working class/middle class; fantasy/reality; what is actual/what would be ideal. Tom Leonard is in touch with them, grappling with them, speaking urgently about them.

Tom is a stoater of a poet. Pun intended. In terms of content, language, theme and style, he is a radical innovator. If there is hope — socially, politically, culturally — in Scotland today, and there is, then it is due in large part to the work of writers like Tom, Liz Lochhead, Agnes Owens, Jim Kelman, Alasdair Gray and Alan Spence. Through their work we are hearing the voices of the majority who do not live in rural circumstances, who do not speak Scots, and who do not speak standard English either.

33. Key Texts in Community Education in Scotland

Since 1986 I have been teaching the Community Education core course on the postgraduate MSc/Diploma in Community Education at Edinburgh University. Key Texts in Community Education is a tidied-up version of my lecture notes on the *Alexander Report*, the *Carnegy Report* and *Training for Change*. It combines extract and summary with critique as it traces the evolution of community education in Scotland.

*

What we are going to do is try to trace, mainly from written evidence — from three key texts — the evolution of a new profession, which is just twelve years old. It's a profession, or service, in which a lot of hopes were invested. In a sense it belongs to that era, the late 1960s, when hopes were high and central government set up committees to investigate and restructure various aspects of public service provision. You could argue that the *Alexander Report, Adult Education: The Challenge of Change*, arrived too late. The Committee of Enquiry was established in 1970 and didn't report until 1975, by which time there was an economic crisis, which persisted and worsened. It was hardly an auspicious time for a new service to get off the ground, a service which depended for the realisation of its hopes not only on the integration of two previously separate services, but on the expectation that the state would invest substantial amounts of new money. Alexander spelled out what was wanted: an extra million pounds per year at 1974 prices as a permanent addition to the bill, plus an extra £70,000 a year for five years.

Before we begin to look at the *Alexander Report* in depth, let me remind you of two important human factors. We shouldn't over-estimate their importance, but we should be aware of them. The world of the youth service and the world of adult education were very different. Adult education was organised by men in suits, well-groomed men in collars and ties and polished shoes. They ran classes in evening institutes, usually in schools used at night, or in a few cases in specially adapted adult education centres. They were a respectable lot. They saw themselves as educators. They had degrees. The youth service was different. It was also run by male workers, but they tended to be more informal, with open-necked shirts, jerseys, and sleeves rolled up. They ran youth clubs, with table tennis, dancing, football, other sports, and perhaps work-camps or community service. They had youth work training. There was often a social class division between these two services, a blurred division rather than a sharp one. Adult education classes attracted more middle-class, better-educated, older people, while youth work had a rougher element along with the respectable kids, it had more of a working-class presence and, of course, by definition, it was young.

These two worlds had fairly negative views of each other. Adult education tended to look down its nose at the youth service. It wasn't rigorous, it wasn't education, just containment. Ping-pong and coca-cola. The youth service regarded adult education with a certain amount of contempt: it was too formal, too polite, nose-in-the-air, middle class, cut off from real people with real problems in the real world. This factor of inter-service rivalry really existed, but has now largely receded into the background. It's reflected to some extent in the other human factor I want to touch on: the rivalry between the two types of training agency. By and large adult educators got their training in universities. Youth workers were trained on the job, as assistant leaders, and got in-service training at weekends, or else through doing full-time training courses at Colleges of Education. There was (and still is) a rivalry between these two types of training agency. It is not the same as the first rivalry, but influences and is influenced by it. It wasn't only a matter of degrees: most college staff did have degrees, though they often got them by routes other than that of going straight from school to university. It had to do with the relative status of the two types of agency and with the orientation of the training provided. The universities had a basically conceptual and historical orientation, whereas the colleges were centred more on practical skills.

I don't want to overemphasise these factors, but they are there, and they have been at work in some of the difficulties and conflicts experienced in Community Education over the past twelve years. It could be argued that, even if you agree with the Alexander prescription for an integrated Community Education service, it singularly fails to take into account as a factor in the process of integration, the human relations issues arising out of these inter service and inter-institutional rivalries.

Turning to the Alexander Report, it is worth stressing that it is a report about adult education. Its aim is to advance the cause of adult education, and its chosen method is the creation of a Community Education Service incorporating adult education with youth and community work. It is concerned with *voluntary leisure time courses for adults which are educational but not specifically vocational*. It takes careful note of the present position: a provision involving just over 4 per cent of the population, 72 per cent of them women, mainly middle class, generally well educated, and with a disproportionately high number of people over fifty-five. The report describes adult education students as 'the older, the better educated, the more affluent'. (Brian Groombridge was making a similar point when he asserted that adult education was stuck in a lower middle-class ghetto.) The main subject areas are categorised as physical training, needlecraft, and handicrafts and hobbies. Local Education Authorities provide for 87 per cent of the total number of students, Extra-mural Departments 10 per cent, the WEA 2 per cent, and the central institutions 1 per cent.

Alexander wants to expand the volume of provision, and to redistribute it. He aims to double the number of students by the mid 1980s. He calls for 200 more full-time workers, and for more emphasis *generally* on the socially, educationally and economically disadvantaged, and *specifically* on such special groups as young mothers, the elderly, those with literacy problems, immigrants, prisoners, the physically and mentally handicapped, shiftworkers, those working unsocial hours, people in long-term residence in hospital (whether physically or mentally ill, or geriatric), and people living in what are described as areas of multiple deprivation. The report has a cultural deficit view of these groups: it uses the phrase cycle of deprivation, leading to a notion of education as remedial.

Returning to the key structural prescription, listen carefully to the words used. Adult education is to be seen as an *element* in community education, an element with specific characteristics and requirements, but sharing *common aims* with the other element ʼuth work), and needing its resources and expertise. You'll notice far this is from the later concepts of generic community ʼon and a single community education process. As I've already ʼander is not calling just for crude expansion, but for ʼ qualitative improvement. He suggests that the ʼuld use a Community Development approach to ʼvement. He argues for research into what subjects, ʼd methods will prove attractive in different areas ʼmilieux. He attacks the division between ʼal provision. He proposes certain new

structures: a national community education council (happened),
Scottish Education Department grants towards the teaching costs in
developmental work (didn't happen), regional advisory councils
(tried in one region but didn't really prosper), and the creation of
adult education centres (hardly any).

Although the report touches on the question of the numerical
balance of full-time staff as between adult education and youth work
(7:500 or 1:7), it doesn't tackle the problems of integration inherent
in such an imbalance, contenting itself with soft soap about both
services having the same objectives, and the potential gains through
economies of scale. As you know, this was the argument used in
every case of structural integration and increases in scale in the
organisation of government services in the '60s and '70s, often —
incredible as it may now seem — in combination with arguments
about the devolution of decision-making to local levels.

At the time, Henry Arthur Jones, quoting the limerick:

> There was a young lady from Riga
> Who went for a ride on a tiger.
> They came from the ride with the lady inside,
> And a smile on the face of the tiger.

implied that there was a danger of adult education getting swallowed
up by the youth service. He was proved right in one sense but wrong
in another, for it was generic community education that was to
swallow up the resources available for both adult education and
youth work, as we shall see.

In discussing the development of training the report called for
flexible entry so that people without first degrees could get in, and
for expansion in the role of the Universities. Universities, Colleges,
employers and the Open University were to collaborate to provide
in-service training for full and part-time staff. With regard to the
principles underlying training, the report called for a *common
purpose*, cutting out wasteful duplication and competition. It argued
that training for each sector (adult education, youth work, and
community work) should not be isolated, and

> the *common core* of knowledge and expertise concerned with
> adult education should be included within training schemes for
> each of the other sectors.

Discussing how the sectors should relate, Alexander describes
adult education and youth service as having overlapping functions
and that there should be *common elements* in the training of both
groups. These terms *common elements* and *common core,* used in
evolving and finally quite different ways, reverberate down the
history of community education in Scotland over the last thirteen

years. The struggle around their meaning was the focus of a running
battle between Colleges and Universities seeking to defend or expand
their share of the market for training in a context of shrinking
resources.

Here are a few of the remaining Alexander recommendations:
— a dual fee system, of economic fees side by side with aided fees,
  whose aim was to free resources for priority work;
— fees to be waived altogether for the sixteen to eighteen-year-olds,
  pensioners and the disadvantaged;
— flexibility on minimum class numbers;
— incentives to employers to grant paid educational leave;
— management councils for adult education centres, with staff and
  student representation;
— students' associations where centres were big enough;
— the WEA to concentrate on the educational needs of the socially,
  economically and educationally disadvantaged; education
  authorities to seek its help in making the relevant provision;
— the establishment of a residential college for industrial relations
  training;
— education authorities to establish counselling services;
— each education authority to appoint an assistant director with
  specific responsibility for adult education.

How are we to assess the Alexander Report? My view is that it is a
workmanlike job, well researched and thorough. Its various recommendations hang together, and all run in the same direction. The whole
package depends on the availability of a considerable amount of new
investment in full-time staff, buildings, and training, which never
appeared. In another sense it is very much of its time. It is structural,
integrative, expansionist, top down, and male. It has a passive-objects-
of-improvement attitude to people. It avoids saying anything about
class or other conflicts of interest. It is outer-orientated, rather than
inner-orientated. It is rational and orderly in the Scottish way, but it is
not philosophical: it doesn't wrestle with questions of value or
ideology. It speaks the language of service and provision. Finally, its key
recommendation, the integration of adult education and the youth
service, failed to achieve its stated aim of the expansion, redirection and
qualitative improvement of adult education in Scotland.

Let's pass on to the report of the Working Party on Professional
Training for Community Education, known as the *Carnegy Report*.
The Working Party was created, very shortly after Alexander was
published, by the Scottish Institute of Adult Education and the
Standing Consultative Council on Youth and Community Service,
and it reported in February 1977, reflecting an eagerness to get
training for the new service under way. We are only a little way

into Carnegy, however, when we realise that things have moved on. There is reference to:

> the common core of knowledge and skills required by almost all community education workers

already a fundamental departure from Alexander. Grand claims are made for community education:

> the significance of community education for the well-being of society, for the quality of life in communities, and for the personal fulfilment of individuals is now widely recognised

and

> the benefits of community education to society are out of proportion to the meagre expenditure of public money on it and the small number of staff engaged in it. . . Community education workers are multipliers who stimulate and mobilise many times their own number

and

> Community education taps the springs of voluntary initiative and service.

This is clearly promotional hyperbole since, at the time of writing, the service was just getting off the ground. It may be that it was felt necessary to hype community education in order to gain extra resources in a time of economic stringency. But the trouble with hype is that gaps can open up between claim and performance. Carnegy sets itself the task of creating a general impression of what community education is, but not giving a precise definition. This is justified, it claims, because

> it is the needs and responses of individuals and groups which must determine the nature of community education. . .

This is the first of many refusals to define community education. As the needs and responses change, the report goes on, so should the nature and specific aims of community education. Having refused to be specific, the report proceeds to produce a very clear statement of the *general* characteristics of community education:

> We consider the concept of community education to be consistent with current international thinking about education

as a whole, as represented for example by the phrases 'education permanente', 'recurrent education', and 'continuing education'. It reflects a view of education as a process (a) which is life-long; (b) in which the participants should be actively and influentially involved and the traditional stress on teaching outweighed by the emphasis put on learning; and (c) in which the needs of the participants rather than academic subject divisions or administrative and institutional arrangements should determine the nature and timing of provision. The distinctive contribution which the concept of community education may be said to bring to these international concepts is its emphasis on the process as one in which the benefits to and the contributions of the individual are matched by those of the groups and communities to which he or she belongs; and one which can be enjoyable as well as beneficial, relaxed as well as rigorous. Community education recognises the educative influences and the educational potentialities inherent in a local community and operating through multifarious groups and agencies, formal and informal, industrial, commercial, religious, social and recreational as well as explicitly educational.

We therefore see community education as a constantly evolving process of interaction between the needs of people and the educational resources of the community, a process to which fixed boundaries cannot be set. . .

This is elegant and clear, and much of it is admirable. As an abstract statement, it says nothing about the concrete realisation of its ideals. Perhaps we cannot take it to task for avoiding what it does not set out to do, but the absence of any models of practice fills me with unease, because it opens the gate to omnipotence. The association of the educative and the educational is valuable, insofar as it brings closer together categories traditionally kept apart. But I suspect that it conceals a confusion of learning with experience. While all learning involves experience, not all experience results in learning. Finally, a service which refuses to define the boundaries of its own process is a service which is going to have problems.

The report proceeds to a statement of general aims, which can be summarised as follows: to involve people as individuals and in groups and communities in, first, *ascertaining* their needs for opportunities to:

(i)   discover and pursue interests;
(ii) acquire and improve knowledge and skills;
(iii) recognise their personal identities and aspirations;

(iv) develop satisfactory inter-personal relationships;
 (v) achieve competence in their roles in family, community and society;
(vi) participate in shaping their physical and social environment and in the conduct of local and national affairs;
and second, *meeting* these needs, once ascertained, in co-operation with others, and by finding appropriate educational resources.

Once again this statement cannot be faulted for its clarity, its comprehensiveness, or its ambition. But is it realistic? Can it be done by one service? Where are people to find these resources? I want to spell out what I suspect you will already have guessed about my own view. I would prefer the adoption of a more modest list of aims combined with some sense of how they might be achieved. There is a virtue in making choices, prioritising objectives and concentrating resources, rather than spreading the butter so thin it disappears. To use a different metaphor, the Carnegy Report had its eye on the beautiful panorama, rather than on the road ahead.

Proceeding further, we come across another feature that has become characteristic of community education: an *excessive* admiration for the effectiveness, the untutored brilliance, of voluntary participants:

> circumstances will occur where the proper role of the professional should be at most that of releasing and supporting voluntary initiative and . . . admiring and learning from the insights and natural skills of non-professionals.

Now this is true, and worth stressing, but it can also contain something unhealthy: a negation of the positive aspects of professionalism, a romanticising of 'the people' and their 'natural skills'. This is connected in my mind with what was to become the caricature of the community education worker, a scruffy, unkempt individual who gave no lead and upheld no standards of performance. This negation of professionalism, which I confess I shared for a time, can be seen as an antithetical reaction to the experience of the paternalistic professional. Its *reductio ad absurdum* would be to hand back the salary.

Later, an attempt is made to categorise the kinds of full-tme workers the report envisages will be required. The four categories proposed are staff concerned with:
— animation, groupwork and tutoring;
— organisation and management;
— advisory and specialist functions are a remove from participants;
— formulating policy, administration, and managing staff.

In one sense this is accurate enough, but in another it subtly presages the process of devaluing practice. I am referring here to that process, found in most professions in the last twenty years, and specifically in community education, of leaving the practice work to lower grade or part-time staff, the other side of the coin being the scramble to get into policy-making, administrative and managerial positions. Is this an aspect of the process of bureaucratisation?

The central shift from Alexander in Carnegy is the introduction of the concept of a common core of knowledge and skills required by all categories of community education staff, which includes *education, psychology, sociology, social administration, community work, group work, politics, and leisure.* The list is so long that it leads me to wonder about the danger of the dilution of quality, of a relatively shallow *tour d'horizon* approach being adopted in all these areas. Yet the Carnegy Report claims to be concerned with high standards.

The list of areas of knowledge is followed by a list of skills, which is very impressive, but also very long. Again I ask myself, how could people learn *all* those skills? I was aware, in the late '70s and early '80s, of the annual trail of newly trained or just-appointed community education workers coming to see me at the WEA. The story was always the same: I'm supposed to be doing adult education but I've got no idea how to go about it.

It should be stresed, however, that Carnegy does recognise the existence of processes specific to each of adult education, youth service and community work.

An unfortunate though presumably unintended effect of the Carnegy Report's rejection of the binary system of training was to give a further twist to the destructive competition between the colleges and the universities.

The Carnegy Report introduced the word 'generic' into the glossary of community education. As first employed, it is inter-changeable with the word 'common' and used to refer to the skills held to be shared by those professions said to be 'related' to community education: teaching, social work, and leisure and recreation.

In summary, the Carnegy Report opts for an idealising description of community education, using hyperbole to sell the fledgeling service, with the danger of opening up gaps between claim and performance. At the same time, training in the original areas of practice, though still held to be important, can be regarded as having been diminished in value as the concept of the common core of knowledge and skills required for community education is introduced.

The evolution of community education — and the process of

revising Alexander — takes further steps in *Training for Change,*
subtitled *A report on community education training,* issued eight
years later, in 1984, by the Scottish Community Education Council.
By this time the service has had a chance to show what it can do, still
without the hoped-for extra cash.

The key concept is now *core plus options,* with core defined as
relating to the process of community education, and options to the
wide variety of specialist settings in which the process is put into
practice. We are moving further away from Alexander towards the
concepts of generic community education and generic workers, to
whom specialists are in some sense inferior. The net effect is to raise
the status of community education and community education
process, and to lower the status of adult education, youth service,
and community work. They are no longer areas with their own
processes, they are mere settings, equivalent in status to other
settings like outdoor activities, dance, play leadership, and adult
basic education.

As a document, *Training for Change* is full of contradictions. One
moment it recognises adult education, youth service, and community
work. The next, we are back to the community education process.
There are moments of self-critical frankness such as this:

> It is not surprising, therefore, that the introduction of a
> community education service led, initially, to confusion
> amongst staff as to their roles. Previously a youth and
> community worker or an adult education organiser, the newly
> designated community education worker was now to deliver
> lifelong learning, supporting individual and group
> development from pre-school children to the elderly,
> incorporating, along the way, provision for disadvantaged or
> special needs groups. In this 'cradle to the grave' education the
> possibilities were endless, and the generic community
> education worker was born. For some time the experience was
> overwhelming and they retreated to what they knew best,
> while others began to exploit the freedom of their role by
> carrying on within their traditional areas of activity but with
> some new emphasis in their work. In the early stages after
> reorganisation there was little evidence of the formulation of
> new policies or practices which might reduce the tensions
> faced by the community education worker. Some of the
> tensions remain today, and there is evidence that a recognisable
> and accessible developmental structure of education has not
> been fully achieved. There is substantial evidence that the
> mainstream curriculum tends to be static, ad hoc, remains

located in leisure, social and recreational areas avoiding
cognitive and issue-based learning.

There is an attempt to look at the third strand — community work
— and a recognition that community education staff feel they lack
the skills to tackle it. But the report doesn't draw the obvious
conclusion, that there is a particular set of skills, and a process, in
community work, which people need to learn in depth, and which
differ from, though it overlaps with, the processes of youth work and
adult education. Instead, reference is made to the need for trainees to
learn about local authority structures and social policy issues.

Training for Change goes on to sketch in some of the 'additional
responsibilities and interests' which community education has
'developed' in the last eight years: ABE, vocational training,
unemployment, poverty, welfare rights, information technology,
resource centres, women's education, children's play, the disabled,
multi-cultural education, older people, community schools, and so
on. It summarises community education as a 'rapidly expanding field
of practice', meaning of course not more workers but more
responsibilities for the existing workers. We are close, in fact, to the
rag-bag concept of community education, and to a picture of a
passive profession with a low self-image which gets new tasks flung
at it whether it wants them or not. The report does not complain. It
classifies all such work as community education, and in the same
breath, not surprisingly, asks itself what the central concept of
community education is.

In seeking to answer its own question, *Training for Change* starts
off with a pretty hard challenge from Professor Nisbet, who lambasts
community education for failing to define its theoretical basis and
the anti-theory attitudes of its practitioners, and specifies four 'fears'
which are in fact criticisms aimed at the heart of community
education. These are:
(1)   practice without theory leads to judging provision by scale
      rather than purpose;
(2)   community education is in danger of becoming a series of
      unco-ordinated and unrelated responses;
(3)   community education is in danger of being seen as only for
      people in deprived areas;
(4)   practice paid for by public funds must be theoretically justified.

Instead of responding to this challenge in a lively fashion, the
report says, simply, that it agrees with Nisbet. Seeking to restore
community education's dignity, it embarks on an attempt to define
its aims, starting with those identified by Carnegy. This is followed

by a list of people and activities to which these aims are said to be applicable. They are applicable to *everybody* and to a vast range of activities: leisure and recreation, knowledge and skills, personal and social learning, environmental and political change. They are appropriate to other professions as well. What the report succeeds in doing here is reverting to the Carnegy position and somehow evading Nisbet's challenge. I ask myself: what is the meaning of this repeated concern with other professions? Is it the anti-compartmentalising tendency, or does it in fact reflect community education's continuing uncertainty about its own professional identity? Are they trying, by association, to borrow status from professions like social work which have succeeded in establishing a core of task and expertise? Is community education really aware of its lack of coherence and is this the drive behind the insistent search for a common core of knowledge and skills? The report seems unable or unwilling to make exclusive choices.

Training for Change concedes that community education is seen as an umbrella term, but asserts that there really is a central process, visualised as the hub of a wheel, holding all the activities and settings together. They offer a definition:

> Community education is a process which involves the participants in the creation of purposive developmental and educational programmes and structures which afford opportunities for individual and collective growth and change throughout life.

The process is described as having six functional tasks:
(1)   identification of issues, demands and needs;
(2)   design of programmes/structures/learning to meet the needs;
(3)   promotion of these;
(4)   managing, supporting and delivering them;
(5)   publicising them (the difference between tasks three and five is not made clear);
(6)   continuous assessment/evaluation.

The report admits that workers will need specific knowledge of one or more specific areas, as well as a knowledge of the generic process, and this leads them to their conclusion: that what is required is a core-plus-options model.

For a moment we are allowed again to glimpse some of the evidence demonstrating the unwisdom of the whole drift of *Training for Change*'s thinking. Reference is made to the fact that the national bodies representing both adult education and youth service feel that the quantity and quality of work in these areas is being impaired. Again, they deal with the damning criticism by agreeing with it.

The cure is to be threefold. First, it is recommended that the amount of training time spent in fieldwork placements is to be increased to 50 per cent of the total, thus bringing about a different relationship between theory and practice, and a greater attention to the employers' requirements with regard to training. It is recognised that the quality of placements and of fieldwork supervision will have to be improved. Secondly, the modularisation of training, that is to say the adoption of a system of free-standing forty-hour units of learning which can be articulated (joined up) in what is held to be a flexible variety of ways, thus improving access and reducing rigidity. Thirdly, the creation of a national-and-regional training scheme structure consisting of four area training councils and a national training council.

Course members must decide for themselves what to make of all this. I confess to a distrustful attitude towards pseudo-scientific, ultra-rational, totalising systems. Modularisation can be regarded as a diversion of time and resources away from the long-overdue task of mobilising everyone available to train the vast body of part-timers on whom the community education service depends. The aim of changing the relationship between theory and practice is a good one, and it is right that there should be a greater emphasis on fieldwork practice experience. I argued at the time that the resources called for in the report to create the structure of national-and-regional councils should be diverted into the creation of fieldwork teaching units located in practice agencies throughout Scotland. These considerations, however, must be regarded as academic in the light of the fact that the whole package of recommendations was rejected by the Secretary of State three years later. Yes, *three years later*, an illustration of the masterly use of delay as an instrument of policy perfected by British administrators in colonial settings, and applied with devastating effect throughout the whole community education period in Scotland.

How are we to assess *Training for Change*? It reflects the anxiety of a profession about the core of its identity, the quality of its practice, the absence of boundaries, and the poverty of its theory. It attempts to identify a core. It can be seen as grasping at the quasi-technological straw of modularisation as a means of prising resources for training from a tight-fisted central government.

Widening the lens now, how can we summarise the development of community education from Alexander through Carnegy to *Training for Change*? We have been watching the formation and early stages in the evolution of a new profession, with dimensions of internal conflict, identity uncertainty and a search for identity, with moments of omnipotence and grandiosity. alternating with moments of doubt about competence and direction. More specifically, we see a shift from the initial focus on adult education and its expansion and redirection towards those who are disadvantaged, towards a view of adult education and youth service as regions of the wide newly designated territory of Community Education, and a further shift towards the notion of a single imperial entity, generic community education, with its single process, its collection of settings, and its hierarchical ranking of generalist over specialist workers.

There is one final pressing question. Suppose the notion of a single process proves to be unhelpful in the longer run? If so, is the concept of community education still valid? If it is, how can the identity of the service be strengthened, boundaries set, and the self-worth of the staff established in their own eyes? If it is not, how are we to promote the causes of adult education, youth work, and community work? So many questions, as Brecht wrote — and behind them, such a lot of anger.

34. Adult Education: national disgrace

This letter, concerned with cuts in central government grants to the Extra-mural Departments of Scottish Universities, was printed in *The Scotsman* on 18th October 1986.

*

159 Dalkeith Road,
Edinburgh,
October 14, 1986

Sir, — I was dismayed to learn from Basil Skinner's letter of the substantial cuts in the Scottish Education Department's grants to Scottish university extra-mural departments, and particularly to the Extra-mural Department of Edinburgh University.

The poverty of funding for adult education in Scotland is appalling. It is a national disgrace.

The Secretary of State's Committee of Inquiry into Adult Education, chaired by Sir Kenneth Alexander, observed in its 1975 report 'Adult Education: The Challenge of Change' that just under 4.5 per cent of the post-school population attended adult education courses in 1972-73. Since then, following a peak (or rather, a foothill) of 4.9 per cent in 1975-76, numbers have fallen steadily to 3.5 per cent (representing 171,463 enrolments) in 1978-79, the last year for which figures have been made easily available. It is understood that they are still falling.

By way of contrast, the Alexander Report recommended the creation of 200 additional posts, the expenditure of an extra £1 million (at 1974 prices) and set the objective of doubling student numbers by the mid-1980s! Within this perspective, the task of the universities and their extra-mural departments was seen as crucial.

Their roles of providing the highest level of academic study and liberal education for individual students were recognised. In encouraging them to adopt a community development approach to stimulating demand for adult education among those sections of the population not currently taking part, the report stated explicitly that this would require 'a substantial injection of resources of all kinds'.

The report also recommended additional appointments to increase the awareness among the general public of the potential contribution of the universities, the provision of courses for professional groups, and opportunities for informed public discussion of controversial issues of public policy.

During the last ten years, adult and community education bodies in general, and extra-mural departments in particular, have striven to respond to the challenge presented by Alexander. The Edinburgh Extra-mural Department has made a very valuable contribution, providing such innovative, effective and popular courses as New Horizons (for returners to study), Wider Opportunities for Women (for returners to work), Employment Refresher Courses (for unemployed men and women), Human Relations and Counselling Courses, Christian Studies, and Looking at the Lothians.

Alas, successive Governments, both Labour and Conservative, have failed to provide the new resources required. The present Government prefers to switch resources away from liberal education into training with a narrowly utilitarian orientation, for jobs which do not exist.

Apart from the inherent absurdity of such a project, there is a failure to understand that skills training which fails to set the learning of skills in the context of the wider and deeper development of the person will fail to attain its own objectives.

The officials of the Scottish Education Department are in an unenviable position: pressed on the one hand by Government Ministers to cut expenditure and hold it at present levels, and on the other by demands for increased expenditure from various sources, they are obliged to take resources from one valuable area of work to fund another. They have to rob Peter to pay Paul.

If we believe, with Dante, that we are born to seek knowledge and virtue, and that our search will be helped by the availability of a wide range of opportunities for further learning throughout our adult lives, then we would seem to have no alternative but to make the resourcing of adult and community education a political issue in the run-up to the next General Election.

Colin Kirkwood

35. Issues in Adult Education Training

For many years I was a member and later secretary of the Scottish Institute of Adult and Continuing Education's Training Committee. One of our major preoccupations was the training of part-time tutors. We were invited to prepare a collection of papers for a special training number of the Institute's journal. 'Issues in Adult Education Training' was my own contribution to the collection, which was published in the *Scottish Journal of Adult Education* in the spring of 1987. My major objective was to reaffirm the primacy of questions of orientation and value over questions of technique, while not devaluing the latter.

*

Part-time tutors' motives for seeking training

Part-time tutors of adults have a variety of motives for seeking training. Most of these motives relate to practical aspects of their task. Tutors look to training to improve their skills, including how to set learning objectives, build curricula, increase their repertoire of teaching/learning methods, sharpen such communication skills as preparing a presentation, listening, re-presenting, summarising, stimulating and using discussion, and helping their students learn how to learn.

They also want to know more about group dynamics; more specifically, what happens in a learning group within, between, and among its members, the roles of group tutor, leader or co-ordinator, and how to tackle some of the problems that can arise in group learning situations. Further, tutors want to find out more about their roles in relation to the learning objectives and difficulties of *individual* students.

Finally, there is a cluster of motives relating to factors outside the immediate learning situation: in taking part in training..., tutors are seeking ideas, collaboration and support from their fellow tutors, and from their employer or supervisor. They are sometimes responding to pressure from the employer to take part in training. And they may wish to obtain a professional qualification, or some recognition of satisfactory completion of training, in order to improve or safeguard their employment prospects.

Mobilising resources for part-time tutor training: a case study

From 1969 until 1972 I worked as an area principal for adult education in north-east Derbyshire. My arrival happened to coincide with the beginning of dramatic developments in training. This was the mobilisation of the available resources for a systematic programme of training for part-time adult education tutors employed by local education authorities in the area covered by the East Midlands Advisory Council for Adult Education, including Derbyshire, Leicestershire, Nottinghamshire, and the burghs within their boundaries. The initial push seems to have come from the professional adult educators themselves, particularly the divisional adult education officers. The HMI for the region was involved, as were the staff of the Department of Adult Education at the University of Nottingham, who played key roles both in training the trainers and in the actual training sessions with part-time tutors.

The exciting thing about this project was its inclusiveness, the sense of a shared movement and purpose. It really did seem to be a mobilisation: the area principals, the divisional adult education officers, the county training officer, the staff of the university, the HMI, and a large number of heads of centres and part-time tutors employed by the county. The number of tutors taking part was impressive, given that it was optional: they were not paid for taking part, and got no increase in pay as a result, though a certificate of attendance was issued, and successful completion increased their chances of continued employment. The programme lasted thirty-six hours in the first year, leading to a modular programme in the second year, and the opportunity to take a university certificate in the third.

Discovery Learning

The format used was a series of all-day Saturday meetings, with lectures, workshops and plenary sessions, plus a residential weekend. The emphasis was on practical approaches to curriculum building and the use of a range of teaching/learning methods, with stress on getting tutors to expand their repertoire beyond the traditional exposition and demonstration. There was input on how adults learn, and emphasis on relating conceptual knowledge to practical experience. Much was made of discovery learning. We watched the famous Belbin film about steam engine drivers being taught to drive electric trains. This involved learning about electric circuits, to which the film showed two alternative approaches: first the exposition-and-demonstration method, using chalk and talk, and second the discovery method, which involved each driver finding out how to connect up the components of his own miniature circuit for himself. It was claimed that the second method was a quicker and more effective way of grasping electrical processes than the first. Seeing that film was one of those illuminating experiences, permanently influencing my views on the methodology of adult learning in favour of learning-by-doing, though I have never accepted the implicit devaluation of exposition and demonstration.

Resistance to Change

These experiences in Derbyshire had their lighter side. The dressmaking, woodworking, and metalworking tutors were among the hardest to budge when it came to changing attitudes to methodology. The tutors knew that the LEA professional staff and the university lecturers were entirely ignorant of the mysteries of their respective crafts. The lecturers and adult education organisers knew that in some of the craft classes students just told the tutors what they wanted to make, and the tutors would either make it for them, or do the hard bits and use the students as unskilled labour. There was also a wish to challenge the exclusively practical orientation of these classes and their social-club atmosphere. An invisible wrestling match went on between the two sides throughout the training process. I can recall the withering contempt of some of the male craft tutors for ivory tower academics, and the triumphant air of one lecturer when introducing a film of a dressmaking class in which articles of clothing were being made out of an intricate material belonging to some sixteenth- or seventeenth-century genre, offering scope for enriching the educational process by discussing the history of its mode of production and its social uses. Shortly afterwards a lady was found who enthusiastically took on board the desired learn-by-doing and intellectualising orientations in the teaching of dressmaking. She was given extra classes and used as a stick to beat the unreconstructed. The latter, however, had the last laugh, because their classes were popular, and the last thing we wanted was to preside over a big drop in enrolments.

Micro-Teaching

Part of the residential weekend was devoted to what is now called micro-teaching. Tutors were asked to bring with them a prepared chunk of around thirty minutes teaching/learning in their subject, and to do this session live with a small group of tutors from other disciplines who would be their students. This would be followed by group assessment of the strengths and weaknesses of each session. Micro-teaching can be a good way of getting tutors to think about the learning experiences their students are having, if participants take part in the right spirit, and if the assessment sessions are well handled. It deepens their awareness by placing them in swift succession in the roles of student and tutor, and the feedback confronts them with the success or failure of their normal methods. It is also useful for full-time staff (who may be organisers rather than teachers in their professional work) because it gives them insight into the problems with which their part-time tutors are struggling.

With hindsight, the weakness of these training experiences lay in the excessively narrow conception of what counted as adult education, and in the emphasis on curriculum and method over such questions as value, purpose, and who education is for. It was training in methods for tutors on the existing class programme. Having said that, I agree with Neil Tempest* when he describes it as 'an attempt to lift adult education out of the old evening institute days and ways'. It was training of a high quality. Collaboration across institutional and divisional boundaries was a great source of strength. It helped to reduce the envious belittling of other people's work to which we are all given. Overall it gave participants a sense of being part of a service which took itself seriously and was concerned about standards of quality. And it demonstrated a commitment to the professional development of part-time staff, bringing them out of isolation and into productive association, creating a sense of an adult education movement.

Training based on the ideas of Paulo Freire

In the late 1970s, a series of courses exploring the ideas and methods of the Brazilian adult educator, Paulo Freire, were organised through the WEA in Edinburgh. There were four such courses altogether. Two were close reading groups, based on Freire's book *Pedagogy of the Oppressed*. The main course, combining study of Freire's ideas and methods with discussion of community action and community education projects, was run as an in-service training course for community education, community development and social work staff in Lothian, both in the statutory and voluntary sectors. The fourth was an evening course aimed at the general public, attracting

---

* Neil Tempest was at that time Divisional Adult Education Officer in North-East Derbyshire. I am indebted to him for reminding me of many aspects of the training programme.

teachers, lecturers, housewives, and members of churches, trade unions and political parties.

I felt Freire's ideas were crucial for a number of reasons. First, he represented a refreshing counterweight to the excessively empirical and pragmatic tendencies in British adult education. Freire treated theory seriously. On the other hand, his theory, though rich and elaborate, was not purely abstract. It illuminated the lives and educational experiences of oppressed people, and the blocks to participation they encounter. Freire appeared to have succeeded in overcoming the division between the ghettoistic localism that characterised some British approaches to community education, and the macro-economic/political analyses that were posed as the alternative. In struggling to create an education which would treat students as subjects in their relations with each other, the teacher, and the world, Freire showed that education was not a separated-off domain, but should concern itself with real circumstances, real problems, at both macro and micro levels. In other words, education *was* concerned with politics. On the other hand, in his consistent challenges to sectarian, determinist and authoritarian tendencies on the left (which tend to regard education as the transmission of a correct consciousness to supplant the false consciousness imposed by oppressive élites), and in his insistence on no political interference from governments, he showed that education was not simply the pursuit of political objectives by another means.

Freire was also important because his methods pointed to ways of overcoming the false polarisation of experience and academic knowledge, showing instead how they can be related without reverting to worship of the latter. Finally, Freire did not accept the fashionable option of negating the authority of the tutor. He was concerned with enabling people to move beyond magical and naive stages of consciousness, in which god-like powers are ascribed to tutors and other figures of authority, but not to the point of *destroying* their authority, or the value of their knowlege.

The exploration of Freire's ideas by participants in these courses was to influence the growth of the writers' workshop movement in Scotland, the approach to education with unemployed people developed by the WEA and Edinburgh University Settlement, and Lothian Region's Adult Learning Project in Gorgie/Dalry.

Key themes in adult education and training

While it is important that training should connect with the motivation of those who seek it — motivation related to felt needs for learning about practical approaches and obtaining personal support — it is also important to explore fundamental assumptions and educational values. In a very real sense these values underlie and are embodied in all educational situations.

Autocratic Authority

The last twenty years have seen challenges to the autocratic conception of the teacher's authority, the arrangement of seats in ranks, the obligatory silence, the orientation of individual competition, and the examination system. Alternative visions of education have been advanced, proposing a relationship of dialogue and respect between teacher and students, semi-circular or circular seating arrangements, and an orientation of mutual help in classwork and homework. We are concerned here with a crucial cluster of themes: the nature of the authority of the tutor, the authority of the students, and the relations between student and student and student and tutor.

Student Control

These challenges have not been static once-and-for-all statements. On the contrary, they have been dynamic; their content has undergone change and development, and has evoked equally dynamic responses (such as the Black Papers and the research by Neville Bennett and his colleagues). As the 1970s advanced, however, a tendency to think in polarised opposites intensified in some educational circles. From the traditional magisterial conception of the authority of the teacher (sometimes characterised as patriarchal, hierarchical, or even just male), there was a swing towards negotiation of the curriculum, or outright student control. This was often accompanied by rejection of the very notion of authority per se. Authority was seen simply as domination.

Experience and Knowledge

This leads on to another key theme in the politics of education: the relationship between experience and knowledge, and the connected but not identical relationship between the affective and the cognitive. Just as the authority of the teacher was challenged, so was the authority of knowledge: from a posture of obeisance before the academic tablets of stone (books, research findings, learned papers, lectures) there was a swing towards a high valuation of the expression of personal or shared experience and opinion, or towards a relativistic conception of knowledge.

Another related theme is the relationship between education and politics. From being regarded to a large extent as a separated-off domain-in-itself, education came to be seen by some as a colony of the imperial power of politics, one domain among many in which it was felt that desirable political objectives could be pursued. There has been a small but vocal minority who regard education as serving political objectives in a simple fashion: from that viewpoint, education is a transmission belt for the correct facts, analysis or political policies, whether overtly or covertly, and whether expository, participatory or discovery modes of teaching and learning are used.

Choice of Methods

Some of the effects of these powerful themes have already been alluded to. They can be seen more clearly when we look, for example, at choices of teaching/learning methods. Their effect has often been to narrow the range of methods that are regarded as acceptable. Thus, exposition, extended presentations from books (as opposed to short extracts), and structured discussion controlled by a co-ordinator, have all tended to be seen in a negative light. Instead, what is often disproportionately favoured is loosely structured, barely- or un-co-ordinated discussion, or group work exercises around worksheets containing sequences of questions or tasks (which are often individually or cumulatively slanted towards particular learning outcomes).

The case I am arguing here is twofold: first, that values have become unproductively polarised, and that a process of reintegration is now needed; and secondly that these and other important themes clearly pervade what may appear to be purely practical technical matters like curriculum building, methods and skills, and that opportunities to examine them should therefore be built into training courses.

Mature Integration

In moving towards a conclusion, I would like to mention two recent examples of training for WEA staff in Scotland, which, though small in scale, demonstrated a mature integration of some of these polarised themes. In these instances, I felt I was observing and taking part in training experiences in an expository mode, with good orderly use of verbal and (in one case also) visual presentation, with questions posed and answered, with discussion co-ordinated both by the main tutor and by the group as a whole, through disciplined and attentive listening and responding. There was an organic feeling about these sessions, one with Cathy Sandler on Second Chance to Learn, the other with Ann Dale on Educational and Psychothera-peutic Processes. Both demonstrated how the abandonment of the god-like status of the teacher need not lead to the negation of her authority, neither in the dimension of her knowledge, nor of her role in co-ordinating the group. Nor need it lead to a dive into a relativistic morass in which standards, competence, quality, insight, wisdom, and inherited bodies of knowledge are thrown out of the window. The experiences of participants were positively valued, knitted into the process, but not worshipped as the one true god, nor manipulated to lead to conclusions predetermined by the tutor.

With hindsight, it seems to me that we have lived through a period in which two false absolutes held sway one after the other, two caricatures: worshipping the tablets of stone, then reinventing the wheel. I am not arguing against the value of using students' experiences, but against their romantic deification, and against anything-goes attitudes. It is important for us to work out how things sometimes went awry in the latter part of the 1970s. As well as losing the best effects of the traditional method of logical exposition or demonstration by someone who has knowledge or expertise, we also lost — in the shoddier, more laid-back versions of participation — the good learning that can grow out of experiential or discovery methods when they are well used.

Authority and Collaboration

Adult education training and practice should be neither authoritarian nor permissive. Our work should be founded on the authority of the tutor's knowledge *and* his/her competence as a facilitator of learning; and on the authority of students who are also knowers and responsible agents in seeking to know more, voluntarily accepting and collaborating with the tutor's authority in order to achieve their objective. The metaphor of negotiation, which implies bargaining between two sides with fundamentally opposed interests, seems to me inappropriate as a means of conceptualising this relationship.

The danger of reversion to authoritarian or manipulative styles never disappears, nor does the temptation to go native, to wish or pretend to be in the same position as your students. There is a contradiction between these two roles which is benign and productive, rather than antagonistic. I would argue that this contradiction is resolved to some extent at least in the process of teaching and learning, when it is effective.

36. Divorce Advice and Counselling for Men (review)

Relationships between men and women was one of the most difficult issues of the seventies and early eighties. It was also the hardest to write about, partly because its root-system penetrated so deeply into your own personality, and partly because, if you were a man, it seemed as if the women's movement had put an interdict on the expression of views which did not correspond with their line. The difficulty was magnified in intensity if you actually agreed with large parts of the feminist case. The result was silence except from those 'new men' who enthusiastically tried to become the sort of guys they thought the feminists wanted. The feminists and the new men produced images which grossly misrepresented actual men, and the causes of male behaviour, to the point, sometimes, of unrecognisability. Both sexes suffered as a result of this feminist imperialism, which was simply a reversal of, or antithetical reaction to, patriarchal imperialism. Reviewing Jane Forster's paper was a pleasure precisely because she was interested in finding out what real men (as opposed to bogey-men) were thinking and feeling. This review appeared in Lothian Marriage Counselling Service's autumn newsletter, in 1988.

*

Men and women are another country to each other, the literal *embodiment* of otherness. There are various ways of dealing with such differences. At one extreme, there is fantasy, and at the other, investigation. Much of the feminist literature of the 1970s demonstrated a view of men based largely on fantasy. The great strength of Jane Forster's excellent monograph, *Divorce Advice and Counselling for Men*, is that it takes the investigative approach. It summarises the findings of the existing literature, and it reports on and analyses the work of a small pilot Divorce Counselling and Advice Service provided in Edinburgh by Family Care, in which the author was involved.

Divorce Advice and Counselling for Men by Jane Forster (Occasional Paper No. 3, Scottish Marriage Guidance Council, 1988).

Jane Forster writes clearly. Her thinking is logical and incisive. She manages to combine thoroughness and brevity. Hardly a word is wasted.

She begins by referring to the myths about men and divorce: that men don't care, get off scot-free, and soon forget. She summarises the research evidence on the feelings aroused in men by divorce: loss, anger, bitterness, victimisation, and yearning for the lost partner and the children. She focuses on the facts that divorced fathers usually become the non-custodial parents, that many of them lose contact with their children, and that it is in this group that the evidence of physical and mental ill-health is likely to be greatest. Since the children who keep contact with their divorced fathers are more likely to be in good psychological health, she concludes that services for divorcing men might set themselves the objective of increasing the number of men remaining in touch with their children.

Her comments on male psychology are in line with Janette Chisholm's recent remark that 'men in our society are not allowed to be helpless'. She touches on our need to be in control, to succeed, to hide our vulnerability, our tendency not to be in touch with feelings at all, and therefore, not to be good at expressing them. She explains convincingly why men are less likely than women to seek counselling or social work help.

In her account of the Pilot Project, she emphasises that the sample was very small and that the conclusions cannot therefore be generalised. While one approves of her caution, the truth is that careful, sustained, in-depth work with a small group is more likely to yield valuable insights that can be applied elsewhere, than academically respectable, empirically measurable, basically shallow large-scale investigations, however randomised their samples, because what they measure is often not significant.

Of the divorced or separated men who sought help in the project, some had been drinking to excess, some had been close to suicide, some had run up large debts, and some had been on drugs. They tended to have started on their own to climb out of the pit of despair, which underlines, for me, the pathetic investment we men have in self-sufficiency. For most men, seeking help is *humiliating*.

The author identifies three broad categories of motive for seeking help: seeking factual information; being on the brink of making an important decision; and wanting to unburden and disentangle feelings. It is another reflection of the problem identified in the previous paragraph that, sadly, the last group was the smallest.

Her conclusion is that counsellors and social workers should anticipate and prepare for a majority of one-meeting relationships with such men, adapting their methods to the men's need to focus

L

on information-getting and to stay in control. I think that is adapting to a pathological norm. On the contrary, it seems to me that counsellors need to create an atmosphere which helps men to get out of their habit of walking the tightrope of information and control.

Jane Forster discusses the pros and cons of female and male counsellors where men are concerned, concluding that neither has unqualified advantages. The key issue, she argues, is to establish the nature and boundaries of the relationship.

She also discusses the scope for counselling men in work settings, concluding that there is some way to go before that is a realistic option, though workplace advertising of counselling services may be valuable. Finally, she considers the involvement of children and wives in the counselling sessions, especially in the early stages of the separation process, concluding that: 'the overriding need seemed to be to allow the man space to explore his personal thoughts and feelings . . . involving the other partner in these situations would actually inhibit the exploration. . . .'

My only serious point of difference with the author relates to her proposal for Divorce Resource Centres. I have two objections: first, I would argue that the evidence she presents can be taken equally to support the case for generic or multi-focus counselling services, as for such a narrow focus; and second, the creation of such centres would give a further twist to the cultural process by which we are being encouraged to regard marriage as a short-term relationship, and marriage partners as consumer goods to be traded in when they begin to wear out.

At fourteen pages, *Divorce Advice and Counselling for Men* is short, pleasantly produced and easy to read. It is the third of Scottish Marriage Guidance Council's series of occasional papers. It is an excellent piece of work, and I recommend it highly.

37. The Ideological Make-up of Community Education

This outline was prepared for the Annual General Meeting of the Scottish Association of Community Education Staffs (SACES) held at Livingston in September 1988.

*

For the purposes of this outline, ideology is taken to mean a cluster or constellation of interrelated concepts and values which, taken together, make up a meaningful totality that stands on its own. This does not mean that it is independent of other concepts, values or ideologies. The ideological make-up of a particular sector, such as community education (hereinafter CE), is that totality of interrelated concepts and values which characterise the sector as a whole. No one has the ideal or perfectly informed vantage point from which to know the ideology of any one sector. The methods available to us are *exposure* to the complex, evolving reality of its origin, constitution, structure, practice, and to what is said and written about it, including its key texts; *investigation; clarification; evaluation;* and finally *presentation.* It is an ongoing, collaborative venture in which people work together, learn from and challenge each other. The contributions of individual investigators are significant dimensions of such collaborative processes.

In preparing this outline I am drawing on the following sources: my own experiences in Scotland, England and Italy as a learner, adult educator, community worker, teacher of community education and community development, and activist in working-class localities; my understanding of the formation and evolution of the CE service in Scotland; miscellaneous research findings, and the following specific texts: *Community Education: An Agenda for Educational Reform,* edited by Allen, Bastiani, Martin and Richards (Open University Press, Milton Keynes, 1987); *Issues in Community Education,* edited by Fletcher and Thompson (Falmer Press, Lewes,

1980); *Living Adult Education: Freire in Scotland,* by G. and C. Kirkwood (Open University Press, Milton Keynes, 1989) plus various articles and papers published in *SCAN, Network* and *Adult Education* over the years.

The ideology of CE as it presents itself in practice and in various writings is a mish-mash of contradictions, an overcooked soup in which various component vegetables and cereals can occasionally be sighted. This lack of clarity has increasingly been recognised, and the task of clarification is being undertaken on a serious basis.

I propose to contribute to the effort of clarification by identifying eight broad strands of CE, with distinctive yet interwoven ideologies. These strands are:

1. Mainstream CE, Scottish version
2. Mainstream CE, English version
3. Freirean thinking and practice in CE
4. Feminist thinking and practice in CE
5. Ideal CE
6. British colonial CE
7. Socialist CE
8. A right-wing view of CE.

There is no implication of greater or lesser approval in the choice or sequencing of these strands. They are offered as descriptions of what exists. I am leaving out of consideration other ideologies washing around the shores of CE, and to a greater or lesser extent penetrating it, such as open learning and skills training for jobs, because, though important, they are not specifically community education ideologies.

Each strand operates on the basis of some sort of understanding of two key concepts, *community* and *community education.* Both concepts contain dimensions of fact and dimensions of value, and one of our problems is that the facts and/or values can sometimes vary from strand to strand. What we each mean by, and how we deal with, these two concepts, is a basic problem for everyone concerned with CE. I propose not to cover old ground again by offering definitions, but to signal the necessity for each of us to try and work out where we stand on both of these.

1. Mainstream CE, Scottish Version

The Scottish version is essentially a marriage of youth and community work and adult education, coloured with community development ideas. The question of whether or not it includes community schools is open to doubt: in terms of sentiment, it probably does, but in terms of administrative reality, community schools are a separate though allied domain.

Key texts are the *Alexander Report*, the *Carnegy Report*, and *Training for Change*.

The Scottish version regards the vagueness of the term CE as a positive advantage: as functionally ambiguous. It is said to be all-embracing. Some critics would say that this is part of its problem: it has difficulty in drawing exclusive boundaries round itself and is vulnerable to the periodic inclusion of new tasks in its remit, by Ministers or senior civil servants.

It is characterised as informal in style, responsive to popular demand, reflecting local communities, embodying voluntarism, and stimulating self-help. It claims to work with everyone, from the cradle to the grave, and places emphasis on the value of people's experience. There is a strong undercurrent of hostility to knowledge and to teaching in Scottish CE. And there is stress on people doing it themselves, doing what they want, and taking control of their own lives.

It can be argued that the ethos of Scottish CE is a reaction to the ethos of traditional formal education in Scottish schools, colleges and universities. It can also be argued that its ethos owes much to the fact that it is a non-statutory sector, and that therefore the activities in which it involves people are non-compulsory.

As far as professional workers are concerned, the key feature of Scottish CE is the concept of the generalist or generic worker. This derives from the integrative anti-specialist trend of the 1960s, and specifically from the model of the generic social worker. Specialism and specialists have thus tended to be downgraded: this has applied, for example, to youth work, adult education, and adult basic education. While the high tide of the generic concept and the devaluation of specialism has passed, it is still powerfully influential.

The generic worker is seen as having wide-ranging organisational and groupwork skills, capable of engaging in youth work, leisure and recreation, community arts, community centre work, local festivals, adult basic education, issue-based adult education, work with the physically and mentally handicapped, provision for the elderly, community action on local issues, etc. They have been regarded as multipliers, either because they touch and facilitate the lives of many groups, or through their roles as organisers and deployers of part-time specialists.

Most workers accept this concept and struggle to fulfil it. Some have found that difficult. There has been some de facto specialisation, some demand for specialist in-service training, and for changes in deployment policy to allow both specialisation and teamwork.

Some keywords in Scottish CE are:

(as it affects participants) leisure, enjoyment, expression, creativity, activity, freedom, choice, disadvantage, and community control

(as it affects the roles of workers in relation to participants) access, availability, responsiveness, outreach and relevance.

A key theme in Scottish CE revolves around the meanings attached to the concepts of professionalism and authority. There is a strong anti-professional, anti-authority current, reflected in the idea that activities should be user-led, that the role of the worker is to be informal, approachable and responsive, a facilitator whose task is to work him/herself out of a job. There is a strong identification with those who have failed at school (or been failed by the schooling system), and an implicit blaming of teachers and the education system as a whole. Teaching is eschewed in favour of experience; study in favour of activity; and the institutional world of education in favour of the community.

The problem here is that there are positive values on both sides of these polarities, and it is the present writer's view that CE needs help to emerge from the locked, polarised position in which it has placed itself on these issues.

2. Mainstream CE, English version

CE in England is about community schooling at both secondary and primary levels, and also about community work and adult education in deprived/disadvantaged/working-class communities.

Key texts include: *The Village College* (Henry Morris); *Educator Extraordinary: the Life and Achievements of Henry Morris* (Harry Ree); *The School and Community* (Cyril Poster); *The Plowden Report*; various books by Eric Midwinter; various articles by Keith Jackson and Bob Ashcroft; *Adult Education, Community Development and the Working Class* by Tom Lovett.

These are really separate strands which sometimes entwine, occasionally merge, and generally remain apart. They are, however, *viewed* as a totality. The English picture is thus different from the Scottish.

Morris's view of the school was that it should be a powerhouse in the community, an integrative, generative and regenerative force. He worked in rural Cambridgeshire in the 1920 and '30s, and was concerned about economic decay, depopulation, and the political vacuum left in local government by the decline of the squirearchy. He wanted to create comprehensive institutions of education covering fairly large areas, taking in all secondary-aged children and acting as a centre for all adult education and community life. The school was to be a beautiful, significant building in the landscape, a true centre placing education at the heart of the life of the district.

Morris's ideas are said to have contributed both to the movement for comprehensive education and to the movement for community schools. These two movements are seen as distinct but related. The campaign for comprehensivisation spread in the post-war period and had largely triumphed by the end of the 1960s. The community schools movement also spread in the post-war period, but more slowly, and may still be gathering momentum.

The key ideas here are two-way communication and traffic between the school and its setting; dual use of premises; the involvement of people in the outside community in the life of the school, and in the management of the school; various forms of outreach from and engagement by the school in the life of the surrounding community; changes in the design of school buildings, and in the approaches to curriculum development, teaching, learning, and assessment. It should be stressed that the notion of economies of scale seems to have provided part of the motivation for the development of community schools in many counties. The concept of community espoused is therefore wider than that of the local neighbourhood.

The primary school as community school is a more recent concept, dating from the publication of the Plowden Report, *Children and their Primary Schools,* in the late 1960s. This gave rise to the creation of a number of Educational Priority Areas throughout Britain, of which the best known was the Liverpool EPA led by Eric Midwinter. Here a key concern was the contradiction between the culture of the school and the culture of the home and community (and here community does mean local neighbourhood). The aim was to bring about fruitful home-school links and diminish the cultural discontinuity. There was a recognition that children learn more outside school than inside, and it was argued that there was a need for relevance in the curriculum, with parental involvement in school, and home visiting. This view was challenged by those who argued that the discontinuity or value-dissonance between the school and a deprived community was a positive feature, and that working-class children were entitled to a perspective that revealed their living conditions as intolerable. This view favoured the transcendent, universalistic value of subjects like geography or foreign languages, over against the notion of basing the curriculum on getting to know the locality.

The Liverpool EPA was associated with attempts to involve working-class adults in education, for example through participation in discussion groups on themes of interest or concern to them, in settings acceptable to them. This work, associated with the name of Tom Lovett, links in with the third broad element in the English CE picture, the adult education and community development work developed by Community Development Projects such as the Home Office CDP, YVFF (now CPF) and their multiple derivatives throughout the 1970s.

The English CE mainstream has many elements in common with the Scottish, but also some divergences. Its key concepts are accessibility, attractiveness, relevance, two-way traffic between home and school, partnership between parents and teachers, and the renegotiation and redefinition of the relationships between professional educators and learners.

Writers like Ian Martin, recognising the vagueness of the term CE, regard its 'functional ambiguity' as both negative (e.g. it avoids having to address issues like class) and positive (e.g. it permits a blurring of boundaries between educational establishments and their surrounding communities, between teachers and students, work and leisure, professional and lay person, producer and consumer).

Some recent developments in English CE thinking are discussed in section 7 below.

3. Freirean ideas in CE settings

Key text: *Pedagogy of the Oppressed* by Paulo Freire (and his other works).

Freire's ideas have become steadily more influential in CE settings in Britain. Initially their influence was at the level of ideas, and got stuck there, perhaps because it was felt to be difficult to translate them into practical approaches in contemporary Britain. The gibe 'airy Freire', coined by a community worker in Edinburgh, makes the point very neatly. There is now an increasing number of field workers trying to understand and apply his ideas in Scotland, England and Ireland. In *Living Adult Education: Freire in Scotland*, an account of the work of the Adult Learning Project in Gorgie/ Dalry, Gerri Kirkwood and I try to explain Freire's ideas and to describe learning programmes and action outcomes in which they are applied in practice.

The heart of Freire's position is the struggle to create a world in which it will be easier to love, and each person's struggle to become fully human, in their relationships with each other and with the world. The key to his educational approach is the investigation, by professional workers in collaboration with volunteers from an area, of the important themes in the lives of those who live there. These themes are named in relation to significant situations, which are codified, and the codifications are arranged in a meaningful sequence. Participants from the area then take part in a series of decoding discussions, in which the process of exploration goes from descriptive through affective to analytical levels, with movement backwards and forwards between the codified situation and the real life situation.

An analysis of the results of the decoding process leads to the preparation of learning programmes, using experts from various disciplines. Learning groups are established operating according to the broad sequence: say your own word/contribution by expert/ dialogue. The final stage of the process is action by participants on some issue or area of concern requiring change in their real world.

The Freirean process may seem rigid from this summary, but in fact it is capable of great flexibility and variation. It is founded not on a set of techniques but on a view of human beings as subjects capable of knowing the world through investigation, coming to realise that they can emerge from a fatalistic position of submergence, and through dialogue with each other act on the world to change it.

The visit of Paulo Freire to Scotland in May of this year, the work of ALP, the new initiative in Tayside, the creation of the Freire network, and the work of Sister Doreen Grant and her team in Strathclyde, are all signs of the impact of Freirean ideas on CE in the Scottish context. A view of the influence of Freire in England can be found in the writings of Paula Allman.

4. Feminist thinking in CE settings

There are many women involved in CE fieldwork, but very few in promoted posts. In the absence of statistical evidence, I would guess that the majority of participants in CE initiatives in Scotland (defined as those activities CE workers engage in or support during their working hours) are women. The kinds of analysis developed by feminists in the last twenty years therefore have a bearing on CE. A key text here has been *Learning Liberation: Women's Response to Men's Education* by Jane L. Thompson. Practice initiatives have been taken in the areas of youth work with girls, away-days and weekends for women, women's studies, women and health, women and mental health, women and history, etc. A group of women in the Chester area have prepared a feminist model of CE, which is reproduced here from Ian Martin's chapter in *Community Education: an Agenda for Educational Reform*:

Table 1.3: *Radical feminist model of activity*
Implicit model of society/community: Radical feminist

Premise	Gender-related inequality
	Oppression of women
Strategy	Positive discrimination/action
	Gender role analysis
	Separate provision
	Reconstruction of female knowledge and
	reality
Initial focus	Girls'/women's groups
	Women's studies
	Feminist education
Key influences	'Discounted' women in history
	Mary Wollstonecraft
	Virginia Woolf
	Jane Thompson
Twentieth-century	Suffragette movement
origins	World Wars I and II
	Modern birth control
	'Sexual revolution'
Dominant themes	Separatism/Collectivism
	Control/autonomy
	Nature of oppression
	Family, education and work
	Personal politics
	Nature of learning process
	Excavation and analysis of women in history
	Redefinition; female continuity, identity and
	knowledge

5. Ideal Community Education

This strand is not one which has been identified as such in any writing about CE with which I am familiar, but in my view it is implicit in much CE thinking, writing and practice. Basically I am arguing that a view (in fact several overlapping views) of community and community education as *ideals* exists, containing the following elements:

●Human beings live and work in communities, and this is a fact of central significance about all human societies. It is both a descriptive fact and a normative fact: that is, community inevitably exists where people exist, and human beings need community as a positive value.

●What is meant by community is disputed but there are enough common features in the varying definitions or notions for it to have a meaning. Some of these are:

— participants or members
— groups, organisations, institutions, nations, international/supranational organisations
— territory (at various levels of scale from the home, neighbourhood, district, region, nation, subcontinent, continent, world)
— social activities
— social relationships
— feelings.

The most interesting discussion of community I have come across is by David Clark in his chapter in *Community Education: an Agenda for Educational Reform,* from which the above list is drawn. His view of community is expressed as follows:

> the strength of community within any collective is demonstrated by the degree to which its members act in an ecumenical and autonomous manner.

The term 'ecumenical'* here refers to *solidarity* in a group, but a particular kind of solidarity whose boundaries go beyond those of the particular group, relating to the communal requirements of the world or society as a whole (i.e. it is not a solidarity characterised by hostility to other groups).

The term 'autonomous' here refers to the dignity and significance felt by the individual person in such a community and includes dimensions of enlightened self-interest and of altruism.

Ideal community education, in David Clark's view, aims to enable members of any collective to become increasingly ecumenical and autonomous, and has to do with the maturation of the individual, the group, and society as a whole.

Clearly there are other strains of ideal CE, but what they seem to have in common is a lack of interest in or emphasis on those factors which divide people and set them at odds, such as class, wealth, poverty, race, gender, competitiveness, etc. Perhaps it would be more accurate, from the point of view of ideal CE, to say that it seeks to achieve convergence, ecumenicity, and the resolution of conflict or division.

---

* ecumenical: of or representing the whole Christian world or universal church, general, universal, Catholic (from he oikoumene, the inhabited earth).

6. Colonial Community Education

I have given elsewhere a detailed account of the evolution of
community development and community education in British
colonial contexts and have argued that it was brought home and
applied in the UK in the 1960s and '70s. Reasons of time and space
prevent the elaboration of this strand here, except to say that various
elements, such as the emphasis on locality, popular culture and
custom, relevance, self-help projects, popular celebrations and
festivals, local economic development, adult education (including
literacy), women's groups, the encouragement of initiative,
preparation for self-government, harmonious collaboration
between government bodies and local communities, are all to be
found in the CE programmes implemented by Britain as a colonial
power in Africa, India and the Caribbean. They all characteristically
involve the eschewing of universalistic forms of knowledge such as
foreign languages, world history, or philosophy in favour of
practical, local, co-operative activities.

7. Socialist Community Education

A socialist theory of CE has emerged in the 1980s. It seems partly at
least to be a response to the Thatcherite attack on state education,
and an attempt by some Labour-controlled LEAs in England to
revive and redirect the flagging movement for comprehensive
education. I am drawing here on Ian Martin's chapter in *Community
Education: an Agenda for Educational Reform,* but I stress that I do
not mean to imply that Ian's view of CE is simply a political
programme. In fact his view incorporates elements of the other
strands identified in this outline, and belongs to the Mainstream
English version of CE. His is a sophisticated, inclusive analysis
distinguished by a conceptual clarity rare in CE writing.

His basic premise is that CE is committed to public sector
provision, that is, to comprehensive and continuing education. He
writes:

> If 'community' stands for the world outside the institutional
> framework of Education with a capital 'E', Community
> Education is a commitment to education for all.

Community Education as a normative (rather than merely
descriptive) concept is about the ownership of education as public
property. It implies that education is for communities of all interests
and ages, belonging to everyone and not just to the academically
successful or the most articulate. For this to become a reality, CE

must be accessible, attractive and relevant to people. Ian Martin attacks the supermarket approach to CE, which he identifies (wrongly, in my opinion) with the free market in the economic sense. Community educators, he argues, must be proactive not reactive:

> This means taking the initiative by going out into the community to find out what people want, deliberately moving from 'normative' to 'expressed' and 'felt' definitions of need.

He regards the totality of people's life experiences as educative, and in arguing for two-way traffic between home and school, he identifies another central feature of his view of CE: that it is about renegotiating and reconstructing the ways in which the education system relates to communities (of interest or of residence). Traditional formal education, he argues, cultivates in the learner dependence, deference, malleability, passivity, and a 'consumer' attitude. It legitimises control of people. CE, by contrast (which, on this view, is not a sub-sector on the margins of formal education, but a project to transform education), develops a relationship of more equal partnership between teacher and parent and teacher and learner, and is about processes with unpredictable outcomes:

> . . . which professional educators should not and cannot expect to predetermine and control.

That is, he is challenging the view that containment and control should be defining features of professionalism. What he does not do, though, is to clarify what he regards as the positive features of professionalism.

In discussing relevance, Martin takes account of criticism aimed at the notion of a localised, community curriculum. He writes:

> CE is about making education relevant to the interests, concerns and issues which people define as significant.

but

> Relevance should be about means rather than ends, about where the learning process starts rather than where it leaves off.

and

> the eventual outcome may be a redistribution of opportunities for more traditional forms of educational activity and achievement.

and finally

> Who is to dismiss the 'relevance' of traditional forms of
> abstract and universalistic knowledge in terms of the access
> they confer to positions of power and authority in our society?

8. A right-wing view of Community Education

Is there a right-wing view of CE? That is a genuine question. I am not
sure, but an attempt at a truly inclusive outline seems incomplete
without at least raising the question. Many on the right would be
happy to dispense with the services of large numbers of professional
CE workers paid for by the state. But they might well subscribe to a
positive view of CE as something people should do, or should be
encouraged to do, by and for themselves. The key features of such a
view of CE would be self-help, individual responsibility,
voluntarism, the family as the basic unit in society (or the nation, if
you don't believe in society), the local neighbourhood as a locus of
mutual support (e.g. neighbourhood watch schemes), an emphasis
on the fight against crime, and the belief that such CE should be
achieved at no or low cost to the state.

Conclusion

There are certain key issues in CE which need to be addressed if we
are to move from confusion in the direction of clarity.
— the nature of the *authority* of the CE worker
— what does the worker's *professionalism* consist of?
— the *role* or *roles* of the worker
— how should workers be *deployed*?
— the *boundaries* of the CE *service*
— the relationship of *activity, experience* and *knowledge* in CE
— the relationship of *content* and *process* in CE practice.

CE in Scotland, like other aspects of our experience in recent years,
has been characterised by radical rhetoric and conservative practice.
There is a challenge to those engaged in policy reviews to be much
clearer about what they want from CE, how the service should be
structured, where it should be located administratively, and how
field staff should be trained to achieve the aims set for the service.

38. Reflections on experiences of counselling men, and some theoretical and historical considerations

This paper was written early in January 1990 at the request of the Steering Committee of the Scottish Health Education Group's Better Health for Men project.

*

> The chronic aggression which has always seemed to be the hallmark of 'man' is but a defence against and a veneer over basic ego-weakness.
>
> Harry Guntrip

A key issue in the concealment of vulnerability. Many of the men who seek counselling are intensely vulnerable, whether they present as hard men or soft men or any combination of the two. Images of 'armour' and 'weak spots' come to mind. It's often difficult for men to get in touch with their vulnerability. For some, on the other hand, it has become overwhelming.

There's often an underlying issue of early loss of touch, which I like to describe as sensuous nurture. This is present in different forms depending on the culture. For example, many middle-class men have had the amputating experience of being sent far from home/mother/father to boarding school at the age of four or five. But there are lots more who stayed at home and don't recall anything in the way of touching or cuddling. You don't need to be far away to be out of touch.

Come to think of it, I don't believe I've been in a counselling relationship with a man who remembers much in the way of stroking or touching as a small boy. A small number of exceptions to this recall invasive or abusive touching. By contrast, the majority of women clients recall a lot of touch/stroke/cuddling experiences, though these are not always unproblematic.

I think there's a connection between the absence of the *integrated* experience of being touched, stroked and cuddled, and being aware of feelings. Many men have difficulty in getting in touch with feelings or expressing them except in overwhelming, momentary or awkward ways.

When some men do get in touch with vulnerable parts of themselves, and their feelings, or when they manage to face up to the past absence of touch or present difficulties around touch, strong feelings of anger, fear, persecution, despair, or emptiness may come to the fore. These feelings can sometimes be so intense as to merit the description 'violent'.

How do these men cope in their lives? Some barely cope at all: their lives are a switchback of elation and depression, usually with the latter in the ascendant. A common solution is to place great reliance on reason, order and productive work. This is widespread and takes various forms: for example, having a grasp of a wide range of facts/information/knowledge which the man needs to display — that's his mode of relating; another is being well organised and systematic; another is to work very hard for long hours, often for most of the man's waking hours; another is to engage in energetic, demanding or competitive sport; another is to work very productively, that is, the man places a high value on the need to produce, on what is produced, and on the valuing of the productions by others. Another solution is excessive drinking, and another is violent behaviour. These last two ways of coping are not unconnected with the previous list. They may even provide a clue as to the true aim of placing such reliance on reason, order and production. All these coping mechanisms are ways of relating to the *outer* world. The first three share common themes of control and the release of contents or energy. In the other two control has been lost. The point is that they are all also ways of dealing with the *inner* world. For many men it is difficult to free-associate, to give up orderly rational discourse of one sort or another because it involves loss of control of the inner world. These various coping methods have often become habitual, even integral to the man's character.

A linked area of difficulty is relationships with women. Sometimes such relationships are impossible to form, or they can only be formed around sexual activity narrowly defined. More often the men find themselves baffled, outmanoeuvred or rebuffed in their relationships with women. Even talking to women can be problematic. Deep feelings of anger and resentment are often directed towards them.

I want now to say something about how to see this sort of evidence, because how we construe it is crucial. The main theory on offer is that variety of feminism which sees men as a sex as the oppressors and women as a sex as the oppressed. The evidence of human history and of all extant societies, according to the theory, is that men have the power and control and that women are exploited and objectified. Society is male. The system is male. Men must stop controlling women, they must relinquish their power or share it with women. The strategy, at the societal level, involves a long march through the institutions to press for the appointment of women in promoted posts, women managers and directors, women MPs, and for the adaptation of working conditions to take account of pregnancy and childcare. At the personal level, male violence should be identified, exposed and condemned. The individual man must be confronted with, and personally acknowledge, the reality of his violence towards his wife or his children. He must take responsibility for his behaviour, recognise that it is unacceptable, and change it.

This theory implies a simple, Manichaean world. Women are good and men are bad. It is only a short step to link this male oppression of women with white oppression of blacks, straight oppression of gays, and capitalist oppression of proletarians.

My view is that this theory, while it accords well with some aspects of the evidence, ignores, distorts or discounts other aspects, and is far too simple. But I acknowledge one of its central claims: it is true that the most powerful institutions in human societies are dominated by men. And when we look at the history of culture, the evidence is the same: most of the dominant figures have been men.

But there is a catch in my acceptance of this element in the crude feminist thesis. I insist on holding it closely to the evidence it adduces, and on watching how the evidence is described, explained and conceptualised. The evidence to which the theory correctly points is that most of the dominant positions in contemporary and historical societies are or have been held by men. Thus, for example, armies are dominated by hierarchies of men, governments, government departments, corporations, institutions, they are all dominated by hierarchies consisting mostly of men. The error in the crude feminist thesis is this: to infer from the fact that most oppressors are men that most or all men are oppressors; and to infer from the fact that some male behaviour is oppressive that oppression is part of the essence of maleness. As soon as this error is recognised its significance becomes apparent. There is a logical and evidential confusion at the heart of the crude feminist thesis between the category of oppression and the category of men.

This distinction between the category of men and the category of oppressors is not an academic one. The crude feminist thesis is correct in denouncing the reality of oppression and in asserting that much oppression is historically enacted by some men. But it completely fails to give a satisfactory account of how men are oppressed by the present arrangements. What is required is a radically more complex and more accurate picture which includes the theoretical and evidential possibility that women can sometimes be oppressors, that men can sometimes be oppressed, and that human beings can sometimes be oppressed by arrangements which are neither intended nor recognised as oppressive. In other words it suggests that a true picture of human oppression would be complex and particular rather than simple and general, that it would involve the assessment of inner and outer, invisible as well as visible, early childhood and adulthood dimensions, and recognise the simultaneity of contradictions.

Incomplete diagnoses lead to incomplete prescriptions. My sense of it is that the crude feminist prescription which results, as it does, in the arrival of women in managerial and governing positions in the public realm, which I warmly support, at the same time fails to go to the heart of oppression. On its own, it will result simply in the more effective domination of the mass of men and women by both male and female oppressors.

A more fundamental exploration of the theory and practice of oppression in human societies and in human relations would require us to trace the historical development and use of hierarchical military command structures *and* indirect, horizontal, manipulative styles of control, neither of which are the exclusive prerogative of either sex, but which are extensively deployed by both.

When we return to consider the phenomena encountered in the counselling relationship with men, the crude feminist thesis loses more of its credibility. The feared male oppressor emerges often as vulnerable, frightened, empty, out of touch with his feelings and with large parts of his potential self, having difficulties in the areas of physical and personal intimacy, outmanoeuvred in relationships, and unable to assert himself in a dialogical, responsive way. Some monster! Hardly the male oppressor of feminist demonology. For many men, any relationship which is not functionalised or otherwise ritualised is difficult. If I were to risk further generalisations — and I am willing to do so, because although each man is unique and particular common patterns can be discerned — they would be in the form of questions for further exploration. Why is it that so many parents touch girls and not boys? Why is it that girls are encouraged to express their feelings, and affirmed when they express feelings of vulnerability, and boys are not? Why is it that boys are punished physically more than girls? Why are boys not encouraged to dress expressively? Why blue for boys and pink for girls?

These are truly intended as questions, declarations of an intention to search for understanding, and affirmations that we don't really know the answers.

I imagine that this hurried paper will be challenged along the following lines: if you don't agree 100 per cent with what you call the crude feminist thesis, what other thesis are you proposing? My answer would be in several parts. First, the relations between men, women and children have so often in history been the subject of authoritative general prescriptions, that an orientation of curious attention to what particular people have to say for themselves might just be worth trying for a while. Second, I favour a view of human beings as persons struggling to be true to themselves, to come into their own, as persons-in-relations-with-other-persons: I am a personalist, if you like! Third, I think that in our understanding of the dialectic of inner and outer, the outer — that is to say, the empirically measurable dimensions of reality — has carried excessive weight and that the time has come to allow our subjectivity to come more fully into the picture. Finally, the object relations tradition in psychoanalysis, associated with Ronald Fairbairn, Harry Guntrip and Jock Sutherland, has a lot to commend it. For me, these words of Guntrip's are full of resonance where men are concerned (he is referring to psychotherapy):

> the provision of a kind of personal relationship in which the alienated stunted self is given the potential for a healthy growth and development which puts it in touch with other persons . . .

and (referring to good early relationships):

> the foundation of the experience of ego-reality and selfhood, the feeling of in-beingness as a definite self. . . .

Guntrip, in his *Psychoanalytic Theory, Therapy and the Self*, describes the 'vacuum of ego-unrelatedness' which he calls the schizoid state, a state of depersonalisation, as having the following characteristics:
(1)   the person is *withdrawn* and *regressed* in fear
(2)   the person is *repressed* because the 'weak infant' is unacceptable to consciousness
(3)   the person is *dis-integrated* in the beginnings of his ego structure
(4)   the person is *unevoked* in his potentialities. (My italics.)

This appears to suggest that underdevelopment, distorted development and fragmentation result from particular experiences of upbringing. I would like to explore further my hunch that these insights apply specifically to the upbringing of male children. I must spell out my belief that both men and women are involved, in complicated, partly unconscious ways, in the process of stunting and smashing boys.

I like to recall Jean-Luc Godard's phrase in his film *Pierrot Le Fou*: 'il faut constamment reinventer l'amour'. We must reinvent the upbringing of boys. But can we do it without also reinventing the upbringing of girls? The two are connected. And it is the grown men and women, damaged as we are, who must do the reinventing. Surely it will involve much deeper and more unpredetermined communication between men and women than has seemed possible so far in human history. I am not posing men against women or women against men, but I am proposing a recognition of the reality of actual differences, biological and cultural, and the possibility of better communication and collaboration.

Afterword

In the introduction I argued that the good energy of the late sixties and early seventies was dissipated by splitting, oppositionalism, a return to old forms, failure to listen to ordinary people, and failure to generate the new concepts and structures required for fundamental democratisation.

Here I want to focus on current possibilities in Scotland, because I am a Scot and committed to our historical emergence as a people, an emergence which has personal, familial, communal, national and international dimensions. I am not anti-English, but I am opposed to the dominance exercised by concentrations of wealth and power in London over the lives of people in the rest of these islands. It is for the people of Wales, Northern Ireland and England to shape the societies they want to live in, and for all of us to develop the new forms of interdependence and collaboration we will undoubtedly require.

Fundamental democratisation — which Paulo Freire describes as involving the emergence of the people onto the stage of history as subjects, not objects — runs the risk of being interpreted as requiring mere structural changes unless it is accompanied by the reorientation which it actually implies. In order to ensure that the dimension of reorientation is highlighted, the concept of fundamental democratisation needs to be linked with the concept of liberation. Liberation is not liberalism, not libertarianism, not libertinism. It is based on the biblical exodus of the children of Israel from Egypt in search of a land flowing with milk and honey. It involves risking the loss of security afforded by living in bondage, in favour of taking personal, communal and national responsibility for choosing our own values and creating our own society. In other words, it commits us to the search for a way of life. It involves the engagement of the people, the exercise of real leadership, and the denunciation of adventurism and empty rhetoric. It involves the exposure of both ambivalence and ambiguity, by making explicit the contradictions they conceal, so that they can be explored and resolved and choices made. The aim of liberation is to create the good society in which every human being can find a meaningful and dignified place. Because this aim involves all the people, the idea of posing class against class is inappropriate. Creating the good society has at its core the struggle for social justice, and this distinguishes it from designer socialism, which is willing to contemplate managing the continued existence of an excluded underclass.

The strand which unites these concepts of fundamental democratisation, people as subjects not objects, liberation, and the good society, is the possibility of the reality of love. This possibility is to be distinguished from the concept of care in the British tradition of state welfarism. (I do not mean to reject the concept of care, but to suggest that it requires rethinking, following its association with a tendency to objectify the 'client'.) Love can only become a reality at personal and interpersonal levels, although its presence or absence can also be sensed at communal and societal levels. What needs to be transcended is the tradition of treating people as objects, the immobilising, standardising provision of housing, jobs, health, income support and education by state bureaucracies. What is being advanced here is not the argument of the Right that government should withdraw and create a so-called 'free' market for predators. The good society will recognise and exercise responsibilities in all areas listed above. What is required is that we should win back from the Right the concepts of responsibility and enterprise. The good society will structure and regulate means whereby all citizens, as whole persons in collaboration with each other, can be responsible and enterprising in relation to their own and other people's needs. It will be a society characterised by the simultaneity of autonomy and interdependence, in which learning, collaboration, love and enterprise are integral to its functional processes.

In Scotland, the post-war Labour-Tory consensus — the triumph of Fabianism — installed as its final achievement a reformed system of local government, institutionalising the rational management of the population through large-scale structures. The reform of local government produced inflated bureaucracies which consume human and natural resources unproductively. Bureaucracy can be seen as a distorted form of creativity. It has got a firm grip on Scottish society in the last fifteen years, although its growth may recently have slowed down. Unlike cancer, bureaucracy can be reversed, but not until it is understood. One misunderstanding prevalent in Scotland is that bureaucracy and the representative-democracy version of accountability are mutually opposed. On the contrary, the evidence is all around us that the growth of bureaucracy and the elaboration of the machinery of accountability to elected representatives at local government level have gone hand in hand.

The roots of the growth of bureaucracy, in the short term, are the belief in the efficacy and rationality of large-scale organisations, in the use of elongated and elaborated hierarchies as the means of controlling such structures, exclusive faith in the 'representative' conception of democracy, faith in state provision of services, and — last but by no means least — the endemic trade union versus management, management versus trade union Punch and Judy show. Why do the Scots still place their faith in a bureaucratic corporatism which manages a greater part of our national resources than in any country outside the Soviet bloc? The answer, in brief, is: poverty, castration, fear of freedom, distrust of our leaders, and doubts about our capacity for self-government. There are historical layerings here. The Reformation and its legacy of Calvinism was a mixed blessing: whatever good it achieved it did not generate popular self-confidence. The Union can be seen as an act of betrayal of the Scottish people by their own leaders. Since then the Scots have been unsure of their leaders, and the leaders themselves have been ambiguous men, half committed to those who chose them and half to their own search for power on some wider stage.

Another factor deriving ultimately from the Union is a deep-seated devaluation of Scottish culture at the most intimate levels. Nowhere is this seen more clearly than in attitudes to popular speech and its relationship to written language. The majority of Scots grow up feeling inferior and inhibited, linguistically and culturally. The existence of a certain Scottish omnipotence does not contradict this fact, but reinforces it. We enact a storyline which derives from a Derby/Culloden complex. Arrogant and omnipotent, we set off to conquer the world. This omnipotent energy carried us to within striking distance of power and the challenges and responsibilities that might entail. Then we take fright and run for home, expecting and frequently receiving from someone in authority a hammering of truly annihilating proportions. This swing from omnipotence to impotence is re-enacted again and again: the Darien scheme, the referendum, and the defeat of Ally's army which, in its omnipotent phase, was celebrated as follows:

> We're on the march with Ally's army,
> We're going to the Argentine,
> And we'll really shake them up,
> When we win the World Cup,
> For Scotland is the greatest football team!

Between the far distant factors (the Reformation, the Union, and their aftermath) and the post-world-war-two factors (the relief of poverty provided by the welfare state, now threatened by the witch

Thatcher, producing the close-ranks corporatist reflex) — lies the
medium term and another deep-seated source of our fear of freedom.
A great part of the urban population of the central belt consists of
people who have been economically, culturally and psychologically
traumatised for generations. We are all more or less deeply touched
by these experiences. I am referring to the people driven from the
Highlands and Islands by their own chiefs, and from Donegal and
the west of Ireland by famine and poverty. These uprooted, excluded
people lost their links with the land, finding their way into the
industrial ghettoes where they suffered degraded housing and
employment conditions for the rest of their lives. The psychological
impact of these losses and traumas has never been seriously
considered as a powerful continuing factor in history. They are
explored in such works as James 'B.V.' Thomson's *The City of
Dreadful Night* and Patrick McGill's *Children of the Dead End*. An
analogous experience (the transition from the Island of Wyre to
Greenock) is recounted by Edwin Muir in *An Autobiography*. They
have been passed down through generations and we bear the marks
on our souls. These experiences account for much of the hatred and
fear characterising the relationships between men, women and
children, and they account for the sense of castration, which affects
both sexes, but historically was much greater for the men who had to
suffer the economic and role castration of unemployment. At least
the women could go on bearing and rearing children.

At the heart of the Scottish experience is not the romance of ghosts,
castles and tartans, but uprooting, loss, castration, humiliation, mutual
hatred, envy, hopelessness, and lack of self-belief. The simplest way of
grasping this fact is to think of it as the loss of the experience of growth,
of culture in its root sense, of synthesis, in personal and family life, in
work, and in the relationship with the natural world. The state
provision of housing, social security, health, secondary education and
full employment in the post-war period was a great advance, but it
failed to address these deeper themes. It is sometimes argued that it is
negative to focus on such matters. They can be dealt with confidentially
by the Social Work Department. We should accentuate the positive. We
should focus our attention on hope and possibility. Of course, that is
true. But a hope that is solidly based will grow only from confronting
the reality of fear, abuse and loss of self-regard. It is also argued that our
problems are economic and political, rather than psychological, and
that they can only be solved by economic and political policies. Of
course, psychological insight which ignores the realities of political
economy will have less impact than it otherwise might. But political and
economic policies which ignore psychological realities will be equally
ineffectual. That is the lesson of the post-war period.

The central challenge for Scots is bravely to confront our psychological and political/economic problems as dimensions of a complex totality. At the heart of such an endeavour is taking responsibility for what we are, and the circumstances in which we find ourselves, the recognition of our need for help and learning at personal and inter-personal levels, and undertaking the search for a mature autonomy-within-interdependence which will enable us to escape from the dependence/independence dichotomy. It will involve recognising our identity as a nation, and taking on the task of governing ourselves and developing interdependent links with other nations.

Labourism has played on our insecurity and our fear of freedom, by denouncing Scottish nationalism as separatist and by opportunistically *reflecting* our hostility to Thatcherism rather than helping us to *reflect upon* it and advance to the stage of taking responsibility. The current (September 1989) 49 per cent level of support for Labour in the opinion polls is a fearful, defensive vote based on the paternal promise to protect, achieved as a result of hugging close to the contradictions contained in social research findings, most notoriously with the 'Independence in the UK' policy of spring 1989. At local government level — and in the name of socialism! — Labour has helped to build and now presides over a two-class society of providers and receivers, in housing, education and social work. Of all these policies the most shameful has been the systematic creation of housing apartheid in Scotland — in the name of socialism! How many Labour MPs, councillors and apparatchiks choose to live in the houses they provide for their voter-natives?

The struggle for liberation on which we are slowly finding the courage to embark will not be about manning barricades and throwing bombs. Nor will it involve standing around in the rain listening to Labour spokesmen mouthing their hackneyed denunciations of Thatcher and invoking the golden age. It will be about the dawning realisation that we can do more, so much more, than rent life from Labour, and that if — unlike Margaret Thatcher — we have a vision of the good society, then we can build it for ourselves.

Classified Bibliography

Bibliographies are usually described as 'select' or 'classified'. This one has some of both qualities, but it is also an experiment in re-mapping. The classification combines established categories (such as Adult and Continuing Education) with new ones (such as Men, Emotions and Relationships). It is interdisciplinary, with multiple entries where appropriate. I hope it will be useful to students of education and community work, to other specialists, and to the general reader.

*

Adult & General Education

Adult Education: a plan for development (the Russell Report), HMSO, London, 1973.

Advisory Council for Adult and Continuing Education, *Adults: their educational experience and needs*, Leicester, 1982.

Advisory Council for Adult and Continuing Education, *Continuing Education*, Leicester, 1982.

Advisory Council for Adult and Continuing Education, *Education for Unemployed Adults*, Leicester, 1982.

Aldred, Chris, Doonan, Shelagh and Marshall, Margaret, *Getting Started: a basic education pack for tutors/organisers working with women in informal learning groups*, WEA, London, 1982.

Alexander, Sir Kenneth, et. al. *Adult Education: the Challenge of Change*, HMSO, Edinburgh, 1975.

Alfred, David, 'The Relevance of the work of Paulo Freire to Radical Community Education in Britain', in *International Journal of Lifelong Education*, volume 3 no. 2, 1984.

Arbetsgrupp vid Brevskolan, *The Study Circle: a brief introduction*, Brevskolan, Stockholm, 1978.

Armstrong, Anne Kathleen, *A comparison of the thought of Coady and Freire,* Centre for Continuing Education, University of British Columbia, Vancouver.

Brattset, Hallgjerd, *What are the Characteristics of the Study Circle,* Norsk-Voksenpedagogisk Institutt, Trondheim, 1982.

Bright, Barry P. (ed.), *Theory and Practice in the Study of Adult Education: the Epistemological Debate,* Routledge, London, 1989.

Bristol Women's Studies Group, *Half the Sky: an introduction to women's studies,* Virago, London, 1979.

Brown, Cynthia, *Literacy in 30 Hours: Paulo Freire's Process in North-East Brazil,* Writers' and Readers' Publishing Co-operative, London, 1975.

Charnley, A.H., McGivney, V.K., and Sims, D.J., *Education for the Adult Unemployed: some responses,* National Institute of Adult & Continuing Education, Leicester, 1985.

Cherry, Chris and Turnbull, Moira (eds.), *Women Start Here: parts one and two,* Scottish Adult Basic Education Unit, Edinburgh, 1983.

Collins, Denis, *Paulo Freire: His Life, Works and Thought,* Paulist Press, New York, 1977.

Costigan, Margaret, *You Have the Third World Inside You: an Interview with Paulo Freire,* Workers' Educational Association, Edinburgh, 1980.

Donovan, Judy, et. al. *Experiences of a Changing Kind: adult education in psychiatric hospitals and day centres,* MIND/WEA Yorkshire North District, London/Leeds, 1985.

Edwards, Judith, *Learning Together: a study skills handbook,* WEA West Lancashire and Cheshire District, Liverpool, 1985.

Entwistle, Harold, *Antonio Gramsci: conservative schooling for radical politics,* Routledge and Kegan Paul, London, 1979.

Fieldhouse, Roger, *The Workers' Educational Association: Aims and Achievements 1903-1977,* University of Syracuse, 1977.

Flude, Ray and Parrott, Allen, *Education and the Challenge of Change: a recurrent education strategy for Britain,* Open University Press, Milton Keynes, 1979.

Forgacs, David (ed.), *A Gramsci Reader,* Lawrence and Wishart, London, 1988.

Freire, Paulo, *Cultural Action for Freedom,* Penguin, Harmondsworth, 1972.

Freire, Paulo, *The Politics of Education: Culture Power and Liberation,* Macmillan, London, 1985.

Freire, Paulo, *Pedagogy in Process: the Letters to Guinea-Bissau,* Seabury Press, New York, 1978.

Freire, Paulo, *Pedagogy of the Oppressed*, Penguin, Harmondsworth, 1972.

Freire, Paulo and Macedo, Donaldo, *Literacy: Reading the Word and the World*, Routledge and Kegan Paul, London, 1987.

Freire, Paulo, *Education for Critical Consciousness*, Sheed and Ward, London, 1974.

Freire, Paulo and Shor, Ira, *A Pedagogy for Liberation: dialogues on transforming education*, Macmillan, London, 1987.

Gelpi, Ettore, *A Future for Lifelong Education Volumes 1 and 2*, Manchester, 1979.

Gerver, Elisabeth, *Computers and Adult Learning*, Open University Press, Milton Keynes, 1984.

Groombridge, Brian, *Television and the People: a programme for demoratic participation*, Penguin, Harmondsworth, 1972.

Hawkins, John N., *Mao Tse-Tung and Education: his thoughts and teachings*, Linnet Books, 1974.

Ireland, Timothy, *Gelpi's View of Lifelong Education*, Manchester Monographs, 1979.

Jackson, Keith, 'The Marginality of Community Development: Implications for Adult Education', in the *International Journal of Community Development*, summer 1973.

Jackson, Keith and Ashcroft, Bob, 'Adult Education, Deprivation and Community Development — a Critique', Institute of Extension Studies, University of Liverpool, Liverpool, 1972.

Jackson, Keith, 'Adult Education and Community Development', duplicated paper, date unknown.

Jackson, Keith, 'University Adult Education and Social Change in Urban Society', Department of Adult Education and Extra-Mural Studies, University of Liverpool, date unknown.

Jackson, Keith, 'Adult Education in a Community Development Project', duplicated paper, 1973.

Jackson, Keith and Ashcroft, Bob, 'Adult Education and Social Action ', in *Community Work One*, edited Jones & Mayo, Routledge & Kegan Paul, London, 1974.

Jarvis, Peter, *The Sociology of Adult and Continuing Education*, Croom Helm, London, 1985.

Jarvis, Peter (ed.), *Twentieth Century Thinkers in Adult Education*, Croom Helm, London, 1987.

Jarvis, Peter, *Adult and Continuing Education: theory and practice*, Croom Helm, London, 1983.

Jarvis, Peter, *Adult Learning in the Social Context,* Croom Helm, London, 1987.

Jennings, Bernard, *Albert Mansbridge and English Adult Education,* Department of Adult Education, University of Hull, 1976.

Jennings, Bernard, *Knowledge is Power: a Short History of the WEA 1903-78,* Department of Adult Education, University of Hull, 1979.

Kirkwood, Gerri, 'Adult Education in the Community: Should the Educator Take a Back Seat?', text of a talk given to a gathering of community educators in Leicestershire, 1989.

Kirkwood, Gerri and Kirkwood, Colin, *Living Adult Education: Freire in Scotland,* Open University Press, Milton Keynes, 1989.

Kirkwood, Colin and Griffiths, Sally (eds.), *Adult Education and the Unemployed,* Workers' Educational Association, Edinburgh, 1984.

Kirkwood, Colin, 'Community Work and Adult Education' in *Staveley, North-East Derbyshire, December 1969-December 1971* (M.Sc. dissertation), University of Edinburgh, 1976.

Lawson, K.H., *Analysis and Ideology: conceptual essays on the education of adults,* University of Nottingham, Department of Adult Education, 1982.

Lawson, K.H., *Philosophical Concepts and Values in Adult Education,* Department of Adult Education, University of Nottingham, 1975.

Lovett, Tom (ed.), *Radical Appproaches to Adult Education: A Reader,* Routledge, London, 1988.

Lovett, Tom, *Adult Education, Community Development and the Working Class* , Ward Lock, London, 1975.

Lovett, Tom, Clarke, Chris and Kilmurray, Avila, *Adult Education and Community Action,* Croom Helm, London, 1984.

Mackie, Robert (ed.), *Literacy and Revolution: the Pedagogy of Paulo Freire,* Pluto Press, London, 1980.

McGivney, Veronica and Sims, David, *Adult Education and the Challenge of Unemployment,* Open University Press, Milton Keynes, 1986.

Millar, J.P.M., *The Labour College Movement,* N.C.L.C. Publishing Society, London, 1979.

Munn, P. and MacDonald, C., *Adult Participation in Education and Training,* Scottish Council for Research in Education, Edinburgh, 1988.

Parker, Andrew, 'Democratic Education', unpublished paper, circulated 1975.

Paterson, R.W.K., *Values, Education and the Adult,* Routledge and Kegan Paul, London, 1979.

Rogers, Jennifer, *Adults Learning,* Open University Press, Milton Keynes, 1977.

Rogers, Carl, *Freedom to Learn for the '80s,* Merrill, Columbus, Ohio, 1983.

Schuller, Tom and Megarry, Jacquetta (eds.), *World Yearbook of Education 1979: Recurrent Education and Lifelong Learning,* Kogan Page, London, 1979.

Schuller, Tom, *Is Knowledge Power? Problems and Practice in Trade Union Education,* Aberdeen People's Press, Aberdeen, 1981.

Senior, Barbara and Naylor, John, *Educational Responses to Adult Unemployment,* Croom Helm, London, 1987.

Shor, Ira, *Freire for the Classroom: a Sourcebook for Liberatory Teaching,* Boynton Cook, Portsmouth, USA, 1987.

Shor, Ira, *Critical Teaching and Everyday Life,* University of Chicago Press, Chicago, 1987.

Spencer, Bruce (ed.), *Adult Education with the Unemployed,* University of Leeds, Department of Adult and Continuing Education, Leeds, 1986.

Steward, Tim and Alexander, David, *Information and Guidance on Adult Learning Opportunities in Scotland,* Scottish Academic Press, Edinurgh, 1988.

The 1919 Report, republished by the Department of Adult Education, University of Nottingham.

Thompson, Jane L., *Learning Liberation — Women's Response to Men's Education,* Croom Helm, London, 1983.

Thompson, Jane L. (ed.), *Adult Education for a Change,* Hutchinson, London, 1980.

Tight, Malcolm (ed.), *Adult Learning and Education,* Croom Helm, London, 1983.

Woolfe, Ray, Murgatroyd, Stephen and Rhys, Sylvia, *Guidance and Counselling in Adult and Continuing Education,* Open University Press, Milton Keynes, 1987.

Youngman, Frank, *Adult Education and Socialist Pedagogy,* Croom Helm, London, 1986.

Community Education and Community Schools

Alexander, David, Steward, Tim, and Leach, Tom, *A Study of Policy, Organisation and Provision in Community Education, Leisure and Recreation in Three Scottish Regions,* University of Nottingham, 1984.

Alexander, Sir Kenneth, et al., *Adult Education: the Challenge of Change,* HMSO, Edinburgh, 1975.

Alfred, David, 'The Relevance of the Work of Paulo Freire to Radical Community Education in Britain', in *International Journal of Lifelong Education*, volume 3 no. 2, 1984.

Allen, Gareth, Bastiani, John, Martin, Ian and Richards, Kelvyn (eds.), *Community Education: an agenda for educational reform*, Open University Press, Milton Keynes, 1987.

Bennett, Neville, *Teaching Styles and Pupil Progress*, Open Books, London, 1976.

Bidwell, Laurie and McConnell, Charlie (eds.), *Community Education and Community Development*, Dundee College of Education (now Northern College of Education, Dundee Campus), Dundee, 1982.

Carnegy, Elizabeth et. al., *Professional Education and Training for Community Education (the Carnegy Report)*, HMSO, Edinburgh, 1977.

Cowburn, Will, *Class, Ideology and Community Education*, Croom Helm, London, 1986.

Dewey, John, *Democracy and Education*, Macmillan, New York, 1916.

Dewey, John, *Experience and Education*, Collier MacMillan, London, 1963.

Fletcher, Colin and Thompson, Neil (eds.), *Issues in Community Education*, Falmer Press, Lewes, 1980.

Goodman, Paul, *Compulsory Miseducation*, Penguin, Harmondsworth, 1975.

Grant, Doreen, *Learning Relations*, Routledge, London, 1989.

Grant, Nigel, *Society, Schools and Progress in Eastern Europe*, Pergamon Press, 1969.

Grant, Nigel, *Soviet Education*, University of London Press, 1965.

Illich, Ivan, *Deschooling Society*, Penguin, Harmondsworth, 1973.

Judge, Jon, *Education in the USSR: Russian or Soviet?*, in Comparative Education, vol. 11, No. 2, 1975.

King, Kenneth (ed.), *Education and the Community in Africa*, University of Edinburgh Centre for African Studies, Edinburgh, 1976.

Kirkwood, Gerri, 'Adult Education in the Community: Should the Educator Take a Back Seat?', text of a talk given to a gathering of community educators in Leicestershire, 1989.

Kirkwood, Gerri and Kirkwood, Colin, *Living Adult Education: Freire in Scotland*, Open University Press, Milton Keynes, 1989.

Levitas, Maurice, *Marxist Perspectives in the Sociology of Education*, Routledge and Kegan Paul, London, 1974.

Lewis, L.J. (ed.), *The Phelps Stokes Reports on Education in Africa,* Oxford University Press, London, 1962.

MacKenzie, R.F., *State School,* Penguin Education, Harmondsworth, 1970.

MacKenzie, R.F., *The Unbowed Head: events at Summerhill Academy 1968-74,* Edinburgh University Student Publications Board, Edinburgh, 1978.

Midwinter, Eric, *Patterns in Community Education,* Ward Lock, London, 1973.

Midwinter, Eric, *Education and the Community,* Allen and Unwin, London, 1975.

Neill, A.S., *Summerhill,* Penguin, Harmondsworth, 1968.

Nisbet, John, Hendry, Leo, Stewart, Chris and Watt, Joyce, *Towards Community Education: an evaluation of community schools,* Aberdeen University Press, Aberdeen, 1980.

O'Hagan, Bob, *The Struggle for Community Education: structure and process in five Rochdale schools,* MPhil Thesis, Cranfield Institute of Technology, 1985.

Ocitti, J.P., *African Indigenous Education as practised by the Acholi of Uganda,* East African Literature Bureau, Nairobi/Kampala/Dar-es-salaam, 1973.

Plant, Raymond, *Community and Ideology,* Routledge and Kegan Paul, London, 1974.

Poster, Cyril, *Community Education: its development and management,* Heinemann, London, 1981.

Ranger, Terence, 'African Attempts to Control Education in East and Central Africa 1900-1939', in *Past and Present,* No. 32, 1966.

Reimer, Everett, *School is Dead,* Penguin, Harmondsworth, 1981.

Scottish Community Education Council, *Training for Change: a report on community education training,* Scottish Community Education Council, Edinburgh, 1984.

Shor, Ira, *Freire for the Classroom: a Sourcebook for Liberatory Teaching,* Boynton Cook, Portsmouth, USA, 1987.

Simon, Brian, *Intelligence, Psychology and Education: a Marxist critique,* Lawrence and Wishart, London, 1971.

Wallis, J. and Mee, G., *Community Schools: claim and performance,* University of Nottingham, 1983.

Community Development, Community Work, Community Action

'The Professional Radical, 1970' (Article on Saul Alinsky), *Harper's Magazine*, January 1970.

Bailey, Roy and Brake, Mike (eds.), *Radical Social Work*, Edward Arnold, London, 1975.

Batten, T.R., *Communities and their Development*, Oxford University Press, London, 1957.

Berger, Peter L., *Pyramids of Sacrifice: Political Ethics and Social Change*, Allen Lane Penguin Books, London, 1974.

Biddle, William and Loureide, *The Community Development Process: the Rediscovery of Local Initiative*, Holt, Rinehart and Winston, New York, 1965.

Bidwell, Laurie and McConnell, Charlie (eds.), *Community Education and Community Development*, Dundee College of Education (now Northern College of Education, Dundee Campus), Dundee, 1982.

Brokensha, David and Hodge, Peter, *Community Development: an Interpretation*, Chandler Publishing Company, San Francisco, 1969.

CDP Inter-Project Editorial Team, *Gilding the Ghetto*, The Russell Press, Nottingham, 1977.

Cockburn, Cynthia, *The Local State: management of cities and people*, Pluto Press, London, 1977.

Community Development and National Development, United Nations, New York, 1963.

Community Development, Central Office of Information Reference Pamphlet No. 76, HMSO, London, 1966.

Dickie, M.A.M., 'Community Development — Scotland', in the *Community Development Journal*, vol. 3, No. 4, 1968.

Ferguson, Ron, *Geoff: the Life of Geoffrey M. Shaw*, Famedram Publishers, Gartocharn, 1979.

Hope, Ann and Timmel, Sally, *Training for Transformation: a handbook for community workers, Books 1, 2 & 3*, Mambo Press, Gweru, Zimbabwe, 1985.

Huizer, Gerrit, 'Community Development, Land Reform and Political Participation', in *Peasants and Peasant Societies*, ed. Shanin, Teodor, Penguin, Harmondsworth, 1971.

Jackson, Keith, 'University Adult Education and Social Change in Urban Society', Department of Adult Education and Extra-Mural Studies, University of Liverpool, date unknown.

Jackson, Keith, 'Adult Education and Community Development', duplicated paper, date unknown.

Jackson, Keith, 'Adult Education in a Community Education Project', duplicated paper, date unknown.

Jackson, Keith, 'The Politics of Community Action', duplicated paper, 1972.

Jackson, Keith and Ashcroft, Bob, 'Adult Education, Deprivation and Community Development — A Critique', Institute of Extension Studies, University of Liverpool, Liverpool, 1972.

Jackson, Keith and Ashcroft, Bob, 'Adult Education and Social Action', in Community Work One, edited by Jones & Mayo, Routledge and Kegan Paul, London, 1974.

Jackson, Keith, 'The Marginality of Community Development: Implications for Adult Education', in the International Journal of Community Development, Summer 1973.

Jones, D. and Mayo, M., Community Work One (see also subsequent volumes), Routledge and Kegan Paul, London, 1974.

King, Kenneth J., The American Background of the Phelps-Stokes Commissions and their Influence in Education in East Africa especially in Kenya (Ph.D. Thesis), University of Edinburgh, 1968.

Kirkwood, Colin, 'New Ways of Meeting the Needs', unpublished paper, Department of Education, University of Edinburgh, 1976.

Kirkwood, Colin, Community Work and Adult Education in Staveley, North-East Derbyshire, December 1969-December 1971 (M.Sc. dissertation) Department of Education, University of Edinburgh, 1976.

Lancourt, Joan, 'Organising for Social Change: What Alinsky Organisations Have Taught Us for the 1970s', Brandeis University, Waltham, Massachusetts, 1977.

Landry, Charles, Morley, David, Southwood, Russell and Wright, Patrick, What a Way to Run a Railroad: an analysis of radical failure, Comedia, London, 1985.

Lapping, Anne (ed.), Community Action, Fabian Society, London, 1970.

Laver, Richard and Ward, Kevin, 'Sponsored and Spontaneous Community Work: The Dangers and the Potential', duplicated paper, July 1975.

Lees, R. and Smith, G., Action Research in Community Development, Routledge and Kegan Paul, London, 1975.

Lewis, L.J. (ed.), The Phelps Stokes Reports on Education in Africa, Oxford University Press, London, 1962.

Lovett, Tom, Clarke, Chris and Kilmurray, Avila, Adult Education and Community Action, Croom Helm, London, 1984.

Lovett, Tom, *Adult Education, Community Development and the Working Class*, Ward Lock, London, 1975.

Marris, Peter and Rein, Martin, *Dilemmas of Social Reform*, Penguin, Harmondsworth, 1974.

Mayo, Marjorie, 'Community Development: a Radical Alternative?, in *Radical Social Work*, ed. Bailey, Roy and Brake, Mike, Edward Arnold, London, 1975.

Mayo, Marjorie (ed.), *Women in the Community*, Routledge and Kegan Paul, London, 1977.

McConnell, C.S., *The Community Worker as Politiciser of the Deprived*, no publisher identified, 1977.

Milson, Fred, *An Introduction to Community Work*, Routledge and Kegan Paul, London, 1974.

Morrell, Derek, 'Social Work and Community', text of talk given in April 1968.

O'Malley, Jan, *The Politics of Community Action: a decade of struggle in Notting Hill*, Spokesman Books, Nottingham, 1977.

Plant, Raymond, *Community and Ideology*, Routledge and Kegan Paul, London, 1974.

Ranger, Terrence, 'African Attempts to Control Education in East and Central Africa 1900-1939', in *Past and Present*, No. 32, 1966.

Wass, Peter, *Community Development in Botswana, with special reference to the evolution of policy and organisation, 1947-70*, Ph.D. thesis, Edinburgh University Department of Education, 1972.

Weiner, Ron, *The Rape and Plunder of the Shankill: community action, the Belfast experience*, no publisher identified, 1975.

Women, Adult Education and Community

Aldred, Chris, Doonan, Shelagh and Marshall, Margaret, *Getting Started: a basic education pack for tutors/organisers working with women in informal learning groups*, WEA, London, 1982.

Aldred, Chris, *Women at Work*, Pan Books, London, 1981.

Bristol Women's Studies Group, *Half the Sky: an introduction to women's studies*, Virago, London, 1979.

Carpenter, Val and Young, Kerry, *Coming in from the Margins: youth work with girls and young women*, Youth Clubs UK, Leicester, 1986.

Cherry, Chris, Galford, Ellen, Pitman, Joy, Mitchell, Lorna, Markham, Stephanie, *Hens in the Hay*, Stramullion Co-operative, Edinburgh, 1980.

Cherry, Chris and Turnbull, Moira (eds.), *Women Start Here: parts one and two*, Scottish Adult Basic Education Unit, Edinburgh, 1983.

Fell, Alison, Pixner, Stef, Reid, Tina, Roberts, Michele, Oosthuizen, Ann, *Licking the Bed Clean*, Teeth Imprints, London, 1978.

Lochhead, Liz, *True Confessions and New Clichés*, Polygon, Edinburgh, 1985.

Mayo, Marjorie (ed.), *Women in the Community*, Routledge and Kegan Paul, London, 1977.

Mohin, Lilian (ed.), *One Foot on the Mountain: an anthology of British feminist poetry 1969-1979*, Onlywomen Press, London, 1980.

Norwood, Robin, *Women who love too much*, Arrow Books, London, 1989.

Stirling Women and Writing Group, *Recurring Themes*, Workers' Educational Association, Edinburgh, 1985.

Thompson, Jane L., *Learning Liberation — Women's Response to Men's Education*, Croom Helm, London, 1983.

Men, Emotions and Relationships

Alighieri, Dante, *The Divine Comedy: a new verse translation by C. H. Sisson*, Carcanet New Press, Manchester, 1980.

Barker, Sebastian, *Who is Eddie Linden?*, Jay Landesman, London, 1979.

Boyle, Jimmy, *A Sense of Freedom*, Pan Books, London, 1977.

Buchan, John, *Sick Heart River*, Hodder and Stoughton, London, 1950.

Camus, Albert, *The Outsider*, Penguin, Harmondsworth, 1981.

Conrad, Joseph, *Heart of Darkness*, Penguin, London, 1985.

Craig, Carol, 'On Men and Women in McIlvanney's Fiction', in *Edinburgh Review*, No. 73, ed. Peter Kravitz, Polygon, Edinburgh, 1986.

Davidson, Toni (ed.), *And Thus Will I Freely Sing: an anthology of gay and lesbian writing from Scotland*, Polygon, Edinburgh, 1989.

Douglas, George, *The House with the Green Shutters*, Mercat Press, Edinburgh, 1986.

Flaubert, Gustave, *The Legend of St Julian Hospitator*, in Three Tales, Penguin, Harmondsworth, 1961.

Friel, George, *The Boy Who Wanted Peace*, Polygon, Edinburgh, 1985.

Goethe, Johann Wolfgang Von, *The Sufferings of Young Werther*, Penguin, London, 1989.

Gray, Alasdair, *Lanark*, Canongate, Edinburgh, 1981.

Greene, Graham, *A Burnt-out Case*, Penguin, London, 1988.

Greene, Graham, *The Heart of the Matter*, Penguin, Harmondsworth, 1981.

Guntrip, Harry, *Schizoid Phenomena, Object Relations and the Self*, Hogarth Press, London, 1980.

Guntrip, Harry, *Psychoanalytic Theory, Therapy and the Self*, Hogarth Press, London, 1977.

Hay, J. MacDougall, *Gillespie*, Canongate, Edinburgh, 1979.

Hind, Archie, *The Dear Green Place*, Polygon, Edinburgh, 1984.

Homer, *The Iliad*, Penguin, Harmondsworth, 1984.

Homer, *The Odyssey*, Penguin, Harmondsworth, 1946.

Hopkins, Gerard Manley, *Selected Poems and Prose*, Penguin, Harmondsworth, 1963.

Jenkins, Robin, *The Cone-gatherers*, Paul Harris Publishing, Edinburgh, 1980.

Kelman, James, *A Disaffection*, Secker and Warburg, London, 1989.

Leonard, Tom, *Intimate Voices 1965-1983*, Galloping Dog Press, Newcastle upon Tyne, 1984.

Marlowe, Christopher, *Doctor Faustus*, in the Complete Plays of Christopher Marlowe, Penguin, Harmondsworth, 1969.

Marlowe, Christopher, *Tamburlaine the Great*, in the Complete Plays of Christopher Marlowe, Penguin, Harmondsworth, 1969.

Marlowe, Christopher, *The Jew of Malta*, in the Complete Plays of Christopher Marlowe, Penguin, Harmondsworth, 1969.

McGrath, Tom and Boyle, Jimmy, *The Hard Man*, Canongate, Edinburgh, 1977.

McIlvanney, William, *The Big Man*, Sceptre, London, 1986.

Melville, Herman, *Billy Budd, Sailor*, Penguin, Harmondsworth, 1970.

Miller, Arthur, *Death of a Salesman*, in Collected Plays, Cresset Press, London, 1958.

Miller, Arthur, *All My Sons*, in Collected Plays, Cresset Press, London, 1958.

Osborne, John, *Look Back in Anger*, Faber, London, 1962.

Owens, Agnes, *Gentlemen of the West*, Polygon, Edinburgh, 1984.

Sartre, Jean-Paul, *Nausea*, Penguin, Harmondsworth, 1963.

Segal, Lynne, *Slow Motion: changing masculinities, changing men*, Virago, London, 1990.

Seidler, Victor J., *Rediscovering Masculinity: reason, language & sexuality*, Routledge, London, 1989.

Shakespeare, William, *Sonnets,* in William Shakespeare: the Complete Works ed. Peter Alexander, Collins, Glasgow, 1962.

Sharp, Alan, *A Green Tree in Gedde,* Richard Drew, Glasgow, 1985.

Solzhenitsyn, Alexander, *One Day in the Life of Ivan Denisovich,* Penguin, Harmondsworth, 1963.

Spence, Alan, *Its Colours they are Fine,* Collins, London, 1977.

Stewart, Ena Lamont, *Men Should Weep,* 7:84 Publication, Edinburgh, 1982.

Sutherland, John D., 'John Buchan's "Sick Heart" — Some Psychoanalytic Reflections', in *Edinburgh Review* no. 78/9, 1988.

Tamez, Elsa, *Against Machismo,* Meyer Stone Books, Illinois, 1987.

Torrey, E. Fuller, *The Roots of Treason: Ezra Pound and the Secret of St Elizabeth's,* McGraw Hill, New York, 1984.

Trilling, Lionel, *The Middle of the Journey,* Penguin, Harmondsworth, 1963.

Unemployment: Experiences and Responses

Advisory Council for Adult & Continuing Education, *Education for Unemployed Adults,* Leicester, 1982.

Charnley, A.H., McGivney, V.K. and Sims, D.J., *Education for the Adult Unemployed: some responses,* National Institute of Adult & Continuing Education, Leicester, 1985.

Hayes, John and Nutman, Peter, *Understanding the Unemployed: the psychological effects of unemployment,* Tavistock Publications, London, 1981.

Kirkwood, Colin and Griffiths, Sally (eds.), *Adult Education and the Unemployed,* Workers' Educational Association, Edinburgh, 1984.

McGivney, Veronica and Sims, David, *Adult Education and the Challenge of Unemployment,* Open University Press, Milton Keynes, 1986.

Seabrook, Jeremy, *Unemployment,* Granada, London, 1983.

Senior, Barbara and Naylor, John, *Educational Responses to Adult Unemployment,* Croom Helm, London, 1987.

Sinfield, Adrian, *What Unemployment Means,* Martin Robertson, Oxford, 1981.

Spence, Alan, *Sailmaker,* Hodder and Stoughton, London, 1988.

Spencer, Bruce (ed.), *Adult Education with the Unemployed,* University of Leeds, Department of Adult and Continuing Education, Leeds, 1986.

Language, Literacy, Writers' and Readers' Workshops

Alighieri, Dante, *De Vulgari Eloquentia,* translated by A. G. Ferrers Howell, Rebel Press, Bideford, 1980.

Alighieri, Dante, *The Divine Comedy: a new verse translation by C. H. Sisson,* Carcanet New Press, Manchester, 1980.

Brown, Cynthia, *Literacy in 30 Hours: Paulo Freire's Process in North-East Brazil,* Writers' and Readers' Publishing Co operative, Edinburgh, 1980.

Castlemilk Writers' Workshop, *Mud and Stars: poems and stories from Castlemilk Writers' Workshop,* Workers' Educational Association, Glasgow, 1985.

Cherry, Chris, Galford, Ellen, Pitman, Joy, Mitchell, Lorna, Markham, Stephanie, *Hens in the Hay,* Stramullion Co-operative, Edinburgh, 1980.

East End Writers' and Artists' Group, *East End Writers and Artists III,* Glasgow, 1983.

Edinburgh Unemployed Writers' Workshop, *Write Now,* Workers' Educational Association, Edinburgh, 1982.

Fell, Alison, Pixner, Stef, Reid, Tina, Roberts, Michele, Oosthuizen, Ann, *Licking the Bed Clean,* Teeth Imprints, London, 1978.

Finlay, Ian Hamilton, *The Dancers Inherit the Party,* Migrant Press/Wild Hawthorn Press, Edinburgh, 1962.

Finlay, Ian Hamilton, *Glasgow Beasts, an a Burd, haw, an Inseks, an, aw, a Fush,* Wild Flounder Press, Edinburgh, 1962.

Freire, Paulo, *Cultural Action for Freedom,* Penguin, Harmondsworth, 1972.

Freire, Paulo, *Education for Critical Consciousness,* Sheed and Ward, London, 1974.

Freire, Paulo and Macedo, Donaldo, *Literacy: Reading the Word and the World,* Routledge and Kegan Paul, London, 1987.

Hayton, Alan, *Far Cry from 1945: poems by Alan Hayton,* Pertinent Publications, Wishaw, 1982.

Hoggart, Richard, *The Uses of Literacy,* Penguin, Harmondsworth, 1966.

Kay, Billy, *Scots: The Mither Tongue,* Grafton Books, London, 1988.

Kelman, James (ed.), *An East End Anthology 1988,* Clydeside Press, Glasgow, 1988.

Kirkcaldy Express Group Writers' Workshop, *Free Expression: poetry and prose by members of the express group writers' workshop,* Workers' Education Association, Edinburgh, 1986.

Kohl, Herbert, *Reading, How to,* Penguin, Harmondsworth, 1974.

Kravitz, Peter (ed.), *Edinburgh Review 77: Tom Leonard number,* Polygon, Edinburgh, 1987.

Leith Writers' Workshop, *Multi-Stories: a selection of stories and poems from Leith Writers' Work-shop,* Workers' Educational Association, Edinburgh, 1983.

Leonard, Tom, *Intimate Voices 1965-1983,* Galloping Dog Press, Newcastle upon Tyne, 1984.

Lochhead, Liz, *Dreaming Frankenstein and Collected Poems,* Polygon, Edinburgh, 1987.

Lochhead, Liz, *True Confessions and New Clichés,* Polygon, Edinburgh, 1985.

Lochhead, Liz, *Tartuffe: a translation into Scots from the original by Molière,* Polygon/Third Eye Centre, Edinburgh/Glasgow, 1985.

Mace, Jane, *Working with Words: literacy beyond school,* Writers' and Readers' Publishing Co-operative, London, 1979.

Mackie, Robert (ed.), *Literacy and Revolution: the Pedagogy of Paulo Freire,* Pluto Press, London, 1980.

McCaffery, Juliet and Street, Brian, *Literacy Research in the UK: Adult & School Perspectives,* RaPAL, Lancaster, 1988.

Mohin, Lilian (ed.), *One Foot on the Mountain: an anthology of British feminist poetry 1969-1979,* Onlywomen Press, London, 1980.

Morley, Dave and Worpole, Ken (eds.), *The Republic of Letters: working class writing and local publishing,* Comedia, London, 1982.

Spender, Dale, *Man Made Language,* Routledge and Kegan Paul, London, 1982.

Stirling Women and Writing Group, *Recurring Themes,* Workers' Educational Association, Edinburgh, 1985.

Street, Brian, *Literacy in Theory and Practice,* Cambridge University Press, Cambridge, 1984.

Tollcross Writers' Workshop, *Clock Work: stories and poems from Tollcross Writers' Workshop,* Workers' Educational Association, Edinburgh, 1981.

Tollcross Writers' Workshop, *Clock Work Two: more stories and poems from Tollcross Writers' Workshop,* Workers' Educational Association, Edinburgh, 1983.

Wandor, Micheline and Roberts, Michele (eds.), *Cutlasses and Earrings: feminist poetry*, Playbooks, London, 1977.

Scottish Experience and Culture

Beveridge, Craig and Turnbull, Ronald, *The Eclipse of Scottish Culture*, Polygon, Edinburgh, 1989.

Boyle, Jimmy, *A Sense of Freedom*, Pan Books, London, 1977.

Brown, Gordon and Cook, Robin (eds.), *Scotland the real divide*, Mainstream, Edinburgh, 1983.

Brown, Gordon (ed.), *The Red Paper on Scotland*, Edinburgh University Student Publications Board, Edinburgh, 1975.

Carmichael, Kay, 'A Balanced Society', in *Cencrastus*, No. 34, Edinburgh, 1989.

Carmichael, Kay, 'Freedom and Order', in *Cencrastus*, No. 34, Edinburgh, 1989.

Carter, Ian, 'A Socialist Strategy for the Highlands', in *The Red Paper on Scotland*, ed. Gordon Brown, Edinburgh University Student Publications Board, Edinburgh, 1975.

Craig, David and Manson, John (eds.), *Hugh MacDiarmid Selected Poems*, Penguin, Harmondsworth, 1970.

Davidson, Toni (ed.), *And Thus Will I Freely Sing: an anthology of gay and lesbian writing from Scotland*, Polygon, Edinburgh, 1989.

Davie, George Elder, *The Crisis of the Democratic Intellect*, Polygon, Edinburgh, 1986.

Davie, George Elder, *The Democratic Intellect*, Edinburgh University Press, Edinburgh, 1961.

Douglas, George, *The House with the Green Shutters*, Mercat Press, Edinburgh, 1986.

Dudley Edwards, Owen (ed.), *A Claim of Right for Scotland*, Polygon, Edinburgh, 1989.

Eliot, T.S. (ed.), *Edwin Muir Selected Poems*, Faber and Faber, London, 1965.

Ferguson, Ron, *Geoff: the Life of Geoffrey M. Shaw*, Famedram Publishers, Gartocharn, 1979.

Finlay, Ian Hamilton, *Glasgow Beasts, an a Burd, haw, an Inseks, an, aw, a Fush*, Wild Flower Press, Edinburgh, 1962.

Finlay, Ian Hamilton, *The Dancers Inherit the Party*, Migrant Press/Wild Hawthorn Press, Edinburgh, 1962.

Garioch, Robert, *Collected Poems*, MacDonald Publishers, Loanhead, 1977.

Gibbon, Lewis Grassic, *A Scots Quair*, Hutchinson, London, 1978.

Grant, Nigel, et al., *Scottish Education: a Declaration of Principles*, Scottish Centre for Economic and Social Research, Edinburgh, 1989.

Gray, Alasdair, *Unlikely Stories*, Canongate, Edinburgh, 1984.

Gray, Alasdair, *Lanark*, Canongate, Edinburgh 1984.

Gunn, Neil, *The Serpent*, Souvenir Press, London, 1986.

Harvie, Christopher, *No Gods and Precious Few Heroes: Scotland since 1914*, Edward Arnold, London, 1987.

Hay, J. MacDougall, *Gillespie*, Canongate, Edinburgh, 1979.

Hayton, Alan, *Far Cry from 1945: poems by Alan Hayton*, Pertinent Publications, Wishaw, 1982.

Hind, Archie, *The Dear Green Place*, Polygon, Edinburgh, 1984.

Humes, Walter M., *The Leadership Class in Scottish Education*, John Donald Publishers, Edinburgh, 1986.   .

Jenkins, Robin, *Fergus Lamont*, Canongate, Edinburgh, 1979.

Jenkins, Robin, *The Cone-gatherers*, Paul Harris Publishing, Edinburgh, 1980.

Kay, Billy, *Scots: The Mither Tongue*, Grafton Books, London, 1988.

Kelman, James, *A Disaffection*, Secker and Warburg, London, 1989.

Kelman, James, *The Busconductor Hines*, Polygon, Edinburgh, 1984.

Kelman, James, *Greyhound for Breakfast*, Pan, London, 1988.

Kelman, James, *Not Not While the Giro and other stories*, Polygon, Edinburgh, 1983.

Kelman, James, *A Chancer*, Polygon, Edinburgh, 1986.

Kesson, Jessie, *Another Time, Another Place*, Hogarth.

Kesson, Jessie, *The White Bird Passes*, Hogarth.

Kravitz, Peter (ed.), *Edinburgh Review 77: Tom Leonard number*, Polygon, Edinburgh, 1987.

Laing, R.D., *The Divided Self*, Penguin, Harmondsworth, 1969.

Leonard, Tom, *Intimate Voices 1965-1983*, Galloping Dog Press, Newcastle upon Tyne, 1984.

Leonard, Tom, *Situations Theoretical and Contemporary*, Galloping Dog Press, Newcastle upon Tyne, 1986.

Leonard, Tom, *Two Members' Monologues & a Handy Form for Artists for use in connection with The City of Culture*, Edward Polin Press, Glasgow, 1989.

Lochhead, Liz, *True Confessions and New Clichés*, Polygon, Edinburgh, 1985.

Lochhead, Liz, *Dreaming Frankenstein and Collected Poems*, Polygon, Edinburgh, 1987.

Lochhead, Liz, *Tartuffe: a translation into Scots from the original by Molière*, Polygon/Third Eye Centre, Edinburgh/Glasgow, 1985.

MacGill, Patrick, *Children of the Dead End: the autobiography of a navvy*, Horsham Galiban, 1982.

MacKenney, Linda (ed.), *Joe Corrie: plays and theatre writings*, 7:84 Theatre Company, Scotland.

McGrath, Tom and Boyle, Jimmy, *The Hard Man*, Canongate, Edinburgh, 1977.

McGrath, John, *The Cheviot, the Stag and the Black, Black Oil*, West Highland Publishing Company, Kyleakin, Isle of Skye, 1974.

McIlvanney, William, *Docherty*, Sceptre, London, 1987.

McIlvanney, William, *The Big Man*, Sceptre, London, 1986

McIlvanney, William, *Walking Wounded*, Sceptre, London, 1990.

Milton, Nan, *John Maclean*, Pluto Press, London, 1973.

Muir, Edwin, *An Autobiography*, Hogarth Press, London, 1980.

Muir, Edwin, *Scott and Scotland*, Polygon, Edinburgh, 1982.

Muir, Edwin, *Scottish Journey*, Mainstream, Edinburgh, 1979.

Owen, Robert, *A Statement Regarding the New Lanark Establishment*, The Molendinar Press, Glasgow, 1973.

Owens, Agnes, *Gentlemen of the West*, Polygon, Edinburgh, 1984.

Scott, P.H., *In Bed with an Elephant: the Scottish experience*, Saltire Society, Edinburgh, 1985.

Scott, P.H., *1707: The Union of Scotland and England*, Chambers, Edinburgh, 1979.

Scott, Sir Walter, *Waverley*, Penguin Books, London, 1972.

Scottish Constitutional Convention, *Towards a Scottish Parliament: consultation document and report to the Scottish people*, Scottish Constitutional Convention, Edinburgh, 1989.

Sharp, Alan, *A Green Tree in Gedde*, Richard Drew, Glasgow, 1985.

Sillars, Jim, *Scotland: the case for optimism*, Polygon, Edinburgh, 1986.

Smout, T.C., *A History of the Scottish People 1560-1830*, Fontana, Glasgow, 1979.

Smout, T.C., *A Century of the Scottish People*, Collins, London, 1986.

Spark, Muriel, *The Prime of Miss Jean Brodie*, Penguin, London, 1965.

Spence, Alan, *Its Colours they are Fine*, Collins, London, 1977.

Stein, Jock, *Scottish Self-Government*, some Christian viewpoints, The Handsel Press, Edinburgh, 1989.

Thomson, James, *The City of Dreadful Night: and other poems*, Reeves and Turner, London, 1888.

White, Kenneth, *The Bird Path: collected longer poems 1964-1988*, Mainstream Publishing, Edinburgh, 1989.

Political and Cultural Analysis

Allen, Karen and Radcliffe, Nick, *Towards a Green Scotland: contributions to the debate*, Scottish Green Party, Edinburgh, 1990.

Ascherson, Neal, *Games with Shadows*, Radius, London, 1988.

Berger, Peter L., *Pyramids of Sacrifice: Political Ethics and Social Change*, Allen Lane Penguin Books, London, 1974.

Beveridge, Craig and Turnbull, Ronald, *The Eclipse of Scottish Culture*, Polygon, Edinburgh, 1989.

Brown, Gordon and Cook, Robin (eds.), *Scotland: the real divide*, Mainstream, Edinburgh, 1983.

Brown, Gordon (ed.), *The Red Paper on Scotland*, Edinburgh University Student Publications Board, Edinburgh, 1975.

Brown, Gordon, *Where there is Greed: Margaret Thatcher and the betrayal of Britain*, Mainstream, Edinburgh, 1989.

Carmichael, Kay, *Freedom and Order*, in Cencrastus, No. 34, Edinburgh, 1989.

Carmichael, Kay, *A Balanced Society*, in Cencrastus, No. 34, Edinburgh, 1989.

Carter, Ian, 'A Socialist Strategy for the Highlands', in *The Red Paper on Scotland*, ed. Gordon Brown, Edinburgh University Student Publications Board, Edinburgh, 1975.

Cockburn, Cynthia, *The Local State: management of cities and people*, Pluto Press, London, 1977.

Cooley, Mike, *Architect or Bee? the human/technology relationship*, Langley Technical Services, Slough, 1980 (repr. Hogarth Press, 1986).

Cornforth, Maurice, *Communism and Human Values*, Lawrence and Wishart, London, 1972.

Craig, Cairns, 'Where are we in history?' in *Radical Scotland*, No. 42, Edinburgh, 1989/90.

Davie, George Elder, *The Crisis of the Democratic Intellect*, Polygon, Edinburgh, 1986.

Davie, George Elder, *The Democratic Intellect*, Edinburgh University Press, Edinburgh, 1961.

Dudley Edwards, Owen (ed.), *A Claim of Right for Scotland*, Polygon, Edinburgh, 1989.

Entwistle, Harold, *Antonio Gramsci: conservative schooling for radical politics*, Routledge and Kegan Paul, London, 1979.

Fanon, Frantz, *The Wretched of the Earth*, Penguin Books, Harmondsworth, 1969.

Forgacs, David (ed.), *A Gramsci Reader*, Lawrence and Wishart, London, 1988.

Freire, Paulo, *Pedagogy of the Oppressed*, Penguin, Harmondsworth, 1972.

Freire, Paulo, *The Politics of Education: Culture Power and Liberation*, Macmillan, London, 1985.

Freire, Paulo, *Pedagogy in Process: the Letters to Guinea-Bissau*, Seabury Press, New York, 1978

Fromm, Erich, *To Have or to Be?*, Sphere Books, London, 1979.

Fromm, Erich, *The Fear of Freedom*, Routledge and Kegan Paul, London, 1961.

Groombridge, Brian, *Television and the People: a programme for democratic participation*, Penguin, Harmondsworth, 1972.

Hall, Stuart and Jacques, Martin (eds.), *New Times: the Changing Face of Politics in the 1990s*, Lawrence and Wishart, London, 1989.

Harvie, Christopher, *No Gods and Precious Few Heroes: Scotland since 1914*, Edward Arnold, London, 1987.

Hoggart, Richard, *The Uses of Literacy*, Penguin, Harmondsworth, 1966.

Humes, Walter M., *The Leadership Class in Scottish Education*, John Donald Publishers, Edinburgh, 1986.

Kelman, James, 'A Reading from Noam Chomsky and the Scottish Tradition in the Philosophy of Common Sense', in *Edinburgh Review* No. 84, Edinburgh, 1990.

Koestler, Arthur, Silone, Ignazio, Gide, André, Starkie, Enid, Wright, Richard, Fischer, Louis and Spender, Stephen, *The God that Failed: six studies in communism*, Hamish Hamilton, London, 1951.

Koestler, Arthur, *Darkness at Noon*, Penguin, Harmondsworth, 1976.

Kolakowski, Leszek, *Marxism and Beyond*, Paladin, 1971.

Leonard, Tom, *Glasgow, my big bridie*, Third Eye Centre, Glasgow, 1983.

Leonard, Tom, *Situations theoretical and Contemporary*, Galloping Dog Press, Newcastle upon Tyne, 1986.

Leonard, Tom, *Intimate Voices 1965-1983*, Galloping Dog Press, Newcastle upon Tyne, 1984.

Leonard, Tom, *Two Members' Monologues & a Handy Form for Artists for use in connection with the City of Culture*, Edward Polin Press, Glasgow, 1989.

Levitas, Maurice, *Marxist Perspectives in the Sociology of Education*, Routledge and Kegan Paul, London, 1974.

Lyons, John, *Chomsky*, Fontana/Collins, Glasgow, 1975.

Mackie, Robert (ed.), *Literacy and Revolution: the Pedagogy of Paulo Freire*, Pluto Press, London, 1980.

Mackintosh, J.P., *The Devolution of Power: local democracy, regionalism and nationalism*, Penguin, Harmondsworth, 1968.

Marris, Peter and Rein, Martin, *Dilemmas of Social Reform*, Penguin, Harmondsworth, 1974.

Marx, Karl, *Capital, volumes 1 and 2*, Penguin, Harmondsworth, 1976 and 1978.

Marx, Karl, and Engels, Frederick, *Selected Works*, Lawrence and Wishart, London, 1977.

Memmi, Albert, *The Coloniser and the Colonised*, Orion Press, New York, 1965.

Nairn, Tom, *The Break-up of Britain*, NLB and Verso Editions, London, 1981.

Nairn, Tom, *The Enchanted Glass: Britain and its monarchy*, Radius, London, 1988.

Newman, Oscar, *Defensible Space: people and design in the violent city*, Architectural Press, London, 1973.

Nyerere, Julius K., *Ujamaa: Essays on Socialism*, Oxford University Press, London, 1968.

Orwell, George, *Nineteen Eighty-Four*, Penguin, Harmondsworth, 1981.

Owen, Robert, *A Statement Regarding the New Lanark Establishment*, The Molendinar Press, Glasgow, 1973.

Porritt, Jonathon, *Seeing Green: the politics of ecology explained*, Basil Blackwell, Oxford, 1989.

Scottish Constitutional Convention, *Towards a Scottish Parliament: consultation document and report to the Scottish people*, Scottish Constitutional Convention, Edinburgh, 1989.

Sillars, Jim, *Scotland: the case for optimism*, Polygon, Edinburgh, 1986.

Simon, Brian, *Intelligence, Psychology and Education: a Marxist critique*, Lawrence and Wishart, London, 1971.

Smout, T.C., *A History of the Scottish People 1560-1830*, Fontana, Glasgow, 1979.

Smout, T.C., *A Century of the Scottish People*, Collins, London, 1986.

Stein, Jock, *Scottish Self-Government*, some Christian viewpoints, The Handsel Press, Edinburgh, 1988.

The British Road to Socialism, Communist Party of Great Britain, London, 1978.

Tressell, Robert, *The Ragged Trousered Philanthropists*, Granada, London, 1981.

Vincent, John J., *Liberation Theology from the Inner City*, Edinburgh Methodist Mission, Edinburgh, 1989.

Williams, Raymond, *Culture and Society 1780-1950*, Penguin, Harmondsworth, 1977.

Williams, Raymond, *The Long Revolution*, Penguin, Harmondsworth 1971.

Williams, Raymond, *Keywords: a Vocabulary of Culture and Society*, Fontana/Croom Helm, Glasgow, 1979.

Williams, Raymond, *Communications*, Penguin, Harmondsworth, 1962.

Williams, Raymond, *Culture*, Fontana, Glasgow, 1981.

Human Relations: Counselling, Groupwork, Psychotherapy

Alighieri, Dante, *The Divine Comedy: a new verse translation by C. H. Sisson*, Carcanet New Press, Manchester 1980.

Axline, Virginia, *Dibs: in search of self*, Penguin, Harmondsworth, 1986.

Balint, Michael, *The Basic Fault*, Tavistock/Routledge, London, 1989.

Bion, W.R., *Experiences in Groups*, Associated Book Publishers, London, 1968.

Bowlby, John, *Attachment and Loss: volumes 1-3*, Penguin, London, 1989.

Brown, Dennis and Pedder, Jonathan, *Introduction to Psychotherapy*, Tavistock Publications, London, 1979.

Buber, Martin, *I and Thou*, T. & T. Clark, Edinburgh, 1970.

Cardinal, Marie, *The Words to say it*, Pan Books, London, 1984.

Casement, Patrick, *On Learning from the Patient*, Tavistock, London, 1985.

Chaplin, Jocelyn, *Feminist Counselling in Action*, Sage Publications, London, 1988.

Cherry, Chris, Robertson, Marea, and Meadows, Flora, *Personal and Professional Development for Group Leaders*, Scottish Health Education Group, Edinburgh, 1990.

Davis, Madeleine and Wallbridge, David, *Boundary and Space: an introduction to the work of D.W. Winnicott*, Penguin, Harmondsworth, 1983.

de Mause, Lloyd (ed.), *The History of Childhood*, Souvenir Press, London, 1976.

Dinnage, Rosemary, *One to One: experiences of psychotherapy*, Penguin, London, 1988.

Donovan, Judy, et al., *Experiences of a Changing Kind: adult education in psychiatric hospitals and day centres*, MIND/WEA Yorkshire North District, London/Leeds, 1985.

Douglas, Tom, *Groupwork Practice*, Tavistock Publications, London, 1976.

Douglas, Tom, *Basic Groupwork*, Tavistock Publications, London, 1978.

Egan, Gerard, *The Skilled Helper*, Brooks Cole, Belmont, California, 1982.

Fairbairn, W. Ronald D., *Psychoanalytic Studies of the Personality*, Routledge and Kegan Paul, London, 1986.

Fewell, Judith and Woolfe, Ray, *Groupwork Skills: an introduction*, Scottish Health Education Group, Edinburgh, 1990.

France, Ann, *Consuming Psychotherapy*, Free Association Books, London, 1988.

Freud, Sigmund *(translated by James Strachey, edited by Albert Dickson)*, The Pelican Freud Library, volumes 1-15, Penguin, Harmondsworth, 1986.

Fromm, Erich, *Greatness and Limitations of Freud's Thought*, Sphere Books, London, 1980.

Gay, Peter, *Freud: a life for our time*, Dent, London, 1988.

Guntrip, Harry, *Schizoid Phenomena, Object Relations and the Self*, Hogarth Press, London, 1980.

Guntrip, Harry, *Psychoanalytic Theory, Therapy and the Self*, Hogarth Press, London, 1977.

Harris, Thomas A., *I'm OK — You're OK*, Pan Books, London, 1979.

Hassan, Janet, *Human Relations*, in Adult Education and the Unemployed, eds. Kirkwood and Griffiths, Workers' Educational Association, Edinburgh, 1984.

Heimler, Eugene, *Survival in Society*, Weidenfeld and Nicolson, London, 1975.

Herman, Nini, *Why Psychotherapy?*, Free Association Books, London, 1987.

Jacobs, Michael, *Psychodynamic Counselling in Action*, Sage Publications, London, 1988.

Jones, Maxwell, McPherson, Frank, Whitaker, Dorothy Stock, Sutherland, J.D., Walton Henry, and Wolff, Heinz, *Small Group Psychotherapy*, Penguin, Harmondsworth, 1971.

Jung, C.G., *Analytical Psychology: its theory and practice*, Ark Paperbacks, London, 1986.

Kindred, Michael, *Once upon a Group . . .* , published by the author, Southwell, Notts, 1988.

Korb, Margaret, Gorrell, Jeffrey and Van De Riet, Vernon, *Gestalt Therapy: practice and theory*, Pergamon Press, New York, 1989.

Laing, R.D., *Wisdom, Madness and Folly: the making of a psychiatrist*, Macmillan, London, 1986.

Laing, R.D., *The Divided Self*, Penguin, Harmondsworth, 1969.

MacMurray, John, *The Self as Agent*, Faber and Faber, London, 1936.

MacMurray, John, *Reason and Emotion*, Faber and Faber, London, 1936.

MacMurray, John, *Persons in Relation*, Faber and Faber, London, 1961.

Mearns, Dave and Thorne, Brian, *Person-Centred Counselling in Action*, Sage Publications, London, 1988.

Miller, Alice, *The Drama of Being a Child*, Virago Press, London, 1989.

Mitchell, Juliet, *Psychoanalysis and Feminism*, Penguin, Harmondsworth, 1975.

Mitchell, Juliet, *The Selected Melanie Klein*, Penguin, Harmondsworth, 1975.

Noonan, Ellen, *Counselling Young People*, Methuen, London, 1983.

Norwood, Robin, *Women who Love too much*, Arrow Books, London, 1989.

Perls, Frederick S., Hefferline, Ralph F. and Goodman, Paul, *Gestalt Therapy: excitement and growth in the human personality*, Penguin, Harmondsworth, 1976.

Pincus, Lily and Dare, Christopher, *Secrets in the Family*, Faber and Faber, London, 1978.

Pincus, Lily, *Death and the Family: the importance of mourning*, Faber and Faber, London, 1976.

Pitt-Aikens, Tom and Ellis, Alice Thomas, *Loss of the Good Authority: the cause of delinquency*, Viking, London, 1989.

Rogers, Carl, *On Becoming a Person: a Therapist's View of Psychotherapy,* Constable, London, 1982.

Rushforth, Winifred, *Something is Happening,* Turnstone Press, Wellingborough, 1981.

Segal, Hanna, *Introduction to the Work of Melanie Klein,* Hogarth Press, London, 1978

Skynner, Robin and Cleese, John, *Families and how to survive them,* Methuen, London, 1978.

Sutherland, John D., *Fairbairn's Journey into the Interior,* Free Association Books, London, 1989.

Sutherland, John D., *The Psychodynamic Image of Man,* Aberdeen, 1983.

Tillich, Paul, *On the Boundary,* Collins, London, 1967.

Trower, Peter, Casey, Andrew and Dryden, Windy, *Cognitive Behavioural Counselling in Action,* Sage Publications, London, 1988.

Williams, Martin and Lockley, Paul, *HIV — AIDS Counselling: a training manual,* Scottish Health Education Group, Edinburgh, 1989.

Winnicott, D.W., *The Child, the Family and the Outside World,* Penguin, Harmondsworth, 1976.

Winnicott, D.W., *Playing and Reality,* Penguin, London, 1988.

Winnicott, D.W., *Home is where we start from,* Penguin, London, 1986.

Woolfe, Ray, Murgatroyd, Stephen, and Rhys, Sylvia, *Guidance and Counselling in Adult and Continuing Education,* Open University Press, Milton Keynes, 1987.

Woolfe, Ray, *Counselling Skills: a training manual,* Scottish Health Education Group, Edinburgh, 1989.

Index

369